Praise for

Marmee & Louisa

"It's hard to imagine that anything new could be said about the life of Louisa May Alcott. . . . Yet . . . LaPlante isn't just any biographer. . . . An intimate portrait of mother and daughter, showing how their lives were profoundly intertwined. . . . Fascinating."

—*The Boston Globe*

"Meticulously researched . . . LaPlante shatters myths about the supposedly passive Marmee, replacing them with a portrait of a woman who fought for a woman's right to education, professional and maternal satisfaction, and power."

—*People* Magazine

"Engrossing . . . LaPlante, a descendant of the Alcotts, pursued this untold story after discovering forgotten journals and letters in an attic trunk. In her skilled hands these documents yield Abigail unabridged: a thinker, writer, activist, wife and mother who held fast to her convictions in the face of terrible suffering. . . . In bringing to life the woman who made Louisa May Alcott's work possible, LaPlante shows . . . there's even more to admire in the real Abigail than in the fictional Marmee. . . . This is a biography of Louisa, too."

—*The Washington Post*

"Abigail May Alcott . . . [or] 'Marmee,' as her daughters called her, was a fine writer, an indefatigable reformer, a devoted teacher—and, above all, Louisa's literary lodestar. . . . [After] the wildly popular *Little Women* . . . [Bronson Alcott] was, he crowed, 'the Father of Miss Alcott.' At last, people came to hear him lecture. To his credit, though . . . he mentioned in passing that Louisa's mother hadn't yet received 'her full share.' To her credit, LaPlante evens the score."

—*The New York Times Book Review*

"[An] involving mother-daughter portrait . . . Although bitter ironies mark each woman's story, vividly set within the social upheavals of the Civil War era, their profound love, intellect, and courage shine."

—*Booklist*, starred review

"Revelatory . . . Convincing . . . Abigail's daughters were her dreams made manifest."

—*The Seattle Times*

"The eye-opener of Eve LaPlante's marvelous new dual biography . . . is that Abigail was every inch the social philosopher that Bronson was when it came to . . . abolition and women's rights. . . . A romance."

—Maureen Corrigan, *National Public Radio*

"This revealing biography . . . will forever change how we view the characters and their relationships in Louisa's novels. . . . Louisa drew heavily from Abigail's life experiences in her own writings. . . . Revel in LaPlante's biography . . . and then turn to a bonus . . . companion volume, *My Heart Is Boundless*, writings of Abigail May Alcott."

—*USA Today*

"The single most memorable character from a 2012 book . . . [is] Louisa May Alcott's mother . . . one of the subjects of Eve LaPlante's *Marmee & Louisa* . . . whose activist life and tart, intelligent writing just blew me away."

—*Salon*

"Superbly crafted . . . An impeccably documented and verified biographical masterpiece . . . A genuine story of women who were heroines of their time . . . An intensely moving story whose truth is all the more powerful for being fleshed out in such an engaging and heartfelt style."

—*Bookreporter*

"Thoroughly researched and moving."

—*Kirkus Reviews*

"Nineteenth-century New England literature buffs and Alcott aficionados will appreciate this well-wrought study."

—*Library Journal*

"LaPlante has turned up more material on Abigail May Alcott than most scholars thought possible."

—*Washington Independent Review of Books*

"Compelling."

—*Publishers Weekly*

"An important book . . . Writing engagingly and with precision, Eve LaPlante sheds new light on the Alcott story, a story that is in some ways the story of America."

—Jon Meacham, Pulitzer Prize–winning author of *Thomas Jefferson*

"'Let the world know you are alive!' Abigail Alcott counseled her daughter, who amply did, having inherited her mother's spirit and frustrations, diaries, and work ethic. . . . LaPlante beautifully resurrects her here. A most original love story, taut and tender."

—Stacy Schiff, Pulitzer Prize–winning author of *Cleopatra: A Life*

"[A] heartwarming and thoroughly researched story of family interdependence very much in the style of Louisa's own unforgettable *Little Women*. No other biographer has examined so thoughtfully and with such compassion the mother-daughter relationship that supported both women through decades of adversity and brought a great American novel into being."

—Megan Marshall, author of *Margaret Fuller: A New American Life*

"Louisa May Alcott's mother . . . juggled work and family in ways that will be strikingly familiar to many contemporary readers. . . . The engrossing story of a vibrant, talented woman whose life and influence on her famous daughter has, until now, been erased."

—Anne-Marie Slaughter, Princeton University

ALSO BY EVE LaPLANTE

My Heart Is Boundless (editor)

Salem Witch Judge

American Jezebel

Seized

Marmee & Louisa

*The Untold Story of Louisa May Alcott
and Her Mother*

Eve LaPlante

SIMON & SCHUSTER PAPERBACKS

New York   London   Toronto   Sydney   New Delhi

Simon & Schuster Paperbacks
A Division of Simon & Schuster, Inc.
1230 Avenue of the Americas
New York, NY 10020

First Simon & Schuster trade paper edition November 2013

SIMON & SCHUSTER PAPERBACKS and colophon are trademarks of Simon &
Schuster, Inc.

For information about special discounts for bulk purchases, please contact
Simon & Schuster Special Sales at 1-866-506-1949 or
business@simonandschuster.com.

The Simon & Schuster Speakers Bureau can bring authors to your
live event. For more information or to book an event contact the
Simon & Schuster Speakers Bureau at 1-866-248-3049 or
visit our website at www.simonspeakers.com.

Permissions and credits for quotations in text and
insert illustrations are on page 356.

Book design by Ellen R. Sasahara

Manufactured in the United States of America

1   3   5   7   9   10   8   6   4   2

Library of Congress has cataloged the hardcover edition as follows:
LaPlante, Eve.

Marmee & louisa : the untold story of Louisa May Alcott and her mother /
by Eve LaPlante. — 1st Free Press hardcover ed.
p. cm.
Includes bibliographical references and index.
1. Alcott, Louisa May, 1832–1888– Family. I. Title.
PS1018.L37 2012
813'.4— dc23
[B]
2012016132

ISBN 978-1-4516-2066-5
ISBN 978-1-4516-2067-2 (pbk)
ISBN 978-1-4516-2068-9 (ebook)

To David

Mothers are the *best* lovers in the world;
but I don't mind whispering to Marmee, that
I'd like to try all kinds. It's very curious, but
the more I try to satisfy myself with all sorts
of natural affections, the more I seem to want.

—Louisa May Alcott, *Little Women,* 1868

Contents

A Note on the Text

All dialogue and other quotations are from written records, in most cases the letters, journals, and other writings of the Alcotts and their relatives and friends. Nineteenth-century punctuation and spelling stand except when they might obscure meaning. Please see the Notes for sources and citations.

Introduction

W ho is Louie?" my oldest daughter asked, holding up a small book with a worn, embossed cover. She and I were kneeling on the dusty floor of my mother's attic, rummaging through a huge metal trunk containing our ancestors' belongings. The trunk had arrived decades earlier following the death of an aunt, who likewise had inherited it from her aunt. Inside the trunk, beneath feathered ladies' hats and a nineteenth-century quilt, my daughter had found an 1849 edition of *The Swiss Family Robinson,* inscribed as a gift:

> *June 21st / 55.*
> *George E. May*
> *from his cousin*
> *Louie*

"That's Louisa May Alcott," I realized, remembering that relatives knew her as Louie or Cousin Louisa. In June 1855, our great-uncle George E. May was ten years old and his first cousin Louisa May Alcott, who hoped he would enjoy the tale of a shipwrecked family, was twenty-two. She was staying with other maternal cousins in Walpole, New Hampshire, spending her days gardening and hiking, forming a theater troupe, and inventing "little tales" that she hoped to sell. Her parents and younger sisters would soon join her in Walpole, a "lovely place, high among the hills," to live in an uncle's spare house. Deeply in debt, they could not afford to pay rent. Their only regular income in 1855 was her older sister's small salary as a teacher in Syracuse, New York, where she boarded with George's family. Louisa's father, Bronson, recently returned from an unprofitable lecture tour of the Midwest, was planning a solo trip to England—"not a wise idea," according to Louisa. Her mother, Abigail, had left jobs in Boston as a social worker and employment agent. The novel *Little Women,* which would give the Alcotts their first taste of financial security, was still thirteen years in the future. But Louisa had already published poems, short stories, and a book of original fairy tales, the start of her remarkable career.

In another trunk my daughter and I found the brittle, handwritten memoir of George's older sister, my great-great-grandmother Charlotte May, who had grown up with Louisa and whose wedding Louisa had recently attended. Charlotte and Louisa, born a few months apart in the winter of 1832–33, had played games, invented stories, and wandered the woods and hills surrounding their childhood homes. A packet of letters tied with a ribbon contained Charlotte's scribbled descriptions of her and Louisa's teenage escapades in Syracuse in the late 1840s. Louisa signed letters to Charlotte, who lacked sisters, "Your sister-in-love."

Charlotte and George May's father, the Reverend Samuel Joseph May, was likewise his nieces' "uncle father." Samuel Joseph had introduced his youngest sister, Abigail May, to Bronson Alcott in 1827 and spent decades providing their family with much-needed financial and emotional support. Samuel Joseph's published memoir, stuffed with letters in his elegant hand dated from the 1820s to the 1860s, was also in my mother's attic, along with a crumbling copy of his 1869 *Recollections of Our Antislavery Conflict* and an 1823 Bible that belonged to his wife, Lucretia, who became Abigail May Alcott's closest friend.

At the time of these discoveries, I knew next to nothing about the Mays and the Alcotts, and little of Louisa except for her juvenile fiction, *Little Women, Little Men,* and the rest, which I had devoured as a child. But the treasures in the attic compelled me to explore the mysteries of the May-Alcott family. Their faded, cracking pages led me to read Louisa's novels and stories for adults, her letters and journals, and the writings of her parents, sisters, and other close relatives.

In the process, I encountered a paradox. While Marmee, Abigail May Alcott's alter ego in *Little Women,* is universally acknowledged as the central figure in her children's lives, the flesh-and-blood Abigail seemed in the standard rendition of the Alcott saga to be practically invisible and almost mute. Abigail's letters and journals, unlike those of her daughter and husband, remained unpublished and largely unexplored.

The more I learned about the Alcotts, though, the more I saw Louisa and Abigail as a pair, each one the person in the world to whom the other felt closest. It was clear that this mother and daughter shared a profound intimacy that had light and dark facets, in which a fierce commitment to female independence coexisted with a mutual dependency. Abigail, I realized, was a vibrant writer, brilliant teacher, and passionate reformer who spent decades working to abolish slavery, ameliorate urban poverty, and allow women to be educated, vote, and engage in public life. She nurtured and fostered Louisa's career as a writer and entrepreneur, encouraging her daughter, rejection after rejection, to persist. Louisa in turn dedicated all her early work, starting with her first novel at age sixteen, to her mother, who possessed a "nobility of character and talents," Madelon Bedell observed in her biography of the family. "Louisa was to take these sensibilities and talents and transform them into art and literature. . . . If her fame continues to endure and her mother's name is unknown, nonetheless the achievement is a dual one; behind the legendary figure of Louisa May Alcott stands the larger-than-life model of her mother, Abby May." Louisa created "a distinctly mother-centered . . . fictional universe," according to another scholar, Monika Elbert, "in which children seek a nurturing home, husbands [seek] maternal warmth in their wives, and orphans [seek] a mother-surrogate." Over the years, in fact, Louisa functioned as partner, provider, nurse, and even mother to Abigail. "The great love of [Louisa May] Alcott's life . . . was doubtless her mother, whom she idealized as Marmee in *Little Women,*" Elizabeth Lennox Keyser wrote. In short, Abigail was Louisa's muse.

Yet Abigail's story seemed never to have been told. Basic facts, such as the place of her birth, remained undiscovered. Abigail was always portrayed as a housewife, while her husband was seen as Louisa's mentor. "Louisa May Alcott was so dominated by her father," the biographer Susan Cheever wrote, "that it is hard to unravel their lives from each other. . . . In every big decision [Louisa] made, her father hovers in the background. His hold on her was incalculable." Madelon Bedell referred to "Bronson Alcott's great-granddaughter" as if she were not also descended from Abigail. "Even though [Bronson is] hardly present in [*Little Women*], his was the powerful personality that lay at the heart of the legend" of Louisa May Alcott. Collections of American literature invariably described Louisa as the student of men: "Raised in Concord,

Massachusetts, and educated by her father, Alcott came under the influence of the great men of his circle: Emerson, Hawthorne, the preacher
Theodore Parker, and Thoreau." Even a feminist study of nineteenth-
century women writers suggested that Abigail exerted no intellectual
influence on Louisa, who "was taught by her father and also introduced
to men of great influence, including Ralph Waldo Emerson, Nathaniel Hawthorne and Henry David Thoreau." No anthology or biography portrayed Louisa as "taught by her mother and also introduced to
women of great influence, including Elizabeth Palmer Peabody, Lydia
Maria Child, and Margaret Fuller." Yet that statement, I discovered, is
equally true.

Perhaps Abigail's absence shouldn't have surprised me. Invisibility is
the lot of most women of the past. With few exceptions, women appear
in historical records only when they were born, married, and died, if
they are remembered at all. The eleven-page chronology of Louisa's life
compiled by the editors of her published papers mentions her father
repeatedly but her mother just four times:

> Abigail May is born
> Bronson Alcott and Abigail May are married in Boston
> Mrs. Alcott's final illness begins
> Mrs. Alcott dies

A woman who was pregnant at least eight times and bore five children
was not credited in the chronology with even giving birth: "Louisa May
Alcott is born." One might infer that Abigail was barely present in the
Alcott home and had not a thought in her head.

How is it that the woman behind Marmee, the cornerstone of Louisa's most famous work, would have had nothing to say? One possible
explanation is that Abigail is hiding in plain sight. As readers of *Little
Women,* we feel we know Louisa's mother because we know the mother
in Louisa's book. As a result, Louisa's literary creation may obscure the
flesh-and-blood Abigail.

There is another explanation for our lack of knowledge of Abigail,
or so we've been led to believe. Abigail's letters and journals were all
destroyed, burned by her husband and daughter after she died. Louisa
wrote in her journal in the spring of 1882, "[I] Read over & destroyed

Mother's Diaries as she wished me to do." Apparently, she and her parents wished to eradicate these papers in order to maintain the family's privacy, to protect Bronson's reputation, and, ironically, to preserve Abigail's image as an avatar of docile, nineteenth-century womanhood. The biographer John Matteson concluded that "instead of weaving her mother's writings into a published work, [Louisa] chose to commit the great majority of them to the flames. Her decision has cost historians priceless insights into the mind of an extraordinary woman"—an extraordinary woman who cannot be known. According to conventional wisdom, Abigail's inner life was a mystery because she left no significant record of her thoughts.

The conventional wisdom turned out to be wrong. Louisa did weave her mother's writings into published works. Throughout the 1860s, as she composed short stories, adult novels, and *Little Women,* she pored over her mother's private journals, mining them for material. Her claims of burning the family papers are exaggerations. Louisa wrote to a friend in January 1883, "My journals were all burnt long ago in terror of gossip when I depart & on unwise use of my very frank records of people & events."

In fact, however, hundreds of pages of Louisa's journals are in the archives at Harvard University, which holds the largest collection of Alcott papers in the world. These archives also contain hundreds of pages of Abigail's diaries as well as thirty-six years of Abigail's personal correspondence with her brother Samuel Joseph. These letters have "a remarkable vivacity," in the words of Madelon Bedell. "In some ways, Abby was a better writer than her more famous daughter." Cornell University's collection of May Papers contains more unpublished family diaries and personal correspondence. Unknown papers of the Alcotts continue to be discovered. The historical society of a village in western Maine where Abigail worked in 1848 referred me to a local historian, who revealed to me that he had letters written by Abigail that year to his great-grandmother. In addition to visiting his farmhouse in the foothills of the Mahoosuc Mountains and reading those letters, I explored the sites of Abigail's and Louisa's lives in Washington, D.C., Pennsylvania, New York, and throughout New England.

My research exploded a number of myths about the Alcotts that have arisen as a consequence of *Little Women.* Unlike the fictional March

family, the Alcotts were homeless for decades. Abigail regularly begged
for money from family and friends. Her marriage was deeply distressed.
For years she functioned as a single parent, whose despair over her husband's inattention, absences, and inability to earn a living caused her at
least once to pack and move out with her four children. For Louisa, who
was ten years old, seeing her parents' marriage disintegrate motivated
her to become her mother's provider and support. For much of Louisa's
childhood her father, even when at home, often seemed absent. Her
mother, in contrast, was always present, urging her on and serving as her
intellectual mentor and literary forebear.

In addition to challenging the myths and misconceptions about the
Alcotts and especially about Abigail, *Marmee & Louisa* offers answers to
questions that readers continue to ask about Louisa. Why did she never
leave home? Why did she not marry? Who was the real Mr. March?
Where did Louisa May Alcott find the material to describe a happy childhood?

While writing this book, I came to see that many of the dilemmas that
Abigail and Louisa faced in the nineteenth century were not unlike the
dilemmas we face today: How to balance work and love? How to combine a public life with a private one? How to live out one's ideals without
doing harm? How to hold one's children close while encouraging their
independence? How to find a voice in a world that does not listen?

Marmee & Louisa is the story of two visionary women, perhaps the
most famous mother-daughter pair in American literary history. Louisa
and Abigail were born into a world that constrained and restricted them,
but they dreamed of freedom. The story of their struggle to forge a new
world begins with Abigail. Indeed, we cannot understand Louisa without knowing her mother. You may find, as I have, that aspects of Abigail's life are strangely familiar, as if we had encountered her before. In
a way we have, through her daughter's writing. The imaginative child
of an inspirational mother, Louisa studied Abigail's life and character,
appropriated them, and embedded them in her fictional worlds.

Chapter One

A Good Child, but Willful

On Wednesday, October 8, 1800, in a large frame house on Milk Street overlooking Boston Harbor, Dorothy Sewall May delivered her fourth living daughter, whom she named Abigail, after her husband's mother. "[I was] a sickly child, nursed by a sickly mother," Abigail recalled, linked from the start to her own "Marmee."

Dorothy Sewall May's "most striking trait" was "her affectionate disposition," according to Abigail. "She adored her husband and children." This natural tendency was intensified because Dorothy had been orphaned at twelve when her father died of a stroke, a year after the death of her forty-year-old mother. Thereafter Dorothy had lived with her eldest sister, Elizabeth Sewall Salisbury. Elizabeth's husband, Samuel, was a merchant whose apprentice, Joseph May, Dorothy married in 1784.

By the time of Abigail's birth sixteen years later, the Mays had three boys—ages twelve, five, and three—and four girls: thirteen-year-old Catherine; Louisa, who was eleven; two-year-old Elizabeth, whom they called Eliza; and the new baby. Dorothy had no formal education and her husband had abandoned Boston Latin School in his early teens to work for Dorothy's brother-in-law. Nevertheless, she determined to send their boys at age five to dame, or ma'am, schools run by women and then to "man schools" to prepare for Harvard College, from which her brother, father, grandfathers, and great-grandfathers had graduated. As for her daughters, Dorothy encouraged them to follow a year or two of dame school with reading, singing, and sewing at home, where she provided tutors in dancing and music. The girls could read freely, for the Mays had house servants and a library stocked with the classic historians, philosophical works of Priestley and Paley, and the poetry of Pope, Addison, and Shakespeare.

The year after Abigail's birth, the family moved three blocks south to a "plain but comfortable" wood house with a large garden and orchards at No. 1 Federal Court, a "sunny and cheerful spot" off Federal Street that is less than a block from South Station in modern Boston. Around that time, Abigail's frail, forty-three-year-old mother suffered a miscarriage that ended her thirteenth and final pregnancy.

At midday on Thursday, April 29, 1802, when Abigail was eighteen months old, her six-year-old brother Edward arrived home from ma'am school "full of glee" and eager to play, according to her four-year-old brother, Samuel Joseph, who was known in the family as Sam Jo. The brothers were close, Sam Jo said later: "We slept together, ate together, and he taught me all the sports. I every day awaited his return" from school.

Following the family's midday meal, the two boys ran out to the garden, leaving their sisters inside with their mother. Edward climbed to the roof of a barn and pretended to be a chimney sweep. Minutes later, having concluded his sweeping, he prepared to descend from the barn by stepping onto the post of an old wooden chair. The chair post splintered beneath him, a broken spindle pierced his side, and he dropped to the ground. Screams from servants alerted Dorothy, who raced from the house, carried her six-year-old inside, and called for a bath. Servants rushed to the well and the stove. Not until Dorothy removed Edward's shirt did anyone see the fatal wound.

Dorothy fainted, Sam Jo recalled, and all around the dying boy was "confusion and dismay." Servants ran to summon the doctor and Joseph May, who raced home from his marine insurance office near Long Wharf. Amid the chaos Edward's body was cleaned, dressed, and laid out in the best room.

"Some strange awful change had come over my beloved Edward," Sam Jo said. "Eyes shut, body cold," he gave "no replies to the tender things said to him" and took "no notice of all that was being done to him." But Sam Jo would not abandon his brother's body. He begged his parents to let him sleep with Edward one last time. That night in bed he kissed his brother's "cold cheek and lips, pulled open his eyelids, begged him to speak to me, and cried myself to sleep because he would not."

The next morning the children watched their father place Edward into his coffin "in order that it might be laid away in the ground." The parents and older sisters continually assured the younger children that "Edward is still living; he has become an angel and gone to heaven."

Throngs of relatives and friends and Joseph May's colleagues in shipping and insurance attended the funeral. James Freeman, America's first Unitarian preacher and one of Joseph's closest friends, performed the funeral service at home. Pallbearers carried the little coffin out to a carriage. Black-clad mourners followed the carriage on foot up the hill to the burial ground beside King's Chapel, where Joseph was warden and coauthor of the new hymnal. Young men bore the coffin into the burying ground beside the stone church, while Sam Jo pleaded to see what they were doing to his brother.

His uncle Samuel May, his father's younger brother, carried the boy into the graveyard and down the steps to the family burial vault. From the safety of his uncle's arms Sam Jo surveyed the coffins of his brother Edward, his other deceased siblings, and his paternal grandfather, who had died in 1794. "Our kind uncle," Sam Jo said later, "opened one of the coffins and let me see how decayed the body had become." Uncle Sam allowed him to kiss his brother one last time. "Edward's body is going to decay and become like the dust of the earth," his uncle reassured him, while "his soul has gone to live in heaven with God and Christ and the angels."

Over the years Sam Jo would recount this experience for Abigail, who was too young to recall the details. The night after the funeral, alone in bed for the first time without his brother, Sam Jo had a vivid dream. The ceiling of his room seemed to open, revealing a bright light. From "the midst of it came our lost brother, attended by a troop of little angels. He lay by me as he used to do, his head on my arm," and said, "How happy I am in heaven."

This dream recurred nightly until "by degrees" Sam Jo's grief abated. "But I have never forgotten my almost twin brother" and the "heavenly vision" that provided "the deepest religious impression that my soul ever received." That vision, he told Abigail, motivated him to devote his life to God.

Edward's death caused other revolutions. Joseph and Dorothy May, who had lost five babies, were devastated. Dorothy drew even closer to her two surviving sons and four daughters. Meanwhile, their oldest son, Charles, an indifferent scholar, determined in his teens to go to sea. Charles's departure when Abigail was small reduced the siblings at home to four girls and a single boy. This fundamental May quintet, as described decades later by Abigail to her daughters, would become a model for *Little Women*'s central characters, the four "March" sisters who share their remarkable Marmee with "Laurie," the privileged boy next door.

Edward's death forged an unexpected bond between little Abigail and her sole brother at home. A year after Edward's death, when Sam Jo began attending school, two-and-a-half-year-old Abba, as she was known in the family, begged him to take her along. He and their sisters persuaded their parents to allow Abba to join them at school. By the time she was four she was learning to read and write under the tutelage of her seven-year-old brother, who delighted in walking his "darling little sister" up the cobbled road from home to Mrs. Walcutt's Dame School on High Street.

This bond was unusual in Boston and the wider society, which assigned boys and girls to separate realms. Privileged boys were trained at school to excel in the public sphere, while their sisters were prepared at home to manage a family. Sons, expected to succeed in the world, were prepared with the finest education available, while daughters were prepared to marry well, a task that required no outside education.

These different modes of education, the Mays and their peers believed, suited the genders' inherently distinct natures. Women were considered emotional, nurturing, and intellectually inferior to men, who were all "rational, selfish, and intellectually superior," according to the historian Eve Kornfeld. Middle-class boys "studied the classics, mathematics, natural science, history, and theology" and learned "an aggressive language suitable for debate," while their female peers studied "literature, art, languages, dance, and music" so as to speak "a docile language intended to soothe and to smooth over controversy." This cultivation at school and at home of boys' and girls' apparently distinct interests and talents seemed to provide "further proof of the natural gulf between the male and female worlds."

Sam Jo and Abba May departed from this pattern. Beginning soon after Edward's death, they were each other's best companion and ally. Sam Jo dutifully followed the male path by attending a private academy for boys, Harvard College, and Harvard Divinity School. "My generous father," he recalled later, "thought the best patrimony he could give his children was a good education, so we [boys] were sent to the private schools in Boston that enjoyed the highest reputation." Unlike many of his peers, however, Sam Jo also developed in the wake of his brother's death a passion to rectify the world's wrongs. Among those wrongs was his clever little sister's inability to secure an education like the one that his gender granted him. As a result, he set out to share his man's education with Abba, who concluded in early adolescence that a girl's education was "deficient." Her brother encouraged her to read his books, improve her writing, and think for herself. By the time they were young adults, due to a series of family tragedies Abigail and Samuel Joseph were the only May siblings still living save Charles, who remained away from New England for decades to come. Abigail's remarkable bond with Samuel Joseph contributed to her lifelong determination that women should not only be educated but also have a voice in running the world.

The setting of Abigail May's early life was still in many respects the town from which Paul Revere and William Dawes had ridden just a quarter century before. Dawes, in fact, was Abigail's uncle. In 1800 Boston was still a "pretty country town" with fewer than twenty-five thousand inhabitants, most of them descendants of English settlers, occupying detached houses surrounded by gardens and orchards on a peninsula of roughly one square mile and several adjoining villages. Many Bostonians farmed. Some still shepherded their milk cows to graze on the Common, which descended to a marshy bay along the Charles River. The town had not yet begun its great nineteenth-century transformation, in which cows were banished, pastures and hills smoothed, marshes and bays filled, and brownstones built. In this "handsome" Boston of Abigail May's youth, according to a visitor, "Town and Country seem married."

Growing up on the peninsula's less populous south side, the May children could step into the sea at high tide hardly two minutes from home. Clipper ships passed to and fro. In the evening "the sea dashed under the windows," Abigail's friend Lydia Maria Child recalled, and was "often sparkling with moon-beams when we went to bed." To the southeast the Mays could see from their windows the town's wharves, Gallows Bay, the mud flats of Dorchester, and the harbor islands, most prominently Castle Island with its star-shaped fortification. Looking north their view was of numerous steeples and the town's four great hills. Atop the tallest, Beacon Hill, were the new State House, designed and built in 1798 by Charles Bulfinch, and the elegant home of the late John Hancock, the revolutionary hero and first governor. Hancock, too, was Abigail's uncle, the late husband of her "Aunt Q," Dorothy Quincy Hancock. During Abigail's early years, her Aunt Q still lived in that grand mansion replete with books, paintings, silver, and mahogany furniture, where she had hosted John Adams and General Lafayette. The old woman often invited Abigail and her sisters in for treats. Decades later, in her great-niece Louisa's *Old-Fashioned Girl,* Aunt Q would be immortalized as Grandma Shaw's late aunt, Governor Hancock's widow, with her red-velvet-lined carriage, her "great garden," and her memories of feeding General Lafayette and his troops during the revolution. In fact, Aunt Q's poignant recollections of her only son and daughter, both of whom had died early, may have enhanced her fondness for her nieces and nephews. Aunt Q, like Abigail, had been the youngest, "most petted" of her family. Each year on Abigail's birthday, her aunt reminded her that October 8 was also the day on which "My Mr. Hancock" had died, seven years before Abigail was born.

A revolutionary spirit imbued Abigail's childhood. Many Bostonians had opposed the American Revolution when it happened, but not the Mays. When Abigail was small, her father recounted for her the resolute response of his "strong" mother to a British soldier's petty robbery. Passing by the May house, the soldier had reached into an open kitchen window and grabbed food from the table. "Your grandmother quickly shut the window down upon his arm and held it as in a vise," Joseph May said. Not until a British officer arrived to arrest the offender did Madam Abigail Williams May loosen her grip on the sash. Like other Bostonians opposed to British rule, the Mays left during the Siege of Boston. They boarded with cousins in Pomfret, Connecticut, and did not return to Boston until the British evacuation in the spring of 1776. Joseph was too young to participate in the New England portion of the Revolutionary War, but in his twenties he joined the Independent Corps of Cadets, rose through its ranks, and always desired to be called "Colonel" rather than "Mister" May.

Colonel Joseph May was proud of his heritage. His ancestors, English Puritans with Spanish, Portuguese, and Jewish forebears, arrived in Plymouth in 1640 and settled on the mainland just west of Boston, in Roxbury. An early-eighteenth-century May acquired a large lot on Boston's south side along the slender neck connecting Boston to the mainland except at extreme high tide, when the town briefly became an island. Joseph May was the third child of the carpenter Samuel May's second marriage, to a farmer's daughter named Abigail Williams. Joseph grew up in "Squire May's great house" on the neck at the corner of Orange (now Washington) and Davis streets. Joseph's father, who left the house each morning with a tool bag over his shoulder, was a skilled architect and designer who became a "considerable" dealer in lumber, which he received at a wharf below the house.

Joseph's parents raised nine children, all girls except Joseph and the youngest, Sam, who did not arrive until Joseph was sixteen. A "merry, active" boy accustomed to female company, Joseph was chastised for talking in class. "Sewing being tried" as a cure "proved a failure," so the teacher had him memorize the psalms, the music of a devout Puritan life. This led to his lifelong love of poetry and song, which he passed on to his children. Joseph's youthful gift for singing psalms by heart "drew the attention of the neighbors," who "would stand him up on a folded window shutter before a shop" near his house and call for him to recite "one psalm after another." As his "closing achievement," the boy would sing all 176 verses of the 119th psalm "without an error," prompting applause. In 1770, after the Boston Massacre, Joseph's parents left their church because its minister ridiculed the patriots' cause. They soon joined Old South Church, where their son Joseph found a musical home: "He sat in the singers' seats and sang [psalms] with them when but twelve years old." From age nine Joseph attended Boston Latin School until the British military occupation in 1775 prompted the family's yearlong exile in Connecticut, which ended his schooling after only a few years.

Upon his family's return to Boston in 1776, sixteen-year-old Joseph began a career in business. He was apprenticed to Stephen Salisbury, a prosperous Worcester, Massachusetts, merchant who owned a waterfront store in Boston. Joseph spent four years working for Salisbury and his brother Samuel, whose wife, Elizabeth Sewall Salisbury, had taken in her younger sister Dorothy Quincy Sewall after their parents' deaths. Despite Dorothy's higher social status and her age two years his senior, Joseph May courted his employer's charming young sister-in-law.

At twenty-one Joseph went into business for himself. He opened a store, Patten & May Company, selling flour and produce at No. 3 Long Wharf. His partner, Thomas Patten, was a distant relative who traded flour and other goods in Baltimore, Maryland, and Alexandria, Virginia. Patten & May prospered, enabling Joseph to pledge himself to the young lady he had admired for nearly a decade. On December 28, 1784, at King's Chapel, the ambitious young businessman married the twenty-six-year-old "daughter of [the late merchant] Samuel Sewall, [deacon] of the Old South Church," and his late wife, Elizabeth Quincy.

Dorothy Quincy Sewall came from an illustrious family. She and her future children, as she would remind them, were "thrice related to the Quincys." A direct descendant of the first Edmund Quincy, progenitor of the clan, Dorothy was a cousin of Abigail Adams and of numerous justices of the Supreme Judicial Court of Massachusetts, the oldest independent judiciary in the Western Hemisphere. Dorothy's paternal grandfather, the renowned eighteenth-century pastor Joseph Sewall, whom she had known in her childhood, served Old South Church for half a century and made it "a shrine of the American cause." Her older brother Samuel Sewall was a member of the United States Congress and chief justice of the Massachusetts Supreme Judicial Court. Many male cousins were judges. According to a historian, during "the 122 years from 1692 to 1814, eighty-four [years] saw some member of the Sewall family in the highest court of Massachusetts."

For the first fourteen years of Dorothy and Joseph May's marriage, their family and his business grew. However, in 1798, when they had five living children and she was pregnant with Abigail's next older sister, Elizabeth, disaster struck. Without Joseph's knowledge, his partner had speculated on land in what is now the state of Mississippi, using Patten & May as collateral. Thomas Patten had invested $22,000 (equivalent to

$310,000 in the year 2000) in huge tracts of land sold by Georgia politicians for roughly a penny an acre in a massive fraudulent scheme known as the Yazoo land scandal. Public outrage across the South prompted lawsuits, which nullified the deals. Patten & May became bankrupt. To repay the huge debt he had unknowingly incurred, "Mr. May gave up everything he possessed, even offering the gold ring on his finger."

Following this loss, Abigail's father experienced "a very serious and protracted illness" in which his "mental suffering was great." By the time of Abigail's birth in the fall of 1800, Joseph's health was restored, but his worldview was forever changed. Conservative by nature, having courted a young relative of his well-to-do employer and determined to make money by advancing in the mercantile world, he now considered material wealth harmful to spiritual health. "The sufferings which this disaster caused revealed to him that he had become more eager for property than was creditable to his understanding or good for his heart," his friend the Reverend Dr. Greenwood observed. "After some days of deep depression, [Joseph May] formed the resolution never [again] to be a rich man . . . [and] to withstand all temptations to engage again in the pursuit of wealth." To the dismay of some of his children, "he adhered to this determination" in the future by resisting "very advantageous offers of partnership in lucrative concerns."

Abigail knew her father only after his business failure. But her oldest siblings, like the elder sisters in *Little Women,* "could remember better times." In the novel one sister asks another, "Don't you wish we had the money Papa lost when we were little?"

Like the virtuous Marches invented by his granddaughter, Joseph May responded to loss by beginning again with a new emphasis on duty. "Life was not given to be all used up in the pursuit of what we leave behind us when we die," he often told Abigail. This idealism was enabled by his fortunate choices, particularly his choice of a well-connected wife. In their privileged, insular postrevolutionary world, Dorothy May's wealthy cousins and family friends rallied around them. The Marine Insurance Company, a firm created in 1799 by members of the Cabot and Sargent families, offered Joseph May a lifetime job as its first and only secretary. This sinecure, which he held for decades, provided a relatively modest "competence only for his family" that "never exceeded fifteen hundred dollars a year," equivalent to $25,000 at the turn of the twenty-first century. Various kin, notably Dorothy's younger brother Joseph Sewall, a dry-goods importer significantly more prosperous than his brother-in-law, purchased a new house for the May family.

That house, on the "sunny" spot on Federal Court into which they moved not long after Abigail's birth, is where she was raised and later brought her daughters Anna and Louisa to visit. "Of necessity simple and without show," the house "lacked no comforts, and was full of hospitable and kindly feeling and deed," according to a family recollection. During Abigail's childhood her father was "most attractive in conversation, with . . . a ready wit, giving hours of every day to reading and retaining the fruits of it for the advantage and entertainment of others, ready to participate in the occupations and amusements of those about him, and joining in their music," singing psalms, hymns, and songs. Joseph read aloud to his children and led them in daily prayer and reading of the Bible, in the King James translation.

Dorothy shared "fully with her husband in the hospitable spirit of the house." Even more than her husband, she was "keenly alive to all the joys and trials of her children and of their young friends." In 1819, when Sam Jo's college friend from Maine, George Barrell Emerson, was "seriously ill," Abigail recalled, "my mother had him brought to Federal Court where he remained very sick 5 months." Throughout college Emerson dined every Saturday with the Mays. "I never enjoyed music more entirely than I did then and there in the rich harmony of this exquisite family-choir," he remembered. "Dear Louisa [Abigail's sister] and S[am] J[o] made sweet music for us," Abigail wrote to her daughters, "and the beloved presence of my mother and father and Eliza filled our house with glee, when we all joined in the chorus of the 'Woodland Hallow' or 'Auld Lang Syne' or 'Home Sweet Home.' . . . I have never seen more contentment and happiness—we had music, health, love, and good will."

Amid the cheer were rules regarding appropriate behavior. For Abigail and her sisters, one model of female acquiescence was their Aunt Q, who lived until Abigail was nearly thirty. In 1810 Dorothy Quincy Hancock returned, after a brief second marriage in New Hampshire, to the Hancock mansion beside the State House. The property, built in 1737 by John Hancock's superbly wealthy uncle Thomas Hancock, extended from Mount Vernon to Joy streets. It encompassed walled gardens of flowers, rare trees, and shrubs. Aunt Q later moved to 4 Federal Street, nearer the Mays, where she regaled her nieces with stories of the War for Independence, whose first shots she had heard.

"Shall I tell you the story of the Lexington Alarm?" Aunt Q asked Abigail and her sister Eliza as the girls leaned into her cushioned chair. Late at night on April 18, 1775, twenty-six-year-old Dorothy Quincy had been trying to sleep on the second floor of the Lexington parsonage while her fiancé, John Hancock, the president of the Continental Congress, and Samuel Adams paced in the parlor below. Dorothy had been introduced to Hancock by his aunt Lydia, who raised him as the sole heir to her and her late husband's massive estate. Aunt Lydia had recently invited Dorothy to live in the Hancock mansion. Dorothy was of good family and, according to John Singleton Copley, who painted her portrait, displayed "unusual attractions."

In Boston in early April 1775, General Thomas Gage had ordered British regulars to arrest Hancock and Adams for treason on account of their vocal opposition to the Stamp Act, tea tax, the British blockade of the port of Boston, and the Boston Massacre. King George III's troops also sought a stock of munitions hidden in Concord, the next town. But armed members of the Lexington militia had encircled the parsonage, protecting Hancock and Adams.

Roused by the chaos, Dorothy Quincy donned her cloak and bonnet and descended to the parlor. Before dawn Paul Revere arrived. He advised Hancock and Adams to depart quickly, before British troops surrounded the house. "It was not till break of day that Mr. Hancock could be persuaded" to leave, Aunt Q recalled. "He was all the night cleaning his gun and sword, determined to go where the battle was."

Around daybreak a British soldier, unaware of Hancock's and Adams's presence, knocked on the door, seeking directions to Concord. Upon his departure Dorothy and the Lexington minister stuffed valuables in the cellar and garret. Hancock, Adams, and Revere fled in Hancock's coach, which later returned to retrieve Dorothy Quincy and Aunt Lydia. During their flight Dorothy's first thought was of her widowed father, Judge Edmund Quincy, still in Boston, which was occupied by British troops. "I told Mr. Hancock that I wished to go to my father," Aunt Q recalled. "He said to me, 'No, madam, you shall not return as long as there is a

British bayonet left in Boston.' To which I replied, 'Recollect, Mr. Hancock, I am not under your control yet.'"

But she soon would be under his control, as her nieces Abigail and Eliza were well aware. On August 28 of that year, during a recess of the Second Continental Congress, she married Mr. Hancock in Fairfield, Connecticut. The couple traveled to Philadelphia, where he continued leading Congress and became the first signatory of the Declaration of Independence.

Aunt Q's life with Mr. Hancock exemplified the model marriage of her class and time. In law and in fact, the husband controlled his wife, children, assets, and property. The virtuous femininity displayed by Dorothy Hancock in Philadelphia, where she was the only woman sharing a disorderly boardinghouse with scores of male Continental Congressmen, impressed John Adams. In a November 4, 1775, letter to his wife, Abigail Adams, John described Dorothy Hancock's "modest decency, dignity and discretion. . . . She avoids talking upon politics. . . . She is unusually silent, as a lady ought to be." Aunt Q exemplified the conventional female role of household manager and hostess: she had no education, no career, and no public voice.

Abigail's mother's marital arrangement was marginally different, due to her superior connections and her choice of a mate less privileged and less educated than her male relatives. Dorothy's lineage gave the Mays the status of "Boston Brahmins," a people, according to Oliver Wendell Holmes Sr., who possessed "houses by Bulfinch, . . . ancestral portraits and Chinese porcelains, . . . humanitarianism, Unitarian faith in the march of the mind, Yankee shrewdness, and New England exclusiveness." Brahmins arose, the historian George Fredrickson explained, from a "union of new wealth and old learning" caused by the "extensive intermarriage . . . of rising merchant families with other families known not for their worldly success but for their long lines of clergymen and Harvard graduates."

Dorothy Sewall May's lineage did not prevent her growing feeble during Abigail's childhood, while her confident, ebullient husband remained active into his seventies. Joseph May was known widely for his efforts "to relieve the needy and the sick, and minister to the dying." In 1811 he was one of the men who founded Massachusetts General Hospital to treat the city's poor. (Private doctors cared for the wealthy.)

Dorothy was doubtless as clever as her husband, and as eager to improve the world, but the restrictions on female behavior, exacerbated by her physical decline, prevented her passions from flowering anywhere outside the home. Years later, Abigail remembered that her mother, whose "own education had been a limited one . . . was constantly solicitous that her daughters should be educated as fit companions for man."

Abigail's desire was to be educated, full stop. She did not relish a marriage like her aunt's or her mother's. Alone among her female relatives, Abigail determined to be different. Although she adored her mother and sisters and considered women's work essential, from childhood she longed for the experiences of her brother Sam Jo. She wished to read history and literature, to learn Latin and Greek, and to use her mind to improve the world, as he was encouraged to do. Her society did not value these goals in a girl, but her brother and mother honored her ambition and encouraged her to educate herself.

In the fall of 1810, when Abigail was ten, she received a gift of a blank journal and the suggestion that she write therein. The donor was likely her mother, a proud great-granddaughter of colonial America's most famous diarist, Judge Samuel Sewall, whose portrait had always hung in her house. The toothless old man in the painting, Dorothy told her daughter, kept journals of his thoughts and experiences for more than sixty years starting in 1667, when he arrived at Harvard College. He became chief justice of the Supreme Judicial Court in 1715, the year in which his grandson, Dorothy's father, was born.

The judge was impressive in other ways, Dorothy said as she and Abigail walked in Boston's Granary Burying Ground, where she pointed out his grave. In Salem in 1692 he sat on the court that convicted and executed twenty innocent people as witches. Alone among the eight judges of that court, Sewall realized his judgments were wrong, publicly repented for them, and devoted the rest of his life to trying to reform the world. In colonial New England, where slavery was commonplace, he composed and published America's first abolitionist tract, *The Selling of Joseph*. Sewall also supported the right of Native Americans to be educated, Dorothy told Abigail, and promoted "the right of women." In his diaries, which Dorothy's older brother Samuel had inherited from their father, the judge gave his wife control of his money because she had "a better faculty than I at managing Affairs. . . . She shall now keep the cash; if I want I will borrow of her." Most remarkable, according to Abigail's mother, Sewall concluded late in life that women are fundamentally equal to men.

This was a novel concept. Abigail knew her mother and father were not equal. Nor was she equal to her brother. Sam Jo and other boys were allowed to play freely in the garret, the garden, and the Common; girls were not. She and her sisters accompanied their brother to school for a few years, but only he was prepared for college.

When Abigail was eight or nine, Sam Jo left dame school to attend an exclusive private boys' school, Chauncy Hall. The school was created by Joseph May and other fathers of teenage boys to compete with Boston Latin, established in 1635. For several years Sam Jo studied Latin, Greek, rhetoric, and mathematics with the Reverend Elisha Clapp at an annual cost of a hundred dollars, the equivalent of $1,500 in 2000. A "very puny" boy surrounded at home by sisters, Sam Jo had abhorred the occasional whippings he had received at the hands of previous male teachers.

One morning in late August of 1813, when Abigail was twelve, Sam Jo left home before dawn in a stagecoach to cross the Charles River for Harvard. At fifteen, he was the fifth generation of the family to attend the college. He, his cousin and chum Samuel E. Sewall, and sixty other young men gathered on Harvard Yard before filing into University Hall, itself still under construction, to take written and oral examinations in Latin, Greek, mathematics, and the physical sciences.

While her brother read the classics and philosophy at college, Abigail remained at home with her mother and sisters. Though she was determined to learn all she could, she was a sickly child: "Illness much interrupted" her home schooling. Later, recalling her childhood for her daughters, Abigail remembered lying sick in bed watching her mother's and sisters' anxious faces hovering above her. Roughly one in two children did not survive past age five. Dorothy May, who could not forget the pain of losing Edward, sometimes read to Abigail the Old Testament story of the prophet Elisha's encounter with a dead boy:

> And when Elisha was come into the house, behold, the child
> was dead, and laid upon his bed. He went in therefore, and shut
> the door upon them twain, and prayed unto the LORD. And he

went up, and lay upon the child, and put his mouth upon his mouth, and his eyes upon his eyes, and his hands upon his hands: and stretched himself upon the child; and the flesh of the child waxed warm . . . the child sneezed seven times, and the child opened his eyes. . . . And when [the child's mother] was come in unto him, he said, Take up thy son. Then she went in, and fell at his feet, and bowed herself to the ground, and took up her son.

Abigail's mother spoiled her, Abigail felt. "Owing to my delicate health, I was much indulged. . . . I was allowed to read a good deal, fed on nice food, and had many indulgences not given my sisters and brothers." Perhaps as a result, "I was rather a good child, but willful." A favorite childhood activity was reading aloud "to my mother and sisters when they were employed" with household chores. She learned to sing hymns and songs but could not play the piano because her right hand had been badly burned when she was six months old. Abigail rarely socialized outside her family: "I never cared much for society. Parties I disliked." In her early teens, though, she "danced well" at Mr. Turner's Dancing School, she confided to her journal, and had "for partners some boys who afterward became eminent Divines."

When Abigail was twelve her parents employed for her a private tutor. Eliza Robbins, the author of children's textbooks, allowed "no drone or loafer near," Abigail recalled. "She made each girl use the talents she had, to the best advantage."

But this instruction too was insufficient to Abigail's intellectual ambition. At fourteen she began corresponding with her brother at college about philosophy and the humanities. She read John Locke on the origin of ideas—whether ideas are innate or products of experience—and was impressed by his theory of the mind as a blank slate. "What you say relative to [the need for universal] education is certainly true," Sam Jo wrote to her. "Nothing is of unimportance in the formation of the mind." Besides guiding Abigail's studies, he tutored schoolboys in Concord, Hingham, Nahant, and Beverly during summers and for a year after college, becoming one of the first instructors ever to employ a new device called a blackboard. Teaching was to be a central part of his life's work, as it had been for countless earlier ministers, whose duties often included the education of young men.

Abigail's much older sister Louisa, who was abroad in Canada in 1816, coached her in spelling, grammar, and writing, useful skills even for a woman. In a letter that year, Louisa exhorted her teenage sisters Eliza and Abigail, "Endeavor to accomplish a little reading every day, and at night write me what you have read. Give me your opinion of the Style, etc., of the book you are engaged in. . . . I feel anxious to have your minds well studied with everything useful, and as highly cultivated as any woman in the country. I do not wish to confine you to one kind of reading. . . . Devote most of your time to history and biography; blend with it poetry, the drama; and sometimes a well chosen novel will not be amiss. . . . A great deal may be gained from the Tales of Miss Edgeworth . . . [whose morals] are pure . . . [and style is] delightful."

Meanwhile, their eighteen-year-old brother had to decide on a career. In choosing the ministry, he followed the path laid out by his maternal great-grandfather, the Reverend Joseph Sewall. More significantly, preaching provided a pulpit from which to improve the world, to do for others what he had always done for Abigail. Then a slender young man of average height with a sweet temper, dark hair, glistening hazel eyes, and "a beaming face" that, according to acquaintances, radiated "kindness and cheer," Samuel Joseph "had but to perceive a social wrong to go about righting it." All his life he had a gift for acting upon his passion for radical causes without ever seeming self-righteous or strident. A "very happy, joyous child," by his own account, he had been "rather a favorite among" his "many friends." Mr. May, as he was known as an adult, seemed to be, like Mr. March in *Little Women,* "a minister by nature as by grace."

His and Abigail's desire for reform arose not only from their Christian faith but also from their Puritan ancestors, who founded America with the hope of creating a purer society. The Mays and their peers abandoned Puritan doctrine but maintained the Puritan view of religion as central to the community and the individual. Anyone seen driving out of Boston "on Sunday, either in the morning or in the afternoon, would have lost credit." Dorothy and Joseph May had "a deep interest in religious thought and inquiry." Twice each Sunday they attended services at King's Chapel, where Abigail's early "love of sacred music was intensified . . . by the grand harmonies of the organ and my father's fine bass voice." The Mays had switched to King's Chapel from Old

South after the American Revolution because they preferred its minister, James Freeman, who rejected the Creed, the Trinity, the liturgy in the Book of Common Prayer, and the prehuman existence of Jesus Christ. They were early Unitarians, a liberal sect of Protestantism only a few decades old. The Puritans' Congregational Church, founded on John Calvin's theology, had taught that God is all-powerful, humanity is depraved, and individuals are predestined for salvation or damnation. Unitarians rejected these beliefs, praying instead to a kindly God who promotes the welfare of humans, each one virtuous and worthy of salvation. They believed humans could make themselves perfect. "I must reverence human nature," the Reverend Dr. William Ellery Channing, who mentored the young Sam Jo, wrote. "I cannot but pity the man who recognizes nothing godlike in his own nature."

In many ways, though, Unitarians still experienced the world as Puritans. Abigail and her siblings inherited from their parents and ancestors a commitment to morality and the belief that more was expected of them than of others. Their progressive politics were a liberal, rational extension of the Puritan impulse toward salvation. Boston Brahmins were a model people, they felt, and theirs should be a model city. They had, in addition to Dr. Channing's sermons on the "perfectibility of human nature," according to Abigail's contemporary Edward Everett Hale, the Unitarian "Dr. Joseph Tuckerman determined that the gospel of Jesus Christ should work its miracles among all sorts and conditions of men; they had a system of public education which they meant to press to its very best; and they had all the money which was needed for anything good. These men subscribed their money with the greatest promptness for any enterprise which promised the elevation of human society." Convinced that "if people only knew what was right they would do what was right," Joseph May and his peers founded the Massachusetts General Hospital, its "annex for the insane," and institutions to train the deaf and the blind—much as their seventeenth-century ancestors had established Boston Latin and Harvard College.

Harvard Divinity School, which Samuel Joseph May entered in 1818 when Abigail was seventeen, was the ideal training ground for a Unitarian divine. Founded only two years earlier, the divinity school was dominated by professors of theology who rejected orthodox Calvinism in favor of "Liberal Christianity," which "*dictated* nothing, except personal purity and righteousness . . . [and] fidelity to our highest sense of the true and the right," as Samuel Joseph recalled later. He studied the Bible, Scottish Common Sense philosophy, and John Locke. When he came home in 1820 with his doctorate, he handed his father the final receipt for his Harvard education, at just under two hundred dollars a year. Joseph May folded the receipt with "an emphatic pressure of his hand" and said, "My son, I am rejoiced that you have gotten through, and that I have been able to afford you the advantages you have enjoyed. If you have been faithful, you have now been possessed of an education that will enable you to go anywhere."

Joseph May advised his son, "Stand up among your fellow-men, and by serving them in one department of usefulness or another, make yourself worthy of a comfortable livelihood, if no more." He added a warning: "If you have not improved your advantages, or should be hereafter slothful, I thank God that I have not property to leave you that will hold you up in a place among men, where you will not deserve to stand."

Abigail never heard such a message from her father. It never occurred to him to secure for her any formal schooling. Her husband, not she, needed an education. Her duty, her father explained when she was ten and "inexperienced in the ways of the world," was to be good and therefore happy, quoting the old maxim, "To be good is to be happy." Goodness in a woman entailed "attention, kindness, gentleness, good nature, and a desire to please," which would "procure friends [and] diffuse pleasure all around." She should demonstrate "industry, patience, perseverance, fidelity . . . moral virtue, piety, and resignation." Nowhere in Joseph May's list for Abigail were his admonitions to a son: Stand up among your fellow men . . . Improve your advantages . . . Go anywhere . . .

Soon after Abigail's seventeenth birthday her father advised her to marry a first cousin, Samuel May Frothingham, the twenty-eight-year-old son of Joseph May's closest sister, Martha, and her husband, a prosperous Portland, Maine, judge named John Frothingham. Joseph May believed that his nephew, who lived and worked in Boston, would be a good match for his youngest daughter. It was not uncommon for first cousins to marry, sometimes to maintain family fortunes, but even Abigail's ancestor the repentant witch judge had questioned the lawfulness of the custom.

Abigail liked her cousin, but she had never considered marrying him. Nor had she seriously considered marrying anyone. She felt that marriage might not suit her. She knew of no woman whose marriage she wished to emulate, although two of her three older sisters had married— Catherine in 1808, when she was twenty-one, and Eliza, at age seventeen, in 1817. Catherine had died, probably in childbirth, in 1815. She had left a husband and a five-year-old son, Charles Windship, for whom Abigail sometimes cared.

Bending to paternal pressure, Abigail consented to her cousin's frequent visits. Soon after her eighteenth birthday, she and Samuel May Frothingham were, she told her daughters later, "virtually betrothed." But she continued to doubt the wisdom of the union. Years of watching her mother's poor health and stifled passions prompted in Abigail a desire to avoid a commitment based on duty. Marriage should be based on love, she felt, not obedience. It should make one happy. Her conception of marriage exemplified a broad social change throughout the Western world. Only around 1800 did people begin to adopt the "radical new idea" of marrying based on love rather than on economic or social factors, and allowing young adults "to choose their marriage partners on the basis of love." It is also possible that Abigail resisted the idea of marrying within her family. "Marry her cousin!" a young woman exclaims in a story that Louisa wrote decades later: "That has been the bane of our family in times past. Being too proud to mate elsewhere, we have kept to ourselves till idiots and lunatics begin to appear." It would be better to choose "the freshest, sturdiest flower . . . to transplant into our exhausted soil."

"I do not love my dear cousin," Abigail finally told her parents. Therefore, he could not make her happy, and she could not marry him.

Abigail's mother accepted her decision not to marry her cousin, but her more conventional father could not. "To be good is to be happy," he reminded his willful daughter. Samuel Frothingham was worthy and capable of supporting her, so she should marry him. Abigail and her father battled quietly over the matter for months. To defuse the conflict, Samuel Joseph suggested she leave home for a year to study on the South Shore with his friend John Allyn, a Harvard-educated minister, and his schoolteacher sister, Abby. Samuel Joseph thought Abigail would benefit not only from time apart from her father but also from the Allyns' attentions. Confident in her brother's judgment, Abigail traveled thirty miles to the coastal town of Duxbury to live and study with the Allyns.

For most of that year eighteen-year-old Abigail learned Latin, French, geometry, astronomy, chemistry, botany, American and world history, moral philosophy, and natural theology under the "most valuable" supervision of Abby Allyn. In imitation of her brother and his classmates, she "read History" in a manner "very enterprising," she reported, "making notes of many" scholarly books, with an emphasis on the Scottish Enlightenment. Among the books she studied were David Hume's *History of England,* Edward Gibbon's six-volume *Decline and Fall of the Roman Empire,* the just-published *View of the State of Europe During the Middle Ages* by Henry Hallam, William Robertson's *History of Charles V,* Oliver Goldsmith's four-volume *History of England,* Charles Rollin's *Ancient History of the Egyptians, Carthaginians, Assyrians, Babylonians, Medes and Persians, Macedonians and Grecians,* and *The Golden Sayings* of Pythagoras. She "did not love study," she observed, "but books were always attractive."

Her brother sent her bundles of books and suggested she read one article from the *Rambler Journal* each morning "until you can remember the train of thought and the leading ideas." Lest her zeal cause her excessive exertion, he advised caution. "Do not be alarmed by the number of Books which it is desirable you should read; nor be induced to read with too great rapidity. . . . Haste in reading is a great waste of *mind* as well as *time*: of mind because it weakens the power of observation; of time because nothing is in fact accomplished." Finally, "Do not think that all knowledge is to be obtained from books, and that you are . . . only learning when sitting in your little chamber. Let your mind be constantly employed upon something. . . . Indulge your curiosity."

Looking to the future, Abigail could envision herself as a teacher, like her brother and Miss Allyn. While her brother's path to the ministry was closed to her, Miss Allyn proved to be "a model worthy of imitation. By her character I form my own, and the very improbability of being like her incites me to constant exertion. . . . I may yet earn my bread by the knowledge this year has afforded me and spend . . . [my] life in teaching a school." Abigail loved to write, too, and was praised for her "flowing, full pen." In her heart of hearts, writing—which she called her "old passion"—was what she wished to do.

Although still nominally engaged to her cousin, Abigail felt no strong tie to Boston, except to her sisters and mother, whose health continued to decline. More and more Abigail felt the tug of scholarly and professional pursuits. That year she set herself the goal of translating portions of the Gospel of John from the Latin Vulgate into English, as she had seen her brother do at Harvard. "If I should not succeed I should be mortified to have you know it," she confessed to her parents. "I wish my pride was subdued as regards this." Nonetheless, working two hours every Sunday for several months, she accomplished the task she had set for herself.

An ambitious young woman, Abigail did not want to be thought inferior to a man. In fact, she said, "I am not willing to be found incapable of anything."

Chapter Two

Drawing Toward Some Ideal Friend

I n early August 1819 at the Allyn house in Duxbury, Abigail received a letter with shocking news. Suddenly and unexpectedly, Samuel May Frothingham was dead. She took the stagecoach to Boston to join her family in mourning her dear cousin.

This tragic loss might have been expected to resolve her conflict with her father but apparently it did not. Soon after her cousin's funeral she returned to Duxbury to continue her studies, and at the end of that year she informed her father she would return home only if he agreed to the condition that she "be allowed to refuse visiting." She would no longer submit to the expectation that she receive eligible young men. "I must be permitted this winter to withdraw," even "if I incur the epithet[s] pedantic or unsocial or misanthropic," she resolved. Should her withdrawal arouse criticism, she would "trust that time will obliterate the fiction of opinion, and confirm the decisions of truth."

Nineteen-year-old Abigail dreamed not of marriage but of teaching school and learning more about the world. She wished to avoid "those gay scenes where once was my delight" in order to study without distraction and to "fix my habits of attention and reflection," she told her parents. "I cannot let this winter pass without much improvement in mind and habits. I feel as if I had just begun life. . . . And I am every day more convinced that there are no real enjoyments but those which philosophy dictates and religion sanctions." Her father reminded her that a passion for intellectual achievement diverted her from a young woman's expected path. He must have agreed to her condition, though, because she returned to Boston at the end of 1819 to live with her parents and her sister Louisa.

At home she soon discovered that Louisa shared her interest in education. Several female friends had already started schools in their homes; teaching was one of the few careers open to affluent single women. Abigail and Louisa talked about teaching together, which suited Abigail, who did not feel sufficiently confident to create a school on her own. "Louisa's capability joined with my industry shall make us independent of our relations and happy in ourselves," unlike the model woman of their day.

In 1821, to Abigail's dismay, her sister Louisa accepted a marriage proposal from Samuel Greele, a Harvard graduate of 1802 and church deacon whose first wife had been their late first cousin Lydia Sewall. Because a married woman had even fewer employment opportunities than her unmarried peers, Louisa's marriage would preclude any sisterly school.

Meanwhile, in March 1822, her other surviving sister, Eliza May Willis, who was twenty-three, fell ill and died of unknown causes in Portland, Maine. Eliza left a husband, Benjamin Willis Jr., a three-year-old son, and an infant daughter. In a letter to Eliza at the boy's birth in 1819, Abigail had anticipated the opportunities enabled by his gender: "Soon he will be rivaling his Aunt [Abigail] in 'amo,' 'amas, 'amat.' . . . And may he, like her, thirst for knowledge, but, unlike her, may he be earlier gratified and better able to receive the draught, which intoxicates weak minds, but renders strong minds stronger." Abigail's desire for a man's education had not yet caused her to reject the notion that a woman's mind is inherently weaker than a man's. Following her sister Eliza's death, Abigail assumed a traditional female role with her little nephew and niece, Hamilton and Elizabeth Willis, as she had with her sister Catherine's son, by taking "care of them in their childhood a good deal," often in her parents' house on Federal Court. She came to see her motherless niece and nephews as almost her own progeny, referring to them in an 1829 letter to her brother as "my children." Their care was burdensome. "My time is expired, the children are clamorous," she added. "I have three motherless orphans, all suffering for that care which a *Mother* only can give. . . ."

Despite, or perhaps because of, the extensive child care that Abigail provided during her twenties to her late sisters' offspring, she felt unmoored. "I have felt a loneliness in this world that [is] making a misanthrope of me," she told Samuel Joseph, "in spite of everything I . . . do to overcome it." Her mother, now in her early sixties, was too weak to leave her bedchamber. Abigail felt her father's continuing disapproval, and her brother Samuel Joseph was no longer present to steady her. He gave his first sermon on Christmas Day 1820 in Springfield, Massachusetts, and was ordained in Boston eighteen months later by Dr. Channing and Dr. Freeman, founders of American Unitarianism. "Discover what moral evils have sprung up in the present age," Freeman had exhorted him, "and you will exert yourself to eradicate them." Samuel Joseph now preached temporarily at the First Congregational Church of Brooklyn, in Connecticut, a state that had never before hosted a Unitarian minister. In order to decide where to preach permanently, he planned to travel down the eastern seaboard to consider churches that had offered him pulpits, as far south as Richmond, Virginia. In anticipation of his sister Louisa's impending marriage, he invited her to accompany him on the trip. Samuel Joseph and Louisa were away for months, leaving Abigail, in Boston with her orphaned charges, bereft.

Conscious of this, her brother sent her letters describing his and Louisa's adventures. The churches and monuments were impressive, but nothing so impressed him as the sight of human beings in chains. Like their early loss of their brother Edward, this experience changed the trajectory of both his and Abigail's lives.

The most memorable event of the trip occurred as he and Louisa rode in a stagecoach from Baltimore, where slavery was legal, toward the nation's capital, the site of one of America's largest slave markets. "We saw, standing by the road-side, a row of negro men, twenty or thirty in number," Samuel Joseph wrote. "We soon perceived that they were all handcuffed, and that the irons about their wrists were fastened around a very heavy chain that was passed between them [and] attached to the tail of a large wagon." Black women passed along the line "giving to each man a thick slice of coarse bread."

Thinking the men prisoners, Samuel Joseph asked his sister Louisa, "What can they have been guilty of?" A moment later the truth "flashed upon" his mind. "Oh, no, Louisa! They are slaves being taken to market."

"I reckon," a southern passenger said to him, "you and the lady are from New England."

Indeed they were. At home the Mays had heard reports of "the abomination of slavery and the internal slave trade," but they were not yet conscious of the reality of human bondage. "The house-slaves in our kinsmen's families in Baltimore seemed to us like any other domestic servant" in Boston, he said. "But here the monstrous wrong stood palpably before us. I never before felt so grateful that I was not born where human beings can be bought and sold, and treated like cattle. I am ashamed of my country and my race."

The timing of their births had shielded Abigail and her siblings from slavery's role in their lives. Some of their ancestors' fortunes were indeed built on the New England slave trade, which began in the 1640s. They had cousins in Georgia and Maryland who owned slaves. Even some of their Massachusetts relatives owned slaves until 1783, when the commonwealth's highest court banned the slave trade and ordered immediate emancipation. Aunt Q's father, Edmund Quincy, bought and sold slaves as late as the 1770s; her husband John Hancock inherited his uncle's slaves in 1764. Hancock's aunt Lydia at her death in 1776 freed her five slaves, several of whom stayed on as house servants to John and Dorothy Quincy Hancock. Many heroes of the revolution owned slaves. But in the mid-eighteenth century, when bonded white servants were so prevalent that "as much as half of colonial society [was] at any moment legally unfree, the peculiar character of lifetime, hereditary black slavery was not always as obvious as it would become in the years following the Revolution when bonded white servitude virtually disappeared," the historian Gordon Wood explained.

In the postrevolutionary Boston in which the Mays lived, the wealthy had servants, not slaves. Children of Abigail's generation knew free blacks intimately, as their nursery maids. Abigail's first cousin Samuel E. Sewall attributed his adult passion for abolition to his devotion to his black nurse, Flora, who often admonished him, "Swallow your temper." At the age of three, when he heard someone call Flora "black," he retorted, "She's *not* brack, she's b'own." Samuel Joseph May remembered as a boy of seven coming to consciousness in the arms of a black woman he did not know. Finding him bloody and unconscious after a fall, she generously carried him home.

But Abigail and her peers were not familiar with the sight of slaves in irons headed to market like cattle. The image aroused in her twenty-three-year-old brother "thoughts and feelings that a few years afterwards took shape and gave direction to the whole cause of my life." On his return to New England he and Abigail discussed slavery in a new way. It offended them because it undercut their faith in their nation's righteousness and justice. It was wrong.

Abigail had already impressed friends with "her prompt decisions concerning the right and wrong of things," in the words of Lydia Maria Child. In 1836 Abigail called emancipation "a cause worthy [of] the best and most intelligent efforts of every enlightened American. . . . Every woman with a feeling heart and thinking head is answerable to her God if she do not plead the cause of the oppressed, however limited may be her sphere." She predicted in an 1835 letter to her friend Mary Tyler Peabody, "We shall shake hands over the victories of Abolition before long. . . . The dawn is obvious in the dark horizon, depend on it, dearest Mary, we shall live to see the perfect day. Then how those mistaken patriots will exhort the hills to cover them—and the mountains to fall upon them. . . . I mean in particular those men who . . . make the cradle of liberty the coffin of freedom. What they intended for a stumbling block will prove a stepping stone to this righteous cause."

Abigail had a complex view of her privileged past. She honored her revolutionary and Puritan ancestors—particularly Judge Samuel Sewall, who opposed slavery—but she considered the nation itself corrupt because of its foundation in slavery, which its constitution allowed. This set her apart from her father, who regarded slavery as a necessary evil that would eventually fade away. Massachusetts formally banned slavery in 1783, but Boston's elite, including Joseph May, did not demand a halt to the national system of slave labor that contributed significantly to New England's commercial growth. Slavery still thrived in much of the North in the 1830s, George Fredrickson wrote; American "democracy was premised on racism." Most New Englanders opposed abolitionism, considering the idea radical and dangerous. Slavery was too entrenched in American commerce, they believed, to be ended abruptly. If slavery did not gradually disappear, Joseph May and his contemporaries supported "repatriating" freed slaves to Africa. They could not countenance the notion of assimilating freed slaves into American society.

This rejection by powerful Bostonians of the antislavery movement would intensify as New England turned from its maritime economy to a new dependence on manufacturing in mill towns outside cities. By 1840, according to the historian Van Wyck Brooks, the "wheels of the cotton-factories revolved at a furious pace, and the Southern slave-drivers plied their whips to feed the Yankee mills with Southern cotton. . . . The more the prosperity of New England came to depend on cotton, the closer the propertied classes drew to the Southern planters, with whom they felt obliged to ally themselves, yielding to them in all political matters."

In regard to Abigail's mother, there is no extant record of Dorothy Sewall May's personal view of abolition or any public topic, as is typical of women of her time. It seems likely, though, that Abigail and her brother inherited from her their passion for reform. Among all the ancestors she described to them, the one who aroused her greatest pride was the repentant witch judge who more than a century earlier had called for the abolition of slavery.

In October 1823, soon after Abigail's twenty-third birthday, her sister Louisa married Samuel Greele. Abigail experienced this union as a loss. Not only were her dreams of starting a school dashed, but now she was the only sibling left with her parents on Federal Court.

Not long afterward her brother, who was twenty-six, proposed to Lucretia Flagge Coffin, the lovely, eighteen- or nineteen-year-old daughter of a wealthy Boston merchant and his wife. Lucretia, who had been tutored at home in French, Italian, and probably German, took pride in her refined speech, manners, and appearance. She had a "complex about growing old" that kept her from ever revealing her age to her husband and children. Abigail adored Lucretia and dubbed her "Lu," the nickname also of her sister Louisa. Samuel Joseph and Lucretia's wedding, at King's Chapel on June 1, 1825, troubled Abigail less than those of Catherine, Eliza, and Louisa because it seemed to entail gaining rather than losing a sister.

Samuel Joseph and his bride returned to Brooklyn, in eastern Connecticut, where he had decided to remain. His father had advised him to take a more impressive pulpit, with an established congregation in a city, because staying in Brooklyn would provide only "conflict, hard work, and poverty." But Samuel Joseph was drawn to evangelize among farmers, bankers, and laborers in mills and factories, many of them still strict Calvinists who considered Unitarianism heresy. He embraced the challenge of preaching in a rural, conservative part of New England where slaves still toiled. Connecticut's 1784 emancipation law had called only for the gradual freeing of slaves' offspring, so the state still had slaves as late as the 1850s. Brooklyn, about eighty miles southwest of Boston, was not too far to prevent frequent trips home to see his parents and Abigail.

Despite his idealism, Samuel Joseph's progressive opinions soon aroused suspicion in Connecticut. An early follower of Noah Worcester, founder of the fledgling American peace movement, whom he'd met during divinity school, Samuel Joseph formed a Brooklyn Peace Society and gave sermons advocating disarmament. He considered capital punishment "judicial murder" and declined to preach at an 1826 execution. He could not serve as chaplain of a regiment because, he said, his only prayer would be "that they might beat their swords into plowshares and learn war no more."

Perhaps more shocking to his neighbors, the Reverend May preached the virtues of temperance. He and Lucretia agreed to "total abstinence from intoxicating drinks." They requested that their house in Brooklyn be built "without the customary hospitable kegs of rum, thereby audaciously violating precedent." He founded the Brooklyn temperance society, which sponsored parades of a "Cold Water Brigade" to encourage the drinking of water. Temperance, now seen as "the most popular reform movement of the antebellum period," was a sincere response by settled Americans to the growing problem of rampant drunkenness among men. In 1830 an American man drank on average the equivalent of a quarter bottle of whiskey every day. Alcohol consumption increased with the anxiety and powerlessness experienced by a "growing sea of workers who no longer lived under their employer's roofs." Most activists for temperance and prohibition were women. Like the early peace movement, temperance was at odds with social norms. In promoting these causes, Samuel Joseph dared to defy his father, but the defiance of a May son, unlike that of a daughter, did not confound the old man.

In Boston a few weeks after Samuel Joseph and Lucretia's wedding, Aunt Q, now in her late seventies, sat on a balcony to watch the Marquis de Lafayette lead a parade to the Bunker Hill monument to honor the Revolutionary War dead. Nearly a half century before, she and Mr. Hancock had hosted the general, and in October 1781 it had been Lafayette who arrived at their house with news of the British surrender at Yorktown. The general's host now was Aunt Q's nephew and Abigail's cousin Josiah Quincy III, who had been a Federalist senator, congressman, and judge before becoming Boston's mayor. As Mayor Quincy escorted General Lafayette along streets crowded with people and festooned with French and American flags, "the keen-eyed old soldier" spied Madam Hancock. Although "time had wrought many changes in her piquant face and figure, he instantly recognized her and, with the inborn courtesy of a Frenchman, directed his conveyance to stop in front of the place where she sat, and rising, with his hand placed over his heart, made a graceful obeisance which was gracefully returned." His eyes apparently glistened with tears, prompting Aunt Q to "burst into tears" and proclaim, "I have lived long enough."

This scene, as it was later recounted by Abigail to Louisa, appears in *An Old-Fashioned Girl*. Grandma Shaw, who is described as having been a girl during the French general's 1825 visit, recalls that "by and by the general, escorted by the mayor, drove up" to her aunt's house on Federal Street. "Dear me, I see him now! A little old man in nankeen trousers and vest, a long blue coat and ruffled shirt, leaning on his cane. . . . Lafayette bowed . . . to the governor's widow, and kissed her hand. . . . The last thing I remember was hanging out of the window with a flock of girls watching the carriage roll away while the crowd cheered as if they were mad . . . 'Hurrah for Lafayette and Mayor Quincy! Hurrah for Madam Hancock and the pretty girls! Hurrah for Colonel May!'" Louisa neither repeated nor explained the novel's reference to her actual grandfather.

The autumn after Lafayette's tour, it was not the ancient Aunt Q who died but Abigail's beloved mother, at age sixty-six, on October 31, 1825. This was another devastating blow to Abigail. In recent years, as her siblings had married and moved away or died, she had grown closer to the woman who seemed at times her closest companion and best confidante.

With her mother she could share the dreams of studying, teaching, and writing that perplexed her father. In her journal she paid tribute to her late mother: "She loved the doing of a good action better than describing it. She never said great things, but she has done ten thousand generous ones."

Abigail could not have doubted, if the thought even occurred to her, that her mother's life would leave little or no mark on the world. Dorothy Sewall May—of whom there are no extant portraits or journals or letters, although the latter two likely existed—was buried at King's Chapel in early November 1825 with three of her twelve children present: Abigail, Samuel Joseph, and Louisa. Her son Charles had not yet returned from sea, and all the rest of her children were dead.

Without her mother, Abigail felt lonelier than ever. The house that once bustled with her siblings and friends was empty except for her father and servants. Her dislike of socializing isolated her from peers. The present seemed gloomy; the future did not beckon.

A few months after her mother died, her sixty-five-year-old father, still "tall and personable," informed her that he had proposed marriage to Mary Ann Atkinson Cary, the widow of a King's Chapel assistant minister. Madam Cary accepted his proposal, which in itself was not uncommon; many privileged widowers and a few widows married again.

But the proposal distressed Abigail. Madam Cary was thirty-nine, more than a quarter century younger than Joseph May, younger than two of his children, and only thirteen years older than Abigail herself. His action seemed hasty and ill-advised, especially as Dorothy had so recently died. How could a man who so worshipped duty so fail in his duty to his late wife? "My father has been very busy in conjugating the verb to love," Abigail wrote to a cousin, "and I assure you he declines its moods and tenses inimitably."

As headstrong as his youngest daughter, Colonel May married Madam Cary on October 12, 1826, not quite a year after Abigail's mother's death. As the new Madam May moved into Abigail's house, Abigail fled. She traveled by stagecoach several hours south to live with Samuel Joseph and Lucretia, who had rented a house in Brooklyn, Connecticut, while awaiting construction of their new house. Abigail reveled in the company of her brother and sister-in-law. With them, as with her mother, she could indulge her fantasy of a future of writing or teaching.

Unlike the vast majority of her female peers, who were already married, Abigail devoted her twenties to exploring her role as an individual in the world. In the context of her era, she was behaving like a man.

It was her status as a woman, though, that placed Abigail in the bedchamber on June 27, 1827, when Lucretia May gave birth to her and Samuel Joseph's first child. They named the baby Joseph, after his paternal grandfather. Abigail and Lucretia grew even closer as they shared the care of the infant and the house, while Samuel Joseph was often away, preaching to other congregations and raising funds for reform.

One of his missions was to improve Connecticut's notoriously poor common (public) schools, which well-to-do residents mostly avoided by educating their children privately. Unable to avert his eyes from a problem, the Reverend May leapt into action. He formed a society to raise money for a statewide convention on public education. In early 1827 he wrote letters seeking speakers, advice, and support. One of the teachers he contacted was a young man from Wolcott, Connecticut, known for his unconventional teaching methods. He unscrewed the fixed desks and chairs in his classroom, decorated it with greens, and asked his students questions rather than filling them with answers, as was the norm. In the spring Samuel Joseph invited A. Bronson Alcott to come to Brooklyn to discuss rejuvenating the common schools.

On the July afternoon that Mr. Alcott knocked on the parsonage door, Samuel Joseph was not at home and Lucretia must have been occupied upstairs with their new baby, because Abigail opened the door. Before her stood a tall young man with a long face, piercing blue eyes, and disheveled blond hair. He introduced himself and said he was calling on Mr. May. She welcomed him into the parlor and introduced herself as the younger sister of the minister, who would return soon. Until then she could entertain her brother's guest.

As Mr. Alcott described his classroom in Cheshire, Connecticut, Abigail was struck by his volubility, intelligence, and charm. Especially striking was his tranquility, a remarkable calm that she and many others found alluring. Hearing "the grand diapason of his rich words," another acquaintance observed, was "like going to Heaven on a swing." Abigail had never before observed in a man such a delightful mix of traits—personal serenity blended with verbal and intellectual intensity.

Before long she felt sufficiently bold to relate some of her own ideas about teaching. She believed that children should be allowed to "think and reason" and be "active in themselves," rather than "treated like machines . . . to be acted upon." Her particular interest was the education of girls. The deficiencies of her education exemplified a wider problem: "Women are not educated up to their abilities." She hoped to promote female education in order to enhance women's "moral health and intellectual growth. . . . Let us be taught to think, to act, to teach."

Impressed, Bronson noted that his eminent host's lively younger sister was unmarried. There is no extant portrait of Abigail from this period, but later photographs suggest that at twenty-six she was lithe and handsome, with long chestnut hair. She had a quick mind, a forthright manner, and dark, deep-set eyes that seemed to take in everything. Bronson, who had never been on intimate terms with a Boston Brahmin, felt drawn to what he called the "May character. This family," he explained the following year, "is distinguished for their urbanity, and benevolence, their native manners and nobleness of souls, moral purity and general beneficences."

This "young lady apparently near [my] age," whose culture and early life were so remote from his, enthralled him. His first impression, reported in his journal, was of "an interesting woman [I] had often portrayed in [my] imagination. . . . In her [I] thought [I] saw its reality. There was nothing of artifice, or affectation of manners" about Abigail. "All was openness, simplicity," intelligence, and traditionally feminine virtues: "sympathy, piety, exemplified in the tenderness of the eye, in the beauty of the moral countenance, in the joyousness of domestic performance," and "refined and elevated conversation. . . . How could [I] but be in love with [these virtues'] possessor? We conversed on a variety of subjects. She had thought for herself. Her sentiments were also [mine]. Her purposes were like [mine]—the instruction of the young. Everything seemed to favor the commencement of an acquaintance of a pure and sentimental kind."

Abigail knew little of her admirer's background. She was unaware that he was literally a self-made man. "Mr. Alcott," the eldest son of an unschooled couple named Alcox on a hardscrabble farm in a region of Connecticut known for "extreme" Calvinistic theology, had been baptized Amos Bronson Alcox. His early dislike of rote learning prompted him at age thirteen to leave school and read at home among seven younger brothers and sisters. At seventeen he traveled to Virginia and the Carolinas to peddle scissors, puzzles, and trinkets from a cart. Southern planters welcomed the placid Yankee youth into their homes, impressing him with their manners and wealth. He could not make peddling profitable, though; all he accumulated was debt. He returned home "disgraced" and "disgusted" with himself. To elude creditors, perhaps, he re-created himself as a new man, A. Bronson Alcott. Sensing a call to teach, he visited district schools in hopes of understanding the profession. Schools in several rural towns, including his hometown, hired him, but in each post parents objected to his novel methods and eccentric manner, and he was asked to leave. "Those who in modern times attempt in education anything different from the old established modes are by many regarded as . . . dangerous" anarchists, he had observed in his journal in September 1826. "How knoweth this man more than others?" his critics seemed to him to be saying. "Who is he? What is his parentage? *Learn and look, for out of Galilee cometh no Prophet.* Hath he ever been the inmate of a University? . . . Hath he ever taught in our privileged seminaries or Churches? *Where then hath he these things?*" At the time he wrote that account, the year before his encounter with Abigail May, the twenty-six-year-old teacher owed six hundred dollars, triple his annual salary.

To Abigail he seemed, while "not an Educated man," to have skillfully taught himself. He spoke with eloquence of literature and philosophy. He expressed passion for the work of the Swiss educational philosopher Johann Pestalozzi, whose letters Abigail read and admired. Bronson's "modesty" and "earnest desire to promote better advantages for the young" charmed her, as did his determination that the "large fund of one million" dollars—equal to eighteen million dollars in 2000—that the state had provided for education "be used for higher ends" such as raising teacher salaries to "secure better teaching."

In the middle of the young couple's conversation Mr. May arrived, concluding their pleasurable intercourse and commencing a similar encounter of his own. Later, after supper and several hours of conversation with Bronson, Samuel Joseph took his sister aside and said, "He is a born sage and saint . . . radical in all matters of reform . . .

I have never been so immediately taken possession of by any man I have ever met."

During the week that Bronson resided with the Mays, Samuel Joseph observed that his sister could not take her eyes off their guest. This and certain "indications of a mutual attraction" pleased the minister. He and his wife had the satisfaction of a child; now his sister had the possibility of a husband and a family of her own.

At the end of the week Mr. Alcott departed for his home seventy miles to the west, leaving Abigail with her dreams. She felt she had finally found a suitable male companion, to whom she might grow as close as she had been to her mother and sisters, with whom she might open a school. Over the subsequent months she did not see him in person but sent him many letters. Men "are beginning to see that we are intelligent, accountable beings," she wrote to him. "That we are instruments in the hand of the great Artificer [Creator] cannot be denied. Let us then be used as such. Let . . . women be treated as divine agents, not merely as objects of pleasure or sense, created only for convenience and admiration," as were her mother and many of her peers.

In letters she elaborated on the need for women's education, but in her journal she revealed her adoration of her new acquaintance: "He shall be my moral mentor, my intellectual guide . . . my benefactor; he shall see . . . that I am not only his lover, his mistress, but his pupil, his companion." She hoped Bronson would take her brother's advice to seek work in Boston. Then she might see him. As she told Lucretia, "abundant news from Boston," presumably in regard to a school that Bronson might start, prompted Abigail to consider taking a trip there.

That fall, though, Bronson took a teaching position in Bristol, Connecticut. As before and probably for similar reasons, some of his pupils' parents complained and he was asked to leave. Meanwhile, Abigail wrote to him of her desire to be his "female assistant," should he teach in Boston. If he would only "instruct" her, she would be "pleased to associate myself with you for that purpose."

She meant more. "It would add much to my happiness to form an arc in your social circle wherever you may be," she continued. "My words come dripping off my pen so fast that their component parts are lost. You will, I fear, be puzzled to read and more puzzled to understand; but the fear that my thoughts will be chilled by too much attention to their expression, has made my language incoherent, my writing shameful." She may have feared that voicing her feelings was not feminine. "But if amidst the scrawl, you can make out what I most wish to convey, I shall be satisfied." Finally, "I shall pass the winter here and hope to hear from you (if not see you) often."

They did not see each other much that winter, if at all. He visited Boston the following spring, armed with letters of introduction from Samuel Joseph to other ministers and notable men. Bronson called at the mansions of her relatives and family friends, each one more unlike his boyhood farmhouse than the last. He heard a sermon by the Reverend Ralph Waldo Emerson, Samuel Joseph's friend, and met a gifted young teacher named Elizabeth Palmer Peabody, a sister of Abigail's friend Mary. Bronson called on Samuel Joseph's mentor, the esteemed Unitarian minister William Ellery Channing, and spent an afternoon in his parlor on Mount Vernon Street discussing educational and religious reform.

At Channing's urging, Bronson went to hear him sermonize at the Federal Street Church. "How ardent was my drawing toward some . . . ideal friend," Bronson recalled later—unaware perhaps that Abigail longed for that role. "I was led providentially to visit my brother May at Brooklyn, and through him was introduced to Boston" and Channing, "he more than any mind at that time answering to my ideal." Channing told his Harvard roommate Dr. Joseph Tuckerman, whose wife was now Abigail's stepsister, of the young Mr. Alcott. The Reverends Tuckerman and Channing agreed that Alcott might be the man to organize the "infant school" that Boston badly needed. Infant schools, established in urban centers in the 1820s to educate poor children as young as age two, were becoming attractive also to middle-class parents. Bronson, "flattered by the prospects" before him, accepted the offer and prepared to open the Salem Street Infant School in Boston's North End.

In Connecticut Abigail prevailed upon Lucretia, who had regained her "strength & health" since Joseph's birth, to join her in traveling to Boston. By the first of May the two young women and eleven-month-old Joseph May were ensconced amid the stately furniture, English carpets, and fine glassware of Abigail's childhood home. Abigail "says it is quite pleasant at the [house on Federal] Court & that they are very kind to her," Lucretia wrote to her husband, "but there is a something, I can't

tell what, there. I don't feel at my ease." Lucretia sometimes felt uncomfortable with her father-in-law and his young wife, whom they all nonetheless called "Mother." One afternoon, eleven-month-old Joseph sat
at the feet of Lucretia, Abigail, and Louisa as they took tea with Mother.
As Lucretia recounted, "What did Joe do but *piddle* on the carpet. Your
Mother, Abba, Louisa and I [were busy] with cloths, diapers & I can't tell
what. You would have screamed to see our distress."

Abigail had not yet seen Bronson, but she delighted in news of him
from her sister Louisa. "My dear brother," Abigail wrote to Samuel
Joseph, "[I] Hope you get on [in Brooklyn] to your heart's content,
wifeless, childless, sisterless. Noiseless . . . I can as yet tell you no news
[but] Louisa tells me Mr. Alcott is all the 'rage'. The Cabots are head
over heels enamored with his system" of teaching, which involved the
Socratic method, much discussion and journal writing, and minimal
structure and routine. "Susan Cabot says, 'the Infant [school] may make
us much [advantage] as they have a mind to if Mr. A[lcott] will only take
the school.' . . . Louisa has only seen him once. He is constantly with
some of the grandees . . . I have not seen him, do write to him."

Again Abigail wrote to Bronson to offer him her services. In response,
he called on her at her father's house in early June "in relation to the
Infant School, for which she has applied as assistant teacher," according
to his journal.

He politely refused her, without divulging his reason. In his journal
he admitted that he was afraid of losing "Miss May" if he were forced
to depart a school in which she worked. Referring to himself in the first
person plural, as was his habit, Bronson felt "unwilling she should engage
in this school with hopes of continuing in it when we leave, for we are
very desirous—and are becoming every day more interested in her—that
she should assist in the more desirable situation which we propose for
ourselves in a school of higher order. And we have reason to think that
she herself is more interested in the latter situation than in the former,
and would assist us with pleasure." He was "devoted to the teaching of
Infant Schools, and female assistance, if the right kind, is our chief hope.
In the acquisition of this lady to assist us we think we should obtain that
kind of help which is indispensible." The assistance he envisioned from
Abigail was as his wife.

Disappointed by his response to her overture, Abigail defied social norms further the next day. She walked unescorted through the North End, hoping to encounter him there as if by accident. Abigail's boldness may have inspired a grown Jo March near the end of *Little Women* to walk out alone in hopes of running into an older man she loves, Professor Friedrich Bhaer. "I always do take a walk toward evening, and I don't know why I should give it up, just because I often meet the Professor on his way out," Jo thinks to herself, not quite admitting her feelings. In the North End decades before Louisa wrote those words, Bronson spied Abigail on her solitary walk. He said nothing to her, but several days later wrote to her, "I shall hope that you will sometimes visit my little circle in Salem Street. I thought I caught a glimpse of you in that vicinity the other day. Shall I add that only my diffidence prevented me from accosting you there?"

July was agony for both Abigail and Bronson. Feeling melancholy and fearing rejection, he felt unable to speak to her of his feelings. She found him "too vacillating." She knew she loved him. Did he not love her? Each time she broached the subject, he did not know what to say. He alternated "between doubt and certainty." The prospect of marriage "calls forth the most gloomy and afflicting scenes" in his mind. "What a peculiar temperament is [mine]!"

On August 2, seeking somehow to express his feelings, he handed her his journal. She read through the entries explaining his refusal to hire her. This "had the very effect which [he had] hoped." Without delay she spoke the words that eluded him, and he supplied the yes. He revealed to her that "he has been attached to me from the evening" of their first conversation, in Brooklyn, "but circumstances have prevented the disclosure of his feelings. I found it remained to me to make all conscious with him or give him that encouragement and promise that should secure to him my future interest." In addition to defying convention by voicing the proposal, Abigail did not wish him to ask her father for her hand, as all her sisters' suitors had done. Triumphantly she wrote to her brother and Lucretia, "I am engaged to Mr. Alcott, not in a school, but in the solemn, the momentous capacity of friend and wife." It would be a marriage of opposites: "He is moderate. I am impetuous. He is prudent and humble. I am forward and arbitrary. He is poor. But we are both industrious. Why may we not be happy?" This description would prove prescient in that Bronson and Abigail were opposites. Over the years, though, Bronson would demonstrate little of the prudence, industry, and humility that she had ascribed to him. She, on the other hand, would remain as she saw herself then, industrious, impetuous, and forward.

Her refusal to approach marriage in the traditional way continued to perplex her father. Bronson was unlike every other prospective son-in-law Colonel May had considered. The young teacher was charming, no doubt, and admired by Samuel Joseph. But Bronson was penniless, without formal education or family money, and only fitfully employed. While Colonel May had rejected the pursuit of wealth for its own sake, he never questioned the social norm that a man support his family. It is possible that Abigail's father detected in Bronson a quality that Ralph Waldo Emerson would later define: encounters with Alcott invariably ended with his demand, "Give us much land & money."

In answer to Colonel May's concerns about Bronson's ability to support her, Abigail indicated that neither she nor Bronson worried about money. She had great faith in him. His new school was indeed flourishing; by late summer its enrollment had tripled, to sixty students. Despite Bronson's continuing indebtedness, of which Abigail was likely now aware, he aimed to establish what he called a "reign of truth and reason" by "arrang[ing] society—or systems of education—in accord with the laws of our nature." His projects were "opposed to the ruling opinions and prejudices of the age, [so] we shall render ourselves unpopular," he conceded, but "we care little about these things."

Abigail told her brother and Lucretia, "The connection I have found with Mr. Alcott is very essential to me." During their marriage she anticipated that Bronson would guide and improve her character by smoothing her edges. "He is tranquil and firm," she said, "which you know is directly opposite to my constitution, [so] full of emotion, strong prejudices. . . . My dislikes are antipathies, my prepossessions, loves." Her deep emotions and firm convictions, which she shared with her brother and doubtless their late mother, whom she "loved with all the ardor of" her heart and from whom she "imbibed much" of her character, were among their legacies as Sewalls. "With this temperament," she went on, "how important that my future companion should be tranquil and equable. He is all this, which gives me a hope that I too may one day become what my friends may wish." Enumerating her perceived failings, she added, "I do feel most exquisitely. . . . It is a pardonable sin, for it is a natural response. But I have moral strength which restores the equilibrium, and I go on cheerfully."

Conversations with Bronson strengthened her hope that women might play a new role in society. "No woman's intelligence should be trammelled and attenuated by custom as her body is by fashion," Abigail believed. She intended to join her husband in bringing her talents and opinions before the world, which her mother and sisters could not do. "Reason and religion are emancipating woman from that intellectual thralldom that has so long held her captive," she observed. "She is finding her place by the side and in the heart of man, thus compelling him by the irresistible force of merit to accept her as an intellectual companion."

In late summer she escaped the heat by visiting relatives in Hingham on the coast. Upon her return in early September, Bronson called on her at Federal Court. "I do love this good woman," he wrote in his journal. "I love her because she loves me."

Abigail introduced Bronson to all her Boston relatives, including Aunt Q, who invited the couple to dine. "Servants!" Aunt Q exclaimed when a servant she summoned failed to appear, according to Bronson. She praised him for eating two servings of her apple pudding: "You shall have enough, I say!" Her cider-sauce was better than Abigail's mother's, she boasted. While carving her "fine roast beef" she said she'd learned to carve because of Governor Hancock's lame wrist. Aunt Q stuffed Bronson with bread and potatoes and requested he "come again and take tea with her." This "eccentric . . . old lady," he observed, "still considers herself invested with the honors of Revolutionary respect" and "is constantly admitting persons of her acquaintance to see her, being too much absorbed in her own Madamism to call on others." A woman of "fancied greatness," she presumed to entertain him with "her august presence," her table, and her "My Mr. Hancock." Aunt Q's manners demonstrated to Bronson "the influence of station upon weak and ignorant minds, how much circumstances give tone and quality to untaught natures."

Even as Bronson mocked the imperious Aunt Q, his admiration of her world grew. "The morality of Boston is more pure than that of any other city in America," he felt. "Channing is its moral teacher. His system of instruction is that of Christ." This "righteous" city had hosted the momentous event of the past year, his "connexion with Miss May," of which he "anticipate[d] the fullest felicities."

Abigail, meanwhile, anticipated the kind of family she hoped they would create. The mother "is the most interesting as well as important member in the community," she believed. "The father, brother, husband, son all feel her importance and are rational, enlightened enough to acknowledge it." This was not true among the Mays, but it would, she vowed, be true among the Alcotts.

She spent the autumn in Connecticut with Samuel Joseph and Lucretia. More sad news came in November 1828, when her last surviving sister, Louisa May Greele, who had been "miserable" for months with "horrible headaches" of unknown cause, died at age thirty-five, leaving two children. Samuel Joseph and Abigail went to Boston for Louisa's funeral, while Lucretia stayed in Connecticut with her baby. "Dear Lucretia . . . [seems] nearer and dearer to me than any female friend in the world," Abigail wrote, now that her mother and sisters were all gone. Years later Abigail asked her brother to "tell Lucretia her love is more substantial than the world's Gold."

In Brooklyn a week after Louisa's funeral, one-year-old Joseph May developed a cough and high fever. He was so pale and weak by December 11 that Lucretia notified Samuel Joseph, who was still in Boston. "You had best come home soon," she scrawled early the next morning. "7 o/clock the darling is no better, do come soon, yrs in love, LFMay." Before handing her note to a rider for delivery to Boston, she added, "The Dr says he is no better. He is very very sick."

Even before her note could be delivered, a messenger arrived at Federal Court in Boston to say the baby had died. Samuel Joseph "hurried home" to his wife and dead son "with a brain almost bewildered." This loss recalled the loss of his brother Edward, which had proved God's existence, guided him to the ministry, and helped him face death. "I pray God that these impressive lessons may sink deep into my heart," he wrote in his journal, "and induce me to lead a life of greater holiness and devotion to his will and the happiness of my fellow-men."

Abigail was drawn back to Connecticut to comfort her brother and Lucretia. She soon returned to the parsonage with her sister Louisa's children, four-year-old Samuel Sewall Greele and two-year-old Louisa May Greele. For most of 1829 Abigail "had the care of these children, boarding with them at my brother's in Brooklyn, Conn." Lucretia May gave birth to a second son, John Edward, on October 7, 1829, again with Abigail present.

Throughout these months, Bronson occupied her thoughts. In him she had found a man she could love and who could make her happy, she was sure. Like her mother, sisters, and Lu, she would marry and bear children. Unlike them, she would speak and be heard.

In Boston the enrollment at Bronson's school began to decline, reducing his income and rendering his future uncertain, further delaying their wedding. He kept busy with "fearless free-thinking and brisk correspondence with Abigail May." Eager to begin their shared life, she again sought assistance from relatives. Late in 1829 Dr. Charles Windship, her sister Catherine's widower, learned of an opening suitable for Bronson. The Free Inquirers of Boston needed a teacher "willing to leave disputed [religious] points out of his system of teaching and inculcate nothing but what can be demonstrated to the senses and perceptions of the children. Such an individual they will amply reward by a salary of $1000 or $1200 per annum"—more than double what Bronson had ever earned. But Bronson said no. The job was "absolutely wrong," he said. The Free Inquirers "do not love virtue nor truth" and "are indifferent to everything truly good," so "I shall have nothing to do with them." This astonished Colonel May, who continued to worry about Bronson's ability to support a wife and family.

In February 1830, Aunt Q died, at eighty-two, cutting Abigail's living link to the American Revolution. By then Abigail and Bronson had chosen May 23 as their wedding day, despite the problems at his school. Her father, now resigned to her choice and hoping to maintain good relations, invited Bronson to call on him on Federal Court. He gave Bronson his daughter's dowry of five hundred dollars, in several payments, and with his second wife gathered household "sundries" for the young couple's future abode. These included a mahogany washstand, a framed looking-glass, a mattress of horse hair, blankets, a rug, a sofa, a table, lamp oil, silver knives, forks, and spoons, cups and saucers, a "platter, bowls, pitchers, [toilet] chamber and cover," and a pair of fireplace bellows.

In mid-April Abigail returned for the last time from Brooklyn to Boston to prepare for her marriage. On the morning of Abigail's departure, Lucretia described her emotions to Samuel Joseph. "We shall be mourning our loss [of Abigail] & it will be to us a cross that the world can ill supply. She has so long shared our joy & participated in our sorrows & has become so identified with ourselves, that it is like plucking out an eye to part with her & I doubt not that many who know her less intimately & cannot so well estimate the excellent qualities of her mind & heart will share in our grief." Not long afterward, when Samuel Joseph was away from home, Lucretia wrote to him, "I am solitary enough now that you and Abba are so far away."

The Boston to which Abigail returned in 1830 had begun its transformation into a major city, which would soon make it unrecognizable to those who had known it as a country town. "I never desire to go near [Boston] for it is entirely changed to me," Lucretia May wrote later. Boston had become a city in 1822 by a citizens' vote. In 1830 its elected mayor was Abigail's cousin Josiah Quincy, a reformer known for cleaning streets, renovating the waterfront, creating the Faneuil Hall market district, fighting prostitution and public drinking, and removing cows from Boston Common to make of it a leafy public park. The city was growing rapidly, following a period of no population growth during and just after the revolution. Its population now doubled every twenty-five years—from 25,000 inhabitants at Abigail's birth, in 1800, to 60,000 at her wedding, thirty years later. By 1900 Boston would have more than 500,000 residents, a twenty-fold increase in one century. Its character was changing, too, as the maritime commerce that provided livings to Colonel May and his peers gave way to a market economy based on manufacturing. The factory system that began around 1800 would soon be a multimillion-dollar industry dependent on the labor of numerous new immigrants from Europe. As production and exchange moved farther from the home, the divide between the public sphere, limited to men, and the private domestic sphere of women grew wider.

Early on May 23, 1830, at home on Federal Court, Abigail donned a plaid silk walking dress with puffed sleeves that she had chosen for the occasion. She put on a stylish black beaver-fur hat. Her father and stepmother accompanied her to the Stone Church, as they still called King's Chapel to avoid mentioning the monarchy. Joseph May, as a church warden, walked through the vestry before emerging from behind the pulpit to join his wife, Samuel Joseph, sons-in-law, and grandchildren in the family pew, No. 20, to the right of the chancel. Abigail's father was a "noticeable" figure, "with his massive square head, and manly figure," his elegant waistcoat, breeches, and "grey stockings showing the muscular limbs of which he was justly proud, [and] the knee-buckles and shoe-buckles of the gentleman of the old style." Bronson arrived in his best suit, with the long pants that were now in fashion. The Reverend Francis Greenwood, the church's second Unitarian minister and Joseph May's old friend, prepared to perform the ceremony.

During the short wedding service, Abigail was painfully conscious of the absence of her mother and sisters, and of Lucretia, who had stayed in Connecticut with seven-month-old John. Acutely aware of her father's disappointment in her choice of a husband, Abigail found comfort in her brother's glistening eyes and beaming face. He and Lucretia were her dearest friends in the world, she felt. Of Abigail's marriage Lucretia would pray, "May she never have cause to repent her passage & may he whom she has chosen for the deposit of her heart never prove unworthy of the sacred trust she has reposed in him & may they live long & happily a blessing to each other & to all the 'little Alcotts' who may rise toward them."

After the wedding, Colonel and Madam May hosted a party for Mr. and Mrs. Alcott. The company feasted on cakes, tarts, and puddings prepared by servants, oranges and meats arrayed on platters, and glasses of porter, claret, Madeira, rum, and brandy. That evening Abigail and her husband walked the few blocks north to Mrs. Newell's boarding-house on Franklin Street, where he rented a room. This bare chamber was the first of many dwellings they would share. But Abigail felt no fear or worry, only hope. She embraced her beloved and with him went promptly to bed.

Chapter Three

Humiliating Dependence

T wo weeks after her wedding Abigail was pregnant. "I am very well," she wrote to Lucretia in June, before she knew she had conceived. "My husband is all I expected. . . . I have already seen the good effects [of marriage] operating in our lives and conversations. My mind is gradually engaging."

For most of the next decade Abigail would be pregnant or breast-feeding or both. The prospect of a baby pleased her. She longed for a family with whom to re-create the love and security she had known as a child. At the same time, though, she worried about Bronson's employment, which was "inadequate to our support." Less than a month after her wedding, his school had "diminished a good deal in consequence of families going into the country. I hope some good salary offer will be made him ere long. It is important to him, for all financial concerns are very irksome and embarrassing to him. A salary would relieve his mind from all those anxieties which are incident to the fluctuations of a private school."

Bronson did not find a job he felt he could consider until autumn, when a wealthy Philadelphia Quaker named Reuben Haines with an interest in universal education invited him to Philadelphia to create a school with the Scottish educational pioneer William Russell. Bronson's letters of recommendation included several from Abigail's family friends: The Harvard professor George Ticknor noted that Bronson had "married into one of our most respectable families," while the Reverend

Joseph Tuckerman described Bronson as "one of the most child-like and amiable of men." Bronson accepted the job and determined to close what little remained of his Boston school in November and move with his pregnant wife to Philadelphia. Abigail, unlike her wanderer husband, had little experience of travel, having occupied only the houses of her parents and brother. As she prepared for the first move of her married life, she could not have imagined that she and Bronson were establishing a pattern. In their first thirty years the Alcotts would relocate more than thirty times, mostly to rented or borrowed homes.

Abigail faced the future with hope. She was expecting a child, Bronson had found a fine job, and together, she prayed, they would create a loving home. She might teach alongside her husband; surely she would teach her own children. In addition, she would maintain a connection to books, ideas, and the world.

In their boardinghouse room on Tuesday, October 12, 1830, an advertisement in the *Boston Courier* caught her eye. A man named William Lloyd Garrison requested the use for an evening of "a Hall or Meeting-house . . . in which to vindicate the rights of TWO MILLIONS of American citizens who are now groaning in servile chains in this boasted land of liberty." Garrison, a twenty-four-year-old printer from Massachusetts who had recently been released from a Maryland jail for publicly criticizing someone for shipping slaves to New Orleans, was now on a tour of Philadelphia, New York, and New England, lecturing and seeking support for his cause. He promised "just, benevolent, and constitutional measures" to end slavery. If no space were donated, he offered to "address the citizens of Boston in the open air, on the Common."

Abigail was captivated. She and Samuel Joseph had often talked of the evils of slavery. But this man offered something new. He not only condemned the trade but also promised to end it. No church she knew would host such a man. He would likely be thrown in jail or forced out of town. "Too many Boston folk were making a great deal of money out of slavery" to welcome immediate emancipation, the historian Mary C. Crawford observed. "Nearly all of Boston was strongly opposed to Garrison." Prominent Bostonians preferred either gradual emancipation of slaves over many decades or their resettlement to African colonies, such as Liberia.

Until the Civil War, in fact, abolitionists met "strong resistance from nearly all established, conservative Northern interests." Most New Englanders followed Senator Daniel Webster of Massachusetts, "who, with his eye for the 'good in everything,' found something good in slavery: he had visited a plantation in Louisiana, and he was happy to report that the quarters of the slaves were neat and clean and the beds were furnished with mosquito-nets. This was reassuring," Van Wyck Brooks wrote, "to Christian souls who counted on the slaves for their bread." Even Abigail's husband, who had seen slavery firsthand on his peddling trips south, had no moral qualms about it. According to the biographer John Matteson, Bronson Alcott left "no indication that he found anything intolerable or outrageous about slavery in Virginia in the 1820s."

The space Garrison found for his October 15 address was Julien Hall, at the corner of Atkinson (now Congress) and Milk streets, which had recently hosted a temperance meeting and the exhibition of a boa constrictor and an anaconda swallowing mice. Samuel Joseph, who was visiting from Connecticut, and their cousin Samuel E. Sewall—now a Harvard-educated lawyer with a "serious, quiet manner [and] piercing, beautiful eyes," according to an acquaintance—invited Bronson to join them in the all-male audience for Garrison's lecture, "The Genius of Emancipation." On Friday evening the three men left Abigail, who was four months pregnant, at the Alcotts' boardinghouse, where she eagerly awaited their reports.

Abigail's husband, brother, and cousin were already seated in Julien Hall—opposite the house in which she had been born—when the young Garrison arose, "modestly but with an air of calm determination," to begin his address, Samuel Joseph reported later. Slavery is a "stronghold of the devil" that must be stopped, Garrison proclaimed. Every slave in America should be freed, incorporated into American society, and granted all the rights guaranteed in the Constitution, he demanded. He gave legal, moral, economic, social, and political reasons for abolition, and pleaded with his audience to help "save our country from the terrible calamities which the sin of slavery is bringing upon us."

Bronson was not won over. In his journal he summarized Garrison's lecture as "a statement of facts concerning the cruelty with which many slave-holders had treated their slaves at the South. . . . There is sometimes a want of discrimination, perhaps, between the slave-holder who keeps his slaves from motives of expediency and the one whose principles are in favor of slavery." According to historian Sarah Elbert, Bronson had "slept in slave quarters and sold goods to slave owners on his peddling trips. . . . Like many early nineteenth-century citizens of enlightenment, he expected slavery to die a natural death. Having observed what he considered cordial, even friendly, relationships between masters and slaves, he did not remark on the actual deprivations of slave life."

By contrast, Samuel Joseph turned to his companions the moment Garrison finished. "Come, we ought to help him," he said. "Let us go and give him our hands." He strode to the front of the hall. "Mr. Garrison, I am prepared to embrace you. I am sure you are called to a great work and I mean to help you." Many years later he recalled, "That night my soul was baptized in his spirit, and ever since I have been a disciple and fellow-laborer of William Lloyd Garrison."

Samuel E. Sewall also shook Garrison's hand and offered his help. Sewall and May, who had been Harvard roommates for three years, were the first men of Boston to support Garrison's movement. Samuel Joseph May became one of Garrison's closest friends. In the words of the abolitionist Frederick Douglass many years later, "Never . . . was one man . . . more devotedly attached to another than is Mr. May to Mr. Garrison."

Samuel Joseph May's first glimpse of the "peculiar situation," outside Washington, D.C., in 1821, had been quite different from Bronson's. On first meeting Garrison, the young minister now determined to devote himself to the speaker's cause. "Never before was I so affected by the speech of any man," Samuel Joseph told Abigail. She had heard him say this only once before, after his first encounter with her husband. "Garrison is a prophet," Samuel Joseph felt. "He will shake our nation to its centre, but he will shake slavery out of it."

As they left Julien Hall, Samuel Joseph continued talking with Garrison. Someone may have mentioned that May's sister awaited them, because the four men walked to the Alcotts' boardinghouse. Abigail greeted Garrison and talked with him until midnight. "Although [she] lacked the formal education and civic opportunities afforded a male citizen of her class," according to Sarah Elbert, "she was of one mind and heart with her brother" in matters of reform. She, like her brother and cousin, was drawn to the young crusader and determined to help his cause.

As a woman, Abigail empathized with slaves. Middle- and upper-class white women often "identified consciously or unconsciously with other excluded groups," the historian Carolyn Karcher wrote. Women too were excluded "from the benefits that American democracy conferred on their male peers. . . . In the 1830s an awareness of being 'bound with' black slaves would propel a significant number of American women into the abolitionist movement." One of Abigail's peers, the writer and teacher Margaret Fuller, observed a few years later, "It may well be an Anti-Slavery party that pleads for woman, if we consider merely that she does not hold property on equal terms with men; so that, if a husband died without making a will, the wife, instead of taking at once his place as head of the family, inherits only a part of his fortune, often brought him by herself, as if she were a child, or ward only, not an equal partner." In Providence, Rhode Island, a few years later, a woman approached Samuel Joseph after he gave an antislavery speech. She said, "I doubt whether you see how much of your description of the helplessness of slaves applies equally to all women." The abolitionist Sarah Grimké felt that men "made slaves of the creatures whom God designed to be their companions." According to Lydia Maria Child, "Little can be done for the slave while this prejudice [against women] blocks up the way."

The morning after Garrison's speech, Samuel Joseph walked briskly to Garrison's boardinghouse, where Garrison showed the minister letters he had received from noted New Englanders attacking his cause. Immediate emancipation was "misguided," the Reverend Dr. Henry Ward Beecher, of Connecticut, wrote to him. Former president John Quincy Adams, another cousin of the Mays, compared abolition to "pouring oil into a smoking crater." Even the renowned Reverend Dr. William Ellery Channing, one of Samuel Joseph's former teachers, criticized the movement for its lack of "calm."

Not long afterward, May approached Channing, who had been raised in the slave-trading region of Newport, Rhode Island, and had lived on a slave plantation in Virginia. Channing was troubled by aspects of slavery he had just seen in the West Indies, he told May, but he could not countenance Garrison's vulgar tactics and violent language.

"If this is so, Sir, it is your fault," Samuel Joseph responded, looking into his mentor's eyes. "You have held your peace and the stones have cried out. If we, who are obscure men, silly women, babes in knowledge, commit these errors, why do not such men as yourself speak and show us the right way? . . . You, more perhaps than any man, might have so raised the voice of remonstrance that it should have been heard throughout the length and breadth of the land. . . . Why, sir, have you not taken this matter in hand yourself?"

Channing replied, "Brother May, I acknowledge the justice of your reproof. I have been silent too long."

Samuel Joseph seized every subsequent opportunity to speak out against slavery. Two days after meeting Garrison, he was scheduled to preach at New South Church, known as Church Green, located below his father's garden, at the corner of Summer and Bedford streets. On Sunday morning he strode to the octagonal church designed by Charles Bulfinch. Samuel Joseph greeted old friends, heard the service begin, and walked to the pulpit. "I have heard something extraordinary," he said: a lecture by a man with eyes "so anointed that he could see that outrages perpetrated upon Africans are wrongs done to our common humanity," and ears "so completely unstopped of 'prejudice against color' that the cries of enslaved black men and black women sound to him as if they come from brothers and sisters." Shuffles and grunts in the congregation indicated unease. "I have been prompted to speak thus," Samuel Joseph continued, "by the words I have heard during the past week from a young man . . . William Lloyd Garrison, [who] is, I believe, called of God to do a greater work for the good of our country than has been done by anyone since the Revolution. I advise, I exhort, I entreat—would that I could *compel*—you to go and hear him!" Should slavery not be stopped, he warned, "the very foundations of the Republic must be broken up!"

It is not clear if Abigail or any other May was present at Church Green, but the next morning a business associate approached Joseph May on the street. "I hear your son went crazy at Church Green yesterday," he said. "I cannot tell you how much I pity you." This alarmed Colonel May. Everyone he knew considered advocates of immediate abolition to be atheists, infidels, even criminals. Most northerners feared that abruptly ending slavery would offend southern businessmen, split the country, and lead to war. Samuel Joseph "repudiated his social class," the historian Donald Yacovone wrote, by joining Garrison "in forging the American antislavery crusade." Radical abolitionism made Samuel Joseph "an outcast to the Brahmins who dominated Boston society, jeopardized his career as a Unitarian minister, and outraged family and friends." His stepmother, who was "constitutionally conservative," Samuel Joseph observed, and "opposed to my espousal of the Anti-Slavery cause," was astonished by one of his predictions that she recorded in her diary for 1830: "Our son, S. J. May, says that, in ten years from this time, the Anti-Slavery cause must be triumphant." Like Abigail, Samuel Joseph was deeply religious—a believer in God and in the immortality of the human soul—but not "constitutionally conservative." This was a rare mix of traits in their time and place, and one reason that, as Yacovone wrote, "few members of New England's social and economic élite followed May" and his sister "into a life of social protest."

Undeterred, Samuel Joseph returned to his Connecticut pulpit to repeat the sermon he had given in Boston. Over the next year he met frequently with Garrison and Sewall to plan an antislavery society. He helped Garrison start an abolitionist newspaper, the *Liberator,* in early 1831. Garrison settled on the northern slope of Beacon Hill among Boston's free blacks near the 1806 African Meeting House. There on December 16, 1831, amid a bitter storm of wind and rain, May, Sewall, Garrison, and several other men founded America's first antislavery society, the New England Anti-Slavery Society. Samuel Joseph became an agent of the society, speaking at halls and churches throughout New England.

Abigail felt as passionately as her brother about the evils of slavery, but she was not present at any of these meetings. No woman was. Nor did any of the men consider inviting women. It was not proper for a woman to speak in public. Women had been excluded from public meetings since America's earliest European settlements. It was a custom that arose from the Bible, a foundation of early American law. St. Paul, in 1 Corinthians (14:34–35), admonishes women to be silent in church and wives to seek guidance from their husbands. "I permit not a woman to teach, neither to usurp authority over the man, but to be in silence," 1 Timothy 2:12 states. Abigail could no more assist in reforming her society than she could ascend a pulpit to preach.

Now almost six months pregnant, she spent the weeks after Garrison's momentous lecture preparing to move to Philadelphia. In early December she and Bronson boarded a stagecoach with their belongings. Each night they stayed at an inn, and each morning a new horse was hitched to the coach. They moved into a boardinghouse in German-town, a village seven miles north of Philadelphia founded in the late seventeenth century by Quakers and Mennonite German immigrants. In 1688—twelve years before Abigail's ancestor Judge Samuel Sewall published his abolitionist tract—several Germantown Quakers had sent their ruling Society of Friends a two-page petition condemning slavery. But the society ignored the petition and suppressed its message.

In their boardinghouse in Germantown on March 16, 1831, not quite ten months after her wedding, Abigail gave birth to her and Bronson's first child, a healthy girl. Bronson felt joy. "The emotions produced [in me] by the first sounds of the infant's cry make it seem that I am, indeed, a father." They named the baby Anna Bronson Alcott after his adored mother, Anna, and himself. Abigail, exhausted but happy, turned to the tasks of nursing and nurturing a newborn. The baby, she wrote to her brother, "is in good health, perfectly quiet, and is a true May for eating and sleeping. . . . She has given love to life, and life to love."

Anna was nine days old when her father began writing "an Historical account of the Development of the Intellect and Moral Conduct of my little girl, from birth, to be continued as her mind and heart make progress." He aimed to create a "history of one human mind" from infancy "narrated by the parent until the child should be able to assume the work himself, and carried onward through all the vicissitudes of life to its close." Bronson would initiate such a journal for three of his children, a paternal project that was an unusual variation on a common enough New England theme. Puritans used journals to record their observations of the world in the hope of perceiving and understanding God's will; Bronson began his children's journals in an effort to perceive and under-stand the developing human mind. Freed by his gender from the work of caring for the children, he looked to them as experimental subjects in his effort to develop a new educational philosophy. Before Anna's first birthday her father's observations of her led him to a grandiose theory of mind in which "the human soul has had a primordial experience in the infinite Spirit." Abigail left no comment on her husband's research on their children. Despite her fascination with education and children, she was not of a philosophical bent. Philosophy, moreover, did not feed a family.

About a month after Anna's birth, Bronson wrote to his father-in-law requesting money to furnish their new home. Bronson's sponsor in Philadelphia, Reuben Haines, had purchased for the Alcotts a large, two-story stone house with a garden on nearly an acre along Germantown's main road in which Bronson could teach and his family could live. Colonel May demurred. He told his daughter-in-law Lucretia that he disliked supporting those who "liv[ed] beyond their means." Lucretia wrote to Samuel Joseph, "Now that [your father's] feelings are not the kindest toward Abba, I know he will not feel as [generous as] you or I should about it." Samuel Joseph often sent his sister gifts of ten or twenty dollars, but his salary was modest and not always forthcoming. Later that year, likely due to Samuel Joseph's gentle prodding of their father, the Alcotts received two thousand dollars (equivalent to $38,000 in 2000) from an anonymous donor, probably Colonel May. Much of this money went to settling Bronson's ancient peddling debts.

Anna was two months old when Bronson's attention was entirely diverted by the launching of his new school, in their house. His observations of Anna had revealed to him that "infancy is when most good can be done for the improvement of the character." His task now was to improve the characters of his six students, boys and girls of eight to ten years of age, who boarded with his family while receiving regular lessons from him. These "6 children in my family besides a goodly company to dine and be looked after 7 hours in the day . . . unfits one for much mental effort," Abigail complained to Lucretia.

As she coped with new motherhood and a house full of children, Samuel Joseph preached and lectured throughout New England as an agent of the New England Anti-Slavery Society, raising money and support. "He traveled much in those years," his daughter Charlotte recalled, "to preach in other ministers' pulpits or to further the Anti-Slavery cause," which alienated some white members of his congregation.

The Reverend May's wife, house servants, and pulpit enabled him to devote himself to the cause. Lucretia hated his frequent absences from home but generally supported his antislavery work, particularly after she encountered open racism in Connecticut. She shocked a white neighbor there by saying, "I would rather marry a virtuous and sober colored man [than] an intemperate white man." Although the steady stream of "black, white & grey" visitors to her house seemed overwhelming when her children were small, her objections suggested a light touch. In February 1833 she wrote to her husband, "I hope you will 'remember not to forget' that you went to Boston *this time to see your father* & will not give all your time to emancipating slaves & settling all the quarrels in Christendom & educating all the children." A year later she begged him to "leave the slaves alone for one week" to join her and their infant and toddler.

As Abigail's brother railed against slavery in town halls and churches, Abigail struggled through busy days and restless nights. Five-month-old Anna, she informed Lucretia, was "sick with teething and bowel complaints." Before Anna's first birthday Abigail was pregnant again. Late in their second summer in Germantown, Bronson left her, six months pregnant, with their baby and the boarders while he spent several weeks in his hometown, in Hartford, and in Boston. Abigail became "unusually" depressed, she recalled later. "I was suffering under one of those periods of mental depression which women are subject to during pregnancy." In her worst moments she felt she was "decaying" like the corpses in the family vault, somewhere in the bowels of the earth.

Everyone around her, she observed, desired that her second child be male. She resisted this. "I always rejoiced over the birth of each girl-child," she said later to another mother of daughters. "I never was one as Miss [Margaret] Fuller says 'to make the lot of the sex such that mothers must be sad when daughters are born.' Oh no!" She wrote to her brother on the day after Anna's birth, "Lucretia I suppose is ready with her condolence that it is a girl—I don't need it. My happiness in [the baby's] existence . . . is quite as much as I can well bear—indeed I cannot conceive that its being a boy could add thereto." In part because of the deficiencies of her own education, Abigail was determined to raise strong, confident children, male or female, by providing them with a good education and many opportunities.

On November 29, 1832, Louisa May Alcott was born at home in Germantown. Named for her late aunt, the sister with whom Abigail had hoped to start a school, Louisa became Abigail's third precious Lu, after her sister and sister-in-law. Bronson was pleased that Louisa arrived on his "birth day, being 33 years of age."

This baby seemed different to him. Louisa was larger and healthier than Anna at birth, delightfully "fat" and "fine." She had "a fair complexion, dark bright eyes, long dark hair, a high forehead, and altogether a countenance of more than usual intelligence," a friend said of the new baby. In announcing Louisa's arrival to Colonel May, whom he now called Father May, Bronson drew a portrait of Abigail that both sender and recipient must have considered flattering: she was "formed for domestic sentiment rather than the gaze and heartlessness of what is falsely called 'society.'" It is not clear if Bronson knew his wife had been depressed while he was gone, or, if so, that her depression had begun to intensify.

Close female friends of Abigail's were well aware of her condition, however, as well as of some of its causes. "Our dear Mrs. Alcott has an acquisition of another daughter to her family," another friend wrote to Reuben Haines's wife, Jane, when Louisa was just days old. "Mrs. A[lcott] was so ill that at one period [during the birth] I thought she had ceased to breathe but she revived again." Bleeding was still the most common medical treatment for laboring women in distress. Abigail "has been wrought up to a high pitch of excitement from her [hired] nurse's inexperience and neglect of her baby," Louisa. "The little creature was not even properly washed so that its eyes were in a sad condition and its bowels not attended to. The Dr upon one of his visits found the child in almost a dying condition for the want of nourishment, the mother having nothing to give it." A new nurse, who cleaned Louisa and helped Abigail begin to breastfeed her, reported that Louisa was "a dear little pet . . . the prettiest best little thing in the world. You will wonder to hear *me* call any thing so young pretty. But it is really so in an uncommon degree." Two weeks later mother and child were both healthy and Abigail was calling the new nurse "the savior of her infant's life."

Bronson, meanwhile, was struggling to maintain his school. In a familiar scenario, parents of his students had begun to object to his open classroom and untraditional methods. Some parents, finding Mr. Alcott "eccentric" and "peculiar," withdrew their children. By midwinter he had so few students that he could not afford to continue the school, although several of his former students stayed on as paying boarders under Abigail's care.

Running a boardinghouse did not suit her. "It is a thankless employment to take care of other people's children," she wrote to her brother on February 20, 1833. When Louisa was nearly three months old and Anna almost two years, Abigail developed a serious problem with her vision, which would plague her for the rest of her life. "Dear Sam and Lu, I have been wishing to write you for at least 2 months but my eyes have been in no state." She had resolved, "I never want a larger domain than 3 rooms, [with] 1 servant, [only] my husband and children for occupants."

Bronson announced in April that he was moving out, to read literature and philosophy in a rented room in central Philadelphia. Not wishing to part with her husband, Abigail suggested that the whole family move. He refused, saying children do better in the country than the city, so they should stay in Germantown. A separation would benefit them all, he promised. For the next eighteen months—a period that coincided with Louisa's infancy—Bronson spent most of his time in a room near the Philadelphia public library immersed in Coleridge, Wordsworth, Spenser, Carlyle, and in translation Goethe, Schiller, Dante, and Kant.

Abigail was beside herself. Three years married, with a two-year-old and an infant, she felt her life was in shambles. "A full connected letter seems to me now a formidable undertaking," she wrote to her brother and sister-in-law. "We do not earn the bread; the butter we have to think about. . . .

> My eyes are very uncertain, and my time is abundantly occupied with my babies. . . . I am almost at times discouraged if I find the result [of my efforts] prove unfavorable. My Anna is just at that critical period when the diseases incident to [typical of] her age make her irritable and engrossing; and yet so intelligent as to her making inferences and drawing conclusions about everything which is done for her, or said to her, and I live in constant fear that I may mistake the motive which instigates many of her actions. Mr. A[lcott] aids me in general principles but nobody can aid me in the details, and it is a theme of constant thought, an object of momentary solicitude. . . . I know you laugh at me and think me a slave to my children and think me foolishly anxious. I can bear it all, better than one reproach of conscience, or one thoughtless word or look given to my Anna's injury.

Another small school that Bronson had begun in Philadelphia was "slowly gaining confidence and numbers," she reported. "We do not make much noise but shed some light, which travels faster and more direct" than noise, "and its influence is more effective."

She tried to maintain the hope that had come so easily three years earlier. Bronson "soar[s] high and dig[s] deep," she told her brother in

October 1833. Unfortunately, "such minds are somewhat solitary in this world of folly and fashion when a man's hat is the most essential part of his head, and his coat his surest passport to society." She wished "all philosophers would consent to admit in their domestic arrangements a financier . . . They are often (for lack of this) reduced to the most humiliating dependence. Wisdom must be fed and clothed, and neither the butcher [n]or tailor will take pay in aphorisms or hypotheses. There comes then the 'tug of war' between matter and mind." Long before her daughter Louisa, Abigail showed she had a way with words.

On April 24, 1833, in Brooklyn, Connecticut, Lucretia gave birth to her third child and only daughter, Charlotte Coffin May. Charlotte, like her first cousin Louisa, was named for a maternal aunt. At Charlotte's birth her cousin was five months old, and her father, the minister, was engrossed in the scandal that would make him famous.

Chapter Four

Sacrifices Must Be Made

"You and Miss Crandall are trying to destroy our town," a lawyer shouted at Samuel Joseph May. In the spring of 1833, the two men faced each other on the town green in Canterbury, Connecticut. Across from the green and the meetinghouse and beside the home of the lawyer, Andrew Judson, the leader of the American Colonization Society, stood the schoolhouse in which a white woman named Prudence Crandall was teaching a class of Negro girls.

"The idea of having a school of nigger girls so near me is insupportable," Judson railed at the thirty-five-year-old Unitarian minister, who was coordinating Miss Crandall's legal defense, having already raised ten thousand dollars from New York abolitionists. "The colored people never can rise from their menial condition in our country," Judson went on. "Africa is the place for them. . . . They ought not to be permitted to rise here. . . . You and your friend Garrison . . . are violating the Constitution of our Republic, which settled forever the status of the black men in this land. . . . The sooner you abolitionists abandon your project the better for our country, for the niggers, and yourselves."

Calmly, Samuel Joseph replied, "There never will be fewer colored people in this country than there are now. Of the vast majority of them, this is the native land, as much as it is ours. It will be unjust, inhuman, in us to drive them out, or to make them willing to go by our cruel treatment of them. And," he continued, "if they should all become willing to depart, it would not be practicable to transport across the Atlantic

Ocean and settle properly on the shores of Africa, from year to year, half so many of them as would be born here in the same time. . . . The only question is, whether we will recognize the rights which God gave them as men, and encourage and assist them to become all he has made them capable of being, or whether we will continue wickedly to deny them the privileges we enjoy, . . . [and] enslave and imbrute them."

Several months before this heated public exchange, Miss Crandall, a young Quaker schoolteacher from Rhode Island, had announced that her home-based school, in which she taught English grammar, history, geography, philosophy, chemistry, French, drawing, painting, and music to white girls, was open also to "young ladies and little Misses of color." Inflamed by this announcement, neighbors smashed her windows, smeared excrement on her door, and contaminated her well. Most of her white students withdrew from the school. Shops refused to sell her goods. Residents of rural Connecticut, like most Bostonians, rejected biracial education, mixed marriage ("miscegenation"), and racial equality. Canterbury's town meeting soon voted to stop Crandall on the grounds that "once open, this door and New England will become the Liberia of America."

The Reverend May, who lived and worked a few miles up the road in Brooklyn, encouraged Crandall to continue teaching but, in order to defend the principles of racial equality and universal education, to restrict her school to Negro girls. Early in 1833 free black families from along the eastern seaboard responded to her advertisement in the *Liberator* by sending their daughters to live and study with Miss Crandall. She reopened her school in April with twenty female students "of color."

Immediately, to prevent "amalgamation of the two races," the Connecticut legislature enacted a Black Law forbidding the education of Negroes from outside Connecticut except in free public schools. Local authorities arrested and imprisoned Crandall for breaking this law. Samuel Joseph May came to her defense, arranged for her release from the county jail, where she had spent a night, and made his nearby parish the center of her legal strategy. At public events, where her gender prevented her from speaking, he was her representative.

At her August 1833 trial in the courthouse in Brooklyn, the county seat, chief prosecutor Andrew Judson argued that Negroes were neither citizens nor entitled to legal protection or educational privileges. The jury split. At her second trial Crandall was convicted, an outcome that May and Garrison welcomed because they hoped to appeal her case to the Supreme Court of the United States. May had warned Judson: "I will dispute every step you take, from the lowest court in Canterbury up to the highest court of the United States." While Crandall's conviction was soon thrown out on a technicality, the violence against her and her allies continued. In 1834 locals smashed her windows, dumped manure on her lawn, set fire to her house, and burned a cross they had placed on the Mays' front lawn. Fearing for her students' lives, Crandall sent them all home in September 1834 and moved west.

But her point had been made. Her case raised the crucial question, Samuel Joseph observed, of "whether the people in any part of our land will recognize and generously protect the inalienable rights of man without distinction of color." According to the historian Russel Nye, the Crandall case "furnished the clearest example of the issues involved in the question of Negro education" because it "clearly defined . . . the popular fear of racial equality and racial amalgamation." Nye added, "The schools figuring in the greatest disturbances in the North were those which, in defiance of local prejudice, accepted both white and Negro pupils." An academy in Canaan, New Hampshire, inspired by Crandall, admitted fourteen Negro students in 1834. The local town meeting responded by voting to restrain "the Abolitionists," and three hundred men with one hundred oxen dragged the school building from its foundation.

The Crandall case brought Samuel Joseph to national attention and "propelled him to the forefront of the antislavery movement." Later that year Lydia Maria Child, an author and abolitionist who was one of Abigail's closest friends, published *An Appeal in Favor of That Class of Americans Called Africans,* which examined the history, effects, and economics of slavery and racial discrimination and concluded with a call for immediate emancipation. The book cost Child her reputation as the country's most popular woman writer. But she, like the Mays, was compelled to join Garrison. On meeting him, she said, "A new stimulus seized my whole being and carried me whithersoever it would. I could not do otherwise, so help me God." She dedicated *An Appeal* to Samuel Joseph "for his earnest and disinterested efforts in an unpopular but most righteous cause."

The Crandall case forever changed Samuel Joseph, much as his father's business failure had forever changed him. "I felt ashamed of Canterbury, ashamed of Connecticut, ashamed of my country, ashamed of my color," Samuel Joseph recalled. His advocacy of racial desegregation alienated many of his parishioners and eventually propelled him to leave his pulpit and become a full-time antislavery agent. "If it had not been for Miss Prudence Crandall," his daughter, Charlotte, observed later, "he probably would have passed his life" quietly in Brooklyn, Connecticut.

Samuel Joseph's public recognition may have aroused envy in his brother-in-law. "The minister has long preached, and what has he accomplished?" Bronson wondered in his journal during the Crandall controversy. "Look into our civil and political institutions, our religious periodicals, our schoolrooms, our churches; count the various societies whose object is the suppression of some mighty vice which is preying on the heart of society—intemperance, war, slavery, oppressive governments. . . . And when this mighty catalogue has been filled out, then is the answer at hand of what the minister, with all his boasted authority, has done? He has done little because he has not known how. He has preached; but . . . failed. Early education is the enduring power." Bronson felt his own efforts to reform the world through the minds of infants were worthier than his brother-in-law's public advocacy of antislavery, temperance, and equal rights.

Abigail responded differently to her brother's growing fame. In addition to nursing Louisa, running after two-year-old Anna, and caring for her slightly older boarders, she was inspired to read and think even more about antislavery. "I am informing myself as fast as possible," she wrote to Samuel Joseph. "I have been reading for dear life, past numbers of the *Liberator,* and *Emancipator* and some English publications." As for attending meetings, "I will not engage very much in anything apart from my children while they are so young. But I can read and think and talk."

In a Philadelphia schoolroom in early December 1833, less than two weeks after Louisa's first birthday, Abigail gathered with other white and black women to found the Philadelphia Female Anti-Slavery Society. The society's stated goal was "to elevate the people of color from their present degraded situation to the full enjoyment of their rights." Meanwhile, in Boston, her friend Lydia Maria Child was a founder of the Boston Female Anti-Slavery Society. While some men, including Abigail's brother and his ally Garrison, supported women's societies, many male abolitionists did not, and it would not be long before the men would split over this issue. Samuel Joseph was with Abigail at the women's first gathering in Philadelphia, where, a few days earlier, on December 4, he had been among the male founders of the American Anti-Slavery Society. This first nationwide antislavery society aimed to realize the preamble of the Declaration of Independence by guaranteeing all citizens their "inalienable rights" to "life, liberty, and the pursuit of happiness." According to Nye, slavery forced "a growing realization of the need for establishing the meaning of the guarantees of liberty written into the Declaration of Independence and the Constitution." Years later Samuel Joseph regretted "the mortifying fact, that we *men* were then so blind, so obtuse, that we did not recognize those women as members of our [American Anti-Slavery Society] Convention, and [did not] insist upon their subscribing their names to our 'Declaration of Sentiments and Purposes,'" which called for immediate abolition or "disunion," the severing of the bond between slave states and free states.

A more intimate disunion existed in the Alcott family. Abigail, who disliked living apart from her husband, was still depressed and sometimes angry at him. On weekends, when he visited her and the babies in Germantown, she complained that he was "unkind, indifferent, [and] improvident." He could not do otherwise, he replied, because he was by nature "disinclined from making much of outward success. . . . I cling too closely to the *ideal* to take necessary advantage of the practical. . . . I live in Idea." Unfortunately, he explained, "I am an Idea without hands. I find no body for my thought amidst the materials of this age." Privately, he resigned himself to this situation: "Complain not then, my genius," he thought to himself. "Thou shalt know thyself in fit time, and do thy deed before the ages." He conceded he was a negligent husband and father. "My wife and children suffer from this neglect. . . . I may not sympathize . . . in the deprivations to which this course subjects them." To pursue his life's goal of "find[ing] the truths of my own nature," however, "sacrifices must be made."

Perhaps, but the sacrifices were all Abigail's. Having conceived another child late in 1833, she moved with Anna and Louisa into a Germantown boardinghouse to await the baby's birth the following spring. Bronson visited his family on weekends, "unwilling to live with his family, [yet] unwilling to forsake them." Cynthia Barton described this as "an unorthodox arrangement, particularly because it was instigated by a man who believed, before his time, that a father should play an active role in the care and upbringing of his children." Meanwhile, Bronson moved upstairs in his boardinghouse to a desirable top-floor room, feeling "blessed at last with my one little window fronting the City Library and the Athenaeum, with a bed, a trunk for my clothes, a wash-stand, two chairs, and my books. On these," he vowed, "I am to feed and content myself during the summer." Seven miles away, Abigail would have to "feed and content" three-year-old Anna; Louisa, who was seventeen months old; and herself, near the end of another pregnancy.

At the boardinghouse on May 19, 1834, Abigail suffered a miscarriage. She seemed near death to her landlady, who eventually, at Abigail's urging, called a doctor, and Abigail pulled through. To her brother Samuel Joseph, who seemed to her "good enough for heaven and great enough for earth," she wrote not long afterward, "My health is far from good." Two days later Bronson learned of the miscarriage and closed his school for a few days to visit his ailing wife.

During periods of depression Abigail often found comfort in a leather-bound Bible her mother had given her, in which both of them had inscribed their names. Solace came from a favorite hymn that Abigail had sung with her father and now sang with her girls:

> God of the ocean, earth, and sky!
> In thy bright presence we rejoice;
> We feel thee, see thee ever nigh;
> We ever hear thy gracious voice. . . .
>
> God on the lonely hills we meet;
> God in the valley and the grove;
> While birds and whispering winds repeat
> That God is there,—that God is Love! . . .

"God is love," she murmured to her babies when they seemed scared or sad. God is love, she knew, but where was He?

Bronson, whose latest attempt to start a school had come to nothing, concluded that Philadelphia was not ready for him and his ideas. Unlike

Abigail, he longed to return to her hometown. Boston "is the place for me," he had told his mother on the day of Louisa's birth. "There is no city in this country in which there is more mental and philanthropic activity than Boston." One of Abigail's Germantown friends, Mary Ann Donaldson, wrote, "I cannot bear to think of their leaving us to go so far . . . I look upon Mrs. Alcott as a 'bright, particular star' in our hemisphere & shall never cease to regret her removal from it. I do not believe Mr. A[lcott] will succeed any where." Presumably, Donaldson was one of those to whom Abigail "was clearly suggesting that she wanted a separation from Bronson."

In the summer of 1834, when Louisa was twenty months old, family friends again came to the Alcotts' aid. The Reverend Channing found Bronson another possible job in Boston. It was to create a school there, aided by the skillful Elizabeth Palmer Peabody, a woman of thirty who had more than a decade of experience teaching in Massachusetts and Maine. In August the Alcott family took a steamer to Boston so Bronson could consider the offer.

Abigail set up temporary housekeeping in a boardinghouse on Morton Street in the North End and tried to encourage Bronson to accept the job. All her life she had been taught that a husband's obligation is to provide for his family, while his wife supports him at home. She now had the toddlers Anna and Louisa "very much to myself, leaving them for an hour or two with my girl," a servant likely provided by Colonel May, to "go into the parlor for quiet or social purposes, or for a walk, and after they go to bed I occupy the parlor." She informed her brother on September 1, "Mr. Alcott has now gone [back] to Philadelphia [and] will probably pass a day with you [in Connecticut] on his return. He has determined to remain in Boston. He has taken [rented] rooms at the Masonic temple"—a building at the corner of Tremont Street and Temple Place—"and has about 31 children engaged to *begin* with, and Miss Peabody as his assistant. His prospects were never more flattering, but I try to suppress all emotion but that of hope, for I have *always* been woefully disappointed in my expectations, and I mean this time to keep on the safe side." A week later he had four more students. "Everybody I see seems pleased and excited" about the new school, she exulted. "I hope this will be enduring as well as brilliant. Everybody has their ups and downs. This I believe is to be our *up,* turn." She knew she ideal-

ized her husband and risked being his "enthusiast," for which Samuel
Joseph or Lucretia had apparently teased her. But she believed, she
wrote to them, that "there will be a great educational regeneration"
and "my husband is to be the Messiah to announce to the world a new
revelation."

That September, for the first time in more than a year, she and Bronson lived under the same roof, at a boardinghouse on Bedford Street, a
few blocks south of Abigail's childhood home. Within two weeks she
conceived another child. Each morning Bronson rose early to walk four
short blocks from their boardinghouse to the Temple School, as he
called it. He had a large, elegant schoolroom overlooking Boston Common, which funds donated by his new students' families enabled him to
furnish with carpets, movable desks and chairs, and busts or bas-reliefs
of his heroes Socrates, Bacchus, and Milton. Above and behind his own
desk was a sculpture of Christ. His new students were three to twelve
years old and mostly boys, some of whom would later attend Harvard.
Three-year-old Anna Alcott often joined the class, which included the
sons or grandsons of friends and relatives, such as the Tuckermans, who
were related by marriage to Abigail, and Abigail's cousin the lawyer and
politician Josiah Quincy, now Harvard's president. Everyone in town, it
seemed, had a good word for the new school and its master, who reveled
in his newfound success.

Bronson continued to use the Socratic method with his young students, according to Elizabeth Peabody. He would ask them the meanings
of ordinary words and ideas—"What is a nook? What is the object of
coming to school?"—which aroused class discussion and encouraged the
children to explore their own ideas and beliefs. Peabody, in her *Record of
a School,* described his style of teaching: "I am not myself prepared to say
that I entirely trust his associations. But he is so successful, in arousing
the activity of the children's own minds, and he gives such free scope to
their associations, that his personal peculiarities are likely to have much
less influence than those of most instructors. . . . Mr. Alcott relies a great
deal upon Journal writing, which is autobiography, though it hardly
seems so to the writer. To learn to use words, teaches us to appreciate their force. And, while Mr. Alcott presents this exercise as a means
of self-inspection and self-knowledge . . . he knows he is also assisting
them in the art of composition." During their collaboration Peabody told

Bronson he possessed "more genius for education than I ever saw or expected to see. I am vain enough to say that you are the only one I ever saw who . . . surpassed myself in the general conception of this divinest of arts." While she disliked "some of his methods of discipline"—such as punishing a disobedient student by "making the child strike him," to induce shame—she had "no doubt at all, that as far as regards this particular school, the methods have been in every respect salutary."

Boston's embrace of Abigail's husband augured well. She settled herself and the girls into new rented rooms at 3 Somerset Court (now Ashburton Place), behind the Park Street Church and near the State House. Her husband slept by her side every night, as he noted early one October morning in his journal: "My companion and the little ones lie before me, for I am now in the chamber where they repose."

Proximity brought the family new troubles. Louisa and Anna, who for more than a year had spent little time with their father, became objects of his attention. Their behavior, especially Louisa's apparent disobedience, troubled Bronson. At nearly age two Louisa "manifests uncommon activity and force of mind," he observed. She was "much in advance of her sister" at the same age. Although at school he disciplined students by ordering them to hit him, at home, according to the editor of his journals, Bronson sometimes struck Anna and "particularly" Louisa. The polarity he saw between his daughters—"ideal, sentimental" Anna and "more active and practical" Louisa—matched the polarity he associated with himself and Abigail. Placid, blond Anna was like him, he believed, while impetuous, dark-haired Louisa was like his wife. One of Louisa's persistent childhood memories was of her father telling her she was the spirit and image of her mother. When she was only a toddler he wrote in his journal that Abigail "has more sympathy . . . with Louisa" than with Anna. Abigail "comprehends [Louisa's] mind more fully." Abigail and Louisa "are more alike: the elements of their beings are similar; the *will* is the predominating power." A generation earlier, in the May mansion, Abigail's father had also reproved her for being willful.

It was not only Bronson's daughters who received greater scrutiny. Living with his family opened Bronson's eyes to Abigail's apparent failings. Louisa and Anna conducted themselves poorly under his wife's supervision, he felt. "Some habits, I regret to say, have been permitted to attain a strength and fixity that will require no small degree of skill, delicacy, and yet force of discipline to remove . . . more than the mother will be able to put forth." Abigail's maternal gifts were compromised, he believed, by her vision problems and overall "poor health," which denied the girls "that earnest . . . attention and sympathy . . . upon which the tranquility . . . of childhood depend. Morbid affections," which he did not define, "have gathered around their hearts." He was convinced that Louisa and Anna required "a deep and apprehending love" that only he could provide. To repair the damage done by Abigail, he determined on October 26, 1834, to "relieve" her "from the delicate and yet necessary work" of parenting, presumably by limiting her time with the children. "It is my duty to . . . act in the way of example."

Abigail was distraught. She had accepted the limitations her husband imposed on her public activities, such as during their courtship when he refused to hire her as his assistant teacher. But she chafed at his attempt to control her behavior at home, which was, even in society's eyes, her domain. Her own mother had had no role outside the home, but no one had ever tried to prevent Dorothy Sewall May from demonstrating maternal love, as Bronson seemed to be doing to Abigail.

That winter Abigail's belly swelled as it never had before. The prospect of a third child pleased Bronson, who was convinced that this baby would be male. "I am more interested in the domestic and parental relations than I have been," he confessed. "If the Divinity wills, I shall soon behold the little one, a semblance and reduplication of myself and an image of the Infinite and Unshadowed One."

On June 24, 1835, when Anna was four and Louisa two and a half, Abigail gave birth at home to a third healthy girl. She and Bronson named the child Elizabeth Peabody Alcott in honor of his assistant, and he began another "Record of this newcomer."

A month later, Bronson left for a week to visit "the scenes of my early life" in Connecticut, hoping to be "revived" by "the air of my native hills." Back in Boston with his family on August 1, he accepted an invitation from Samuel Joseph to hear the English abolitionist George Thompson speak at Julien Hall. The small audience included "several slave-holders" making "signs of violence," Bronson observed. At the conclusion of Thompson's speech, vigilantes barricaded the door of the hall and shouted, "Hang him! At Vicksburg we would bring Lynch's Law to bear upon him!" Samuel Joseph, in his clerical garb, briefly diverted the vigilantes by walking back and forth in front of them, while other abolitionists quickly removed Thompson by a back door and drove him to safety.

A week or two later, Abigail informed her brother that the Alcotts faced homelessness once again. "Abba is in trouble," Samuel Joseph wrote to Lucretia. "The house where they live is going to be torn down and they must move this week. Where to go to or what to do they know not. But as necessity will compel them to decide, I suppose that they will know in a day or two."

Daily life was chaos for Abigail, who now had to cope with two toddlers and a newborn in addition to her housing and marital troubles. "I have been hanging on the most precarious contingencies—regarding houses—leases—auctions, help—money &c," she wrote in early September to her friend Mary Tyler Peabody, Elizabeth's sister. "Nothing is yet concluded upon, but that patience is to do her perfect work upon me and my soul. . . . I mean to get to housekeeping very soon when or where I know not—and I sincerely regret that that item is not settled. . . . We may yet manage it in the course of next week, you shall be apprized at the earliest moment of our movements. Something like domestic and social enjoyment is in store for us I am sure this winter—I feel it in my bones."

Despite all her difficulties, her girls—two-month-old "Lizzie" at her breast and Louisa and Anna playing at her feet—were endlessly fascinating to her. Louisa was bright beyond her two and a half years. To illustrate this point, Abigail described "my Louisa's definition of patience: Her father was eating a piece of Gingerbread. She wanted a piece of his (having finished her own). He told her she could not have any more until afternoon, and that she must wait patiently. Do you know what patience is? said he. Yes, said L[ouisa], it means wait for ginger bread."

Abigail added, "I could not do better than that myself."

Louisa's precocity was also a cause for worry. A clever daughter augured a clever woman, which the world spurned. "I pray," Abigail wrote to Mary, "that I may have reason to rejoice that our offspring are girls—or incipient women—but I do so dread the contact, the contamination, the conflict with the world that I almost dread a farther development of their virtue lest the suffering be the more augmented from the very contrast of that which is so [evil] in the world—vice in all forms and attitudes—ready to attack, molest, and make afraid" our daughters. "Mr.

Alcott would call this a horrid & skeptical and naughty kind of *assertion,* & cannot dignify it with the name of *reasoning.*" But to her more receptive, female audience, Abigail elaborated on her desire that women's "capabilities are developed and educated." She wondered, "Are we too tired and crucified [for knowledge]? We *suffer* because we *feel* and *die* because we *know.* Woman was told in the beginning that her sorrow should be greatly multiplied unto her; for what? Because she desired knowledge, the knowledge of good and evil." She added, "I am not a great hand at doubtful points of disputation, as some wise-acre has it, but I say that I do think, and know that I do feel."

Louisa had a vivid memory from this period of playing with her father's books on the floor of his study. As a toddler she built "towers and bridges of the big dictionary," looked at its pictures, and pretended to read it in imitation of her parents. If she could find a pen she scribbled on blank pages in books. Ever since, she said later, "books have been my greatest comfort, castle-building a never-failing delight, and scribbling a very profitable amusement."

In keeping with the infant-school philosophy of the need for early education, Abigail and Bronson began instructing their daughters at age two or three in math, reading, composition, history, and geography. "Our lessons went on at home," Louisa recalled. "On Sundays we had a simple service of Bible stories, hymns, and conversations about the state of our little consciences." Abigail found teaching engrossing but overwhelming. Unable to finish a letter to her brother, she explained, "My children are importunate, or I should fill this sheet, for my mind is brim full and stirring with some great thoughts, which I have not time to define or express" on paper.

Like a professional teacher, Abigail read and discussed with others how best to teach children. She believed in "the importance of *moral* education to the young," emphasizing the human "*hearts* out of which are the issues of life. . . . The very bud and blossom of our country is actually withering under the cold cheerless philosophy of '*breaking* the will' and '*subduing* the spirit.'" She critiqued common-school teachers she encountered. One schoolmistress she observed in 1834 appeared to do "an immense amount of mischief by her influence over those little beings; her voice and countenance and stamp of foot [are] enough to make them turbulent and unhappy . . . as bad as having teeth drawn.

She has no self control, and of course can have little or none over the children. . . . She has no more warmth or refinement than a polar bear."

In addition to teaching them at home, Abigail and Bronson allowed three-year-old Louisa and four-year-old Anna to wander freely in Boston, as only boys could do a generation before. "I would rather a child of mind should roam the street and take her chance, than be under" a poor teacher, Abigail had remarked when they were even younger. There were risks to roaming the city streets, Louisa discovered. At age three, before she could swim, Louisa wandered into the Common and fell into the pond. A black boy saw her struggling in the water, jumped in, and rescued her. "I became a friend to the colored race then and there," she recalled. Her mother often said to her, "You were an abolitionist at the age of three." One night after dark the little explorer, unable to find her way home, sobbed herself to sleep on a doorstep on Boston's Bedford Street. The town crier found her there with her head "pillowed on the curly breast of a big Newfoundland, who was with difficulty persuaded to release" Louisa.

An almost identical scene had occurred during Abigail's childhood, Samuel Joseph recalled. Not long after he and his sister Eliza had persuaded their mother to allow them to bring four-year-old Abigail with them to dame school, "she had become so eager to accompany us that she became quite a regular attendant at school. At length, it was regarded as a matter of course that she was to go to school as we [elder children] did. . . . One afternoon, as we were returning home with a party of our fellows and playing by the way, Abby slipped off into a side street, and went to find something curious." Samuel Joseph "commenced a search, but it was in a direction different from that which she had taken." Alarmed, he ran home. "Of course the whole family were sent in requisition to find the wanderer," leaving him and his sister Eliza "at home alone to bemoan our carelessness and indulge our fears for the fate of our little sister. First one, then another, returned from a fruitless search, only to aggravate an alarm, and make more glaring the sin of unfaithfulness to the charge committed to us. Not until late in the evening was our anxiety relieved, when a young man, a cousin, came leading her in, weary and frightened, from a distant part of the city where he found her."

More than three decades later, the Boston of Louisa's early life was disorderly and sometimes violent. Immigrants from Europe flooded the

city. Catholics and Protestants battled for space. Antislavery lectures provoked crowds of angry protesters. On October 21, 1835, when Louisa
was not yet three years old, she could hear from home the noise of a
crowd of more than a thousand rioters as they gathered to denounce
abolition.

That day, members of the Boston Female Anti-Slavery Society had
invited George Thompson to speak at their annual meeting. Antislavery opponents, learning of the scheduled speech, published this advertisement in the morning newspaper: "That infamous foreign scoundrel
THOMPSON will hold forth this afternoon at the Liberator Office, No.
48 Washington Street. The present is a fair opportunity for the friends of
the Union to snake Thompson out. It will be a contest between the Abolitionist and the friends of the Union. A purse of $100 has been raised by
a number of patriotic citizens to reward the individual who shall first lay
violent hands on Thompson."

The angry crowd moved up Washington Street toward Faneuil Hall.
At the office of the *Liberator* rioters kicked in the door. Thompson was
urged not to appear because of the violence, but Garrison attempted to
address the crowd. Seeing him in danger, colleagues tried to pull Garrison from the mob, which followed and seized him. They dragged him
behind the Old State House, tore off his clothes, and tied a rope around
him, intending to hang him. Rescued by the mayor, Theodore Lyman,
Garrison spent a night in prison, the only place where the mayor could
ensure his safety. Abigail insisted that evening that Bronson accompany
her to visit Garrison at the Everett Street jail. The next morning Garrison
slipped away to return to his pregnant wife in Brooklyn, Connecticut.

During the riot Abigail was at home with her children. Hearing
the shouts of the crowd, she rushed to remove a painting of George
Thompson from the wall. Louisa watched her mother hide the portrait
underneath a bed. The toddler crawled beneath the bed alongside the
portrait, saying she wanted to comfort "the good man who helped the
poor slaves."

Around this time Louisa's uncle Sam took a leave from his church
in Connecticut, where he had preached for thirteen years, to work full-
time for antislavery. This move disturbed his father and stepmother,
according to Abigail, who informed her brother, "Some of your family are very much grieved that you are going to leave the dignified and

respectable office of minister of the Everlasting Gospel, and become an itinerant fanatic." For eighteen months as secretary of the Massachusetts Anti-Slavery Society, he traveled around the eastern United States lecturing and writing for antislavery, peace, temperance, universal education, and an end to capital punishment. Mobs in Rhode Island, Maine, and Massachusetts pelted him with rocks, paint, and eggs, stormed his lectures, and drowned him out with drums and shouts. They prevented him from entering some halls and threatened to burn down others. Local officials, businessmen, and militias attacked him five times in Vermont alone. In New York City, a crowd destroyed the home of his wealthy abolitionist friend Lewis Tappan. "Private assassins from New Orleans are lurking at the corners of the streets to stab [Lewis's brother] Arthur Tappan," Lydia Maria Child said, "and very large sums are offered for anyone who will convey Mr. Thompson into the slave States." Garrison stepped out of his house in Connecticut one day to find a gallows and a note, "Judge Lynch's law," on his front lawn.

Unlike some abolitionists, Garrison and May were "nonresistants," who advocated neither resisting nor responding violently to violence. They advised other agents to avoid mobs, to act surprised if a mob occurred, and to continue speaking as long as possible. They tried to publish the perpetrators' names, which was difficult in the mainstream northern press because it generally encouraged violence against the antislavery movement. In 1836 the governor of Massachusetts, Edward Everett, shut down the abolitionist press on the grounds that it was "calculated to excite an insurrection among the slaves." Samuel Joseph came to Boston to address the state legislature, defend the right to free speech and a free press, and call for the press to be restored. The legislature supported the governor, who explicitly denounced May, Garrison, and Samuel E. Sewall as enemies of the Constitution.

The peak of the violence against abolition came in 1835, when American newspapers reported five hundred mob incidents in a single week. These were "respectable mobs," abolitionists noted with irony. Protesters came from "the *higher classes of society*," one of May's colleagues reported, "—men of wealth, of office, of literature, of elegant leisure, including politicians, and that portion of the clergy who naturally associate with that class just described." Another colleague, James Freeman Clarke, said America's "united South had for its allies at the North both the great political parties, the commercial and manufacturing interests, nearly the whole press, and both extremes of society. Abolition was equally obnoxious in the parlors of the wealthy and to the crowd of roughs in the streets, fashion and the mob being for once united by a common enmity. It was against this immense weight of opinions that the Abolitionists contended."

The Mays were shocked by the violence that abolitionists encountered in their hometown. How did a cradle of liberty become "the nursery of illiberality and prejudice?" Samuel Joseph asked Garrison. By dragging slavery "into the full blaze of the noon day," he hoped, "the doom of slavery is sealed." But the life of a reformer on the road was difficult. He missed his family and disliked being vilified by crowds. "I am not made for . . . turmoil," he admitted to his wife. "I long for the quiet of home."

Despite all the violence, 1835 was a wonderful year for Bronson. Elizabeth Peabody published her *Record of a School,* describing his and her classroom, to rave reviews. A magazine called Bronson "one of the best men that ever drew the breath of life." About a month after his daughter Elizabeth's birth, Bronson finally met the Reverend Ralph Waldo Emerson, whose sermons he had heard. Emerson, who had resigned from the Unitarian ministry and begun a career as a writer and philosopher, responded to Bronson as the Mays had earlier, calling him "a wise man" and "a God-made priest." At the Temple School that fall, Bronson began his "Conversations on the Gospels" with children. "We are now going to speak of the life of Christ," he said to his students, "if any of you are interested to understand how Jesus Christ came into this world and lived and acted and went back to God." At home he began holding conversations with adults as "a dispenser of moral truth" in the tradition of Socrates and Jesus Christ. He titled these conversations, "How Like An Angel Came I Down." He had no prepared text, according to Theodore Dahlstrand, but rather employed "an oracular style, with no logical sequence. Bronson made spontaneous pronouncements, as if he spoke truth at all times and no concrete evidence was necessary, because he believed he could intuit the truth, without evidence, from the atmosphere. He modeled himself on Jesus."

Small children, too, Bronson believed, were invested with divine powers. Each morning, he wrote in his journal that fall, he woke to "my little one [Elizabeth] murmuring the spirit's melodies as she reposes on her mother's arm, with opened eyes and loving heart surveying the things of the outward scene and investing them in the glories of her inner life. . . . Verily, the Divine Life is alive in the infant's heart."

Louisa turned three on November 29. At ten that morning Abigail brought the birthday girl to her father's school. His students crowned him and Louisa with laurels, in celebration of their shared birthday. Bronson delivered a "short account" of his life, and one girl read an ode to Bronson. When it was time for treats, Abigail asked Louisa to hand out little frosted fruitcakes she had made. Louisa gave each child a cake until only one remained on the plate. There was still one pupil to serve besides herself. "I saw that if I gave away the last one I should have none," Louisa recalled. "As I was queen of the revel, I felt that I ought to have it, and held on to it tightly till my mother said, 'It is always better to give away than to keep the nice things.'" The three-year-old hesitated. "I know my Louie will not let the little friend go without," Abigail prompted, reaching down to kiss her. "The little friend received the dear plummy cake," Louisa said, "and I a kiss and my first lesson in the sweetness of self-denial, a lesson which my dear mother beautifully illustrated all her long and noble life."

Little Women opens with a similar scene. Marmee asks her daughters to give their Christmas breakfast to a poor family. After a momentary hesitation the girls agree, pleasing their mother. Delivering the feast enables them to enjoy "a happy breakfast, though they didn't get any of it; and when they went away, leaving comfort behind, I think there were not in the city four merrier people than the hungry little girls who gave away their breakfasts and contented themselves with bread and milk on Christmas morning."

Self-denial was hard even for Abigail. She had moved the family four times in the year since their return to Boston, usually to less expensive quarters. They had occupied three boardinghouses—on Somerset Court, Bedford Street, and Beach Street—and now rented a house at 36 Front Street (now Harrison Avenue) on the neck between the tidal waters. Money was a constant worry. In the summer, around the time of Lizzie's birth, Mary Peabody forgot to repay five dollars she had borrowed from Abigail. It was "the last five dollars I had," according to Abigail, who was too proud to ask for it back. "I could not!" Hoping to remind Mary of the outstanding loan, Abigail asked her for "a quarter of a dollar." To her dismay, Mary "left the room as if to look for it [and] never returned." Abigail was often on edge. A letter she received from Mary questioning abolitionism "made her very angry," Mary's sister Elizabeth observed. Abigail "spoke quite sharply about" the letter to Maria Weston Chapman, Garrison's assistant editor at the *Liberator*.

A conflict between Elizabeth Peabody and Bronson strained Abigail's close relationship with Elizabeth, who with her sister Mary occupied the same boardinghouse as the Alcott family. In early 1836, while discussing the Bible with his students, Bronson had asked them questions that seemed to Elizabeth suggestive and inappropriate, such as, Where do humans come from? His manner, she informed Mary, was offensive and "heavy-handed." People in Boston had begun to whisper that Bronson was guilty of blasphemy. Not long afterward, Bronson, who must have heard of the gossip, approached Elizabeth to accuse her of publicly ridiculing him. A heated discussion ensued, which Abigail, ever loyal to her spouse, joined.

In response, Elizabeth decided to sever her professional relationship with Bronson. She suspected that he and Abigail had gone into her room and read her correspondence with her sister. Due to this "breach of honour," she informed him, "our relations are at an end." He in turn accused Elizabeth of writing to her other sister, Sophia, who occasionally substituted for Elizabeth at the Temple School, a letter, which he had presumably found and read, that would make people think he was "a thief and a murderer!" Elizabeth tried not to respond to this accusation, she reported later to Mary. "But as he went on saying what [he imagined] I thought & had said & had done about him . . . This induced me to reply, but it was to little purpose—except that it gave him new grounds of animadversion respecting my tones."

In the heat of the moment Elizabeth said to Bronson, "You consider yourself a thinker superior to all other people."

"You are guilty of littleness in the extreme," he retorted. She asked him to retract this accusation. He said, "I do not see any reason to alter my opinion, except . . . for the worse."

The cause of their rupture, Elizabeth felt, was Bronson's arrogant "self-estimation without a doubt of having the key that unlocks all wisdom. . . . In his own metaphysical system he subjects everything to the test of his talismanic words, and as they answer to them in his predisposed ear, they take their places." She informed Mary, "I do not regret the crisis. It is better we should separate."

Elizabeth Peabody did not sever her tie to Abigail. The two women had "a little talk" and still trusted each other, Elizabeth told her sister Mary. Within days Elizabeth moved out and left the Temple School, which now enrolled forty students.

Bronson would later change his third daughter's name from Elizabeth Peabody Alcott to Elizabeth Sewall Alcott. But the change had not yet occurred on Sunday, May 22, 1836, when Samuel Joseph baptized Bronson's three little girls "Anna Bronson, Louisa May, [and] Elizabeth Peabody . . . at my own dwelling," Bronson reported. "Our friends were present. The ceremony was impressive, interesting."

Although pleased by the baptisms, Bronson was generally "dissatisfied with the general preaching of any sect." Raised in the Episcopal Church, he abandoned formal religion as a young adult and developed a personal theology similar to Unitarianism in that it rejected the Trinity, the doctrine of Original Sin, and the divinity of Jesus Christ. He strongly identified with Christ, signing letters to his children, "Your Ascended Father." Anna wrote at age eight, "I like to read about Jesus, because he is good. Father is the best man in the world now." Henry James Sr. claimed to have asked Bronson if he ever claimed to be Jesus Resurrected, to which Bronson replied, "Yes, often." In his journal he explained, "I preach the Gospel as it is revealed to my own soul. . . . My doctrine is from heaven. . . . I am a meek and simple follower of the Divine Word within, which I must announce and interpret in the face of all obstacles." He could "commune with God in the hearts of . . . my own children, my pupils, the divine and unsoiled Child, even Jesus Christ." His wife's devotional practices were more conventional: she attended church services, prayed regularly, and often led her children in "Sabbath exercises" of psalms, hymns, and Bible reading, as her father had done when she was small. Bronson, however, was convinced that "my own spirit preaches sounder doctrine" than any church, so "I must listen to its divine teachings."

In the fall of 1836, to his delight, Bronson found an extraordinary replacement for Elizabeth Peabody. Twenty-six-year-old Margaret Fuller was the eldest daughter of a Unitarian, Harvard-trained lawyer

and congressman named Timothy Fuller who had given her a rigor-
ous classical, recitation-based education at home. She was thoroughly
grounded in Greek, Latin, French, German, and Italian—more languages
than in the repertoire of most educated men. As a young woman who
had avoided "the feminine subculture of sentimentality," according to a
biographer, Fuller was able to detect and deplore the exclusion of educated, intellectual women from public power. "We women," she would
write in 1845, "have no profession except marriage, mantua-making and
school-keeping." She had learned of the opening at the Temple School
soon after her father died and she accepted the position in order to support her mother and siblings. But she, like Peabody, would discover that
Bronson never paid his assistants their promised salaries.

During the months that Fuller worked with Bronson, she continued
Peabody's practice of recording classroom discussions. Bronson's freewheeling dialogues with the children about common words and religious concepts surprised and troubled Fuller. "I wish I could define my
distrust of Mr. Alcott's mind," she remarked. "I constantly think him
one-sided, without being able to see where the fault lies. There is something in his . . . philosophy which revolts either my common-sense or
my prejudices, I cannot be sure which." Fuller was neither the first nor
the last person to struggle to define the misgivings that Bronson aroused.

Trouble began at the Temple School in the winter, following the
publication of Bronson's *Conversations with Children on the Gospels,* transcribed by Fuller and Peabody and heavily redacted by Bronson. Peabody had succeeded in moderating the explicitness of her descriptions
of his teaching, but Fuller's narration, however oblique, of his conversations with children about sexual reproduction struck most Bostonians
as obscene. The exchange that prompted the most outrage involved a
six-year-old's response to Bronson's question about the nature of birth.
The boy said, "The spirit comes from heaven, and takes up the naughti-
ness out of other people." Newspapers attacked Bronson for blasphemy.
Strangers jeered at him on the street. Once again parents began with-
drawing students from his school. By February his class had shrunk to
twenty-five children, and four months later he had only ten. This exodus
may have been accelerated by the Panic of 1837, America's first economic depression.

But it was all painfully familiar to Bronson. Even after he had auctioned off his books and the elegant furnishings purchased for his class-room and moved his few remaining students downstairs to the Temple basement, he was still more than five thousand dollars in debt. Fuller, Emerson, and other influential friends wrote to newspapers in Bron-son's defense. But six months later Fuller too left his school, moving to Providence, Rhode Island, where she taught children in a more tradi-tional manner and finally received a salary.

Bronson became depressed. "The age hath no work for me," he told Abigail. A man "severely censured," whose work "threatened a mob," he identified with martyrs for antislavery like his brother-in-law and Garrison. Feeling "doomed" and "outcast," he said, "I see not my way." Abigail tried to encourage him, hoping both to boost his spirits and also to motivate him to find paying work. Bronson felt he needed time away from her and the children. He spent several weeks alone at the coast and then visited with Emerson and his second wife, Lidian, at their comfort-able farmhouse in Concord. Emerson's advice was simply "Write!" This filled Bronson, who lacked confidence in his prose, with dread. Writing was no more likely to support his family than teaching had been. He knew he should support his family, but he had no idea how. In a sense, Bronson was as restricted as his wife was by traditional gender roles. Just as she was hemmed in by the expectation that she work only at home, he was constitutionally unable to assume the role of provider that society expected a husband to fill. He felt he was paralyzed, "an idea without hands."

In July, while his wife, children, and mother, who was now living with them, remained in the city, Bronson resorted to Abigail's "good brother's household" in South Scituate, on the South Shore, where Samuel Joseph had recently assumed the pastorate of the First Parish. Samuel Joseph, Lucretia, and their three children lived about a mile from the church in a large, handsome eighteenth-century house between the woods and a river. While Bronson was there his condition improved. "Since I began to breathe this sweet country air, drink this pure water, and taste of my hostess's wheaten loaf," he wrote to Abigail, "I entertain the pleasing hope of returning a somewhat comelier specific of the man Adam than when I left you last." Naturally, he did not drink alcohol with Lucretia and Samuel Joseph. "No need of resorting to the comforting little bottle that you and [my] mother put into my trunk, so womanly."

He described walking along the river, "sitting under the shade," and conversing with Abigail's cousin Samuel E. Sewall and her brother.

The following fall Bronson had only three students. His "school in the [basement of the] Temple was given up," Abigail observed, "and continued in a large room in the house" at 6 Beach Street in Boston where the Alcott family had reconvened. She suffered another miscarriage in February 1838, and earned a little money by taking in "six boys to board." That spring, at Abigail's urging, Lucretia and her daughter Charlotte, Louisa's playmate, spent two weeks with the Alcotts, traveling to and from Boston in Lucretia's private stagecoach. Abigail and her daughters spent most of the summer in South Scituate with the Mays. On one of Bronson's July visits to South Scituate Abigail became pregnant once again.

Seeing that his latest school had failed, Bronson began to muse about moving to the country, perhaps to Concord, which reminded him of his "native hills." There he could receive more "children into my household as boarders and pupils," he told Abigail, although she felt boarders added to her housework and diverted her attention from her own girls. "I miss the influences of Nature," he said. "The city does not whet my appetites and faculties. Life is got at too great an expenditure of labor." City dwellers, he said, worshipped the "Mammon-King; [their] Gospel is of Profit and Loss."

It is not clear when Abigail realized that her husband would not or could not reconcile himself to earning "filthy lucre." He loved what money could buy, but he hated the earning of it. During their four recent years in Boston, for instance, he had taken in $5,387 and spent twice that. Abigail, who had been raised to believe that a wife should respect and obey her husband and provider, could not forever avoid acknowledging her husband's inability to provide for their family. Having admitted this, she would of necessity wonder, Can I myself support the family?

Hope arrived that fall, or so it seemed, in a letter from England. James Pierrepont Greaves, a mystic "socialist" who had worked with the Swiss educational theorist Johann Pestalozzi, informed Bronson that he and other English reformers were so impressed by Bronson's work, as described in *Record of a School* (1835) and *Conversations on the Gospels* (1836, 1837), that they had formed an institute in his name. Alcott House, in Surrey, southwest of London, was dedicated to simple living, vegetarianism, communal celibacy, and early education. In addition, a London publisher wished to reprint *Record of a School*. Greaves invited Bronson to England to visit Alcott House. Overjoyed, Bronson said to Abigail, "Friends in England . . . appear to take that interest in my labors which my countrymen have not yet shown." She offered hopefully, "You shall cross the water to find the sympathy and appreciation denied you at home."

Still, the prospect of being pregnant and alone with three children to feed and clothe frightened her. One evening in February 1839, as her husband read aloud from his journal, Abigail erupted in anger. His descriptions of her were ugly "caricatures," she said. If Emerson or anyone else heard such unfair characterizations, she would be embarrassed. She promised, "Those must come under the ban of my scissors some day." They must have, because they do not survive in his journals.

In late March, exhausted from his teaching and the evening lectures for adults that he often gave, he closed the school's winter term. "I need a short respite," he said, so "I purpose spending a few days with Emerson at Concord." Abigail, nine months pregnant, remained in Boston with the children from his school and her daughters, ages nine, six, and three. In a letter to his mother, Bronson wrote, "I am full of hope, as usual. . . . As to money, I take no second thoughts about it. . . . It only needs for me to be faithful to my principles, to reap not bread nor shelter nor raiment alone but, what is better, a useful name and peace of mind."

The need for bread, shelter, and raiment did give Abigail second thoughts, however. Indeed she could think of little else. She was sick of begging for food and rent money from relatives and friends. When the girls needed dresses, Abigail sewed them herself. As soon as Anna and Louisa could safely hold a needle, she taught them to sew. The three of them spent countless hours together before the fire, minding little Lizzie and repairing their ragged clothes. "Needlework," Louisa remembered, "began early," often accompanied by literature. "Every day we sewed while mother read to us, [Sir Walter] Scott, [Maria] Edgeworth, Harriet [Martineau], [Fredrika] Bremer, or any good story she found, also books on health, history, & biography." This training "made us independent, not ashamed of work & accomplished in the domestic arts without which women are very helpless. The books so read are remembered with peculiar interest."

Privately, Abigail's worries seemed to intensify along with her expanding belly. Another child, however delightful, was another responsibility. Lacking household help, she arranged for her two younger daughters to stay with relatives during her labor and confinement. Three-year-old Elizabeth went to Grandfather May's house, where servants could watch her. Louisa, now six, was sent to Cambridge to spend a few days with cousins. Anna, nine, could mind herself at home.

Bronson, unlike his wife, could not contain his eagerness for the next baby. His ability to reproduce himself filled him with awe. "My Body," he wrote in his journal, "is an engine of marvelous analytic powers. . . . The Soul climbs out of itself, weaving its net of cellular tissue and incarnating members. . . . Fluids form solids. Mettle [sperm] is the Godhead proceeding into the matrix of Nature to organize Man. Behold the creative jet! And hear the morning stars sing for joy at the sacred generation of the Gods!" The spiritual aspects of reproduction, which he had discussed several years earlier with his pupils at the Temple School, continued to amaze him. "Life is ever throbbing in the soul of Man, and investing him with the immortality which is its essential being," he went on in his journal. "In his fleshly heart the Universal Spirit throbbeth; and his life is summed up and numbered by the pulsations that stir within this central member. And here, in this corporeal vesture, doth the spirit first incarnate itself and display its subtle plying. From this, as from a fount, doth the Infinite gush forth into the light of Life. Behold the first shaping in the maternal womb, where the humanity of the soul is assumed!"

In a letter to his mother, to whom he described himself as a "Hoper," Bronson exulted, "A young Hoper is on his way into the midst of us, and before I write again, will be a cradled Babe with a name. His sisters will jump for joy." Thinking perhaps of God's promise to King David to send a redeemer to save Israel, he wrote. "I say *He,* because I am to have a Boy according to the Promise."

Chapter Five

This Sharp Sorrow

On April 7, 1839, Abigail delivered a "fine boy, full grown, perfectly formed" but dead. "Why," she cried, "after nine months of toil, a severe and tedious labor, a yearning panting hope of a living son, [are we] pierced with this sharp sorrow?" To her Puritan forebears, a dead baby was considered a message from God that the parents had sinned. Abigail pondered the meaning of the "mysterious little being" that made her "drink from death's bitterest beaker. . . . Oh, for that quickening power to breathe into its nostrils the breath of life." She could only "wait, pray, hope, live, watch!" For the rest of her life the anniversary of the stillbirth would give "a gray tinge to the world and my Soul."

Bronson felt despair and anger, too. "My thrill of Hope proved a pang of grief," he wrote in his journal. The baby boy was "a Joy in a Winding Sheet" that seemed, mysteriously, "a true son of its mother." In his own attempt to pinpoint the cause of the stillbirth, Bronson wrote, "So a mother, in a fit of rage, poisons the fountain at which her child draws sustenance, and he dies, slain by her choler. . . . Beware. . . . It is of the family of demons, insane, rabid." Abigail was to blame for the baby's death, he believed. Her response to this does not survive.

It fell to Bronson to carry the tiny swaddled body to the May crypt at King's Chapel, where it would join the bodies of Abigail's mother, sisters, and brother. Joseph May, now in his late seventies, asked to accompany his son-in-law to the burial vault to deposit the remains of a boy

who, had he lived, would surely have been of the sixth generation of Abigail's family to attend Harvard. In the family tomb the two men lingered
to view the remains of Colonel May's second wife, Mary Ann, who had
died two months earlier, at fifty-one.

About a week later Bronson decided to leave for the country on his
own. "I go forth from the city in faith," he told Abigail.

"I distrust this" plan, she replied. "I see not whence shall come the
bread for me and the little ones."

"Neither do I see with eyes of sense, but I know that a purpose like
mine must yield bread for the hungry and clothe the naked, and I wait
not for the arithmetic of this matter." He justified his withdrawal from
the role of provider because of the greater role he saw for himself, as a
philosopher. "Plato held that the philosopher might withdraw from the
state . . . and the like freedom was clearly intimated . . . in Christ's teaching also." On April 29 Bronson went to Concord for a visit with Emerson, the sole person under whose "ministry [he] could sit."

For her part, Abigail found solace in the company of her friend Lydia
Maria Child, who came to stay with her after the stillbirth. She and Lydia
had met fifteen years earlier at a gathering at the May house. Close in
age, they were both the youngest daughter of a feeble mother in a large,
patriotic family. Both adored an older brother who went to Harvard and
became a Unitarian minister. "Denied the education lavished on" her
brother, according to a biographer, Lydia Maria Child taught herself and
"became an early feminist"—being in this way too like Abigail.

But unlike Abigail, Lydia Maria Child had a public career. Her first
novel, *Hobomok, a Tale of Early Times,* featured an interracial Anglo–Native
American couple. She published it at age twenty-two, in 1824, when
"authorship was still almost entirely the prerogative of an educated male
élite." No woman "could expect to be regarded as a *lady* after she had written a book," Child was told, so she used a pseudonym, "an American."
Her next success was a children's magazine she founded in 1826. In the
1830s she wrote popular books of practical, domestic advice for women—
The Mother's Book, The Frugal Housewife, and *The Family Nurse*—all based
on the notion "It is better to give than to receive." Child was unhappily
married to the improvident lawyer and writer David Lee Child, whom she
had to support. Her worldview, like Abigail's, combined orthodox Puritan values with liberal Unitarianism, and she too was drawn to abolition

and women's rights. "In toiling for the freedom of others," she explained, "we shall find our own."

As Abigail struggled to recover from the stillbirth and to care for her three little girls, the members of the Massachusetts Anti-Slavery Society divided over the question of whether to include women. Many abolitionists believed the movement should be "gentlemen only"—no female members, speakers, agents, or participation in the antislavery association—while Samuel Joseph May and Garrison disagreed. Earlier that year, at a packed convention in Boston that Abigail had urged Bronson to attend, the men of the Massachusetts society battled over the "woman question." Amid the meeting's noise and chaos, Bronson rose from his bench, not to take a side on the issue at hand, but to make a memorable statement. "You are all wrong, blind, and carnal," he said to the bickering abolitionists, whose attention he now had. "I am as pure and as wise as was Jesus Christ," he went on. "The reason is, I eat nothing but pure vegetables. The rest of the world eats animal flesh, and that is just what *you* are: cattle, sheep, fowl, and swine."

A Wesleyan minister from western New York named Luther Lee broke the stunned silence. "The speaker told us that we are just what we eat," he offered. "He also told us he eats nothing but vegetables. Does it not follow, by parity of reason, that he is a potato, a turnip, a pumpkin, or a squash?" The house erupted in cheers. There is no record of when Abigail or Louisa, who was only six, learned of this statement by Bronson, as recalled by the Reverend Lee, or of any comment by either of them on its content.

In the vote on the "woman question" that followed the rowdy debate, Garrison and May's side won. In response, the "gentlemen only" group seceded from the Massachusetts society and joined instead the American and Foreign Anti-Slavery Society, which explicitly excluded "women and non-resistants" such as Garrison and May. In an unprecedented move Garrison and May asked Lydia Maria Child and Maria Weston Chapman, the leaders of the women's society, to join the Massachusetts society's committee to draft its resolutions. Samuel Joseph encouraged the women's involvement in part, he confided to Garrison, because "I like to preach from their texts."

Although he was now a strong advocate for the women's cause, it had taken Abigail's brother years to embrace the notion that women could break from their traditional role. Even as he had encouraged his sister's private education and welcomed women as members of antislavery societies, he had held to the Pauline view: women should have no public role as speakers, property owners, leaders, or professionals. Not until a day in March 1838, when he heard a young white woman recount in public her experience growing up with house slaves, did Samuel Joseph begin to question that social norm.

On that late winter day, the lobby and grand staircase of the Massachusetts State House were packed "with people of both sexes, 'black spirits and white,' to hear a lady from S. Carolina . . . declaim upon the subject of abolition," a Boston newspaper reported on March 9, 1838. "For a female, she exhibited considerable talent as an orator. She appeared not at all abashed in exhibiting herself in a position so unsuited to her sex, totally disregarding the doctrine of St. Paul, who says, 'Is it not a shame for a woman to speak in public?' She belabored the slaveholders. . . . Her address occupied about two hours and a half in the delivery, when she gave out. She, however, intimated that after taking breath for one day, she should like to continue."

The "lady from S. Carolina" was thirty-two-year-old Angelina Grimké, making a speaking tour of the east coast with her older sister Sarah. The Grimké sisters, abolitionists who had been raised on a southern plantation with personal slaves, challenged not only the institution of slavery but also the ideas of men and women occupying separate spheres, and of "female subordination" to men. "The time has come for woman to move into that sphere which Providence has assigned her, and no longer remain satisfied in the circumscribed limits with which corrupt custom and a perverted application of Scripture have encircled her." A woman should not be "a second hand agent," Grimké told the Boston crowd, which included the Reverend May. "Whatever is morally right for a man to do is morally right for a woman to do." She continued, "It is not the cause of the slave only that we plead, but the cause of woman as a moral, responsible being."

With the Grimkés, as with Garrison, Samuel Joseph instinctively felt a kinship. As he spoke with them, word of the southerner's speech spread through the city, and a riot erupted outside the State House. Without delay Samuel Joseph invited the Grimkés to stay with his family in South Scituate. During that week, at close quarters with Angelina and Sarah Grimké, Samuel Joseph came to understand how Abigail and other women could conflate their own plight with that of slaves. "It was a miserable prejudice," he concluded, "that would forbid women to speak or act in public. . . . I could not believe that God gave [women] such talents as they evinced" but kept them "buried in a napkin."

Feeling that the scales had been removed from his eyes, Samuel Joseph asked the Grimkés to speak at his church and in neighboring parishes. This alienated many of his congregants and also his wife, Lucretia, who could not abide the idea of a woman preaching. Still, Samuel Joseph persisted in this new cause so close to Abigail's heart. In the late 1830s, when every other minister in Massachusetts signed a petition stating that women's participation in public affairs "threatens the female character with widespread and permanent injury," according to a historian, the Reverend May refused, becoming "one of the country's first feminists."

Meanwhile, Abigail's husband, who had returned from Concord in time to begin a spring semester, concluded his teaching career. At 6 Beach Street in Boston on June 22, 1839, Bronson closed his last school for the last time. The class he had taught at home for about a year had dwindled to three students. "My labours are not appreciated," he felt. He never taught schoolchildren again.

Not long after the Grimkés left South Scituate, the Mays hosted Abigail and her daughters there, as they had for several summers. The six-year-old cousins, Charlotte and Louisa, and eight-year-old Anna spent July and August swimming in the North River, climbing trees, and romping in the woods. Louisa loved "the Book of Nature," her father observed when he visited. She and her sisters were "unwilling to pass their time within doors, or fix their thoughts on formal lessons. I spend an hour or more in the morning . . . with them [inside], but to small profit. Their thoughts are on the distant hill, the winding river, the orchard, meadow, or grove."

Decades later Louisa recalled, "Active exercise was my delight from the time when [I was] a child of six. . . . I always thought I must have been a deer or a horse in some former state, because it was such a joy to run. No boy could be my friend till I had beaten him in a race, and no girl if she refused to climb trees, leap fences, and be a tomboy." In adulthood she attributed this early sense of her own freedom to "my wise mother," who, "anxious to give me a strong body to support a lively brain, turned me loose in the country and let me run wild, learning of Nature what no books can teach." Later, as a teenager, Louisa could walk twenty miles in five hours. "I remember running over the hills just at dawn one summer morning, and pausing to rest in the silent woods, saw, through an arch of trees, the sun rise over river, hill, and wide green meadows as I never saw it before. Something born of the lovely hour, a happy mood, and the unfolding aspirations of a child's soul seemed to bring me very near to God; and in the rush of that morning hour I always felt that I 'got religion,' as the phrase goes. A new and vital sense of His presence, tender and sustaining as a father's arms, came to me then, never to change."

Samuel Joseph, Louisa's beloved uncle Sam, now in his early forties with three children, seemed to Louisa a pillar of strength and kindness. He was never difficult and cranky like other men. Like a character she created years later in a novel, he was "a quiet, studious man . . . busy with his . . . small parish . . . [and] rich in . . . attributes . . . [that] attracted to him many admirable persons, as naturally as sweet herbs draw bees." His wife was gentle and sophisticated. Their home was always noisy with antislavery talk and visitors "black, white & grey," as her aunt Lu liked to say. Uncle Sam led prohibitionist parades of hundreds of children—his "Cold Water Brigade," as he called them—along Main Street carrying silk banners and chanting, "So here we pledge perpetual hate! To all that can intoxicate!" and "Cold water is the drink for me!" At a public "Execution of King Alcohol" on the town green, Uncle Sam wielded the ax. According to a local newspaper, "Every rum-seller in South Scituate capitulated before the Reverend May's moral weapons." Best of all, in Louisa's opinion, with Uncle Sam and Aunt Lu there was always enough to eat.

While his wife and children were ensconced in South Scituate, Bronson spent part of the summer touring eastern Massachusetts and offering conversations on "Self-Culture" to paying adults. The venture was unprofitable. Pressed to produce income, Bronson considered a return to peddling. One night he dreamed he was a peddler again, engaging strangers in impromptu conversations. When he mentioned this to Abigail, she and her relatives urged him against peddling, which seemed undignified and had never provided him with a solid living.

Before Louisa's seventh birthday on November 29, 1839, the Alcotts were reunited again in Boston at the Beach Street house. Around this time, according to Bronson's journal, he conveyed to Louisa that she, alone among his daughters, was noisy and misbehaved. His gift to Louisa on their shared birthday that year was a note that read in part:

> You feel your CONSCIENCE, and have no real pleasure unless you obey it. It asks you always to BE GOOD. . . . How kindly it bears with you all the while! . . . How it smiles upon you, and makes you Glad when you Resolve to Obey it! How terrible its Punishments! It is GOD trying in your SOUL to keep you always Good.

Not long afterward, Abigail became quite ill, perhaps as a result of another pregnancy. Nearly forty years old, Abigail was pregnant for the eighth or ninth time and could not care for her children. She sent Anna to the family of an uncle, Dr. Charles Windship, the widower of Abigail's sister Catherine. Lizzie returned to Grandpa May's house. Louisa went to stay with unnamed relatives in Cambridge, where she missed her mother terribly, according to letters she sent home. Abigail was apparently too sick to write, so Bronson replied, "You want to see us all I know. . . . Be a good Girl and try to do as they tell you. You shall see us all in a few days. You was [sic] never away from home so long before. It has given you some new feelings."

Abigail must have recovered her health and sent for the girls in the winter, because the entire family left Boston in April 1840 to fulfill Bronson's dream of moving to the country. The five Alcotts settled into a rented cottage on more than an acre about a mile from the village of Concord, near a bend in the Concord River. Bronson dubbed the house Dove Cottage after Wordsworth's country home, dug a garden, and aimed to farm like his father. "Abba does all her [house]work and the children all go to School in the village close by," he wrote to his mother. His wife, seven months pregnant, now seemed "as energetic and heroic as in her best days," he informed Samuel Joseph, who was so accustomed to the Alcotts' requests for money that he had mentioned to Abigail that his own funds were short. In a recent letter to Abigail that Bronson may have seen, Samuel Joseph had referred to Bronson's "poetical wardrobe." Perhaps embarrassed, Bronson tried to reassure his brother-in-law that he would repay his debts. "Again I have planted myself," Bronson began, "and . . . I feel . . . more assured of the fitness of my present position than ever, to fulfil[l] the great ends of life. . . . Debts, I will pay in all honour whensoever I may. I regret chiefly that your wonted generosity, must for the present, be so slimly requited. . . . I am not insensible to these favours of friends. I wish, sometimes that God had withheld some portion of the gifts with which he has blessed me, so that I might dwell in closer sympathy with the outward interest, and enter with a keener delight into the secular labors of men. O' it is the hardest of all trials to be sundered from your kind." He went on, "I fear you have suffered from [your] generosity. But I knew not how to prevent it. [My] time of Public Favor has not come. . . . The Saints are popular in Heaven alone: on Earth they are held in low esteem."

In June, anticipating Abigail's confinement, Bronson sent Louisa back to Boston to stay with Abigail's father, who now lived at the corner of Washington and Oak streets downtown. Her older and younger sisters were allowed to remain at home, apparently because their father found them more pliable than Louisa. "Two [children] make peace," he explained to nine-year-old Anna; "three [b]ring discord."

Louisa ached for her mother and resented being with Grandfather May while everyone else in the family was at home. On June 24, to her dismay, she missed Lizzie's fifth birthday. Her father wrote to her, "We all miss the noisy little girl who used to make house and garden, barn and field ring with her footsteps." His advice to his forlorn seven-year-old was to "be good, kind, gentle, while you are away, step lightly, and speak soft, about the house [because] Grandpa loves quiet, as well as [do] your sober Father, and other grown people." It is not clear that this gave Louisa any comfort.

A month later, when Samuel Joseph paid Abigail a visit in Concord, Louisa was still in exile in Boston. Abigail gave birth to her and Bronson's fourth daughter, again at home, on July 26. They named the baby after her, and called her Abby May. Two of Abigail's teenage nieces, Elizabeth Willis and Louisa Windship, came from Boston to help her for several days.

In early August, after nearly two months away, seven-year-old Louisa finally took the stagecoach from Boston home to Concord. She did her best to help Marmee, the name that she and her sisters often used for their mother, with the baby, and she joined Anna in keeping house. That autumn Louisa gathered apples for winter as her father cut lumber for neighbors. She and everyone else knew her family was in dire straits. They had no money to pay December's rent for Dove Cottage. "The cares of the household are too great for the anxious housewife," Abigail observed. In these months she felt "an exquisite sense of weariness," she wrote in her journal. She had become a beast of burden, "a noble horse harnessed in a yoke and made to drag and pull instead of trot and canter."

Learning of their plight, Emerson leapt in with an invitation. The Alcotts could join the Emersons in their large house near the center of town, as Henry David Thoreau had done for several years. Emerson envisioned Concord as a sort of university in which he, Bronson Alcott, the naturalist Thoreau, and other learned men could "have poets & the friends of poets & see the golden bees of Pindus swarming on our plain cottages & apple trees."

Bronson loved Emerson's idea, but Abigail said no. She was devoted solely to her husband and children, as her mother had been, and she did not wish to live with anyone else. "Everyone burns their fingers if they touch my pie," she explained in her journal. Employing a different metaphor, she added, "I cannot gee and haw in another person's yoke." To pay the rent, she promised to take on more sewing and repair more neighbors' shoes.

Her father, at age eighty, died that winter, on February 27, 1841. Samuel Joseph was at his bedside at the end and brought Abigail the news. He told her that just before dying, Joseph May murmured, "And now you must let the old man go." Samuel Joseph embraced him and said, "Father, you shall!"

Joseph May's estate of about $15,000—equivalent to $300,000 in 2000—was divided in seven equal parts. One part each went to his three surviving children, the children of his three deceased daughters, and an adopted daughter named Louisa Caroline Greenwood, who had lived and cared for him in his last years. Bronson's many debtors, to whom he owed more than twice his wife's inheritance, immediately sued the May estate.

Joseph May had predicted this. Any money that came to a woman was legally her husband's, he knew. As his nephew Samuel E. Sewall, the lawyer, explained the law, marriage "conferred on the husband the absolute ownership of all the personal property which his wife had previously owned, and of all which might after marriage come to her. . . . She, on the other hand, if she survived him, had no absolute right to any part of his estate, except a life interest in one third of his lands. Her earnings were his. She could not make a gift or a will, bind herself by a contract, or bring an action in any court without his joining in the suit." So to protect Abigail's inheritance, her father had instructed his executors, Sewall and Samuel Joseph, to serve as trustees, or guardians, of her portion, which was intended, according to his will, for Abigail's "sole and separate use, without the control of her husband or liability of his debts." As a result, her portion of the estate immediately went into probate, where it was protected but inaccessible to her for several years.

In the spring of 1841, five-year-old Elizabeth was the only Alcott child still attending the Concord school. The others were needed too urgently at home. Louisa "plies her hands nimbly with her Mother" at sewing, Bronson observed, "or flies like a bird over the garden." A woman who met the Alcotts around this time remarked that Louisa "is a beautiful little girl to look upon, and I love her affectionate manners. I think she is more like her mother than either of the others."

Abigail, conscious of Louisa's quick mind and deep thoughts and the brevity of her formal education, encouraged her daughter to write. "I am sure your life has many fine passages well worth recording," Abigail advised the child. "Do write a little each day, dear, if but a line, to show me how bravely you begin the battle, how patiently you wait for the rewards sure to come when the victory is nobly won." Louisa began composing little rhymes like the ones her mother often read aloud. Her earliest extant work is a poem, "To the First Robin," which she likely began that spring in their garden when she was eight years old.

> Welcome, welcome, little stranger,
> Fear no harm, and fear no danger;
> We are glad to see you here,
> For you sing "Sweet Spring is near."
> Now the white snow melts away;

Now the flowers blossom gay.
Come dear bird and build your nest,
For we love our robin best.

As "To the First Robin" indicates, Louisa and her sisters had happy times at Dove Cottage. Years later, in "Recollections," she remembered those Concord days as "the happiest of my life." According to a story later told to Louisa by her mother, Mr. Emerson and Miss Fuller called on her parents one afternoon that summer or fall. As her father and the guests stood on the doorstep of the cottage, discussing education and how to raise "model children," Margaret Fuller, who "had no patience" with Bronson after her experience at the Temple School, guessed he was referring to his own children. "Well, Mr. Alcott," she said, "you have been able to carry out your methods in your own family, and I should like to see your model children."

The Alcott girls were playing at a distance from the house. A few minutes later, in Louisa's telling, "a wild uproar approached" and "round the corner of the house came a wheelbarrow holding baby [Abby] May arrayed as a queen; I was the horse, bitted and bridled, and driven by my elder sister Anna, while Lizzie played dog, and barked as loud as her gentle voice permitted. All were shouting, and wild with fun, which, however, came to a sudden end as we espied the stately group before us; for my foot tripped, and down we all went in a laughing heap; while my mother put a climax to the joke by saying, with a dramatic wave of the hand,—'Here are the model children, Miss Fuller!'"

Despite these gay moments, Louisa's father was not well. Realizing with despair that he could not make a living even as a farmer, he fell into another depression. "If his body don't fail his mind will," Abigail reported to Samuel Joseph. "He experiences at times the most dreadful nervous excitation." It seemed to her that "his mind [was] distorting every act however simple into the most complicated and adverse form. I am terror stricken at this and feel as if I would rather lay him low than see his once sweet calm, imperturbable spirit experiencing these fluctuations and all the divine aspirations of his pure nature suffering defeat and obloquy."

Despite everything, she still loved Bronson. But nothing she or the girls did for him seemed to help him. "Why are men icebergs when beloved by ardent nature and surrounded by love-giving and life-devoted beings," she wondered in her journal in August 1841. "Why [does he] so much take, take, [and] so little Give! Give! Women are certainly more generous than men. Man receives, enjoys, argues, forsakes. Man reasons about right. Woman *feels* right. Love is with her instinctive, eternal. With him it is pastime and passion."

In response to her growing anxiety, Samuel Joseph found the Alcotts a "fine house and farm" near his family in South Scituate. Now it was Bronson's turn to refuse. "I do not feel ready to accept them now," he said. He told Abigail that the only reasonable course that remained for him was to cross the ocean to meet his English friends. Emerson—who had just buried his five-year-old son, Waldo—offered Bronson four hundred dollars to cover his passage to England. Eager to make the solo journey, Bronson convinced his unmarried, twenty-four-year-old brother Junius to take his place in Concord, boarding with Abigail and the children while he was abroad. In a letter Bronson apprised Junius of the living situation he could expect at the Alcott cottage: "Here are my wife and children, my house, library, friends, garden . . . all at your profit or service, and you can read, meditate, labour or converse, as you shall incline." This was Bronson's role for himself—to "read, meditate, labour or converse, as you shall incline."

Abigail disliked her husband's plan to leave her and the children but saw no other option. To comfort herself, she quoted the Apostle Paul, "I will hope all things, believe all things." She spent the final weeks of winter "preparing my husband's wardrobe for his voyage." She packed his trunk with loaves of Graham bread, pots of applesauce, apples, and crackers. Anxious about having to assume sole responsibility for four children with no income, she struggled to summon "all the important and agreeable reasons for this absence." She prayed "these trans-Atlantic worthies will be more to him, in this period of doubt, than anything or anybody can be to him here." She knew that his "wife, children, and friends are less . . . [to] him than the great ideas he is seeking to realize. How naturally man's sphere seems to be in the region of the head, and woman's in the heart and affections!"

Decades later, Abigail would recall this "period in my life [as] more full of hardships, doubt, fears, adversities; struggles for my children, efforts to maintain cheerfulness and good discipline, under poverty and debt, misapprehension and disgrace" than any other. In hindsight her actions would seem to her "Heroic." Despite her determination to sacrifice for her husband and children, she often felt weary and troubled. "It seems to me at times," she had confessed to her brother during Louisa's early childhood, "as if the weight of responsibility connected with these little mortal beings would prove to[o] much for me." She could not help but wonder with "earnest inquiry . . . Am I doing what is right? Am I doing enough?" Now, as she anticipated an indefinite future without husband or income, she wrote in her journal, "Oh how great a task this is. . . . It is with a trembling hand I take the rudder to guide this little bark alone."

Chapter Six

Looking to My Daughter's Labors

On the morning of May 8, 1842, the day that Bronson's ship was scheduled to sail, Abigail rose early, "sick and sad." She donned her hood against the chill and "walked away a few minutes" so Anna and Louisa could not see her tears. "Increase my faith!" she prayed. Bronson had gone to Boston the previous day to view his ship's quarters. She did not know how long it would be before he returned from England. Months? More than a year? What if his ship sank? She sought reassurance in the Book of Isaiah. "Must we be robbed of our treasure," she asked herself, thinking of her husband, "to know its real value?"

Bronson awoke that morning at her cousin Thomas Sewall's house on Beacon Hill, where he had spent the previous night, with a powerful sense of guilt. Immediately he wrote a letter to Abigail, vowing to "reward" her "sacrifice." His return to Concord, he promised her, "would be to us a second nuptial eve—a wedding . . . in which our own children shall partake of the sweet sacredness of our Joy," as if the entire family would join in matrimony. Three weeks later, as his ship approached Dover, England, he continued in the same vein. "I have not left you. . . . You have been my companion and company all the way, and have grown more and more precious to me."

Meanwhile, in Concord only a few days after his departure, Abigail was relieved to be able to think "with more composure of Mr. Alcott's absence. . . . My thoughts begin to dwell on the fact of his arriving safely, and the desire for letters" from him. "Is not sorrow, all sorrow, selfish?" she wrote in her journal. She found herself distracted from her worries by the usual work of nurturing and teaching her girls, whose summer frocks needed mending.

The love between her and Bronson did seem stronger in his absence, as he had suggested in his May 8 letter. Two weeks after his departure, in her journal, she called him "Dearest, best of men." She reassured him, as if he were present, "Few know you now; but there are those coming up to the true perception of all that is divine and sublime in your principles and life." She tended to idealize Bronson, as he tended to idealize himself; this instinct intensified in both of them whenever he was attacked. She wrote to her absent husband, "Your life has been more to me than your doctrine or your theories. I love your fidelity to the pursuit of truth, your careless notice of principalities and powers, and vigilant concern for those who, like yourself, have toiled for the light of truth."

On May 23 Abigail observed their twelfth wedding anniversary alone with her children, who were now one, six, nine, and eleven years old. "These years [of marriage] have been great years for my soul," she said. "Wise discipline, circumstances the most diversified, have conspired to bring [my] great energies into action. I have not been always wise, or prudent; I have looked too much to consequences, not enough to principles and motives; but I feel encouraged. Defeat has given me strength." Earlier that month she had expressed this sentiment as a metaphor: "Some flowers give out little or no odour until crushed."

She received no communication from Bronson for six weeks. During this time she liked to imagine him in England, "greeted by friends and coadjutors, surrounded by elements of kindness and love—no longer as exposed to the tempests of wind and water." In truth, he had already arrived at Alcott House and discovered not only that he disliked the English but also that his sponsor, Greaves, had just died. Nevertheless, he sought the friendship and support of Greaves's reform-minded allies, foremost among them "a younger disciple" named Henry Gardiner Wright and Charles Lane, a man so brilliant as to seem Bronson's peer. With them Bronson hoped to return to America to establish "a new plantation," an egalitarian, agrarian, vegetarian community dedicated to his ideals. Even as he sought recruits for his utopian vision, he recognized that "almost every human being is disqualified now for this enterprize."

For Abigail in Concord, two months' contemplation of her life in her husband's absence led to an epiphany. She spent the morning of July 8 at the handsome Old Manse near the North Bridge with her friend Elizabeth Hoar, a judge's daughter who had been engaged to Ralph Waldo Emerson's brother Charles before he died, of tuberculosis, several years earlier. Miss Hoar and Henry David Thoreau were readying the house for the expected arrival of the newlyweds Nathaniel Hawthorne, the author of *Twice-Told Tales,* and Sophia Peabody, an artist who had briefly assisted her sister Elizabeth and Bronson at the Temple School. The Hawthornes' first home was to be the Old Manse, which had belonged to the Emersons' grandfather during the revolution. In this "charmed spot" overlooking the Concord River, its gardens newly adorned by Thoreau with "exquisite" Etruscan vases and "antique flower-stands of old roots of trees," Abigail felt for the first time "dissatisfied with my home."

A few hours later, as she walked back to her cramped, disorderly cottage on the other side of the village, she realized that her family "suffered for want of room. We have always been too crowded up." Consequently, "We have no room to enjoy that celestial privacy which gives a charm to connubial and domestic intimacy. I have suffered in my tastes, and encroached on the rights of my husband and children by this intense proximity."

Despite her anguish at Bronson's leaving and the increased affection that had accompanied his departure, Abigail now admitted in her journal what she dared not say aloud: "I am enjoying this separation from my husband." Although alone and sometimes lonely, especially for her dead mother and sisters, she felt sufficiently strong and cheerful to "meet the demands of my family with swift duty. I am not unhappy." Whereas her absence seemed to make Bronson fonder of her, his absence simply made her happier. She was finding marriage itself perplexing. "Domestic life," she added, "is a problem not easily solved." As hard as it was to raise four children alone, Abigail preferred this separation to her troubled marriage.

To celebrate Abby May's second birthday in late July, Abigail packed a picnic and walked with the girls to the Concord River for a ride in Junius's dory. Each daughter's birthday gave Abigail another opportunity to show her children "the joy I feel in their birth and continuance with me on earth," she observed. "I wish them to feel that we must live for each other. My life thus far has been devoted to them, and I know that they will find happiness thereafter in living for their mother."

For Louisa these were prophetic words, although it is likely that many years passed before she read them in her mother's journal. Already at age nine Louisa displayed "peculiarities and moods of mind, rather uncommon for her age," Abigail had noted. "United to great firmness of purpose and resolution, there is at times [in Louisa] the greatest volatility and wretchedness of spirit—[she has] no hope, no heart for anything, sad, solemn, and desponding. Fine generous feelings, no selfishness, great good will to all, and strong attachment to a few," especially to her mother. The assorted traits she observed in Louisa—"wretchedness of spirit," resolve, volatility, hopelessness, loyalty, and generosity—were also traits Abigail saw in herself.

Meanwhile, in England, Bronson was busy seeking money and members for the "consociate family" he hoped to create in New England, apart from the world's corruption. He was pleased to report to Abigail in a letter that Charles Lane was wealthy. He asked her to visit possible sites in the countryside for their community. She did as he asked but found no available farms she liked.

Moreover, she doubted she would enjoy a consociate family. She had rejected even the idea of living with the Emersons, whom she knew and admired. Now she wondered "whether my capabilities for such an association are at all equal to the demand." She reassured herself that "my powers of adaptation to circumstances have usually been found sufficient to sustain me comfortably to myself and agreeably to others." But she drew a bottom line in her own mind: "My children . . . must be benefited" by any project their father undertook. "If *they* are, surely then am I not injured, for they are the threads wrought into the texture of my life—the vesture with which I am covered. . . . I live, move, and have my being in them."

In Concord she began sharing the effusive letters she received from Bronson with her friends, including the Emersons and Margaret Fuller, who now lived with them. Fuller, according to biographer Joan von Mehren, felt that Bronson's letters demonstrated his "swelling vanity" and "boyish infatuation" with himself. Fuller was "both moved and embarrassed" that Abigail felt "forced to flaunt such specious displays of devotion from a husband whose boundless belief in his own genius had excused him from family responsibilities." Emerson also saw chinks in Bronson's armor, concluding that his impecunious friend "is quite ready at any moment to abandon his present residence & employment . . . his wife & children, on very short notice, to put any new dream into practice which has bubbled up in the effervescence of discourse."

Abigail was not blind to her husband's faults, but at the same time she wanted badly to admire him. Bonded to him in marriage, she was determined that he succeed, despite her own pain. In September, as she awaited his return from England, she wrote, "The lord of our house and life shall find that his servants and lovers"—she was both—"have not slept or idled during his absence from the field of labour. We have toiled" in the garden and the house.

On October 20, after an absence of more than six months, Bronson arrived home with his two new friends, Charles Lane and Henry Wright, whom Abigail initially called "the dear English-men, the good and true." Her husband seemed infatuated with Lane, who he felt possessed "the deepest sharpest intellect I ever met with." Lane arrived in America with a library of a thousand books, abundant cash—the equivalent of nearly fifty thousand dollars in 2000—and a son Louisa's age named William, from whose mother Lane was separated.

The Alcott girls welcomed their father with joy. Louisa, already exquisitely sensitive to her mother's feelings, sensed that in her father's presence all should finally be well. "Mother," she wondered aloud on October 23, "why am I so happy?"

Abigail could not speak. A swell of emotion—"a big prayer"—prevented her. In that moment, "I wished to breathe out my soul in one long utterance of hope that the causes which were conspiring just then to fill us with such pure joy might never pass away—the presence of my dear husband, the gentle sympathy of kind friends," Lane and Wright, "and the inspiring . . . influence of Nature. We have planted and watered in our natural life. . . . May we reap and garner in a divine love!"

Her optimism soon waned. Bronson and his friends—who considered marriage immoral because it separated individuals from the universal "consociate family" they envisioned—seemed to scorn Abigail and condescend to her. The cottage, which was already cramped with five females and Junius Alcott and Charles May, now had four additional male occupants. Abigail's lack of resources and the uncertainty of her family's situation continued to cause her anxiety. But Bronson, Lane, and Wright "all seem most stupidly obtuse on the causes of this occasional prostration of my judgment and faculties," she confided in her journal. "I hope the solution of the problem will not be revealed to them too late for my recovery or their atonement of this invasion of my right as a woman and a mother."

Only a month after their arrival from England, she complained that Bronson and his friends "most cruelly drive me from the enjoyment of my domestic life." With the men "I am prone to indulge in occasional hilarity," a desperate sort of humor, "but I seem frowned down [by them] into stiff quiet and peace-less order. I am almost suffocated in this atmosphere of restriction and form. . . . Perhaps," she realized, recalling her time alone with the girls, "I feel it more after this five months of liberty and option." Indeed, the liberty and option she had experienced in Bronson's absence were now gone.

No married woman in America in 1842 could expect to enjoy liberty and option. Under the English common-law principle of coverture, the husband and father owned his wife and children. A divorced woman lost all rights to her children, including custody, because children were a husband's property. Three years later, in *Woman in the Nineteenth Century,* Margaret Fuller would describe this disparity: "Innumerable . . . profligate and idle men live upon the earnings of industrious wives; or if the wives leave them, and take with them the children, to perform the double duty of mother and father, [the men] follow from place to place, and threaten to rob them of the children, if deprived of the rights of a husband, as they call them, planting themselves in their poor lodgings, frightening them into paying tribute by taking from them the children, running into debt at the expense of these otherwise so overtasked helots. . . . I have seen the husband . . . come to install himself in the chamber of a woman who loathed him and say she should never take food without his company." The law "still reflected the traditional patriarchal view of marriage," according to the historian Nancy Theriot. "Wives belonged to their husbands. . . . Married women held no property in their own right and were not entitled to their own wages. Married women also were not legally exempted from mild physical chastisement or marital rape." In sum, "the entire empire of the mother was within the jurisdiction of the father."

Abigail, in an effort to explain her growing difficulties since the men's arrival, blamed her diet as "not enough diversified." Bronson had turned vegetarian in 1835 after hearing a lecture by Sylvester Graham, who advocated a simple diet based on his own coarse crackers, strict vegetarianism, and chastity. Now Bronson expected his wife and children to follow suit. Flesh eaters "belong . . . to the race of murderers," he said. Charles Lane had a still more restrictive diet. He avoided animal products altogether and consumed only raw food. Bronson had now taken on the cooking, although Abigail still fed the children meat and milk when she could. Her husband's typical feast for company entailed oatmeal pudding, apples, coarse bread, and nuts. Often they had food enough for only two daily meals, each consisting entirely of bread or potatoes and water. Lane criticized even their apples, which were a family staple, for not being "mellow." She felt that "we are not favorably situated here for any experiment of diet—having little or no fruit on the place, [and] no houseroom." Ultimately she blamed herself: "My disrelish of cooking [is] so great that I would not consume that which cost me so much misery to prepare." She also resented Lane for usurping her favorite duty, the children's daily lessons.

"All these causes," she concluded, "combine to make me somewhat irritable, or morbidly sensitive to every detail of life." She often felt "a desire to stop short and rest, recognizing no care but of myself." It would be the rare parent of two-, seven-, ten-, and eleven-year-old children who would not wish sometimes to stop short and rest. "Yet without money we can do nothing," she added ruefully.

At bottom, apparently, she feared insanity. "I hope the experiment [in communal living] will not bereave me of my mind," she wrote in November. "The enduring powers of the body have been well tried. So I wait, or rather plod along, rather doggishly. . . . The mind yields, falters, and fails. This is more discouraging to me than all else. It unfits me for the society of my friends, my husband, and my children." She could not tolerate being unfit for the society of her children. Something would have to change, although she knew not what.

Louisa, so attuned to her mother's moods, was acutely conscious of her pain. Seeing the change in Abigail since the arrival of the men, Louisa began to doubt her father's judgment. She threw contentious questions at him and then, unhappy with his responses, withdrew from him.

Her father sensed her aloofness. In the letter he presented to her on her tenth birthday, he advised Louisa to change. "I live, my dear daughter, to be good and do good to all, and especially to you and your mother and sisters. . . . Will you not let me do you all the good that I would? And do you not know that I can do you little or none, unless you are disposed to let me; unless you give me your affections, incline your ears, and earnestly desire to become daily better and wiser, more kind, gentle, loving, diligent, heedful, serene." Louisa's response to the request that she appreciate her father's goodness does not survive.

The birthday note from her mother, which came with a gift, read in part, "DEAR DAUGHTER . . . I give you the pencil-case I promised, for I have observed that you are fond of writing, and wish to encourage the habit. Go on trying, dear, and each day it will be easier to be and do good." Louisa was fond of writing and would go on trying to make it a habit in order that, as her mother suggested, she be and do good. In addition, her mother thought, writing could serve as a "safety valve to her smothered sorrow which might otherwise consume her young and tender heart." She wrote for Louisa a series of rhymed couplets, beginning, "Oh! may this pen your muse inspire, / When wrapd in pure poetic fire."

Less than a month later, on the day before Christmas, Abigail sought a reprieve from her "arduous and involved" duties of the past three months by making a visit to relatives in Boston. She desired "recreation," she explained. At forty-one years of age, Abigail was "care-worn and depressed" and suffering from vision loss and painful, decaying teeth. Taking a delighted Louisa with her, she announced to Bronson, "We may be [away] from home for some weeks."

"Distance and absence from Home and cares will restore her," Bronson hoped. He felt "very happy" with Abigail gone, he wrote to his brother Junius, who now lived in New York near their sisters and mother, because his friend Charles Lane, "the best substitute for yourself at fireside . . . is near to me."

Several days in Boston with Louisa left Abigail "quickened by a new spirit of confidence and love." One evening she attended a public lecture on education, a topic that continued to fascinate her. Standing up afterward to engage in the discussion, according to an observer, Abigail "quite electrified the audience" with her inspirational public speaking. A note she received that week from Bronson served to remind her of what she called his "perfect trust in God and goodness," particularly now that he was again at a distance." A few weeks earlier, while living under the same roof as her impractical spouse, she had written in her journal, "Give me one day of practical philosophy. It is worth a century of speculation and discussion."

Abigail returned home with Louisa on January 1, 1843, resolved to face the new year with restored confidence and hope. A new year meant a new diary, as it had since Abigail was ten years old. Louisa too was now ten, old enough for a journal. Eleven-year-old Anna had already started hers. Their financial situation was so precarious that she thought the children might benefit from writing to each other as a way of expressing their feelings. To this end, Abigail established a household post office to provide the girls "and indeed all of us" a way of sharing "thought and sentiment," particularly amid conflicts. Hanging a basket by the front door, she explained to Elizabeth, Louisa, and Anna that if any discontent occurred, the post office would provide a "pleasant way of healing all differences and discontents." Anyone could deposit in the basket "letters, notes or parcels," which would "be distributed to the respective owners" each evening after supper. The post office worked well in inducing the children to interchange "notes of reconciliation, reestablishing friendships." Writing helped them, as it helped her, to face and understand their emotions.

Even as her children began to learn how to express their difficult feelings, Abigail had no one with whom to share her own anxiety. Her husband seemed to have withdrawn, physically and emotionally. Bronson may have shared a room with her due to their cramped quarters, but he had not slept in their bed since his return from England, her diary suggests. Charles Lane's devotion to celibacy may have influenced Bronson. Moreover, Abigail felt "greatly beset by men to whom we are owing small sums of money. . . . Mr. Alcott feels that nothing can just now be done but let them wait. I wish I could be more comfortable under this state of things. I have stated my mind [to him] very explicitly, and yet I have not said all I feel, for I do not know how to do it advisedly."

Her husband, she feared, was turning anarchist. In January she overheard him, Lane, and Wright discuss how to "overthrow" the government because of its "errors." In the same month Bronson refused to pay his poll tax, a fixed, per-person tax, prompting Concord authorities to arrest him. He had planned for this act of civil disobedience to send him to jail, but before he was committed Elizabeth Hoar's father, the judge, paid the tax for him, sparing Bronson what Abigail bitterly called "the triumph of suffering for his principles."

In the bitter cold of early March she traveled the few miles to Lexington to discuss her situation with her brother. Samuel Joseph and his family had moved to Lexington in 1842, after his activism cost him his pulpit in South Scituate. The congregation had asked him to depart soon after he invited black parishioners to sit in the front gallery among whites. He had preached, "If a slaveholder, with his gold and fine clothing, were to visit this church he would be given the best seats" on the floor, "but his colored slave, the victim of his tyranny (though he might be a disciple of Christ) would be sent up to the negro pew" in the balcony. Never before had anyone integrated parishioners of different races and classes in the church. Samuel Joseph was now employed by Horace Mann, the pioneering secretary of the Massachusetts Board of Education, in Lexington as the principal of a Normal School, an early teachers' college. His salary was stretched by his need to rent a house, but his family's move to Lexington proved to be a boon to Abigail and her children.

"I am at a loss about money," she told her brother. Although Bronson still had no income, he intended to purchase a house and a farm. In addition to his older, larger debts, she owed $175 to Concord shops. She asked Samuel Joseph how she would pay even their "little debts." She often asked Bronson this "difficult question," but he had no satisfactory answer.

"I am quite at a loss myself," Samuel Joseph said. "I feel dissatisfied that Mr. Alcott finds no means of supporting his family independent of his friends. They have to labor; why should not he?" Bringing his pastoral skills to bear, he said, "I leave it for time to settle. Your husband's unwillingness to be employed in the usual way produces great doubt in the minds of his friends as to the righteousness of his life because he partakes of the wages of others. . . . It is certainly not right to incur debt and be indifferent or inactive in the payment of same."

Abigail marveled at her brother's clarity. He always found a good and loving path. She saw that he was "embarrassed how to proceed, with no means to help us himself and no confidence in the disposition of others to do so."

That spring, following the departure of Henry Wright due to his disillusionment with Bronson's philosophy, Charles Lane agreed to purchase for their community a farm on about eighty acres in the village of Harvard, fifteen miles west of Concord. The property cost $1,800 (equivalent to $43,000 in 2000), and Lane had only $1,500. To cover the balance, the owner offered him and Bronson an interest-free loan, payable over two years in four payments of $75 each (about $1,800 in 2000). Bronson had no money, so someone else had to guarantee the loan.

Emerson refused. "I would as soon exert myself to collect money for a madman," he confided to Margaret Fuller. He had come to hate Bronson's "cold vague generalities" and "majestic . . . egoism." Considering Bronson's character the year before, Emerson had observed, "I know no man who speaks such good English as he. . . . He takes such delight in the exercise of this faculty that he will willingly talk the whole of the day, and most part of the night, and then again tomorrow. . . . Unhappily, his conversation never loses sight of his own personality. . . . His topic yesterday is Alcott on the 17th October; today, Alcott on the 18th October. . . . I do not want any more such persons to exist."

Abigail again asked Samuel Joseph for financial help, but he did not have three hundred dollars to spare. However, to "secure to my sister a house for herself and family," he agreed in April or May to sign the note for the mortgage and to serve as Lane's agent in the sale.

Abigail's "three eventful years in Concord" were nearly over. She hoped that their next home would be happier, more fruitful. Perhaps it would be, for her husband and Lane had decided to call it Fruitlands. But Abigail seemed to be growing frail. Her eyes and teeth were failing her, and each passing year, it seemed, she more closely resembled her own mother. Whenever she prayed, "Give us this day our daily bread," she understood, as she never had as a child, that she meant exactly what she said.

As she packed for another move, she found among her papers a print of an etching she admired of a mother and a daughter. The daughter reminded her of ten-year-old Louisa. On March 12, 1843, Abigail pasted the print on heavy paper and wrote beneath the image, "DEAR

LOUIE . . . In my imagination I have thought you might be just such an industrious good daughter and that I might be a sick but loving mother, looking to my daughter's labors for my daily bread. Take care of it for my sake and your own, because you and I have always liked to be grouped together."

The "industrious good" daughter would spend the rest of her life responding to this message from the "sick but loving mother" who looked to her for her daily bread. Some months later Louisa pasted in her journal the etching and the note from her mother. Beside it she composed a poem about her mother's dream of writing a book:

TO MOTHER

I hope that soon, dear mother,
You and I may be
In the quiet room my fancy
Has so often made for thee—

The pleasant, sunny chamber,
The cushioned easy-chair,
The book laid for your reading,
The vase of flowers fair,

The desk beside the window
Where the sun shines warm and right:
And there in peace and quiet
The promised book you write;

While I sit close beside you,
Content at last to see
That you can rest, dear mother,
And I can cherish thee.

Chapter Seven

To Drag Life's Lengthening Chain

On June 3, 1843, the Alcotts' third day at Fruitlands, after feeding her family and the Lanes and supervising the children's morning chores, Abigail led her four girls outside. Each time they moved she explored with them the world around their new home. Her older children, especially, were increasingly aware of the world. Louisa and Anna, at ten and twelve, were practically young ladies, Elizabeth was almost eight, and Abby May nearly three. The five female Alcotts walked along the ridge between the farmhouse and the woods overlooking the Ascutney, Wachusett, and Monadnock mountains. Abigail pointed out and named the features of "our little territory . . . Hill, grove, forest . . . woodland, vale, meadow, and pasture . . . all beautiful . . . commanding one of the most expansive prospects in the country."

They came upon a pile of wood chips at the edge of the meadow. Kneeling to fill her apron with chips, Abigail encouraged the girls to gather flowers. They scattered and returned with four bouquets. "Like Provident Mother Earth, I gather for use," she said with a smile, "while you collect for beauty. Both give pleasure." This made sense to Louisa: beauty and usefulness are both of value.

"We are transported from our littleness" by lovely vistas, Abigail continued. "The soul expands in such a region of sights and sounds," presenting people with a choice. "Between us and this vast expanse we may hold our [own] hand and stand alone, an isolated being occupying but a foot of earth and living for ourselves," or "we may look again" and be possessed by "a feeling of diffusive illimitable benevolence." Despite all the frustration she felt in her marriage, Abigail was still committed to supporting her husband's goal of living rightly, which he hoped to realize at Fruitlands. But she may not have considered the emotional cost to a child when a parent lives solely for "diffusive illimitable benevolence."

Each time Bronson came to Abigail with a new dream, it seemed, she resolved to do all in her power to make it come true. Of this new "estate" he had proclaimed, "This dell is the canvas on which I will paint . . . a worthy picture for mankind." She in turn prayed that Fruitlands would "prove a happy home" for her children. There she would try to "live the true life, putting away the evil customs of society and leading quiet exemplary lives."

During their early days at the farm Abigail did her best to be, or at least seem to be, optimistic. "Lest you should for one moment be under the apprehension that I am dissatisfied, I hasten to discharge your mind of any such misapprehension," she began her first letter to Samuel Joseph, defensively. "The house is even better (shabby and ill-looking as it is) than I expected, for they described it as being scarcely tenantable—whereas I assure you if all God's creatures were as well sheltered as this, there would be no suffering on this score." The land was "admirable," the "woods, groves, pastures, brooks are delightful," and "the prospect is indescribable," of "lofty hills whose summits pierce the heavens as with a wedge."

Abigail continued, "Mr. A[lcott] is in his element." She was "quite comfortable. . . . Our children are very happy and when the planting is over we shall establish a school." Bronson, Lane, and a hired man were already sowing corn, beans, and potatoes, which they anticipated would yield five hundred bushels, and Bronson was seeking new recruits to join them. "I do feel as if a great work may be effected here," Abigail wrote. "The true life *ought* to be lived here if any where on earth—away from the false and degrading customs of society as now fashioned. . . . We may fail, but it will be something that we have ventured what so few have dared. We have had two beautiful Sabbaths." The "solitude of the place" reminded her of South Scituate, where her brother had spent six years.

She invited Samuel Joseph and his family to visit Fruitlands. Lacking a horse and wagon, she advised him, "instead of stopping at the village of Harvard" two miles away, "tell the stage driver to leave you at [Mr. Edgerton's] this side [of] Still River [village] and some of us will be over

to get you. . . . It will only be a mile—across the fields." She thanked
him for a recent gift of five dollars, "a great comfort as I paid off all my
little [debts] and we owe *nobody nothing* . . . a comfortable feeling after a
perturbation of 10 years." Her feelings were captured "beautifully" by a
hymn they used to sing as children:

> *It surely is a wasted heart,*
> *It is a wasted mind,*
> *That seeks not in the inner world*
> *Its happiness to find.*
>
> *For happiness is like the bird*
> *That broods above its nest,*
> *And finds beneath its folded wings*
> *Life's dearest and its best.*

She did not mention in the letter to her brother that her husband
had grown aloof from her and intimate with Charles Lane. She now
distrusted and disliked Lane. Apparently, the feeling was mutual. "Her
pride is not yet eradicated," Lane wrote to a friend, adding that Abigail "has no spontaneous inclination towards a larger family than her
own. . . . Her peculiar maternal love blinds her to all else." Lane, who
had left his son's mother, was convinced that sexuality was the root of
all evil. Now he was thinking of joining the Shakers, who were celibate
and forswore procreation. He hoped to convince Bronson to join him.

Bronson did seem to be moving in that direction. He continued
to sleep apart from Abigail. In early July, she wrote in her journal, he
"forcibly illustrated" to her the need to renounce sensual pleasure by
marking in chalk on a slate "the † on which the lusts of the flesh are to
be sacrificed," in his words. Bronson urged Abigail to endure "the sacrifices and utter subjection of the body to the Soul," explaining, "Renunciation is the law; devotion to God's will the Gospel. The latter make
the former easy, sometimes delightful." Abigail was now convinced that
Lane posed a threat to her marriage. In fact, according to the scholar
Ronald Bosco, "Lane was a subversive influence on Bronson. Abigail
was right to suspect that this community would not turn out well for
her and her girls."

The two men, having appointed themselves the leaders of their new community, jointly composed its rules, whose austerity the children and Abigail would not fully experience until winter. The men banned all products of capitalism, including wool, cotton, meat, dairy, cane sugar, and tea. Fruitlanders could wear only linen, loose tunics, and pants for both men and women in an era when women universally wore skirts. Every meal was "strictly of the pure and bloodless kind," restricted to water, unleavened bread or porridge, and vegetables or fruits. "No animal substances, neither flesh, butter, cheese, eggs nor milk, pollute our tables or corrupt our bodies, neither tea, coffee, molasses, nor rice, tempts us beyond the bounds of indigenous productions," they wrote. "Our sole beverage is pure fountain water. The native grains, fruits, herbs and roots, dressed with the utmost cleanliness . . . yield an ample store for human nutrition, without dependence on foreign climes, or the degradations of shipping and trade." Cotton depended on slave labor, which Bronson now considered suspect; wool belonged to sheep. No whale oil lamps were entertained, for the oil was the whale's. No beast of burden was permitted. "Only a brave woman's taste, time, and temper were sacrificed on that domestic altar," Louisa pointed out decades later, indignant on her mother's behalf. Even Abigail herself remarked wryly to a nephew that summer, "They spare the cattle, but they forget the women and children."

"Ordinary secular farming is not our object," Bronson and Lane declared in the Transcendentalist journal the *Dial,* edited by Margaret Fuller. "Consecrated to human freedom . . . this enterprise must be rooted in a reliance on the succors of an ever bounteous Providence." They rejected "the cares and injury of a life of gain" and promised never to neglect "the inner nature of every member of the [Fruitlands] family."

The population of their community swelled in July. Visitors that month included Emerson, who was curious to see the farm, the poet Ellery Channing (the minister's nephew), several members of Harvard's Shaker community, Abigail's eighteen-year-old nephew Samuel Sewall Greele, and George and Sophia Ripley, who had founded Brook Farm, a utopian community of about a hundred people in West Roxbury. Six or seven men decided to stay as residents of Fruitlands, doubling the number of mouths Abigail had to feed. Only one newcomer was a woman, the "amiable" and "active" Ann Page, whose presence Abigail appreciated.

Far from living out any utopian ideal, Abigail felt she was running an inn. She alone was responsible for the care of the house, bedding, clothing, washing, and meals, a huge task even with the help of her elder daughters and Miss Page. Abigail struggled to maintain the children's daily lessons, sometimes asking twelve-year-old Anna to supervise them. The girls were no more fond of Charles Lane than she was. Louisa did not like Lane's lessons. "I like [the farm], but not the school part or Mr. Lane," she observed. One day "Mr. L[ane] was in Boston and we were glad." Abigail continued to teach Louisa, Anna, and Lizzie to sew, as her mother and sisters had taught her. She did her best to be a mother to William Lane, who was included in many of the Alcott girls' activities, forming with them a quintet reminiscent of the five siblings of Abigail's childhood.

On Tuesday, July 18, 1843, Samuel Joseph, Lucretia, and their children arrived in a carriage to see how Abigail was faring. As the older Alcott girls played with ten-year-old Charlotte, Abigail talked with her brother and sister-in-law, who had troubles of their own. Samuel Joseph had recently resigned from his job at the Normal School in order to avoid further alienating Horace Mann, who objected to the minister's decision to train a black woman for a teaching career. Other than preaching occasionally at Lexington's First Parish, Samuel Joseph had no work and no way of knowing where he would next be called. In addition, he and Lucretia were planning a trip to Niagara Falls and western New York, a hotbed of abolitionism. But he still provided Abigail a "kind sympathy," for which she was grateful.

August at Fruitlands was busy and "toilsome," even harder for Abigail than July. Bronson seemed to retreat even further. He still avoided physical contact with Abigail and was often away from the farm, traveling around New England, usually in the company of Lane, ostensibly seeking funds to maintain Fruitlands. Bronson returned from several days with Lane in Boston "quite ill" with dysentery and "terrible diarrhea" that left him feeble for weeks. Bronson was "low indeed," Abigail reported to Samuel Joseph, "nor did I see by what human aids he was to be restored." Even after "the acuteness of his disease had passed," he still seemed "not essentially better, and the means he permitted to be used [for healing] were to my mind wholly inadequate." Over and over he murmured, "Thy faith shall heal thee."

Unlike his wife, Bronson had decided to rely entirely on faith. He was "content to wait till the Wise God decree for us all," as he put it, because "a union . . . await[s] us . . . in the life of the Spirit." Abigail, who trusted "common sense" over faith, reported, "I insisted on [Bronson taking] spearmint tea and a total abandonment of vegetable food." The tea, copious blackberries, and a "shower bath" twice a day had "indeed restored him but not made quite whole this dying man." He remained "more nervous and excitable" than usual. A visitor noted "the alteration in Mr. A[lcott], his sepulchral tones, and . . . languor."

Bronson "sees too much company" at Fruitlands, Abigail thought. "His mind is altogether too morbidly active. I thought of proposing to him a little quiet journey as a change—leaving the children with Mr. Lane and Abraham" Everett, another resident. "But he says no." A decade later Bronson noted in his journal that in twenty-four years of marriage, during which he himself traveled extensively, he and Abigail never spent any time together away from home. At Fruitlands he refused a little quiet journey with his wife because, he told her, "I want rest and perfect quiet, that when I journey it will be a long one—and *alone*."

The thought of his death frightened Abigail. As she told her brother, "I do not allow myself to despair of his recovery—but, Oh Sam, that piercing thought flashes through my mind of [Bronson's] insanity." She confessed that "a grave yawning to receive his precious body would be to me a consolation compared to that condition of life. . . . Don't mention this to even Lucretia [May] or Elizabeth," meaning, probably, twenty-four-year-old Elizabeth Willis Wells, the married daughter of their late sister Eliza May Willis for whom Abigail had cared when she was small.

Even writing now seemed a burden to Abigail. "I have written Charles"—her eldest brother, recently returned to Boston after decades away at sea—"a hasty note but now my mind is too much oppressed to do any thing long which is not connected with the condition of things here," she told Samuel Joseph. "I wish you would explain to him more fully how I am distracted—with a large, but fluctuating family—feeble husband—and not wholly persuaded in my own mind that all that *is,* is *best*—I ought not to write to any body. . . ."

With guests she was gloomy and apologetic. She said to one visitor as he departed, "You must come ten years hence for my opinion about Fruitlands."

"Dear Lady," he replied, "you will not be here to answer me."

"Perhaps not. In that case it will speak for itself. It will be a barren wilderness or a fruitful Paradise, I fear, despite of me." Inwardly she thought, "My Genius is too rigidly set in the old mould to make great progress. I abhor Society, as it is, with its fallacies and shams. But I can only be real myself."

Her girls, she felt, also needed to be "real themselves." Conscious of this, Abigail gave Louisa another blank book that summer. "Write in it," she said, explaining that keeping a diary was a long habit in the family, beginning with the male Puritans who regularly recorded their observations and feelings. Louisa began immediately: "Friday, August 4, 1843. After breakfast I washed the dishes and then had my lessons. Father and Mr. Kay [a visitor] and Mr. Lane went to the Shakers and did not return till evening. After my lessons I sewed till dinner. When dinner was over I had a bath, and then went to [a neighbor] Mrs. Williard's. When I came home I played till supper time, after which I read a little in Oliver Twist, and when I had thought a little I went to bed." Louisa concluded her first entry, "I have spent quite a pleasant day."

It was surprisingly satisfying to record her activities and thoughts. Louisa recounted sewing, ironing, and setting the table, her lessons, playing alone or with Lizzie, and picking blackberries and raspberries with Anna and William Lane. Now and then she asked Abigail to read through her entries and comment on them. "I told mother I liked to have her write in my book," Louisa explained. "She said she would put in more and she wrote this to help me: 'Dear Louie,—Your handwriting improves very fast. Take pains and do not be in a hurry. I like to have you make observations about our conversations and your own thoughts. It helps you to express them and to understand your little self. Remember, dear girl, that a diary should be an epitome of your life. May it be a record of pure thought and good actions, then you will indeed be the precious child of your loving mother.'"

Keeping a journal seemed to protect Louisa from pain. On the evening of August 10, after "Mother and Father came home" from a visit to the Shaker community in Harvard that Bronson and Lane had spoken of joining, Louisa and Anna heard their parents arguing. "Though it was unpleasant without," Louisa wrote in her journal, "I was happy within," in part because she had an outlet for the anxiety aroused by her parents' fights.

She and Anna, sensing their mother's growing distress, tried harder to behave. They "deport themselves with more than usual discretion and quietude," Abigail noticed. One late summer evening, as Louisa lay in her bed and "the moon came up very brightly and looked at me," she regretted she "did not mind Mother" that day. She vowed, "I must not tease my mother." A few weeks later, on Abigail's forty-third birthday, Louisa's first thought on waking was "Mother's birthday: I must be very good." She gave Abigail a cross she had made of moss collected in the woods, and a bookmark she feared was "not very pretty." Louisa wrote in her journal, "I wish I were rich, I was good, and we were all a happy family."

Abigail and Miss Page were able to steal a day from their Fruitlands duties at the end of August to visit the nearby Shakers, whose sexual abstinence, farming, and ritual dancing intrigued Bronson and Lane. Neither woman was impressed. "We saw but little of their domestic and internal arrangements, [but] there is servitude somewhere, I have no doubt," Abigail said. The Shaker men had "a fat, sleek, comfortable look. . . . Among the women there is a still, awkward reserve that belongs to neither sublime resignation [n]or divine hope."

Waxing philosophical, Abigail moved from the stifled Shaker women to the lot of women everywhere. "Wherever I turn, I see the yoke on women in some form or another. On some it sits easy for they are but beasts of burden. On others pride hushes them to silence; no complaint is made for they scorn pity or sympathy. On some it galls and chafes; they feel assured by every instinct of their nature that they were designed for a higher, nobler calling than to 'drag life's lengthening chain along.'"

Without defining the group to which she belonged, Abigail considered her own domestic arrangement. "A woman may perform the most disinterested duties. She may 'die daily' in the cause of truth and righteousness. She lives neglected, dies forgotten. But a man who never performed in his whole life one self-denying act, but who has accidental gifts of genius, is celebrated by his contemporaries, while his name and his works live on, from age to age. He is crowned with laurel, while scarce a 'stone may tell where she lies.'"

Miss Page, according to Abigail's journal, replied, "A woman may live a whole life of sacrifice and at her death meekly says, 'I die a woman.' A man passes a few years in experiments on self-denial and simple life and he says, 'Behold a God.'"

"A good remark and true!" Abigail exclaimed. "There certainly is more true humility in woman, more substantial greatness in woman, more essential goodness, than in man. Woman *lives* her thought; man *speculates* about it. Woman's love is enduring, changeless; man is fitful in his attachments; his love is convenient, not of necessity. Woman is happy in her plain lawn; man is better content in the royal purple." Life was fundamentally unfair, she felt, as her daughters were doubtless aware. To be a woman in the world, particularly a married women, was to be subservient and neglected. She found it particularly galling that men, who had so much more power and privilege, often seemed inferior to women in character.

This was aptly demonstrated by her husband, whose behavior became more erratic that autumn. After all his talk of farming, he would not bring in the harvest. In early September he and Lane spent two weeks traveling to Rhode Island, New York City, and Bronson's hometown in Connecticut. Just before the men left the farm Anna and Louisa heard their father call the trip a "separation" and suggest he might never return. During the men's absence Abigail continued the children's lessons. One day she "read [a]loud to Miss Page and the girls *The President's Daughters, a narrative of a Governess* by Frederika Bremer," which contained "fine touches." One passage struck her: "Within the good and happy family all inequalities are smoothed down so as to form a common element of goodness and beauty, in which each member of the family finds his life." If only she could create a family in which all inequalities were smoothed down.

Decades later, in *Transcendental Wild Oats,* her 1873 account of Fruitlands, Louisa recalled the scene that month with an insouciance that may belie her feelings then. Humor was a mask that Louisa used "to keep [at bay] the reality of her passions," a biographer wrote. Louisa described the behavior of "all the men"—her father, Lane, and perhaps a few others—at harvest time:

The rule was to do what the spirit moved, so they left their crops to Providence and went a-reaping in wider and, let us hope, more fruitful fields than their own.

Luckily, the earthly providence who watched over [Bronson] was at hand to glean the scanty crop yielded by the "uncorrupted land," which, "consecrated to human freedom," had received "the sober culture of devout men."

About the time the grain was ready to house, some call of the Oversoul wafted all the men away. An easterly storm was coming up and the yellow stacks were sure to be ruined. Then Sister Hope [Abigail] gathered her forces. Three little girls [Anna, Louisa, and Elizabeth], one boy ([Lane]'s son), and herself, harnessed to clothes-baskets and Russia-linen sheets, were the only teams she could command; but with these poor appliances the indomitable woman got in the grain and saved food for her young, with the instinct and energy of a mother-bird with a brood of hungry nestlings to feed.

Like her "mother-bird," ten-year-old Louisa disliked the stream of strangers who came to see Bronson's experiment, eat their food, and sometimes stay for a few nights or weeks. She wished they would all go away. "More people coming to live with us," she wrote in her journal not long afterward. "I wish we could be together, and no one else. I don't see who is to clothe and feed us all, when we are so poor now." Feeling "dismal," Louisa composed a poem on despondency, which concluded with a wish to "smile through the darkest hours."

Everything was uncertain. "I *believe* that we are to stay here this winter," Abigail told her brother in November, more than a month after Bronson and Lane had returned, "[but] I will predict nothing but try to fortify myself for all the storms and be grateful for all the gales which may be breathed upon me. . . . We are loading up wood and apples as the one thing needful. We all are comfortably fixed for clothing, and come what may I shall try that the peace of these dear children be no more disturbed by discussions and doubts. I and they *will* have comfort, a good fire, cheerful faces and pleasant books." She wrote an affectionate note to Anna: "I feel as if I could fold my arms around you all, and say from my heart, 'Here is my world within my embrace.'" Abigail encouraged the children to play games. Among their favorites were cribbage, casino, Old Maid, and Nine Men's Morris. Each morning, no matter how dreary, her daughters recalled waking to the sound of Abigail singing.

"I am not dead yet, either to life or love," Abigail reassured her brother Charles in a letter. "This is a Hotel where man and beast are entertained without pay, and at great expense. I keep saying 'Oh when will rest come?'" Herself a beast of burden on her husband's farm, she had no heart to expect others to join her there. "I am too generous to tackle anybody [else] into this harrow, for drag as you will you cannot get the ground smooth: the asperities are too sharp, the sinuosities too deep."

She was no longer confident in Bronson's dream. "It is absurd to suppose," as he seemed to do, "that all move in the same circle" as oneself. Abigail wished to "permit each to be good in his own way." Unlike Bronson, "I do not wish to transcend humanity; I wish to transcend nothing but evil and sin." Thinking again of insanity, which she dreaded, "I hope not to transcend my senses; they are the sentinels to guard the citadel of my soul." Finally, she rejected her husband's recent renunciation of sexual passion. "Even our passions are heralds announcing a deep nature. A passionless person is to me a tame, half-whole animal. . . . If rightly governed, [passions] render us invulnerable to All the heresy of Sin."

In addition to all the other physical deprivations, the farmhouse was unbearably cold, which would soon reduce the population of Fruitlands to the original group of Alcotts and Lanes. Abigail tried, without success, to "fortify" herself against "the severe weather" by taking two cold-water showers a day. William Lane "has been sick a fort night," she informed Samuel Joseph in November, "and Louisa with a dreadful cough, pain in her side and head-ache." As for the adults, Bronson remained distant and unhappy. "Mr. Lane looks miserably and *acts worse*." He demonstrated a "contemptible, pitiable moodiness. But no man is . . . always sublime to his *house maid*," Abigail added bitterly, in reference to herself.

Many evenings in November, Louisa and Anna lay silently in their bed as their parents discussed a separation. This made Louisa "very unhappy," she wrote in her journal. "Father and mother and Anna and I had a long talk . . . and we all cried." Then "Anna and I cried in bed, and I prayed God to keep us all together." She feared her father would abandon them and depart again with Charles Lane, dissolving her family. One evening, she reported, "Father and Mr. L. had a talk, and Father asked us if *we* saw any reason for us to separate. Mother wanted to, she is so tired."

Not long afterward, Louisa turned *"Eleven years old. Thursday, [November]29th*—It was father's and my birthday. We had some nice presents. We played in the snow before school. Mother read [the poem] 'Rosamond' when we sewed. Father asked us in the eve what fault troubled us most. I said my bad temper."

Six months had passed since the purchase of the farm, so the first mortgage payment was due. Samuel Joseph, who had doubtless discussed the matter with his sister, simply declined to pay the seventy-five dollars. Without it, the farm went into foreclosure. "Dear S," Abigail wrote with a hint of triumph to Samuel Joseph on November 11, "Your letter [about the mortgage] pleased me better than it did the other proprietors of the Estate," namely Lane and her husband, neither of whom had seventy-five dollars. "I do not wish you to put a cent *here*" at Fruitlands. "I am sifting everything to its bottom, for I will know the foundation, center and circumference," she promised.

Bronson, on the other hand, fell into an "extreme mental depression." Without income or property, estranged from his wife, and feeling himself a failure, he took to his bed, starved himself, and made it known that he wished to die. "Then the tragedy began for the forsaken little family," Louisa wrote in *Transcendental Wild Oats,* assuming an opacity reminiscent of her father's style. "Desolation and despair fell upon [Bronson]. As his wife said, his new beliefs had alienated many friends. . . . He had tried, but it was a failure. The world was not ready for Utopia yet. . . . Then this dreamer, whose dream was the end of his life, resolved to carry out his idea to the bitter end. . . . Silently he lay down upon his bed, turned his face to the wall, and waited with pathetic patience for death to cut the knot which he could not untie. Days and nights went by, and neither food nor water passed his lips."

Despite her eagerness to be rid of the farm, this was agony for Abigail. Her husband was incapacitated. Her children were sick, cold, and hungry. She knew she could no longer remain at Fruitlands. "Mrs. Alcott gives notice," Charles Lane wrote to a friend at the end of November, "that she concedes to the wishes of her friends . . . and shall withdraw to a house which they will provide for her and her four children." She told her brother, "Our situation here [is] quite uncomfortable. . . . We shall probably leave here as soon as we can see our way clear where and how to go." By "we" she meant herself and the children. She could no longer speak for Bronson.

On December 23, 1843, according to Louisa's journal, "In the morning mother went to the Village and I had my lessons and then helped Annie get dinner after which mother came home and Annie and I went on an errand for mother to [a neighbor] Mr. Lovejoy. We stayed a little while to see their little baby boy. I often wish I had a little brother but as I have not I shall try to be contented with what I have got." It is not clear if Louisa had any memory of her stillborn brother, four years before.

Two days later, for the second Christmas in a row, Bronson and Abigail were apart. He had gone to Boston to attend a conference. To celebrate the holiday Abigail prepared small gifts for each child and did her best to have "a little merry-making in the evening with the neighbor's children." But her heart was not in it.

Neither was Louisa's. She "rose early and sat some looking at the Bon-bons in my stocking." By herself she read further in *Pilgrim's Progress,* which fascinated her. "I liked the verses Christian sung and will put them in [the journal]," she wrote on December 25:

> This place has been our second stage,
> Here we have heard and seen
> Those good things that from age to age
> To others hid have been.
>
> They move me for to watch and pray,
> To strive to be sincere,
> To take my cross up day by day,
> And serve the Lord with fear.

Decades later, reading back over this journal entry as the best-selling author of a novel that begins, "Christmas won't be Christmas without any presents," Louisa realized that the "appropriateness of this song at this time was much greater than the child saw. . . . Little Lu began early to feel the family cares and peculiar trials. . . . She never forgot this experience, and her little cross began to grow heavier from this hour. Poetry began to flow about this time in a thin but copious stream."

One of the presents Louisa received from her mother was a poem, which the child transcribed in her journal:

> *Christmas is here*
> *Louisa my dear*
> *Then happy we'll be*
> *Gladsome and free. . . .*

A few days later, extreme winter weather hit central Massachusetts. Snowstorm upon snowstorm left the road to the house "completely blocked up." Abigail could not reach the mailbox until their neighbor Mr. Lovejoy broke a path in the snow. Days were gloomy and evenings, gloomier. Her eyes were "quite troublesome." She could no longer read to the children by candlelight, which they all loved. She played and sang with them "to cheer the scene within to render the cheerlessness without more tolerable."

Sometime that month Abigail had told Mr. Lovejoy that she and her children could not remain at the farm. She needed a place to stay until she could make other arrangements. He offered her three rooms in his house and the use of his kitchen for two dollars a month. She agreed and notified her brother, who sent her ten dollars to shelter her and the girls for five months.

Bronson returned from Boston on January 1, 1844, to learn that his wife and children were leaving. "I have concluded to go to Mr. Lovejoy's until spring, having dissolved all connection with Fruitlands," Abigail announced. The "arrangements here have never suited me, and my children have been too bereft of their mother."

Bronson protested, insisting, "I will not abide in a house set aside for myself and family alone. . . . I cannot consent to live solely for one family."

But Abigail had to live solely for one family. She refused to join another consociate family. "There is nothing there for us," she explained, referring to herself, "no sphere in which we could act without an unwarrantable alienation from our children." She told Samuel Joseph, "I cannot live [Bronson's] principle." Her need to leave Fruitlands was sufficiently strong that she would, if necessary, separate from her husband.

At the same time she resisted the idea of divorce, which violated her every instinct, her inborn sense of duty. She remained devoted to the idea of her husband, if not the actual man, and her dream of all that he might accomplish in the world. There was another reason for her resistance: a divorced woman had no legal right to her children. Abigail "still rested under all the ancient disabilities of the common law," as her cousin Samuel E. Sewall explained. If she did divorce Bronson, he could take the children and prevent her from ever seeing them again.

Only a year later, due to reforms initiated by her cousin and other lawyers, women's marital rights would begin to change. Over the next half century, Sewall would write, "a great revolution in the law respecting this [marital] relation [was] effected, and all of it favorable to wives, recognizing and enforcing their rights to their property, their persons, and their children." Sewall would note with satisfaction in the 1880s that marital law, though still defective, had improved significantly since his cousin Abigail's crisis in 1844.

These legal inequities had already affected Abigail. Had she been a son of Colonel May, she would already have received and gained control of her portion of her father's estate. Her father's estate planning had protected her inheritance from passing to her husband but forced it into probate, rendering it inaccessible for several years. And even after the estate was probated, later in 1844, her portion would be entrusted to male relatives, Sewall and Samuel Joseph, on her behalf.

"The very fault of marriage, and of the present relation between the sexes, [is] that the woman does belong to the man, instead of forming a whole with him," Margaret Fuller wrote in 1845 in *Woman in the Nineteenth Century*. "Now there is no woman, only an overgrown child." In order that "her hand may be given with dignity, she must be able to stand alone."

Abigail did not have the power to stand alone, but she could act. One of her core beliefs, born of her long struggle to find her own, independent way in the world, was that each person has free will and the right to forge his or her own path. When Bronson was in England in 1842 and she alone with the girls, she had written in her journal, "All of us can carve out our own way, and God can make our very contradictions harmonize with his solemn ends." In other words, society's inequities and her marital difficulties were insurmountable, but she was still free to maintain her dignity.

It was decided: they were leaving and the Fruitlands experiment was over. Years later she would recall, "Finding the [Fruitlands] scheme not likely to succeed, I hired a small house in Still River and took my 4 girls with our worldly goods . . . in January 1844." Abigail spent the first few days of that year packing her beloved books—including sixteen Shakespeare plays, poetry and novels, and volumes of philosophy, botany, and herbal therapies—her furniture, and the family's clothes, assisted by Anna and Louisa. At the same time, Charles Lane left with his son and his large library to join the nearby Shaker community. In the middle of January, according to a letter from Abigail to her brother, she and her four daughters bundled up in cloaks and walked the short distance through the snow to the Lovejoy house. There is no evidence of Bronson's immediate actions, and several pages are here torn out of his journal. In addition, he later edited and rewrote portions of Abigail's journals before destroying the originals, so that for this period only his redactions of her journals remain. Scholars have assumed that Bronson's later presence at the Lovejoy house indicates that he moved with his family, but it is equally likely that Bronson remained at Fruitlands alone, without food, money, or support.

"Never had she looked more beautiful as she stood there," the adult Louisa would write of a woman trapped in a destructive love triangle in a story that evokes this drama that Louisa endured as a child. Pauline, the heroine of the story, appears as "an image of will, daring, defiant, and indomitable, with eyes darkened by intensity of emotion, voice half sad, half stern, and outstretched hand on which the wedding ring no longer shone. She felt her power, yet was wary enough to assure it by one bold appeal to the strongest element of her husband's character: passions, not principles, were the allies she desired, and before the answer came she knew that she had gained them at the cost of innocence and self-respect." Seeking revenge against the man who spurned her, Pauline "silently accepted his challenge to the tournament so often held between man and woman—a tournament where the keen tongue is the lance, pride the shield, passion the fiery steed, and the hardest heart the winner of the prize, which seldom fails to prove a barren honor, ending in remorse."

Pauline was Louisa's archetypal fictional heroine, according to Madeleine Stern. "Of all the characters [Louisa] adumbrated in narratives, the one who came most completely to life and who obviously was as intriguing to her author as to readers was the passionate, richly sexual *femme fatale* who had a mysterious past, an electrifying present, and a revengeful future." Similarly, in Louisa's novel *A Long Fatal Love Chase*, which was deemed "too sensational" to publish during her lifetime, the young heroine, Rosamund, seeks "freedom" by marrying a manipulative older man. Upon learning that he is not only evil but also already married, Rosamund flees his villa on the Riviera. He follows her, stalking her across Europe. She evades him by disguising herself as a seamstress, a Catholic nun, and a governess. In the end she can escape her husband only in death.

Abigail neither died nor succeeded in abandoning her marriage. Sometime that month, according to a letter she wrote on January 29, Bronson followed her to the Lovejoy house, where they took him in. Bronson had nowhere else to go. It is not clear if the couple shared a room at the Lovejoys or later, but there is no evidence that Bronson and Abigail—both in their early forties—were ever again physically intimate. Abigail's personal papers burned decades later by Bronson and Louisa "were probably written during critical times," the biographer Cynthia Barton noted, "and were more negative toward marriage and toward Bronson" than the papers that survive. As a result, "just when we'd really like to know how she felt, we can't." To Louisa, Bronson, and possibly other relatives, Abigail's eloquent frankness in recording her thoughts and feelings was "threatening to the Alcotts' posthumous reputation," Barton wrote. Nevertheless, Abigail's actions suggest that she decided to move forward with her husband, rather like a fifth child, in tow. Indeed, a woman who had met the Alcotts the year before had described Bronson's "ultimate providence" as "an excellent wife, who clothed and fed him as a baby, and reverenced him as a divinity."

With the failure of Fruitlands, however, the power shifted in the Alcotts' marriage. For the first time ever, according to Barton, "Abigail took control. She resolved to be less compliant, more vigilant concerning the ramifications of Bronson's schemes for ideal living. As Louisa was to express it years later, [Abigail] became the ballast to Bronson's balloon. . . . They were still dependent on the aid of friends and relatives,

who were vocal in their censure; but Abby finally agreed with them."
Abigail now knew that she could not rely on Bronson to provide for the
family; she would try to rely on herself. This change affected all four of
their children, especially Louisa. Monika Elbert noted that Louisa "suffered the most from the parental union" and, as a consequence, sought
"to reconcile and integrate these contradictory [parental] influences
through her writing."

Abigail's late January letter to Samuel Joseph seemed to lay all the
blame for her family's difficulties on Charles Lane. "All Mr. Lane's
efforts have been to disunite us," she wrote. "I hope we shall be settled
soon to some mode of life which shall either be more independent of the
aid of others or less irksome to ourselves," she went on with her usual
wry fortitude. "Mr. Alcott cannot bring himself to work for gain, but we
have not yet learned to live without money or means." She wished to see
Bronson "a little more interested in this matter of support.

> I love his faith and quiet reliance on Divine Providence, but
> a little more activity and industry would place us beyond most
> of these disagreeable dependencies on friends. For though they
> aid, they censure. . . . Though they give cheerfully of their abun-
> dance, yet they feel that we should earn something ourselves. Mr.
> Alcott is right in not working for hire, if thereby he violates his
> conscience; but working for bread does not necessarily imply
> unworthy gain.

Even now, Abigail felt she had to defend her husband. Meanwhile,
she earned money by sewing for her neighbors. She sold a piece of family silver for ten dollars. She feared offending her maiden aunt Hannah
Robie, who had given her the silver, but felt she had no choice. "This
will be a sad chapter in my book of fate," she lamented in her journal, "if
[Hannah] too in the absence of [my] Mother and Sisters shall go hence
to be no more seen." She felt more dependent than ever on the support
of other women.

Suffering from "soul-sickness" in March, Abigail struggled to seem
cheerful to her girls. She vowed to "take up the daily cross and work on,
isolated and poor, awhile longer. We will economize still further, and
reduce our wants to the lowest possible scale." In April she moved the

family to a small house in a nearby hamlet, Still River, where she was heartened to see Bronson starting to labor "unremittedly in his garden, producing rapid and beautiful changes," turning "stone and rubble, a rude rough chaos," into "neat regular beds and borders."

But Bronson still mourned "my Paradise at Fruitlands." Without Charles Lane he felt "all alone again," he wrote in June. In a letter he begged his brother Junius to rejoin his family: "You seem the sole person in the wide world, designed as a faithful coadjutor [to me] . . . with the constancy of a true lover."

In late June Bronson left again for an extended visit with his brothers and several utopian communities in New York state. For the first time, though, he took a child with him, thirteen-year-old Anna. As the two of them departed, Abigail told her husband earnestly, "I wish you success." Whatever anger at him she may have felt she apparently kept to herself, like Marmee in *Little Women,* who admits, "I am angry nearly every day of my life, Jo; but I have learned not to show it; and I still hope to learn not to feel it."

Anna and Louisa promised to write each other often while Anna was away. Louisa missed her older sister "so much," she soon discovered, that she "made two verses for her," which read in part:

> *Sister, when you are lonely*
> *Longing for your distant home,*
> *And the images of loved ones*
> *Warmly to your heart shall come . . .*
> *"Ever when your heart is heavy,*
> *Anna, dear, think of me."*
> *Think how we two have together*
> *Journeyed onward day by day,*
> *Joys and sorrows ever sharing,*
> *While the swift years roll away. . . .*

Bronson and Anna stopped for about a week in Syracuse, New York, to visit the Mays. Samuel Joseph, Lucretia, who was pregnant, and their children, aged fourteen, eleven, and eight, had recently settled in that bustling city on the Erie Canal, "the great thoroughfare through which the immense travel from the East and the West, and to and from the

Canadas, must almost entirely pass." On Samuel Joseph and Lucretia's trip to Niagara Falls the previous year, he had been invited to preach at the lovely new Church of the Messiah near the canal in central Syracuse. Soon afterward the church's pastor had died and the congregation had called the Reverend May. The Mays occupied a sprawling Federal-style frame house about half a mile from his church. It had a screened-in wraparound porch, several acres of land, vast gardens, a raspberry patch, hens, and a barn for their horses and carriages, as Lucretia continued to keep her own horse-drawn chaise. The Mays employed several servants, and in September 1844 they would have a new baby, George, called "Bonnie" after the ballad "Bonnie George Campbell." In this rapidly growing city on the canal that was America's first efficient highway to the West, the families of bankers, engineers, and inventors had welcomed the minister and his family.

Upstate New York was now home to the reformers Susan B. Anthony and Frederick Douglass and the site of active lines on the Underground Railroad, enabling fugitive slaves traveling from Kentucky and Virginia through Ohio and New York to reach Canada. New York state, which in 1800 had had more slaves than any other northern state, had abolished slavery in 1827. Syracuse, "an island of radical dreams" located only forty miles from Lake Ontario, was now a "convenient shipping-point" to Canada, according to one of Samuel Joseph's colleagues. "I could put [runaway slaves] in a car [in Syracuse] and tell them to keep their seats until they crossed the suspension bridge, and then they would be in Canada." During the decade after 1850—the year Congress severely strengthened the Fugitive Slave Act, which required all Americans to capture and return runaway slaves—a slave passed through Syracuse nearly every day en route to Ontario or Quebec. A historian found that Samuel Joseph "personally aided over a thousand fugitives to reach Canada." The minister fed, bathed, clothed, and sheltered them, accompanied some of them across the border, and toured their Canadian settlements to ensure they were comfortable. Throughout slave states May's name and address were known as conduits to freedom.

Bronson and Anna were still away from home when Abigail's inheritance was finally released from probate in the summer of 1844, more than three years after Joseph May's death. Bronson still resented his exclusion from the May estate. "A little income—her support nearly—

falls to her from her Father's Estate," he informed Junius in August, following his and Anna's return. "But she will bind her interests with mine,
I trust, and rely on something more sure and worthy than Boston Gold;
asserting a true and brave independence by adherence to the . . . labours
of self-support. We shall see. . . ."

Louisa was still only eleven years old that summer, but she too had
been changed by her experiences in the town of Harvard. Fruitlands
had revealed to her the gulf between her parents. And it had affirmed
her sense of Abigail as her best ally. "No one will be as good to me
as mother," she had written in her journal in October. Two days after
Christmas she had added, "Mother often says, if we are not contented
with what we have got it will be taken away from us, and I think it is
very true." Knowing all this, Louisa resolved to be contented with what
she had got. She would labor for her mother's bread, as Abigail had suggested. She would do anything in her power to bridge the gulf between
her parents.

Chapter Eight

The Best Woman in the World

*F*inally, Louisa thought to herself after her family had moved, in 1845, to a ramshackle house in Concord. "I have at last got the little room I have wanted so long, and am very happy about it," she wrote in her journal. More nook than room, Louisa's new bedchamber was on the ground floor of the house purchased early that year with a thousand dollars that Grandfather May had left to Abigail, which her father called "Boston Gold." Eight adjoining acres were a gift from Emerson to her father. To enlarge the house, Bronson had lined the ground with logs and rolled two existing barns onto its sides; Louisa's little room was in one former barn. The Alcotts arrived at Hillside, as they called the house, when Louisa was twelve and her sisters were fourteen, nine, and four years old.

Lying on her bed, with a view of daylilies, lilies of the valley, and the rock garden and wall that her father was building on the hill behind the house, Louisa could finally think, dream, and write uninterrupted. It was bliss. "It does me good to be alone, and Mother has made it very pretty for me," she reported in March 1846. "My work-basket and desk are by the window, and my closet is full of dried herbs that smell very nice. The door that opens into the garden will be very pretty in summer, and I can run off to the woods when I like." According to a male cousin, Louisa could "run like a gazelle. She was the most beautiful girl runner I ever saw. She could leap a fence or climb a tree as well as any boy."

A few months past her thirteenth birthday, Louisa had already "made a plan for my life, as I am in my teens, and no more a child. I am old for my age, and don't care much for girl's things. People think I'm wild and queer; but Mother understands and helps me." Other girls sometimes teased her, and Boston cousins called her a strange, "half-educated tomboy."

Only her mother seemed fully to understand and accept Louisa—perhaps, as both her parents suggested, because she and Abigail were so alike. They both saw clearly, felt deeply, and struggled to express themselves and be heard. Observing her mother's struggles inspired Louisa to be a better person so she could be as helpful as possible to her mother. "Now I'm going to *work really,* for I feel a true desire to improve, and be a help and comfort, not a care and sorrow, to my dear mother," she promised herself.

Abigail encouraged her to write often in her journal and to compose poems so as to be "less excitable and anxious." Just before they moved into Hillside, Louisa had written "little verses . . . with some success," her mother observed. "She is making great effort to obtain self possession and repose" by expressing her feelings in words.

Every now and then Louisa discovered in her journal a message from her mother. "MY DEAREST LOUIE," one note began. "I often peep into your diary, hoping to see some record of more happy days. 'Hope, and keep busy,' dear daughter, and in all perplexity or trouble come freely to your MOTHER."

Knowing that her mother would soon again read her journal, Louisa replied therein: "DEAR MOTHER,—You SHALL see more happy days, and I WILL come to you with my worries, for you are the best woman in the world. LMA."

Even at twelve, Louisa had tried to bolster her mother's confidence. Painfully aware of her mother's ongoing marital troubles, the child had written her a poem of consolation:

> *God comfort thee dear mother*
> *For sorrow sad and deep*
> *Is lying heavy on thy heart*
> *And this hath made thee weep.*

There is a Father o'er us, mother,
Who orders for the best
And peace shall come ere long, mother,
And dwell within thy breast.

Then let us journey onward, mother,
And trustfully abide,
The coming forth of good or ill
Whatever may betide.

Louisa's physical father, meanwhile, continued to be troubled by the "darker temperament" that his second daughter shared with his wife. Biographers have noted that "Bronson assigned great value to physical appearance as a sign of moral thought" and had a "passion for the blond complexion. Blue eyes and fair hair, he thought, were signs of the angelic type, determined in a former state of existence, while the dark eye and the swarthy face betokened the demon." On March 16, 1846, Bronson confessed to his journal that he sometimes wondered if Abigail and thirteen-year-old Louisa were possessed. "Count thyself divinely tasked if in thy self or thy family thou hast a devil or two to plague and try thy prowess and give thee occasion for celebrating thy victories . . . Two devils as yet, I am not quite divine enough to vanquish—the mother fiend and her daughter." He did not define the fiendish behaviors he observed.

In contrast to Louisa, his other daughters seemed more virtuous. Anna and Elizabeth were studious, he noted a month later; "I corrected their Journals which they wrote very faithfully." But "Louisa was unfaithful, and [thus] took her dinner alone." Even five-year-old Abba—whom he punished for not attending her reading and spelling lessons, by making her read aloud before eating dinner—earned his approval. Her "little heart was very sensitive, and [she] felt this gentle reproof of her unfaithfulness." Louisa, however, seemed not to have such a penitent heart.

Perhaps sensing her father's disapproval, Louisa identified with and tried to help her poor mother. At Hillside, according to a family friend, "Both Anna and Louisa strove hard to reinforce the family exchequer." Louisa knew that Abigail felt burdened by her indebtedness to Emerson for all his kindnesses, pecuniary and otherwise, so she hatched a plan to tutor his elder daughter, Ellen, alongside her own younger sisters and a few neighbors. For several summers, then, the teenage Louisa ran a little school in the Hillside barn. She told the children stories her mother had read or told to her. She also invented stories, which the children "went wild" over, according to Ellen Emerson.

Louisa created for her pupils a fairy kingdom, a peaceful place among the flowers that grew around the house. She gave the fairies names and led them on adventures. "Once upon a time, two little Fairies went out into the world, to seek their fortune," Louisa began the story of "Lily-Bell and Thistledown," in which the selfish, prickly Thistledown must undergo an arduous journey to learn how to have a kind heart. In another tale, the pure love of the violet conquers the cruel Frost King, protecting all the flowers from being killed and winning the Frost King's heart. In yet another fairy tale, Louisa created a little Water-Spirit named Ripple "down in the deep blue sea" whose happiness ends when she encounters the mournful mother of a dead boy. The mother begs the spirit to revive her child, as the prophet Elisha does in the Old Testament story that Abigail, like her own mother, had read to her girls. The Fairy Queen advises Ripple to travel to the distant home of the Fire-Spirits, "high up above the sun." There the Fire-Spirits agree to help her in exchange for jewels. She takes the flame they provide back to the sea, revives the child with it, and returns him to his mother. Then she must journey back to the Fire-Spirits to pay them in pearls before returning, happily, to the sea. "I made [Louisa] write them for me," Ellen Emerson recalled of the stories that later became the material for Louisa's first published book.

As the teenage Louisa charmed children in the barn, her parents continued to disagree about the nature of a family. Bronson desired a consociate family and repeatedly urged Junius to return to live with them, but Abigail still wished to live with her nuclear family alone. Whenever guests departed she felt "thrown once more on my own efforts to do and be to my daughters what I believe I am capable of being—and I shall put myself in closer more intimate communication with them than ever." It occurred to her that "a woman who has never known the maternal relation can know but little of the resource of a mother's love to bring about most important and desirable results."

But Abigail still needed boarders to cover her expenses, especially now that they owned a house. A young woman named Sophia Ford lived and ate with them at Hillside, helped teach the children, and assisted with housework. Younger boarders included John Edward May, Samuel Joseph's eldest son. Three years older than Louisa, John Edward was now at the Lexington Classical School, preparing for college.

Settled in upstate New York, forty-eight-year-old Samuel Joseph was now the nation's "first clergyman to advocate female suffrage and women's rights." His 1846 address, "The Rights and Condition of Women," which began as a sermon to his Syracuse congregation, set the tone for the suffrage movement. "Why do half of the people have a right to govern the whole?" he asked. Women cannot "have their wrongs fully redressed, until they themselves have a voice and a hand in the enactment and administration of the laws." He believed the "entire disfranchisement of females is as unjust as the disfranchisement of the males would be. . . . [America's] utter annihilation, politically consid-ered, of more than one half of the whole community . . . is all unequal, all unrighteous. . . . We [men] may with no more propriety assume to govern women than they might assume to govern us. And never will the nations of the earth be well governed, until both sexes . . . are fairly represented." This new concept of gender equality led him to believe that every man and woman is an amalgam of male and female traits: "A perfect character in either man or woman is a compound of the virtues of each." His niece would illustrate this philosophy in fiction, giving female characters masculine names, cutting their hair short, and creating a hero-ine who cries, "It's bad enough to be a girl, anyway, when I like boy's games and work and manners! I can't get over my disappointment in not being a boy. And it's worse than ever now, for I'm dying to go and fight."

While Louisa's uncle loftily campaigned for women's rights, her mother struggled with the practical limitations imposed on women because of gender. Abigail had once thought that the problem of gender inequality could be solved by women's education. But now she saw her own daughters as constrained as she was by the rigid feminine mold, anticipating that as grown women they could not vote, own property, or speak in public. A corset was standard feminine apparel, but to Abigail it felt like a cage. In a corset she could not reach up or bend over, which forced her to ask men for assistance. Years earlier she had begun lacing her corsets loosely and encouraged her daughters to do the same. Now she and her daughters decided to abandon corsets altogether.

The hindrances on women went deeper than apparel, however. While mending and cooking alongside her daughters, Abigail ruminated on the causes of their struggle. "Many of the evils of Woman's life may be traced to the want of education of the *Senses,*" she observed. The expectation that women withdraw from the world prevented them from learning how to feel and experience its complexities, she believed. Women were made "inclining and vacillating, tender and timid. . . . They do not *see* clearly, *hear* distinctly, *feel* deeply. Thus when they describe anything they are not quite sure of the distance, or colour; when they tell anything it is quite certain their statement is a good deal modified, and inaccurate, and their sensations are false or feeble. Girls are taught to *seem,* to appear—not to *be* and *do*." Women are taught to employ "costume, not armor; innocence, not virtue;" and that "beauty, not godliness, should be the foundation of a woman's character."

Abigail aimed to teach her daughters otherwise. She would have Louisa and her sisters know they were equal to boys. Armor, virtue, and godliness should be foundations of their characters. "Strengthen your mind by reflection, till your head becomes a balance for your heart," she told "all the girls," she explained in a letter to her brother. Then "your actions would be more perpendicular, [your] whole life more direct and true."

Samuel Joseph came to visit the Alcotts in the late summer of 1846, leaving his family at home. While in Concord, he received from Lucretia a letter of warning. "Be careful of yourself, avoid eating unwholesome food . . . & remember that disease sometimes lurks even in the *nectar & ambrosia* of Mr. Alcott's utopia." Lucretia had their two-year-old son, George, scribble on the letter, "Come home dear Far," a family name for Samuel Joseph. "I want to see you very much. Mother is very lonesome." As the pastor's reform work sometimes kept him from home a week or more, Lucretia often wrote to urge her "great big darling" to return. "You ought to remember that what is fun to you is dull & lonesome to me." One missive cautions against his generosity: "No money comes so you must not regulate your present expenses by golden hopes and silver anticipations but by the actual state of your purse. 'A word to the wise.' Once more, make haste back, we long to see you, the light of our dwelling is dim and my heart is heavy when you are away." When another minister occupied his pulpit while he was in Buffalo, she wrote to him, "I can't bear these prosaic ministers that must always walk not like snails exactly, with their houses, but with their churches on their backs & are always asking how many families in your parish? How large is your Sunday school? Does Mr. May visit much? Is he absent much? I never can answer a single question save the last." She concluded, "Go to the [Niagara] Falls & see their beauty & magnificence in winter for us all. This will be the only compensation for your long absence. . . . I long, long to see you."

Abigail and Bronson responded differently to separations. Not only was he often away, but she herself developed a habit of departing to visit relatives soon after his return. In 1846 in Concord, while Abigail was in Boston, Bronson wrote to Charles Lane, "Most [women] are quite out of place, if, indeed, there be place yet for them in the eye or heart of mankind." Others in his circle denigrated women. Emerson considered the male mind active and intellectual, the female mind passive and dull, and once remarked of a friend's newborn daughter, "Though no son, yet a sacred event." Women are "all victims of their temperament," Emerson wrote. "A woman's strength is not masculine, but is the unresistible might of weakness." Even Margaret Fuller, after giving birth to a boy, wrote to her sister, "As was Eve, at first, I suppose every mother is delighted by the birth of a man-child. There is a hope that he will conquer more ill, and effect more good, than is expected from girls. This prejudice in favor of man does not seem to be destroyed by his shortcomings for ages. Still, each mother hopes to find in hers an Emanuel."

In the fall of 1846, as Louisa's fourteenth birthday approached, Abigail saved enough money to purchase for her a fountain pen. The message she wrote on the birthday card reiterated their bond. "Dearest, accept from your Mother this pen and for her sake as well as your own use it freely and worthily." Abigail admonished Louisa, "Let each day of this your 15th year testify to some good word or work; and let your Diary receive a record of the same. . . . May eternal love sustain you, Infinite Wisdom guide you, [and] may the sweetest Peace reward you. Mother."

Louisa seemed increasingly serious about writing, as Abigail had hoped. Louisa's "sentimental period," she recalled, began at Hillside when at about fifteen "I fell to write romances, poems, a 'heart journal,' and dream dreams of a splendid future." Almost a young woman now, she chafed at the restrictive feminine role, as Abigail had a generation before. Society did not interest Louisa, except when she joined other teenagers in theatrical performances, games, and sports. Like her mother, she lived in books. Among her favorite writers were Goethe—whose *Correspondence with a Child* she borrowed from Emerson—Charles Dickens, Sir Walter Scott, and the Brontës. *Jane Eyre,* published when Louisa was fourteen and one of her favorite novels, contained passages that echoed her experience. "It is in vain to say human beings ought to be satisfied with tranquility: they must have action; and they will make it if they cannot find it," Jane Eyre says, as if to Louisa. "Women are supposed to feel just as men feel; they need exercise for their faculties, and a field for their efforts as much as their brothers do; they suffer from too rigid a constraint, too absolute a stagnation, precisely as men would suffer; and it is narrow-minded in their more privileged fellow-creatures to say that they ought to confine themselves to making puddings and knitting stockings, to playing on the piano and embroidering bags. It is thoughtless to condemn them, or laugh at them, if they seek to do more or learn more than custom has pronounced necessary for their sex." Young Louisa was inspired by the Brontë sisters, as well as by her mother's friend Mrs. Child, to plot a short story. She thought she might even write a book. Prompted perhaps by her mother's receipt of her inheritance, she would tell the story of a virtuous young woman with a vast inheritance of which she is not aware.

The house bought with Abigail's modest inheritance in fact became the setting for a new stage in Abigail's long mentorship of Louisa. In her mid- to late forties, Abigail knew that her own dreams of a productive public life would never be fulfilled. But her teenage daughters might accomplish more. She had high hopes for Louisa, who seemed to her mother to have "most decided views of life and duty. . . . She reads a great deal. Her memory is quite peculiar and remarkably tenacious. . . . Nothing can exceed the strength of [Louisa's] attachments, particularly for her mother." Strong views and attachments indicated that Louisa had prospects. "I believe there are some natures too noble to curb, too lofty to bend," Abigail observed two years later. "Of such is my Lu."

In spite of Abigail's ambition and desire to improve women's lot, she and her children continued to endure the indignities of poverty. "I am constantly finding myself . . . perplexed for the want of money," she complained to Samuel Joseph in 1846. "My friends are wearied with my applications for help. It does not seem to occur to them," she added resentfully, "that each [of them] putting [aside] a fraction [of money] at intervals for me, would relieve all this distressing embarrassment and give us a comfort which we deserve at their hands. I shall ask no more [of them] but help at the work of life while there is work to do, intelligently, conscientiously, as fast and far as I can, though the world call [me] idle."

Abigail's sense of entitlement may reflect her intense shame. Or perhaps she found it easier to play the loyal wife, to blame her friends and family rather than her husband. He had applied to teach at a district school in Concord, she reported, "but a child is preferred! He asks [for] bread, they will give him a stone. How destitute of sense and sentiment is the world of Concord, looking well to its Pockets! And Places!" She had tried to rent part of a house in Cambridge, "thinking a small school can be obtained for [fifteen-year-old] Anna" to teach in, but was told "that 'Mr. A[lcott]'s religious opinions are repugnant to the Christian world of Cambridge' . . . his not going to Church is an objection. . . . I suggest my willingness to become the matron of an Idiot institution," and in response, "I am warned of the prejudices the public entertain against my husband's theories. Indeed!" she added with her trademark sarcasm. "Believing and practicing the folly of loving our neighbors as ourself. Doing justice and loving mercy. Truly we deserve to suffer!"

Even as a young teenager Louisa "was not unmindful of the anxiety of her parents," her first biographer, Ednah Dow Cheney, wrote. Louisa's "determined purpose to retrieve the fortunes of the family and to give to her mother the comfort and ease which she had never known in her married life became the constant motive of her conduct. It is in the light of this purpose alone that her character and her subsequent career can be fully understood."

At the end of 1846, Abigail reviewed her accounts for the year. Her family had taken in $478 and still owed $254. "These arrearages," she told Samuel Joseph, "are very distressing, because I feel so helpless. Where to curtail? Or how to produce [money] is alike impracticable to me. My children are at no schools, I never rode [a coach] to the amount of one dollar since I lived in Concord, excepting to Boston where I have been called to go on business. I purchase no articles of dress excepting cotton, calico, and shoes. Although much that I receive is useless finery or unconvertible articles of wearing apparel, yet we go without many things which we really need as common comforts. Our food is simple, our recreations not expensive."

A few weeks later she resolved in the coming year "to do more for my children and turn their minds to still greater efforts to save and do. . . . They are bright active beings. I pray to be enlightened on my duty."

Included in her duty: for several days in January and February 1847 she and Bronson hosted an escaped slave on his way from Maryland to Canada. A brief conversation while giving the runaway his breakfast one morning provided Abigail a "meeting [with] God . . . short but real." Decades later Louisa recalled that the young fugitive ate meals with the family, joined them before the evening fire, and cut and piled their wood. Her father, perhaps still uncertain about antislavery, had recently called Garrison "the most intolerant of men," lacking in "comprehension of the whole truth. He does not see it."

In Concord Louisa fell under the spell of her father's friend Henry David Thoreau, a Harvard graduate and native of the town in his late twenties who was living, in Bronson's words, as "a hermit by Walden Pond." Thoreau often took Louisa and her sisters on nature walks in the woods around the pond, pointing out and describing plants, trees, and animals. "Arrowheads and Indian fireplaces sprang from the ground" when Louisa accompanied him. "Wild birds perched on his shoulder. His fingers seemed to have more wisdom in them than many a scholar's head."

Fourteen-year-old Louisa boarded with friends near Boston for part of the summer of 1847, while Anna studied music, French, and German and kept school at home for her younger sisters, Emerson's two girls, and a nine-year-old second cousin, Edward May, who boarded with the Alcotts. Edward was a son of Abigail's cousin Samuel May Jr., an abolitionist Unitarian minister in Leicester, Massachusetts, whose father was Colonel May's only brother. Abigail, who had acquired a keyboard instrument called a seraphine, gave the children regular music lessons, as her mother had done for Abigail and her sisters.

In the fall of 1847, Anna, who was sixteen, took a teaching job in Walpole, New Hampshire, where she could board at no cost with an uncle and cousin. Benjamin Willis, the prosperous widower of Abigail's sister

Eliza, had with his twenty-three-year-old married daughter Elizabeth ("Lizzie") Willis Wells and her husband settled comfortably in southwestern New Hampshire. While Louisa understood the need for Anna to live elsewhere, to earn money, she always preferred that her sister stay home. "I miss [Anna] dreadfully," Louisa wrote in her journal, "for she is my conscience, always true and just and good."

The family was divided even further at Christmastime, when Abigail decided to send twelve-year-old Elizabeth to Boston, where their relative Hannah Robie could feed and care for her in more comfort than Abigail could provide. Robie, now nearly sixty, kept chambers at the homes of her nephews Thomas Sewall in Boston and Samuel E. Sewall in Melrose. Lizzie's departure particularly distressed Abby May. At the Concord train depot on the day Lizzie left, seven-year-old Abby May waved good-bye to her "with tearful eyes, and a sadness at the heart," her mother observed. As Abby May, Louisa, and Abigail returned from the depot in a coach, the child said forlornly, "There is no pleasure now for me in this old, ugly house."

Of the family, only Bronson now loved Concord. Abigail derided "cold, heartless, Brainless, soulless Concord." Their house there was chilly and in need of repair, and she had borrowed so heavily from local merchants that she had no credit. Years later in a burlesque, Louisa mocked "one of the dullest little towns in Massachusetts" as a "modern Mecca" offering "apples by the bushel, orphic acorns by the peck, and Hawthorne's pumpkins, in the shape of pies . . . at philosophical prices." The lodgings of Concord, she wrote, were "filled with Alcott's rustic furniture, the beds made of Thoreau's pine boughs, and the sacred fires fed from the Emersonian wood-pile. . . . Telescopes will be provided for the gifted eyes which desire to watch the soaring of the Oversoul, when visible," over the Concord River.

Bronson, unlike his wife and daughters, was indifferent to the family's diaspora. "Families must swarm sometime. And it is well for [Anna and Elizabeth] to seek fields of richer thyme than grows about the Old Hive, and fall to honey-making for [them]selves," he added, apparently without irony, "since all true and lasting enjoyment must be sipped from the cup by [one's] own exertions alone."

Abigail, of course, did not agree. A child of seven or twelve or even a teenager should not be expected to sip from the cup of her own exertions

alone. A parent's exertions were essential. Having exhausted the generosity of her relatives and friends and having concluded that her husband
would not work for money, she finally determined to go to work herself.

At the end of 1847, in conversation with Lidian Emerson, Abigail
learned of an opening for a matron at a new water-cure establishment
in Maine. The water cure, or hydrotherapy, was a treatment for various
ailments by means of baths, soaks, and wraps in hot or cold water, often
from a natural spring or stream. Scenic resorts in rural villages across
the country offered the cure, as it was commonly called, catering to a
wealthy, mostly female clientele. Rapidly expanding railroad lines, which
had started in Boston in 1833, made these resorts accessible from major
cities. Prominent figures who sought the cure included Harriet Beecher
Stowe, Julia Ward Howe, Nathaniel Hawthorne, Wendell Phillips, Garrison, Theodore Parker, Elizabeth Peabody, and Henry Wadsworth
Longfellow. Lidian Emerson had visited "Dr. Shattuck's Water Cure"
in Waterford, Maine, in August while staying there with her husband's
brilliant and eccentric aunt, Mary Moody Emerson.

"Nothing would please me better" than working for the cure, Abigail
said to Lidian. "What I wish for myself is to be at the head of a water
cure." Abigail believed in water's healing powers. "If I cannot afford to
feed the children, I can wash them, which is almost as essential to health."

Ralph Waldo Emerson, at his wife's behest, wrote to the proprietor
of the spa. "Our neighbor & friend Mrs. Alcott possesses the energy,
experience & economy which the office demands. . . . If there is a place
of this kind to be filled, Mrs. Alcott is ready & willing to undertake it;
and, if you desire it, will come to Waterford at any time, & spend a week
at the House. . . ."

In April 1848 Abigail met in Boston with the spa's physician, Dr.
Kitteridge. She said the job appealed to her. Her only reservations were
"family cares, and the difficulties of removal." Her youngest daughter
was seven, the spa more than a hundred miles away. At nearly fifty, Abigail felt herself growing fat, lazy, and somewhat blind. But she did not
say that to Dr. Kitteridge. She would take the job. No longer willing to
"submit to this life of unproductiveness," she determined that "*Action*
is a duty. *Doing* is coextensive with Being." For a trial period of three
months, the doctor promised her a salary of five dollars a week, plus
room and board.

Louisa resisted this plan as soon as she learned of it. She did not want her mother to leave. Louisa would rather do more sewing and seek other paying work in exchange for keeping their mother at home. Anna, who at seventeen was still teaching in southern New Hampshire, wrote to Bronson to suggest that they sell Hillside and reunite in Waterford, Maine. That way the family could be together.

Bronson replied with his characteristic fatalism. "By some chance as yet unforeseen, we may some or all of us drift even to Waterford hills, but that seems less likely to be our destiny. . . . I honor the good Mother for this brave deed. . . . All Saints and Angels will accompany and bless the dear woman." Considering his own contributions to the family coffers, he added, "Would that some Power as propitious might task my Gifts, and fill my hands too with work and my table with bread. But 'tis not thus with me and I submit to the decrees of fate." Admitting that he was not moved "to any work beyond myself," he concluded with a quote from Milton, "They also serve who only stand & wait."

A few days later, on May 10, 1848, Abigail boarded the train to Boston, accompanied by Abby May and a sixteen-year-old "imbecile" from Nova Scotia named Eliza Stearns. For two years Eliza's parents had paid Abigail to keep and care for their daughter, who was too burdensome to leave with Bronson. Abigail hoped the girl might benefit from the water cure. From Boston the threesome traveled north to Portland and thence to western Maine.

Louisa and Elizabeth, finally home from her winter stay with Hannah Robie, remained at Hillside. Someone had to keep house for Father. In June, about a month after Abigail's departure, Louisa received word that her mother missed her and desired her "company and services." Fifteen-year-old Louisa responded by promising to "fly" to her mother in Maine.

Chapter Nine

Mother, Is It You?

One night in late May, not long after she moved into the water-cure spa, Abigail had a dream that she was home with her girls. In the dream Lizzie was seated at the piano, weeping because Abigail wasn't there to help her find a certain note. Louisa was outside, running up the lane toward the house, her long dark hair blowing up behind her. "Mother," Louisa screamed. "Mother? Is it you?" Abigail woke from the dream in tears, feeling guilty for being so far from her girls.

The sun had not risen outside the bedchamber that she shared with Abby May and Eliza Stearns on the top floor of the spa's dormitory and refectory building, across the lawn from the house that contained the healing baths. The girls were still asleep.

At four each morning Abigail roused Eliza, helped her downstairs, and packed her into wet sheets, one aspect of the cure. Then she raced "through the long passageways to the baths" for her own "plunge" in the water. Returning to her room, she dressed herself and read or wrote beneath a window overlooking a lake and the foothills of the Mahoosuc and White mountains.

By 5 a.m. Abigail would be downstairs organizing the kitchen, seeing the glasses "nicely cleaned, the knives in order, etc." She swept the drawing room, dusted, arranged music books, "unpacked" Eliza, waked, washed, and dressed Abby May, and "set" the two girls "to walking" outside. It was now about six in the morning.

As matron of the spa she was responsible for overseeing all meals. Each one, she wrote in a letter to home, was a tableau "like a scene in a theater." The gathered diners represented "all tastes, all habits, all opinions and divers[e] *notion*alities, as well as *nation*alities." After breakfast each morning she tended to curtains, bed linens, slops, and floors. Before the midday meal she gave Eliza Stearns another wet sheet and put her to sewing or cleaning. At half past twelve she supervised dinner. Then she met with Calvin Farrar, the founder and proprietor of the spa, and a medical expert, Dr. Fisher, to discuss the patrons' dietary needs. She mended and washed linens and gave Eliza a third wet sheet and "washdown." She enjoyed a late afternoon walk, supervised supper at six, and listened to Dr. Fisher play "sweet music" on the parlor piano or took "a little ramble" before collapsing into bed.

Her letters included accounts of her dreams. Like her Puritan ancestors, she saw dreams as windows into truths not otherwise accessible. She often dreamed she was home. In one dream she stood outside Hillside with her husband discussing an "observatory" he wished to erect there. She feared he was too attached to the property, which they could not afford to maintain. "Don't do anything to make this place more attractive," she said in the dream. "I want to find a different home for the girls."

Bronson replied "jocosely"—a word that came naturally to Abigail, even while asleep—that she should not worry because "young girls are very apt to find homes for themselves." Again she awoke in tears.

Despite her anxieties, Abigail made her mark on the resort. Within weeks of her arrival she felt she was "the bone, sinew, and great aorta of the water cure." A travel writer who visited in June to write a newspaper article about the spa provided an objective opinion: "Mrs. Alcott [was] the greatest thing that ever happened to 'down East' . . . and the Waterford Cure House." According to a neighbor in Concord, Abigail was now "a handsome, genial, four-square woman" in her late forties, "quiet and fascinating," and a talented producer of "pies, puddings, root beer, and pea soup."

Less than a month into her stay at the Maine resort, however, Abigail realized the environment was not suitable for children. On a visit to the nearby home of her friend Ann Sargent Gage, a doctor's widow who had Boston roots, Abigail discussed the nature of her concerns. She had observed spa employees engaged in inappropriate behavior, perhaps of a sexual nature, with patrons in the baths. She did not trust one doctor in particular. A different sort of doctor, she told her friend, "would give dignity and character to the Establishment, the lack of which hitherto has I find been a hindrance to many who wished to enjoy 'the Treatment.'"

Abigail felt "selfish" keeping her seven-year-old daughter in Waterford, where she might be exposed to improper behavior, the exact nature of which Abigail did not define in writing. The spa had no provisions for children, and Abigail was too busy to care for her daughter. So she sent Abby May home to Massachusetts and requested that Louisa consider coming to join her at the spa.

But before Louisa could even pack her trunk, Abigail realized that the resort would not suit Louisa any more than it suited her. The establishment was improperly run, in her view, and her work was not adequately remunerated. Her salary was not sufficient for her labor. She was not a woman to abandon paid employment at a task she considered worthy, but she felt she had to leave the spa. The pain and guilt she felt at being so far from her children may have influenced her decision. "I wish I had staid with you," Abby May had already written from Concord. "I wish you would come home soon; when will you come? . . . I wish you would come home."

In late June, after sending word to Louisa to remain at home, Abigail resigned as matron of the spa. It is not clear if she received any of her salary. If so, she had already sent it home. To purchase coach and train fares for herself and her "helpless charge," Eliza, she had to borrow five dollars from Ann Sargent Gage. On or around July 10 Abigail packed her belongings and led Eliza to the stagecoach that took them to the train for home.

A happy reunion ensued in Concord, but a sad truth remained. The Alcotts' situation was dire. Despite her sacrifice, Abigail had changed nothing. They could not afford to keep Hillside and had nowhere else to live. Over their eighteen years of marriage Bronson had proved that he could not support the family, and no one else had succeeded at providing for them in his stead.

On July 13 Abigail placed a five-dollar bank check drawn from the Concord Bank in an envelope with a letter to Ann Sargent Gage in Maine. "There has been no moment, my dear friend, since my arrival at the threshold of my Home that I could pass with you, even to acknowledge the obligation I am under for your many favours during my sojourn in Waterford, and more especially to return your loan so promptly and kindly extended to me, in money for my passage." Abigail felt "truly glad" to return to "love and comfort, two essential elements of my being wholly deficient at" the spa in Waterford, which "infringed too largely" on her physical well-being and "wasted" her energy. Her job had "made a greater sacrifice of home and happiness than I can ever be indemnified for, by any association with men and manners such as have presented themselves at Waterford. . . . [T]he calm peaceful loveful condition of my home will soon restore the balance of my mind and seered heart."

Abigail described for her friend how she coped with the suffering that seemed endemic to women. "Despair is no paragraph in our chapter for the day," she began, almost as if giving a sermon on the sixth chapter of the Gospel of Matthew.

> Our lesson is to do—and bear—toil and stress, and though [we are] doomed to tread the earth with the earthly, we aspire to carry our heads in the heavens with the heavenly. If we must deal with men, we will take sweet counsel of Angels. What a message is in the careless carol of the birds. They take no thought of the morrow. They garner no bread for their journey, yet all are fed. They know that the compassions of the Lord are enduring. And birds would not have them, if grains were not scattered by a gracious Providence for their busy bills to gather. I blush to think that it is man, only man that doubts, and trembles for his substance. Even the sparrow hath more confiding love in the Creator. If we do not already see our father in the vexations of our life, if we seek him in its distractions but find him not, let us trust and love, and he will find and bless us.

Descending from the pulpit, Abigail asked Gage when her adult daughter Rowena would arrive in Boston on her way to Maine from Washington, D.C., "that I and my daughters may see her." This prompted a remark on daughters in general, a subject Abigail gave much thought. "These dear, precious jewels in which you and I, my dear friend, are so regally invested . . . bring a dower in their love, a purity in their gentle hearts, which no royal diadem can surpass in nature or brilliancy." Mentioning that a Concord couple had asked if she could recommend the Waterford spa to their invalid sons, Abigail asked Gage to "ascertain if they have a cook, or a presiding Genius of any sort in the domestic department to which I can look to secure to them the courtesies and comforts of life." It may have been difficult for Gage to imagine a presiding Genius of any sort in the domestic department quite like Abigail.

A few weeks after her return from Maine, having failed there, Abigail sought more paying work. "I have an offer to go as Nurse and companion to a friend of mine in New York for a few weeks. I shall go if she can afford to meet my portions," she wrote in September. "Anything is better than this." Aware that the most practical place to find work was the city of her birth, she corresponded with her moneyed cousins and family friends asking for their help. She hated to beg but would not give up hope. "Despair is the paralysis of the soul," she said to Louisa. "A mother must always find the way, because she has the will to do for her offspring."

Louisa and Anna promised to help, too. Anna, now seventeen, began teaching at a school in Roxbury. Louisa moved to Melrose, north of Boston, to work as a temporary housemaid and laundress at the home of her mother's cousin, Samuel E. Sewall, who had made a small fortune as a lawyer and agent for the Cunard steamship line. Sewall was famous in Boston for working always at a high standing desk, his partner recalled, "in the midst of antique furniture, old bookcases, and dusty books." Elizabeth returned to Hannah Robie's chamber on Beacon Hill so she could attend school in Boston, as Abby May would soon do. Abigail meanwhile traveled between Concord and Boston, seeking employment.

No longer the country town of Abigail's youth, Boston was growing rapidly. The city had 100,000 residents in 1845 and more than 150,000 a decade later, due to an influx of immigrants from Ireland and Germany and refugees from the American South. The city's first slums—in the North End and on Fort Hill around Broad Street above the wharves—provided plentiful labor for the factories, foundries, and shipyards of America's fourth-largest manufacturing center. Overcrowded, dangerous, and filthy, these neighborhoods aroused great concern among settled Bostonians. "The dark lanes and alleys . . . are rarely cleaned," a Harvard Medical School professor observed. "Their wretched, dark, ill-ventilated rooms are scarce ever washed. Their persons are foul. Their clothing dirty. Everything about them is most wretched, most unfit to

minister to self-respect, or to promote physical health, or moral progress. They become—are they not made—intemperate by such hard trial
of virtue."

These were the words of the obstetrician Walter Channing, a brother
of the Reverend William Ellery Channing, in his 1844 *Plea for Pure
Water*. Until then Bostonians had relied for water on cisterns or wells,
many private and some unlocked. Most of these wells were now contaminated by the privies dotting the peninsula. Rapid population growth
overwhelmed the old system, which spread disease and was inadequate
to quench house fires. In the fall of 1848, as the Alcotts prepared to
return, Boston inaugurated a new municipal water system that pumped
clean water from exterior lakes through pipes to the city. In October
Abigail's cousin the former mayor Josiah Quincy spoke before the grand
parade to inaugurate the new system. Water was now a right rather than
a privilege.

At the same time, prosperous relatives and friends of Abigail's were
collaborating to create a charity to employ her called "Dr. Huntington's
Society," much as her bankrupt father had once been given a house and
a job. But Abigail's new work was more challenging than her father's had
been. As a "City Missionary to the Poor," she became one of America's
first paid social workers, in one of its earliest welfare programs. She was
expected to tend to the sick, find work for the unemployed, and circu-
late secondhand clothes among the poor, who were mostly Irish and
other European immigrants and free blacks. She called herself a "sister
of charity," aware that she had long been gifted at such works. A decade
earlier, while struggling to raise three little girls in Boston without an
income or a stable home, she had been lauded by Elizabeth Peabody
as "a visitor of the poor such as I know none other." In 1838, as the
Temple School floundered and Peabody attempted to establish Bronson
as a minister to the urban poor, a scheme that came to nothing, she had
written to the Rev. William Ellery Channing, "Mrs Alcott would be so
invaluable a coadjutor [to Bronson in his urban ministry]! She could
visit the families & hunt up the children. She goes into the Irish hovel
& takes off her things, & with her own hand shows them by doing it
herself, how to wash children, how to prepare food, how to nurse the
sick. She thrives on such labor; her heart is in it; her sympathy for the
poor is like Mr [Orestes] Brownson's a devouring fire that can only be

quenched by doing the things she wants to have done." Abigail's salary, which ranged from thirty to eighty dollars a month, was sufficient in November 1848 to rent a house in the impoverished South End where she worked. Unable to find a buyer for her dilapidated Concord house, Abigail rented it to a tenant for a year for $150.

This change jarred Louisa and her sisters. Hillside had been their home for three years, longer than any other home they had known. Twelve years old when she had arrived, Louisa was now almost sixteen. Years later, though, she minimized the pain of the move. "My father went away to hold his classes and conversations, and we women folk began to feel that we also might do something. So one gloomy November day we decided to move to Boston to try our fate again after some years in the wilderness." Before leaving Concord, the teenager ran alone up the hill behind the house to take a last look at the meadows and woods. Scanning the horizon, Louisa felt "the intense desire of an ambitious girl to work for those she loved." She vowed to herself, "I will do something by-and-by. . . . Don't care what, teach, sew, act, write, anything to help the family; and I'll be rich and famous and happy before I die, see if I won't!"

City life was "very hard" for Louisa, she admitted. "The bustle and dirt and change send all lovely images and restful feelings away." She could not think clearly. She disliked their "small" rented house "with not a tree in sight [and] only a back yard to play in. . . . We all rebelled and longed for the country again." She missed her "fine free times alone, and though my thoughts were silly, I daresay, they helped to keep me happy and good. I see now what Nature did for me, and my love of solitude and out-of-door life."

Everyone in the family but her seemed to have a function. Anna taught. Elizabeth and Abby May went to school. Father went "to his classes at his [rented] room down town" at 12 West Street beside Elizabeth Peabody's bookshop, where he gave his conversations, freewheeling lectures on moral topics, to adults. Abigail "went to her all-absorbing poor." That left Louisa "to keep house" at 29 Dedham Street amid the squalor of Ward 11, her mother's district. "I felt like a caged sea-gull as I washed dishes and cooked in the basement kitchen, where my prospect was limited to a procession of muddy boots."

At the same time, she worried about her mother's health. Social work was even more physically and emotionally demanding than running a spa. Hundreds of people came daily to the Alcott house for help. Abigail, who was open to reforms of all kinds, supported fledgling trade unions, attempted to reorganize city charities to increase their efficiency, and encouraged her donors to provide jobs as well as alms for the poor. "We do a good work when we clothe the poor," she said, "but a better one when we make the way easy for them to clothe themselves. We shall do the best when we so arrange society as to have no poor." She believed the world could—and should—be made better. Each evening after work, according to Louisa, "Mother, usually much dilapidated because she *would* give away clothes, [told] sad tales of suffering and sin from the darker side of life." Louisa understood why her mother identified with the poor: she was one of them. Abigail's "intense labor" to help them was "drudgery," she admitted in a letter to her brother. "My life is one of daily protest against the oppression and abuses of Society. . . . I find selfishness, meanness, among people who fill high places in church and state."

The following summer, in 1849, Abigail was saved once again by well-to-do relatives. While continuing to work among the needy, she moved her family to live rent-free in a downtown mansion at number 88 Atkinson (now Congress) Street, on the corner of Purchase Street. The house belonged to her father's brother Samuel May and his wife, Mary Goddard May, who were temporarily abroad.

Louisa and her sisters delighted in the comforts of their great-uncle's "commodious" house. Their father appreciated the mansion, too, though he hated "feculent," plague-infested Boston. Sometime that summer he became depressed again, according to his journal. He had a vision of his body, buried in Mount Auburn Cemetery. To recuperate, apparently, Bronson left Boston for several months to stay in Concord with the Hosmers, who owned the cottage he had rented a decade before. The Hosmers cared for him and served him "peaches and Apples and Cakes," which would return him to "wholeness," he hoped, "restoration from the dead." He enjoyed walks with Thoreau and long talks with Emerson. Now and then he dreamed of returning to Fruitlands where *"a man once lived,"* he wrote to Abigail, perhaps astonishing her.

Abigail and her daughters returned to the slums that fall. At this point they had to move so often that Louisa and her sisters never unpacked their trunks. Over the winter Abigail began to doubt her ability to continue her arduous work. Even if she did continue, she knew, she, Anna, and Louisa together would not be able to support the family. Moreover, her efforts seemed to address only the symptoms of poverty, not its causes. Her benefactors "are sympathizing in the details of wretchedness," Abigail felt, while "I am busy with the *Causes* of so much poverty and Crime. *Why* is it so? is a better question [about poverty], than what shall we *do*? The former implies prevention, the latter signifies the need of a cure. And for myself I feel that I have much to do to prevent myself from yielding to a false sympathy with the Symptoms, rather than making a stringent effort to overcome the necessity for so much begging and almsgiving!"

Abigail's situation in Boston left her "despondent, quite dejected, feeble," and "disconsolate," she told Bronson after he returned from Concord. She was "embarrassed on every side, with no possible means of relief."

He could not argue with her. "We are [sometimes] spared house rent by the kindness of Mr. [Samuel] May," he said, "but we have no income nor present facilities for earning a support. . . . As far as I am concerned, [support] is a small matter . . . [to a] visionary thinker." But "to the thinker's family . . . it is . . . serious."

Abigail accused her husband of callousness. She had heard that people were gossiping about his "implied indifference" in "permitting her to delve for the family." He refused to discuss further "this subject of family destitution," which in his view reflected the "dislocated state of our social system."

Aware as he was of society's injustice, Bronson remained doubtful of the righteousness of his wife's causes. Most abolitionists were untrustworthy, he confided to Emerson in 1849 after a lecture by Garrison at the Boston Athenaeum. "I scarce never meet a person of this temperament with unmixed pleasure. . . . The spirit and grain of this class is essentially discourteous, and there is fight and desperation in the blood, manners, and speech of the creature . . . as if he were doing Satan's behest in the Lord's name." Bronson then attended a speech by Garrison at Faneuil Hall not long after Daniel Webster had spoken before the United States Senate in favor of slavery. "A little more time must pass to enable the nation to discern the scope and tendency of affairs and Webster's true place, his merits and demerits as a statesman," Bronson noted privately. "While I accept and am proud of the declarations of my friend [Garrison] who pleads the cause of civility and justice . . . I yet must cry out for the awards of justice and civility to Webster, Clay, Calhoun, and the conservatives of slavery even."

Abigail, meanwhile, shared her deepest thoughts with the women, rich and poor, with whom she sewed. "You have come together this evening, my friends, to sew for the poor," she said one evening to a group of her benefactors. "This is praise-worthy," she went on, "but it is not incompatible with the swiftest stitching to deliberate well the principle which moves you to this labor, or the object you would promote, the cause of Pauperism and the best means for its prevention. For while we are doing the one, the other need not necessarily be left undone. And while you seek light to thread your needles, and patterns to shape your garments, let me help to open the shutters and spread the fabric of our social arrangements. We are all part and parcel of this condition of things, and *I* for one am a restless fragment and can't find my niche."

In the spring of 1850, while the Alcotts occupied a cheap rental as they awaited their return that summer to her uncle's mansion, Abigail contracted the "varioloid," or smallpox. Soon the entire Alcott family was afflicted. The four daughters returned to health within a few weeks, but not the parents, and Bronson reported that he was unable to leave the house for months. Louisa, as her parents' nurse, found it a "curious time of exile, danger, and trouble" in which she feared her mother and father were near death. Bronson and Abigail survived, but recovered slowly. Their faces were still pocked in the fall. Abigail said she did not know where she might have contracted smallpox, but Louisa suspected it came "from some poor immigrants whom mother took into our garden and fed one day." Similarly, in New Hampshire in 1856 Louisa thought her sisters caught scarlet fever "from some poor children Mother nursed when they fell sick [while] living over a cellar where pigs had been kept. The landlord would not clean the place till Mother threatened to sue him for allowing a nuisance. Too late to save two of the poor babies or Lizzie and May from the fever."

This was the underside of Abigail's charity work: she gave too much of herself to the world. Decades later Louisa would describe Abigail as "the maternal pelican who could not supply all our wants on the small income which was freely shared with every needy soul who asked for help." During famine, according to legend, a mother pelican spills her blood to feed her children, much as Christ sacrificed his body and blood to atone for human sin. Louisa, who felt obliged to repay her mother for her many sacrifices, may have resented Abigail for sharing her small portion with "every needy soul who asked."

In the wake of the smallpox, one of seventeen-year-old Louisa's role models died. Margaret Fuller had gone to Europe in 1846 as a correspondent for the newspaperman Horace Greeley, "to behold the wonders of art, and the temples of old religion" and "to bring home some packages of seed for life in the new" world. Feeling immediately "at home" in Italy, Fuller sent regular dispatches to the *New York Daily Tribune,* lived through and supported the 1848 revolution, and fell in love with a revolutionary named Giovanni Angelo Ossoli. In the summer of 1850, after Italy's new government fell, she and her family boarded a merchant ship to America. As the ship approached New York City, it ran aground in a hurricane and broke apart. Fuller, Ossoli, and their toddler son drowned.

"It is too tragic to think of," Abigail observed. "Just in the prime of [her] intellectual power. A Book born of her Genius, a Child born of her Love, all Lost in the Deep—Husband, wife, offspring, Book, lost in the Briny Deep. The mysteries of Providence!! I dare not utter here all I feel about it. Surely she must have shrieked, 'My God! My God! Why hast thou forsaken me?'" Some saw in Fuller's death an eerie confirmation of the suspicion that America could not tolerate a female intellectual with a family. "Perhaps it was the most beautiful finish to a woman of Genius," Abigail continued. Had Fuller lived, "care, want, cold, [and] criticism might have invaded her domestic peace or literary aspirations, and she might have become the wretch of outraged genius, or disappointed affection. . . . It is well she rests from trials and labours!"

But Louisa could not rest. In July and August she taught young children at a school in Boston. "School is hard work," she said, "and I feel as though I should like to run away from it." Her students "seem happy, and learn fast, so I am encouraged." But she "missed Anna so much" she was "very blue. I guess this is the teaching I need, for as a *school-marm* I must behave myself and guard my tongue and temper carefully, and set an example of sweet manners." She wrote to a friend, "I . . . prefer pen & ink to birch & book, for my imaginary children are much easier to aaa

manage than living responsibilities." Louisa's students "seem to love her exceedingly," Abigail observed. On September 2, 1850, Bronson noted that he "passed the morning in Louisa's school in Suffolk Street." He read from *Pilgrim's Progress* to her students and admitted to himself, "I never go into a school without some regrets that I may not be there at my post. Had I a hundred and more little ones to meet daily, then would my cup be filled to overflowing, for the pleasure it would give me."

Meanwhile, Abigail, recognizing that she was no longer fit to continue the strenuous work of a "sister of Charity," decided that fall to open in her house an intelligence office, or employment agency for domestic servants, which she called the Ladies' Help Exchange. She advertised "the best American and Foreign Help . . . accomplished cooks, good parlor and chamber girls, nursery maids, seamstresses, toilette women, and dress-makers" for terms of six months. The Alcotts now occupied a rented house at 50 High Street, a tree-lined road above the mercantile offices along the wharves. Louisa called her mother's office "a shelter for lost girls, abused wives, friendless children, and weak or wicked men." Several of their cousins opined that this work was beneath a woman of Abigail's background and stature. "I have outlived the flummery of that," Abigail replied. "If I did not think that I was eminently qualified to extend to the one [the domestic servant] the protection they need in this exacting and cruel work, and to the other [the servant's employer] the agency they require to place the best adapted to each family . . . I should turn in disgust from an occupation which absorbs time, quiet, and domestic privacy."

The irony of the Alcotts' situation in Boston was not lost on Louisa. A few blocks from Abigail's cozy girlhood home, surrounded by their cousins' mansions, the Alcotts were destitute and ignored by most of their wealthy relatives. Louisa sewed, taught, and did housework. She stole moments to read Nathaniel Hawthorne's new novel, *The Scarlet Letter*—"my favorite [as] I like 'lurid' things, if true and strong also"—and her mother's more "wholesome" favorite, the novels of Fredrika Bremer. Louisa continued to write, in order, she told Abigail, to have "something to show that the time has not been wasted. Seventeen years have I lived, and yet so little do I know, and so much remains to be done before I begin to be what I desire—a truly good and useful woman"—like Abigail. Louisa confided in her journal, "I can't talk to any one but

mother about my troubles, and she has so many now to bear I try not to add any more. I know God is always ready to hear, but heaven's so far away in the city, and I so heavy I can't fly up to find Him."

In this moment of doubt Louisa composed a poem on "FAITH" that may seem ironic now:

> Oh, when the heart is full of fears
> And the way seems dim to heaven . . .
> Let not temptation vanquish thee,
> And the father will provide.

It was likely the High Street rental in which Louisa, just eighteen years old, completed her first novel, *The Inheritance.* The novel concerns the complicated legacy of a rich, noble family. Its heroine is an orphaned young woman, Edith Adelon, whom the rich family adopts but mistreats. When Edith is revealed to be the true inheritor of the family's estate, she refuses to accept her inheritance, considering herself unworthy. She even throws into a fire the document proving her right to the estate, much as Louisa would later destroy family papers she deemed embarrassing. All that Edith desires, she explains to an older woman of the family, is to "call you mother and be a faithful, loving child, for you can never know how sad it is to be so young and yet so utterly alone." One's noblest inheritance, Edith realizes, is one's family. This was a message to which Louisa would return again and again, and in essence it was the story of her life. As a gifted writer Louisa was herself the inheritor of an intellectual estate, some combination of her father's charisma and her mother's eloquence. But she, like Edith Adelon, her first literary alter ego, chooses or feels obliged to deny herself the fruits of this inheritance and instead to give it up for the good of her family.

For years Louisa had felt duty-bound to make her mother happy by providing for her. Two years earlier, as she began to conceive *The Inheritance,* at Hillside, she had described her life's goal as making enough money "to pay all the debts, fix the house . . . and keep the old folks cosy." She intended to accomplish this by emulating her mother, who spent most of her days working with her hands. "All the philosophy in our house is not in the study," Louisa once said, thinking of her father's room. "A good deal is in the kitchen, where a fine old lady thinks high thoughts and does kind deeds while she cooks and scrubs."

Her father was still distant and critical of her. In 1850, after reading through her and Anna's journals, he made a stinging comparison between his eldest daughters. Anna's journal concerned "other people," whereas Louisa's journal was "about herself." Louisa was hurt but conceded the truth of her father's remark. Writing did help her to understand and control her emotions, which was one reason she loved to write. "I don't *talk* about myself; yet [I] must always think of the willful, moody girl I try to manage, and in my journal I write of her to see how she gets on." Writing served, in her mother's words, as a "safety valve" for her passionate feelings. If journal writing was therapeutic, story writing was even more so, for it allowed her to let her imagination go wherever it liked. Stories and poems allowed her to explore her self, as her mother had said, her sins as well as her gifts. "[I try to] keep down vanity about my long hair, my well-shaped head, and my good nose," the teenager admitted. "In the street I try not to covet fine things. My quick tongue is always getting me into trouble, and my moodiness makes it hard to be cheerful when I think how poor we are, how much worry it is to live, and how many things I long to do I never can." Louisa's life was so difficult that "every day is a battle, and I'm so tired I don't want to live; only it's cowardly to die till you have done something."

Suicide was on her mind. Louisa wondered if mental illness ran in her family, as it does in some of her stories. Her mother's brother Charles, the mariner, was said to have a mental disturbance. Uncle Junius, her father's brother, seemed strange and unhappy. Grandfather May fell into depression after he lost all his money. Louisa knew that both of her parents had suffered from depression.

Meanwhile, Louisa's beginnings as a writer were deepening her bond with her mother. The proud matron whose health was declining and whose ideals were out of favor sensed that her daughter was genuinely gifted. Louisa, who knew that her mother had dreamed of writing herself, saw Abigail as her only reliable constant, just as Abigail in her youth had seen her own mother.

"I found one of mother's notes in my journal, so like those she used to write me when she had more time," Louisa wrote in the summer of 1850, when she was seventeen. "It always encourages me; and I wish someone would write as helpfully to her, for she needs cheering up with all the care she has. I often think what a hard life she has had since she married—so full of wandering and all sorts of worry! So different from her early easy days, [as] the youngest and most petted of her family. I think she is a very brave, good woman, and my dream is to have a lovely, quiet home for her, with no debts or troubles to burden her. But I'm afraid she will be in heaven before I can do it."

Louisa may have based a scene in *Little Women* on dialogues with her mother during those painful Boston years:

> "Why don't you write? That always used to make you happy," said her mother once, when the desponding fit overshadowed Jo.
>
> "I've no heart to write, and if I had, nobody cares for my things."
>
> "We do. Write something for us, and never mind the rest of the world. Try it, dear, I'm sure it would do you good, and please us very much."
>
> "Don't believe I can." But Jo got out her desk and began to overhaul her half-finished manuscripts.
>
> An hour afterward her mother peeped in and there she was, scratching away, with . . . an absorbed expression, which caused Mrs. March to smile and slip away, well pleased with the success of her suggestion.

Jo wonders why her writing gives readers pleasure. "There is truth in it," her mother replies. "That's the secret; humor and pathos make it alive, and you have found your style at last." Letters of encouragement from her mother, Louisa observed years later, "show the ever tender, watchful help she gave to the child who caused her the most anxiety, yet seemed to be the nearest to her heart till the end."

In Boston in 1850, as Louisa and Abigail leaned on each other, Bronson, now fifty, began a "romance" with a wealthy young woman only a few years older than his daughters. Twenty-four-year-old Ednah Dow Littlehale first appeared in Bronson's journal that January, when she called on him in Boston to discuss his conversations, some of which she attended. As she prepared to depart, he offered to escort her home. "The company of intellectual women has a certain freshness and zest one seldom tastes from intercourse with cultivated men," he wrote afterward. "Sexual qualities seems as needful to the propagation of thought as of human beings." He took Ednah on long walks around the Common and wrote her effusive letters. After a lengthy analysis of her opinion of Thomas Carlyle, in one instance, Bronson promised to await a visit from "My dear Miss Littlehale" in Concord, where he would soon venture. He signed off, "Were I the unforgettable, I should be yours, forever, A. Bronson Alcott."

Bronson's wandering eye troubled Louisa. Although she would befriend Miss Littlehale after the latter's marriage in 1853 to an older artist named Seth Cheney, Louisa remained uncomfortable, it seems, with her father's behavior toward the attractive young woman. Their mutual friend Franklin Sanborn, a Harvard graduate and Concord schoolteacher, remembered being brought by Miss Littlehale to call on the Alcotts in Boston one autumn evening in 1852. The encounter felt formal and stiff to Sanborn. "All through that ceremonious call," he wrote, "Louisa sat silent in the background of the family circle, her expressive face and earnest, almost melancholy eyes . . . fixt on" Miss Littlehale.

Louisa left no record of her feelings that evening. Did she resent her father's flirtation? Was she simply tired? She was, at the very least, busy. Fueled by "the inspiration of necessity," she and Anna had joined their mother at the controls of the family moneymaking machine.

Chapter Ten

A Dead, Decaying Thing

I n late 1849 or early 1850, at Abigail's office on the ground floor of the Alcotts' house on High Street, a well-dressed lawyer requested her services. Scores of people tramped each day through her employment agency, which Bronson, from his upstairs study, called "a confusing business below." The lawyer, James Richardson, sought a young woman to serve as a companion for his invalid sister, with whom he lived. The young woman would be expected to do light housekeeping and be treated as a member of the family in a large, comfortable house in nearby Dedham. After he departed, Abigail turned to Louisa and asked if she knew anyone suitable for the job.

"Only myself," Louisa replied. Like Anna, who had spent the previous summer as a nanny and was now teaching at a school in the Jamaica Plain section of Boston, Louisa would do anything in her power to help pay the bills.

So that winter eighteen-year-old Louisa moved to Dedham. Once she was living in his house, James Richardson tried to seduce her. When she resisted his advances, he ordered her to scrub floors, split wood, and black his boots. After seven weeks of labor she had been paid only four dollars, far less than he and Abigail had agreed. Louisa quit and went home.

Abigail was incensed at the lawyer. She and Louisa agreed she should return his four dollars. Abigail admired Louisa for being "free . . . I am glad the connexion was so loosely sustained, so soon dissolved."

But the other side of pride was shame. Louisa hated the unfairness of poverty. Having to black anyone else's boots made her angry. In her journal she railed against the "male lords of creation" who rule the world.

And she continued to worry about her mother. Abigail, in her early fifties, exhausted from four years of public service, was in poor spirits and "failing" health. Abigail sometimes felt, she said, that she was "a dead, decaying thing"—the lot of most women, it seemed. "Sad that so much time is irrevocably gone—and so little remains," Abigail wrote in her journal. "I am very stupid—stolid—fat and indolent, caring for little, accomplishing less."

The sale of Hillside the next year to Nathaniel Hawthorne enabled the Alcotts finally to move up to Beacon Hill, where their Sewall cousins lived, in 1852. Hawthorne paid $1,500 for the Concord property—$1,000 to Abigail's trust for the house, $500 to Emerson for the land. Emerson gave Bronson the $500, while Abigail's brother and cousin, as her trustees, controlled her $1,000. Abigail used some of her money to rent number 20 Pinckney Street, a Beacon Hill townhouse with room for her family and several paying boarders. Having lost her enthusiasm for social work, she said, "It is more respectable to be in my family than a Servant of the Public in any capacity." To be "used *by* [the public] is *ignoble*."

Meanwhile, Bronson spent several months in Connecticut trying to learn more about his family background and genealogy, according to the late Alcott scholar Odell Shepard. As Bronson earned only $164 that year, "it is not clear how Alcott secured the funds for these extensive researches." Louisa summed up the year in her own journal under "Notes and Memoranda" for 1852: "Father idle, mother at work in the office, Nan [Anna] & I governessing. Lizzie in the kitchen. Ab [May] doing nothing but grow. Hard times for all." Over their four years in Boston, Bronson had earned almost nothing. "Mr. Alcott gave Conversations at various places," Abigail commented in her journal, adding tartly, "I find myself less congenial in these higher harmonies and look on this banquet of beauty and exquisite elegance with incredulity."

As a result of their poverty and their mother's poor health, the older Alcott girls were desperate to make money. For a few months nineteen-year-old Louisa, who now knew that she did not like teaching, "opened a school" at home. She was also submitting short stories to magazines in the hope of making a sale. Her sister Anna, twenty-one, had moved to their aunt and uncle's house in Syracuse to teach classes at an asylum for the insane, where she would work for the next several years. "Self-sacrificing" Anna "disliked it, but decided to go," Louisa noted. In Syracuse Anna's panicked state worried her aunt Lucretia. "I wish the poor child could raise a little more of her own earnings so as at least to have a good supply of meat under clothing," Lucretia wrote to her son Joseph. "But [her] family contrive to use it almost all. She has already anticipated her wage & sent her mother $25. Your Aunt Abba as usual was full of debts & in want of money." Samuel Joseph still sent checks to his sister. "I pity her with my whole heart," he confided to a cousin, "and the more I think of her strange husband, the more I am shocked at his selfishness." From Abigail's brother these were harsh words. As loyal as he was, Samuel Joseph "did not understand during the Alcotts' hardscrabble years how Bronson could not put family first," according to the scholar Catherine Rivard. "Even the great causes, Sam May felt, might consider standing in line behind feeding the children."

The two younger Alcotts were less driven to work, probably on account of their age. Elizabeth, a teenager when they moved to Beacon Hill, spent her days sewing, reading, and keeping house, so that Louisa called her "the home bird" or "our angel in a cellar kitchen." Abby May, a budding artist, was enrolled in a Boston public school in the fall of 1851, at age eleven, and two years later began "getting prizes for drawing," Louisa noted. A crayon drawing of Abigail by Abby May a few years later was "a very good likeness. . . . All of us [were] proud as peacocks of our 'little Raphael.'" Abigail hoped that Abby May's "more structured education would prepare [her] for . . . teaching in the elementary or primary departments of our Schools. She bears the drill of the formal education better than the other girls would have done." Bronson agreed that Abby May's schooling gave her "prospects somewhat fairer than fell to her elder sisters, who, with gifts no less promising, have yet been defrauded of deserved opportunities for study and culture, by the social disabilities under which we have been struggling since the close of my Temple School. It was my hope in that, and afterwards in the Fruitlands endeavour," he continued, "to provide the means of an improved culture in which my children might participate with others to the extent of an enthusiast's dream; but these plans were frustrated, and at the greatest personal hazard and domestic cost. Nor have years of toil and anxiety been adequate to repair the damage.—But the dear intent is all the dearer for its hurts and delays, and shall nevertheless fructify and ripen in some distant generation, of which it is the germ and seed." Little did he suspect that repairing the damage would occur not in "some distant generation" but instead within his own home.

Louisa had just begun to profit from her writing. Her first paid publication, a poem entitled "Sunlight" by the pseudonymous "Flora Fairfield," appeared in *Peterson's Magazine* in the fall of 1851, when she was still eighteen. The same year she sold a short story for the first time. "The Rival Painters. A Tale of Rome," which earned Louisa five dollars, begins with a mother blessing her artist son Guido as he leaves home to make his fortune in the city—just as Abigail had done for Louisa. The mother's advice could have come from Abigail: "Carve thine own fortunes by untiring efforts, . . . Set not . . . too great value upon riches. Walk calmly in the quiet path that leads to thy duty, envying none, loving all. . . . Fear nothing but sin and temptation. . . ." Guido soon falls in love with a beautiful young woman to whom a count has already proposed. The young woman's father tells the two suitors, both of them painters, that they must compete for his daughter by painting a portrait. The Count produces a brilliant painting of the young woman. But Guido wins the contest—and his beloved—with a "strangely beautiful" painting of his revered mother. "The silvered hair lay softly around the gentle face, and the mild dark eyes seemed looking down on her son with all a mother's fondness. . . ." His mother possessed almost godlike powers as nurturer and protector. "And while noble painters and beautiful women paid their homage to the humble artist," Louisa wrote, "high above all the calm, soft face looked proudly down on the son, whose unfailing love for her had gained for him the honor and love he so richly deserved."

"Great rubbish!" nineteen-year-old Louisa said of "The Rival Painters" when it appeared in print on May 8, 1852. Without naming the author, she read it aloud to her mother and younger sisters. Only after her mother "praised it" did she triumphantly announce the author, "Louisa May Alcott!" This first success emboldened her to submit hundreds of poems and stories to periodicals, which purchased many of them for a few dollars each.

In her mother's eyes, Louisa was a "fine, bright girl [who] only needs encouragement to be a brave woman." For her "literary treasures," Abigail bought Louisa a new desk for Christmas. In private she remarked of Louisa, "I am inclined to think the approaching crisis in women's destiny" arising from the equal rights movement "will find a place of no mean magnitude for her."

Abigail had long suspected that Louisa would do great things, although it was hard to imagine exactly what. One of Louisa's jobs during their tenure on Pinckney Street, in 1853, was as a "second girl," a resident domestic servant, in Leicester, Massachusetts, washing linens and clothes for two dollars a week, most of which she sent home.

At the end of 1852 Louisa joined two thousand others at the Music Hall in Boston to hear the abolitionist minister Theodore Parker lecture to "laborious young women." Parker's prayer, she told her mother, was "unlike any I had ever heard." It was "not cold and formal as if uttered from a sense of duty, not a display of eloquence nor an impious directing of Deity in his duties toward humanity." It sounded instead like a "quiet talk with God, as if long intercourse and much love had made it natural and easy for the son to seek the Father." His phrase "Our Father and our Mother God" sounded "inexpressibly sweet and beautiful, seeming to invoke both power and love to sustain the anxious overburdened hearts of those who listened and went away to labor and to wait with fresh hope and faith."

In Syracuse a few months earlier, while visiting the May family, the Reverend Parker had spent a day with Samuel Joseph at an Indian reservation in upstate New York where the latter was trying to establish a library and school. Parker wrote in his journal for February 2, 1852, "To-day I went with Sam Jo May—the best man in this world; and, if there are any better in the next, I shall be all the more glad when I get there—to see the Onondaga Indians. . . . Sam Jo is at work . . . for the Indians, and with the Indians . . . and will do much more."

Samuel Joseph's middle son, Joseph, who was three years younger than Louisa, entered Harvard College in 1853, following at least five generations of men in the family. Abigail and her daughters often hosted Joseph in a spare room on Pinckney Street, where Bronson referred to Joseph as "the Collegian." There is no record of Louisa or her sisters remarking on the inequality of their educations and that of their male cousin, which despite the idealistic efforts of their parents resembled the educational inequities of the previous generation. Louisa's cousin Charlotte, however, did resent her younger brother. Joseph May was their "Mother's undisguised favorite," Charlotte told her daughters later. Charlotte's education entailed a few years at Miss Bradbury's school for girls in Syracuse and a year or two as a boarding student at the Lexington Normal School, where her father was once principal. The year her brother went to Harvard, Charlotte opened in Syracuse "one of those Peabody Sister schools" for boys and girls. "How do you like being a school marm?" Louisa asked her cousin in a letter that year. "Fascinating amusement is'nt [*sic*] it?" Charlotte mentioned that a boy in her class had asked her one day, "Would you ever play cards on Sunday, Miss May?" Sensing that he "wanted a direct answer but an answer that might require courage," Charlotte had replied, "Why, yes, Ross, if I could give pleasure to a lovely or sad or sick old woman, I'd play cards on Sunday." When Charlotte indicated in a letter to Louisa that she, too, wished she were rich, Louisa wrote back, "Dear Lottie don't wish to be rich, for it cannot make you more kind and generous than you already are."

Louisa took a vacation from her labors and her "Pathetic Family," as she now referred to them, at the end of the summer of 1853, when she and her mother traveled together to Syracuse. Louisa stayed a good deal longer than Abigail, who had to return to her younger daughters. In late September, when William Lloyd Garrison and his daughter arrived for a weekend at the May house, Louisa was planning to return to Boston with a care package that Lucretia was preparing for her son at Harvard. "Dear Jody," Lucretia wrote to seventeen-year-old Joseph on September 29, "I have your bundle ready to go by Louisa, and I hope I have not forgotten any of the various articles you wished either of soft or hard ware. If I have notify me & the mistake shall be rectified. The saw you will not find, but I will send that by Mr. Garrison on Monday."

Louisa must have indicated to Lucretia that Abigail needed more paying boarders, and that Joseph's belongings prevented her renting his room when he was not there. "Do you suppose it is convenient for you to go to your aunt Abba's on Saturday?" Lucretia suggested gently to Joseph. "Louisa says she has taken boarders, if so she may need all her rooms. I dare say after a while you will not care whether you go into the city or not."

In addition to running a boardinghouse, Abigail had time to return to her long neglected passion: women's rights. Women in several states were circulating petitions demanding suffrage and equal rights. At her desk on Pinckney Street in 1853 Abigail took up her pen to petition the Massachusetts legislature.

> All women, residents of the Commonwealth, who have attained the full age of twenty-one years, shall be entitled to vote . . . [and] their votes shall be counted as of equal value and potency with those of men. . . .
>
> On every principle of natural justice, as well as by the nature of our institutions, [woman] is as fully entitled as man to vote, and to be eligible to office. . . .
>
> [O]urs is a government professedly resting on the consent of the governed. Woman is surely as competent to give that consent as man. . . . Our Revolution claimed that taxation and representation should be co-extensive. . . . Crowded now into few employments, women starve each other by close competition; and too often vice borrows overwhelming power of temptation from poverty. Open to women a great variety of employments, and her wages in each will rise; the energy and enterprise of the more highly endowed, will find full scope in honest effort, and the frightful vice of our cities will be stopped at its fountain-head.

She submitted her petition, signed by seventy-three women, her husband, brother, and cousin, Garrison, the abolitionist Wendell Phillips, the Reverend Theodore Parker, and many others, to the Massachusetts legislature. A legislative committee promptly rejected it, reasoning that only one percent of the state's 200,000 women had supported this suffrage effort. Similar efforts in Wisconsin, Ohio, New York, and Indiana yielded similar results.

Abigail knew that her efforts to give women the vote, even if they succeeded, would not benefit her. But they could benefit her daughters, who might someday hold property, support themselves, and vote or run for public office. "Keep up," she often said to Louisa. "*Be* something in yourself. Let the world know you are alive!"

Not long after Abigail returned from Syracuse, Bronson headed there himself, at the start of a lengthy trip to the American West. From this year on he traveled west every winter for three to six months, giving conversations as often as he could. This year, as would become his habit, he spent several weeks at the Mays' "excellent" house in Syracuse, where Anna was still teaching and also studying German. "I have had some good hours with Sam and to profitable ends," Bronson reported to Abigail, suggesting a gift of cash. Samuel Joseph invited Bronson to speak at his church, explaining, "I wish to promote your interests here." He introduced Bronson to his friend Gerrit Smith, an abolitionist and philanthropist from Peterboro, New York, who had run as an antislavery candidate for president of the United States.

Samuel Joseph's reform work was expanding as the abolition and women's rights movements grew. He and Garrison, Lucy Stone, Gerrit Smith, and Wendell Phillips had been conveners of the 1850 national women's rights convention, in Worcester, Massachusetts, that nearly a thousand people attended. He, Stone, and Elizabeth Cady Stanton signed the call to the 1852 women's rights convention in Syracuse, which he opened with a prayer. Samuel Joseph's most controversial public act was the "Jerry Rescue" in 1851. Jerry was the nickname of William McHenry, a mulatto man who had lived and worked for years as a cooper in Syracuse after escaping from slavery in Missouri. But the 1850 Fugitive Slave Act prompted Syracuse authorities to arrest, shackle, and jail Jerry. That October Samuel Joseph, Gerrit Smith, and other local abolitionists arranged for thirty men to break into the police station, overwhelm the officers, free Jerry, and smuggle him to Kingston, Ontario. A small injury to a police officer during the raid became national news. Judges indicted May and several other leaders of the raid, but public opposition to the Fugitive Slave Act prevented any convictions. Every October from then on Samuel Joseph organized in downtown Syracuse a huge public celebration of "Jerry Rescue Day," one reason that the city was known as a "laboratory of abolitionism, libel, and treason." The first annual Jerry Rescue Day, in 1852, held in the railroad roundhouse after being banned from City Hall, was attended by three thousand people including Frederick Douglass, who stayed with the Mays.

Bronson headed west from Syracuse at the end of 1853. Abigail, who heard nothing from him for weeks, feared he had died. When a letter from him finally arrived, she forwarded it to Anna in Syracuse with a note: "I had really almost pined for some indication of his whereabouts, and no sign that he even lived since he left Syracuse. . . . He never can realize how much I love him. . . . Long after you and I dear Anna are gathered to . . . the great congregation, his name and excellencies will be monuments on the face of the earth, of priceless value to his descendants." This was not the first or the last time she told her children of their father's brilliance. It was Abigail's habit to idolize her husband and imagine him superior to herself, especially when he was at a distance. She wrote to him in Cincinnati congratulating him on finding "a Cozy home [there] where Art, beauty and hospitality were all inmates. It is too good to believe. Enjoy it dear, all you can."

In February Bronson returned from his western tour. Years later Louisa recalled the "dramatic scene" of his arrival in Boston. The doorbell woke her and her sisters and mother. Abigail jumped from her bed and "flew down" to the door, crying, "My husband!" Louisa and her sisters "rushed after, and five white figures embraced the half-frozen wanderer who came in hungry, tired, cold, and disappointed, but . . . serene as ever." Only the youngest dared ask if he had made any money. With a "queer look" he opened his pocket-book and revealed one dollar. "Promises were not kept," he said, "and travelling is costly, but . . . another year [I] shall do better."

Louisa's memory was somewhat faulty. In fact, Bronson returned to Boston with Anna, who was taking a break from her work in Syracuse to see her family. The recollected scene—of four girls and a loving wife racing to greet their brave father and husband—is more sentimental than the reality of two young women and a teenager greeting their twenty-two-year-old sister who lived elsewhere to help support them, while their haggard mother greeted their itinerant father. Like her mother, Louisa was proud. Appearances mattered to her. If the facts of her life embarrassed her, she would alter details to protect herself.

Throughout that winter and spring Louisa continued writing and marketing her stories. She earned more money now, sometimes fifty dollars a piece, and sold to larger publications, such as the Saturday Evening Gazette. The publisher George Briggs paid her more than thirty dollars (about $700 now) for a volume of the fairy tales and poems she had invented for the children in the Hillside barn, Flower Fables, to be printed and distributed at Christmastime. As often as possible Louisa retreated to a desk in the quiet garret above the third floor of the house, a bowl of apples by her side. To keep warm she donned a heavy green and red wrap she called her "glory cloak" and a green silk cap with a red bow sewn for her by her mother. Louisa was relieved, she wrote to her cousin Charlotte, that Abigail had "at last retired from public life to the bosom of her family. If she would only repose there it would be highly agreeable, but she *wont* [*sic*] and tires herself most perseveringly. . . . We keep her toasting like a large muffin and luxuriating in the rest and quiet she is obliged to take."

Louisa took another trip to Syracuse in June. "Cousin Louisa arrived safely at Colvin Hill at about 12 o'clock," Lucretia informed Joseph in early June. "She was a good deal chilled & fatigued, I thought, but is brightening up and seems quite herself. We were all glad to see her . . . & grateful to any[one] who was willing to come to us, it has been so very lonely without your father & Bonnie [George]," who were in Boston. "They published in our daily [newspaper] that your father was absent, so the usual stream . . . have abstained from visiting us, which is a blessing not in disguise."

Samuel Joseph was in Boston because of a recent demonstration against the Fugitive Slave Act in which his brother-in-law had participated. Although not easily persuaded, Bronson was now an abolitionist who supported violence to promote the cause. In late May 1854 Bronson joined a vigilante company that stormed a Boston courthouse and killed a U.S. marshal in an attempt to free an escaped slave, a preacher from Virginia named Anthony Burns, who had been arrested under the Fugitive Slave Act. Armed troops escorted Burns back into slavery in Virginia, enraging many Americans, even those who were not abolitionists. Attempts by the government to enforce the Fugitive Slave Act proved "a potent propaganda weapon" for abolition and the Underground Railroad, and strengthened Garrison's movement. Many northern states, including New York and Massachusetts, responded by passing laws that freed slaves within their borders. But a few years later, in the infamous Dred Scott case, the Supreme Court of the United States declared unconstitutional all state laws against slavery. The court, Samuel E. Sewall would lament, "has just decided that a negro is not a citizen of the United States, and that Southern slaveholders can carry their slaves through the free States without making them free. . . . I feel ashamed of living in a country where there is such a contemptible President [James Buchanan] and judges." The 1854 Kansas-Nebraska Act, which opened western territories to slavery by allowing their settlers to vote on the matter, also served to unite the North in resistance to southern encroachments. "We have at last come to the point where the slaveholders must be driven back," Samuel E. Sewall wrote to Samuel Joseph that year. "I cannot doubt that the triumphs of freedom are about to commence, and that they will be as rapid as those of slavery have hitherto been."

Home in Syracuse on June 20, 1854, in the study where he received parishioners, with his niece Anna Alcott "well & happily" at his side, Samuel Joseph wrote to his son Joseph, "I have not recovered my serenity, which was so much disturbed by the occurrences in Boston. The most angry, warlike [feelings] have at times been stirred within me. But I know they are not right and so I have been in conflict with myself."

In July, at the Church of the Messiah in which he preached, his daughter Charlotte married Alfred Wilkinson, a young banker she had met on the railroad station platform on her arrival in Syracuse when they were eleven and thirteen years old. There is no record of the wedding guests, but Anna, Louisa, and Abigail would surely have been present. Charlotte May Wilkinson was twenty-one, the same age as Louisa, and similar to Louisa in appearance, according to a family recollection. Five feet, six inches tall and slender, Charlotte had pale skin, "expressive brown eyes, and brown hair rich with tones of red and gold." She was more demure than Louisa, whom a neighbor described as "a big, lovable, tender-hearted, generous girl, with black hair, thick and long, and flashing, humorous" eyes, blessed with good humor, common sense, and the character of "a leader." Charlotte's husband, a son of a Syracuse banker active in Samuel Joseph's church, was a recent graduate of Rochester Polytechnic Institute.

Two months after the wedding Louisa was still in Syracuse. Lucretia wrote affectionately to Joseph, now a Harvard sophomore, on September 29, "I have exchanged your gloves and will send them and your other goods and chattels by L. Alcott who goes [to Boston] next week I suppose. . . . I leave the rest of the [letter] paper at 11 p.m. for your father to fill and hope he will send you something better than my poor brains have been able to, dearest Jody. Ever your loving 'Mum,' L.F. May."

At seven fifteen the next morning, in his study, Samuel Joseph continued the letter to his son while his wife, other children, and niece Louisa slept late. "Our folk not up yet. The savor of a nice beefsteak is ascending from the kitchen, and that will soon bring them down." He went on to give his son advice not unlike that from Abigail to her daughters. "I hear indirectly that you have been called on to deliver an address, or lecture, or speech of some sort. Let us know all about it. The more thoughts you express, the more you will have. And there is no exercise of the mind that is so quickening and strengthening to all our mental faculties as carefully arranging and clearly expressing our thoughts on any subject worth thinking about. I hope too you will take pains to acquire an excellent locution. Do learn to read well, and speak well. Accustom yourself to speak extempore in common conversation, cultivate the habit of saying exactly what you mean to say, of using clear and appropriate language and of finishing your sentences. A slovenly slipshod style in conversation will be very likely to insinuate itself into one's extempore speeches."

That month in Boston, Abigail told Bronson she was terribly worried about money. She had said this to him a thousand times, and he had never known how to respond. Now, though, Anna and Louisa were laboring for the Alcotts' daily bread. In his private opinion, "our good girls are" more capable of earning a living than their mother, who possessed only "the wifely washerwoman's arts and pains-takings." Although Bronson and Abigail owned no land or property, their daughters were becoming their "live-estate." He remarked, "We have reason to be thankful and take in our live-estate since it yields so fair an income."

Chapter Eleven

Left to Dig or Die

On Christmas Eve in 1854, before slipping her first published book into her mother's stocking, Louisa wrote on the title page, "Into your Christmas stocking I have put my 'firstborn.'" At age twenty-two, old enough for marriage and babies, Louisa asked Abigail to accept her compilation of fairy tales, *Flower Fables,* "with all its faults" because "grandmothers are always kind."

To "my earliest patron, gentlest critic, [and] dearest reader," Louisa continued: "Whatever beauty or poetry is to be found in my little book is owing to your interest in and encouragement of all my efforts from the first to the last, and if ever I do anything to be proud of, my greatest happiness will be that I can thank you for that, as I may do for all the good there is in me, and I shall be content to write if it gives you pleasure." She requested that Abigail consider this slender volume "merely as an earnest of what I may yet do; for, with so much to cheer me on, I hope to pass in time from fairies and fables to men and realities."

The next morning, when Abigail reached into her stocking to find the first fruits of her long mentorship of her second daughter, she rejoiced at Louisa's success. She was also pleased that Louisa continued to be modest, sounding "discreet" rather than gloating. "She takes her good fortune in a becoming spirit—just as you could have wished," Bronson said to his wife. The book, Louisa reminded her family, was only tales invented for children. At the same time, it brought in far more than her usual hourly rate, and for much pleasanter work. The *Saturday Evening*

Gazette gave it a good review, which she happily read aloud to her mother. For the first time, Louisa noticed, people other than Abigail seemed to think that "topsy-turvy Louisa [might] amount to something after all, since she does so well as house-maid, teacher, seamstress, and *story-teller*."

Despite their joy at Louisa's literary achievements, mother and daughter both sensed that Abigail was not well. Wornout by six years of work in Boston—"City life being so expensive and [its] labours so oppressive to me," as she put it—Abigail was thinking of moving to Walpole, New Hampshire, where her sister Eliza's widower had offered her a small house on a lane, firewood, and a garden, rent-free. Benjamin Willis, a wealthy ship owner who had lived in a mansion on Fort Hill in Boston, now occupied a spacious colonial with several outbuildings on land along Main Street in the farming village near the Connecticut River in southwestern New Hampshire where Peabodys, Endicotts, and Cabots spent summers. Willis, according to a neighbor, was a "very nervous . . . thrifty" man, who disapproved of his brother-in-law Bronson's insolvency.

In the late spring of 1855, Abigail moved with her three younger daughters—now twenty-two, nineteen, and fourteen years old—to Walpole, where they lived in "near poverty" for nearly two years, Richard Herrnstadt noted. Anna still worked in Syracuse, lived with her May cousins, and continued to send Abigail most of her salary. Bronson traveled between New Hampshire, Boston, and Concord.

That November, not long before her twenty-third birthday, Louisa told her mother that she had decided to leave New Hampshire "to seek my fortune" in the city. She found Walpole "very cold and dull now the summer butterflies have gone." One rainy day in that "dullest month in the year," with her "little trunk of homemade clothes, $20 earned by stories sent out to the 'Gazette,' and my MSS., I set forth with Mother's blessing." In Boston, boarding with Sewall cousins on Beacon Hill, she wrote and sold light tales and poems to the *Saturday Evening Gazette*. Like Anna, she sent home most of her earnings of five or ten dollars for each piece. Her writing was "well paid for," she felt, "especially while a certain editor [Frank Leslie] labored under the delusion that the writer was a man," an illusion that Louisa often enhanced by using only her initials, the "dashing signature L. M. Alcott," or masculine or genderless pseudonyms. "The moment the truth was known," unfortunately, "the price was lowered; but the girl had learned the worth of her wares, and would not write for less, so continued to earn her fair wages in spite of sex. . . . I insisted that if the rubbish was ever worth a dollar a page it was so still, & had my way, steadily increasing the sum as the demand grew." Women writers must "understand the business details of their craft," she wrote later. "The brains that can earn money in this way can understand how to take care of it by a proper knowledge of contracts, copyrights, and the duties of publisher and author toward one another." Louisa also set aside a portion of her earnings for art classes for Abby May.

During the two years her mother and younger sisters lived in New Hampshire, Louisa returned there each spring and summer. Another attraction that drew her back was the community of young intellectuals who acted in the Walpole Amateur Dramatic Company. Louisa, who was tall (five feet, six inches) and lively, with gray-blue eyes, fair skin, a strong chin, and long chestnut hair that she considered her "one beauty," had always loved to act. Her first dramatic experience had been as a child, directing her sisters in the "Louie Alcott troupe." As teenagers she and Anna wrote and performed melodramas. Louisa adapted several Dickens novels for the stage and often assumed the identity of her favorite character, the elderly Mrs. Jarley, of *The Old Curiosity Shop,* with her menagerie of wax figurines. She auditioned for roles and submitted original plays to theaters in Boston, and in New Hampshire she took leading roles in new comic plays. In September 1855 she was Widow Pottle in a drama by J. R. Planché, *The Jacobite,* and Mrs. Bonnycastle in *The Two Bonnycastles,* a one-act farce by John Morton. The following April, having convinced her Syracuse cousins to join her, Louisa played Patty Pottle in *The Jacobite* beside her cousin Charlotte May Wilkinson as Lady Somerford. Charlotte's twenty-six-year-old brother, "Mr. J. E. May," took four small roles in *The Widow's Victim,* a one-act farce by Charles Selby, in which Louisa played Jane Chatterly, an "extremely sensitive, extremely literary, and extremely dramatical" lady's maid. The only reason Louisa did not pursue an acting career, she wrote in 1856, was that a theater manager convinced her "it was such a hard life & few succeeded."

In the spring of 1856 Abigail's sixty-eight-year-old brother, Charles, who had returned to Massachusetts from sea only in the early 1840s, died. Abigail called on Charles's young widow and four small children in Lynn, Massachusetts, where, according to Bronson, she was feeling unwell. She worried that Louisa and Anna might not be able to come home that summer for clean air and rest. As always, Abigail wanted the family together. Lizzie was not well. The summer before she and Abby May had contracted scarlet fever. Abby May, a tall, sturdy fifteen-year-old, recovered quickly from the bacterial infection, but the fever lingered in twenty-year-old Elizabeth. Hearing from their father that Elizabeth was near death, Anna and Louisa raced to New Hampshire to help Abigail. Lizzie came back from the brink, but her untreated infection evolved into rheumatic fever, which permanently damaged her heart. Restoring Lizzie's health became the center of Abigail's life.

Bronson, on the other hand, began an eight-month trip to the West in September 1856. From Connecticut he wrote to ask Abigail to consider another position as matron of a water-cure establishment, which in that state, he thought, might pay $1,500 a year. Abigail, of course, could not leave Lizzie, who continued pale and weak. Over the coming months her three healthy daughters scattered, Anna to her Syracuse job, Louisa to Boston to write, and Abby May to study art while boarding in Roxbury with her adoptive aunt, Caroline Greenwood Bond. Left alone in New Hampshire, Abigail and Elizabeth were "the poor Forlornites among the ten-foot drifts" of snow, in Louisa's words. Throughout that long winter Abigail had a great fear that Lizzie might die, and an urgent need to provide her family a home.

In Syracuse just before Christmas, Anna departed the May house in a coach driven by Dr. Hervey B. Wilbur, her uncle's friend who ran the city asylum where she taught. "The poor child left in quite good spirits outwardly," Lucretia reported to her son at Harvard. "I do believe from all accounts she will be happy [at the asylum] and have some first rate comforts, nice bathing establishment house, warmed by a furnace, and she will not be so much obliged to stint her washing, as she always has done. She has improved wonderfully & yr father says the Dr. [Wilbur] . . . feels he has no common girl." Several months later, during Bronson's stay in Syracuse on his trip home, Lucretia described Bronson as "fussing" and arrogant. "Very few come up to Mr. Alcott's mark," she told Samuel Joseph. As Bronson left the house one day to deliver one of his conversations, Lucretia was "afraid his audience will be very small. . . . I suspect from what I hear [from other ladies] that very few are interested in his manner or matter." Even Samuel Joseph admitted that Bronson's "manner fidgets me."

In Boston that spring, Bronson asked Samuel E. Sewall to help him find and rent "a comfortable house (including my garden of course)." Abby May, "the family genius," wished to live in Boston to study art. Louisa was already in Boston at a boardinghouse. She was proud of having "done what I planned" that spring, "supported myself, written eight stories, taught four months, earned a hundred dollars, and sent money home." Now she planned to "keep house" and do sewing for her cousin Thomas Sewall, on Beacon Hill, "while his girls are away," Bronson informed Abigail.

Filling in as a domestic servant for her rich relatives made Louisa more poignantly aware of the social distinctions of gender and class. Poor people served rich ones, and women of all sorts served men. In "The Lady and the Woman," a work of realistic fiction she published in the *Saturday Evening Gazette* in 1856, a young woman named Kate Loring succeeds in freeing herself from these restrictions, as Louisa herself dreamed of doing. Kate, who merges in herself both "masculine" and "feminine" virtues, is nevertheless able to win the love of a desirable gentleman who at first sees women as only tender, submissive "ladies." Kate describes to him her revolutionary vision of womanhood: "I would have her strong enough to stand alone and give, not ask, support. Brave enough to think and act, as well as feel. Keen-eyed enough to see her own and others' faults and wise enough to find a cure for them. I would have her humble, though self-reliant; gentle, though strong; man's companion, not his plaything; able and willing to face storm as well as sunshine and share life's burdens as they come," equal to any man. Having displayed her courage during a flood by saving a house from destruction, with "a face glowing with exercise, eyes brilliant with excitement, garments dripping, and hair fluttering in the wind, Kate came into the full glaze of the light lit up to guide her home." At the end of the story Kate and her husband clasp hands for their journey "upward, side by side."

Louisa, amid her own sorry life as a seamstress and maid, occasionally allowed herself secretly to "wonder if I shall ever be famous enough for people to care to read my story and struggles." Thinking of Charlotte

Brontë, whose biography she had just read, Louisa wrote, "I can't be a C. B., but I may do a little something yet."

In the summer of 1857 the entire family, including Bronson's elderly mother, who lived with them part of that year, reunited in New Hampshire. Anna and Louisa were disturbed to find Lizzie still so thin, pale, and sluggish. Anna decided to stay to help Abigail rather than return to her job in Syracuse. In July Samuel Joseph visited "Auntie and Uncle Alcott and the girls," he informed a son. Bronson planted and tended a garden, with which he hoped to settle local debts. He promised Anna and Louisa that by fall he would arrange permanent housing for the family. In contrast to his overweight, exhausted, nearly blind wife, Bronson at nearly sixty years of age was fit, "venerable of appearance and possessed of a majestic voice and an utterance remarkably fluent." He enjoyed "a modest fame . . . his acquaintance was wide, and rapidly expanding, [and] he had long been closely associated with persons of high distinction," including Henry James Sr., Henry Wadsworth Longfellow, Horace Greeley, and Walt Whitman.

Over the years of her marriage Abigail had often left to stay with relatives soon after her husband's return from a long trip, and this year was no different. Following the family visits in July, she took Lizzie to stay with relatives and the family of Wendell Phillips in mansions on Boston's North Shore, where she hoped her daughter would be cured by the sea air, frequent baths and carriage rides, and daily walks. In August, perceiving Elizabeth's "brightening prospects," Abigail anticipated several more weeks there and in Boston before she and Lizzie returned to New Hampshire. But Lizzie's condition worsened. Unable to walk more than a few steps, she took to her bed. This hastened their removal to Boston, where Abigail consulted medical experts, to no avail. She spent her days at Lizzie's bedside in Hannah Robie's chamber on Beacon Hill, or reading to Lizzie in the Sewalls' parlor.

Around this time Thomas Sewall offered Abigail's husband a house lot in Malden, but Bronson demurred: Concord "is the place to plant ourselves." In a letter to Bronson, Abigail repeated her reluctance to return to a town where they still had unsettled debts. She felt "anxious and divided in mind" about Concord. She begged Samuel Joseph for "some aid in the way of leaving Walpole honorably," without debt, but he was slow to respond because of family illnesses. Louisa and Anna also argued against another move to Concord. But their father promised, "I can take care of these matters if you will trust me for once a little." Abigail's "reluctances would be overcome," he said, "in two or three years" when he could provide them "a good home" in Concord.

Living with their father in New Hampshire, Louisa and Anna filled in for their absent mother, assuming a traditional female role. They alternated "keeping house," Bronson reported to his wife, behaving like "friendly competitors. . . . Our housekeeping conducts itself neatly under the[ir] alternate weeks' administration, serving us to the old comforts and bountifully, at bed and board," he wrote. "The absent matron would plume herself admiringly, to see how tidily and punctually all things are managed, by her serene substitutes—the newly initiated house-maids two, and who contrive to see company proudly and visit besides—the Artist maiden [Abby May] playing her part handsomely [in these] hospitalities." Bronson was accustomed to receiving his wife's "summons to dinner" and other meals, which Louisa and Anna apparently endeavored to imitate. "Anna is the assiduous housekeeper," Bronson went on, "and keeps her Guests in the best humour with her table and chambers. I find her consulting [your cook]books, and her bread and cakes are excellent. . . . Such order and tidiness it does one good to witness. All the private virtues and accomplishment are embosomed in this modest maiden, and await their times." When not keeping house for their father and grandmother, the two sisters, now in their mid-twenties, wrote, acted in, and directed plays in the Walpole Town House. Seventeen-year-old Abby May was usually exempted from housekeeping, perhaps because her father hoped her work might someday support them.

In early September Bronson visited Concord and set his sights on a house next door to Hillside, which the Hawthorne family now occupied. It was a dilapidated, seventeenth-century house surrounded by shade elms and butternut trees that backed up to an orchard and twelve acres of woodland. "All this I can have for $950," which he expected from Emerson and other friends, he informed Louisa and Anna, "leaving your mother's investments untouched," a promise about which Louisa felt as skeptical as her mother. Bronson continued, "I will take the reins a little more firmly in hand. . . . You may rely upon me for supports of labour and money. . . . [I] shall command the respects of your mother's connexions, and the family all the more favours they may have in their hearts to bestow." He begged his grown daughters, who had likely conveyed to him their frustration at his improvidence, "Let me be the central figure of the Group, and try our family fortunes so, for a little time. . . . Please give me my last chance of redeeming my goodsense and discretion." Louisa and Anna's responses do not survive.

A week or two later Bronson purchased the old house, which still had a tenant and needed extensive renovations, "with Mother's money," according to Louisa's journal. Bronson wrote, "I . . . close my bargain with [the owner] Moore for the place, the papers to be drawn by S. E. Sewall. Sup at Thoreau's and sleep at Emerson's." He decided to call it Orchard House. Louisa and Abigail would give it a different name. To them it was Apple Slump. Louisa said privately, "I never want to live in it."

Abigail, still boarding in Boston, finally consented to move back to Concord. Lizzie, if she was dying, would want the family together, her mother was aware. As the new house was not yet habitable, Abigail rented half a house near the Concord Town Hall, on Bedford Road. In October all six Alcotts reunited there. Anna and Louisa helped their mother care for their mostly bedridden sister, who had been seriously ill for two years.

Louisa turned twenty-five in November. "I feel my quarter of a century rather heavy on my shoulders just now." She seemed to lead "two lives. . . . One seems gay with plays" at the theater, the other "very sad,— in Betty's [Elizabeth's] room, for though she wishes us to act, and loves to see us get ready [for plays], the shadow is there, and Mother and I see it." Louisa often felt that she and Abigail saw the world in similar ways. Watching her at Lizzie's bedside, Louisa was reminded that Abigail had lost all three of her sisters. "Betty loves to have me with her, and I am with her at night, for Mother needs rest. Betty says she feels 'strong' when I am near. So glad to be of use."

"Anxious and restless" about money for basic expenses, Louisa considered taking a job as a governess in Boston. Her parents discouraged her. Abigail needed Louisa's help, and Bronson considered the position beneath her. "I don't relish 'the Governess' in proud people's palaces for any child of mine. There is no better blood nor more noble, to pride upon in any family in Boston . . . than flows in her own veins and holds itself to the old nobilities still."

So Louisa stayed home. Sometimes it seemed she was alone with her parents. Her two healthy sisters were distracted, she sensed, one by her art studies and the other by the courtship of a young man. There is no evidence of earlier courtships, although Louisa and her sisters were close friends with many young men. Louisa and Anna often joked about being old maids, for at twenty-six and twenty-five they were already much older than the typical bride. Their cousin Charlotte May Wilkinson, five months younger than Louisa, was already pregnant with her second child, having lost her firstborn, Margaret, at nearly age two. But a young Concord man, John Pratt, the tall, steady son of a farmer and horticulturalist, had recently been calling on Anna, who was dark-haired like Louisa and Abigail, with large, thoughtful blue eyes and a warm manner. John Pratt, his sister, and the Alcott sisters were members of the Concord Dramatic Union, which staged plays at the local Unitarian Church. It was obvious to everyone that even as Anna continued to keep house for her family she was moving toward a future with someone else. Louisa was not happy to think that Anna might wish to leave home and marry. For Louisa the very idea brought on "lamentations."

In the fall a doctor informed Abigail that Elizabeth might not survive, which focused the attention of the entire family. If Lizzie lived, Bronson observed, "It would be like a resurrection from the dead." A few weeks later, though, he headed west as usual to give conversations as far away as Chicago and St. Louis. Stopping en route in Syracuse in early November, he stayed with the Mays. Samuel Joseph—who reassured Bronson that the Orchard House purchase felt "right"—was preparing to spend several weeks at a water-cure spa at Skaneateles Lake, thirty miles south, where his son Joseph was recovering from an unidentified illness. Samuel Joseph's "parishioners, seeing him worn from preaching and his family trials, kindly sent him to spend some weeks with Joseph, and get leisure, rest, and the benefit of the water cure," Bronson informed Abigail. "Rest is the one thing needful for him, but the Sewall and May ingredients seem hostile to each other . . . so there is neither rest nor repose." Lucretia, who had difficulties with her only daughter, Charlotte, had developed "a nervous weakness" similar to depression, according to a granddaughter. "After her health began to fail, in her need to be alone and out-of-doors" Lucretia often walked northeast on James Street from her house into the country-side, "carrying an Italian grammar as she sat at rest on the farm fences."

To the men in the family, including Bronson, Lucretia was a perfect hostess. Bronson reveled in her hospitality after his brother-in-law had gone to the spa. He occupied one of her many guest rooms and the minister's "warm, comfortable, tidy study" mostly "by myself, as Scholars love to do: Mrs. May and Charlotte keeping the house" and supplying him—as they did all male relatives—with "warm water for bathing and shaving," abundant bread, butter, and apples, "and as much leisure as you choose." The Mays' youngest son, "Bonnie" George, visited the spa and reported that Joseph had recovered and their father appeared "quite gay. Why, you would never think he was a minister."

Meanwhile, in the Alcotts' rented house in Concord, Elizabeth continued to fail. Each week she was paler and weaker. At twenty-two, she looked like an old woman to Louisa. Abigail and Louisa shared the task of watching her, leaving the housekeeping to Anna, who also spent time at the Pratt farm, north of the Concord River beside Punkatasset Hill. Early in 1858 Abigail spoke privately with the doctor, Christian Geist, who said he could no longer give her "much hope." A few days later Louisa noted, "Lizzie much worse. Dr. G. says there is no hope." So Abigail summoned Bronson home from Cincinnati. He arrived in late January. Throughout February, Abigail made sure that Lizzie was never left alone. From time to time the family gathered around her bed, as Abigail's family had done when she was small. Abigail was now Marmee, like her mother before her, and it was her daughter who was dying.

Lizzie felt ready to die; she told her mother, "I can best be spared of the four." Like every Alcott daughter, she was a day worker in the business of maintaining the family. She continued to do needlework until early March, when even her needle became "too heavy."

Abigail and Bronson were sitting beside Lizzie on the evening of Friday, March 12, when Lizzie "reached her arms out of bed to her Father and said take me father into your lap," Abigail reported. "He did so, bracing himself in the large chair. I took her feet in my lap," and Louisa, Anna, and Abby May, "seeing something unusually serene about us, closed in the group." Lizzie smiled contentedly at them all and said, "*All* of us here!" Her next words were, "Air, air," and when the window was opened, "heavenly air. I go! I go! Lay me down gently."

It seemed "she bid us good-by then," Louisa felt, "as she held our hands and kissed us tenderly." Around midnight Lizzie said, "Now I'm comfortable & so happy," and soon she was unconscious. The next day, according to Abigail, who provided her "ether and wine," Lizzie suffered "occasional paroxysms [of] physical distress." Early Sunday morning, while the rest of the family slept, Abigail called Anna, Louisa, and Abby May to Lizzie's bedside. "We sat beside her," Louisa said, "while she quietly breathed her life away," until at three o'clock, "with one last look of her beautiful eyes, she was gone."

Abigail and Louisa dressed Lizzie's body and lay her "on the couch, a form chiseled in Bone, held by a mere integument of skin, no flesh perceptible," Abigail noted. "Her father came" and said, "My child, how beautiful," the three "girls went to bed, and Mr. A[lcott] and myself sat down to try to bring home the lesson . . . that we are wiser for her life, holier for her death." March 14 had dawned "clear and calm," Bronson noted in his journal, and "our daughter Elizabeth ascends with transfigured features to the heavenly airs she had sought so long."

That morning Thoreau and the Emersons called at the house. Near Lizzie's body Louisa found a large, pale green moth with "soft brown spots" and hooked wings "fluttering at the closed window. I let the little emblem of the freed soul fly away from its cell, as she had done from her prison of pain."

Elizabeth Sewall Alcott's last rites were held the following afternoon at home. Abigail asked Emerson, now in his fifties, Thoreau, not yet forty, and two younger men, John Pratt and the schoolteacher Frank Sanborn, to bear Elizabeth's coffin from the house to Sleepy Hollow, a new cemetery that the Alcott girls had known as a picnic place. "We longed for dear Uncle Sam" to preside at the funeral, Louisa told a cousin, "but [Samuel Joseph] was too far away," traveling in Italy, so the Rev. Dr. Huntington of Boston, for whom Abigail had worked, said the service. At her "urgent request" the minister read the simple King's Chapel burial service that had been said for her three sisters, her brother Edward, her mother and father, and her grandparents. She expected it would be said for her, too. It includes portions of the Gospel of John, the 39th and 90th Psalms, and Paul's First Letter to the Corinthians. Louisa, Anna, and Abby May cast handfuls of earth on Lizzie's coffin as the minister intoned, "FORASMUCH as it hath pleased Almighty God to take unto himself the soul of our deceased sister, we therefore commit her body to the ground; earth to earth, ashes to ashes, dust to dust; looking for the general resurrection in the last day. . . ."

Four days after Elizabeth's burial Abigail sat down to write to her brother, who was in Rome. "In the anguish of a bereaved heart we are apt to cry out for help. The body sickens and the soul saddens. We seek sympathy and receive demonstrations that our friends are with us in our trouble." Like Louisa, she blamed herself for Elizabeth's doom. "I dare not dwell on the fever which I conveyed to my home which devoured the freshness of her life, and left her wrecked humanity on the shore of Time for a brief space. I dare not dwell on the helplessness of science which in the person of four 'skillful Drs' I summoned to her aid. The fact is before me: she has faded like a shadow through the valley of death into life and light."

Louisa's first thought after the death of her sister was to visit her cousin Charlotte, the "sister-in-love" whose comfort she needed. But Anna resisted Louisa's plan, saying she couldn't manage without Louisa, and Marmee needed their help. "Louisa is going to stay longer" in Concord, Charlotte's brother John Edward reported in early April, because "Cousin Annie could not let them all go at once." Louisa "will be along in a week or two."

Anna had another reason to ask Louisa to delay her trip. She had happy news that she had likely concealed during Elizabeth's final weeks of life. Anna and John Pratt were engaged to marry, they revealed on April 7. Abigail, delighted, wrapped her eldest daughter and her prospective son-in-law in her arms. Her own troubled marriage—the hard early years, struggles and separations, and a continuing lack of intimacy—had not lessened her faith in the institution of marriage or the importance of family. Indeed, Abigail's unconventional desire that her girls find their way to do good in the world without concern for society's expectations gave them unusual freedom in choosing how to live. Abigail not only supported Anna's conventional choice to marry but also approved of Louisa and May's decisions to stay single while preparing for professional careers. Abigail identified with her daughters, recalled her own difficulties determining how to lead her life, and encouraged them to find the path that suited them. Anna was doing exactly that.

To Louisa, though, Anna's engagement felt like an act of abandon-ment. Ever since Louisa was ten years old, lying in bed beside Anna as their father and mother loudly discussed a separation, Louisa had aimed to keep her family whole. She anticipated the natural dissolution of the family with a gloom like that experienced by Abigail as she faced the prospect of marriage to a man she did not love and all her sisters died, one by one. An engagement was nearly as awful to Louisa as a death. "So another sister is gone," Louisa mourned in her journal. The problem was not John, "a true man, full of fine possibilities . . . a model son and brother." The problem was that she wanted Anna to stay by Marmee and keep the family intact, as Louisa was doing. It is not clear if Louisa admit-ted to herself that a sister's departure increased the burden for the care of their parents on the remaining sisters. The greatest burden, of course, would fall to a spinster daughter. "I moaned in private over my great loss, and said I'd never forgive J[ohn] for taking Anna from me. . . ."

But Louisa's generosity won out. "I shall [forgive John] if he makes her happy, and turn to little May for my comfort." Like Abigail in her twenties, Louisa depended on at least one close female companion. "Lit-tle May" was now eighteen, taller, fairer, and more coquettish than her sisters, with a desire to paint and travel the world.

That summer the Alcotts moved into Orchard House. In nearly forty years of marriage, Bronson and Abigail had moved more than thirty times. The renovations to the new house were not completed, a process that would take years. Bronson's first step was, with Thoreau's assis-tance, to line the hill behind the house with logs and roll an existing two-story tenant house over the logs fifty feet forward to meet the rear of the original two-over-two farmhouse. This doubled the size of the dwelling, providing a third bedroom for the family and three rooms for paying boarders. Behind and to the right of the house he planted a garden that would expand to include rows of beets, spinach, carrots, turnips, pars-nips, radishes, lettuce, onions, leeks, and fennel; mints; patches of three kinds of squash, sweet corn, cucumbers, beans, and cabbages; and small patches of caraway, dill, thyme, and sage. He planted ferns, lilies of the valley, and crocuses, and Concord grapevines beneath the dining room window. "This loved spot, so largely now of my own creation," he said later, was "where I have had . . . the most profitable and agreeable occu-pation since our married life opened. . . . My wife and Louisa are less attached" to it, he knew, but "Anna and [Abby] May partake of my love of it, and cannot think of leaving it."

That fall, hoping to spend the winter writing and painting in the city, Louisa and her younger sister May, who had recently dropped "Abby" from her name, prepared to move to rented rooms in Boston. Before they left, Abigail gave May her deceased sister's miniature 1834 edition of *Diamond's New Testament* "with Notes Explanatory and Practical," which she inscribed, "to Abby [May] from Lizzy's Library, July 1858." At Christmas, while Bronson was on a lengthy trip to and from Chicago, Louisa and May gathered with their mother, Anna, and John at Orchard House.

Late that week Samuel Joseph, whom Abigail had not seen for nearly a year, paid them a visit. He had recently returned from a tour of Europe with his son Joseph. Soon after Lizzie's death, which occurred during his stay in Rome, he had received a letter from Lucretia asking, "Have you written poor aunt Abba? Her heart is full & she feels I doubt not in her desolation as if 'no sorrow was like to her sorrow.' We are all apt to. But time the great assuager reads us other lessons & she & we all can say 'It is well with our children.' 'For He giveth his beloved rest,' & we should not dare to disturb this rest or call them back if we could. They are safe, we know they are safe."

It must have been a relief for Abigail to sit and talk with the only man who sympathized with her so well. As sister and brother reviewed the past year, she called Elizabeth's death "the inexplicable trial of my life." It was, she felt, "an eventful year to us all, but not without its lessons or tests of our faith. When with my sick dying daughter I turned my back forever on [New Hampshire and] its beautiful hills, I felt that although the pastures were green and the hills were covered with the flocks and herds of rich men, I had no bread or honey. For my daughters, I was left to dig or die.

"Since then I have made little or no effort to earn." Alone, without home or income, "I took faithful care of my darling Lizzie till she [was] released from her sufferings by the great Physician of all our woes. . . . I said I had done what I could." Quoting the Gospel of Mark and the Book of Exodus, she added, "Lord, help thou mine unbelief. Save me and mine or Slay us forthwith. We still [have] time to help God before we die."

Louisa, too, took stock at the close of the momentous year of Lizzie's death and Anna's engagement. "Now that death and love have taken two of us away," she wrote in her journal, "I can, I hope, soon manage to care for the remaining four. . . . I can see that these [two] experiences have taken a deep hold, and changed or developed me. Lizzie helps me spiritually, and a little success makes me more self-reliant. . . . No more sewing or going to service for a living, thank the Lord!" Writing, Louisa had realized, "is my salvation when disappointment or weariness burden and darken my soul. . . . I feel as if I could write better now. . . . I hope I shall yet do my great book, for that seems to be my work, and I am growing up to it."

Chapter Twelve

Paddle My Own Canoe

L ouisa wanted to give up. In the autumn of 1858 she had just wasted another day circling Boston in search of employment. Twenty-five years old, with nearly a decade behind her of working or looking for work, she felt she had accomplished nothing. Her father would not support the family, her mother could not, and neither could Louisa, even though she had appointed herself the breadwinner. Now she stood on the edge of the Mill Dam, staring into the fetid water, wondering if she should jump.

There was suicide in the family. In New York State in 1852 her uncle Junius, who lived with the Alcotts when she was nine, had thrown himself into a threshing machine. Her father had considered suicide, certainly at Fruitlands and possibly in Boston in 1849. Both her parents, she was aware, were sometimes depressed. Could Louisa bring herself to die in a whirl of metal and sparks like Junius, or drown herself in the Charles River?

A few days earlier, she had taken the train into the city on her "usual hunt for employment," intending to stay several weeks or months. From the Boston depot near her mother's childhood home, she had walked up to Beacon Hill to spend a few days with her cousins, Samuel E. Sewall's brother Thomas and his wife, Mary, at 98 Chestnut Street, before taking a bed at Mrs. Reed's boardinghouse. Each day she had wandered the city feeling "anxious" and discouraged, she wrote to her mother, "for every one was so busy, & cared so little whether I got work or jumped into the river."

In a "fit of despair" on that October afternoon, Louisa had headed down Beacon Street along the Common, past the State House and the mansion once occupied by her mother's Aunt Q, toward the slender Mill Dam, which spanned the water west of the Boston peninsula. The Back Bay, as the water was known, had been dammed in 1820 to power grist mills, but the project failed. Now "a great cesspool" with "a greenish scum" along its shores, according to a contemporary report, the bay bubbled "like a cauldron with the noxious gases . . . exploding from the corrupting mass below." Louisa looked down into the darkness and "thought seriously of" jumping.

Glancing up, she could see the channel of the Charles River. At high tide it was a gray-blue expanse, at low tide a slender channel amid mud flats. Piles of suburban gravel dotted the flats, part of the city's preparation to expand the land by filling in the bay. Beyond the river were Cambridge and Harvard College, which her male relatives could attend. To her right was the West Boston Bridge and affluent Beacon Hill, where her mother had rented when Louisa was nineteen. To the south, below the Muddy River channel and the embankments of the Boston-Roxbury railroad, was the receiving basin of the Charles River, which filled in at high tide. Louisa breathed deeply. The air reeked of sewage. The dam had failed. Louisa had failed, too. Should she jump?

She could not do it, she told her mother later. It seemed "so cowardly to run away before the battle was over." Moreover, she knew Marmee could not bear another death so soon after Lizzie's. So Louisa turned from the water and marched back to her boardinghouse, resolved to "take Fate by the throat and shake a living out of her. . . . There *is* work for me, and I'll have it." A few days later, after finding a job as a governess, she described the resolution of her despair to her understanding mother, whose response does not survive.

Louisa's flirtation with suicide inspired a scene in a story she composed the following year, "Love and Self-Love." The story's central character, a young woman named Effie, throws herself into a river after discovering that her husband is in love with someone else. Instead of drowning, Effie matures: "the *child* Effie lay dead beneath the ripples of the river, but the *woman* rose up from that bed of suffering." Louisa could have been describing herself. The child Louisa was long gone, after years of worrying over her daily bread. The woman Louisa was now rising.

But what was a woman? What could a woman be? If she worked at a career, she could not be a wife. No professional writer Louisa knew cared for children or a house. Emerson and Hawthorne had wives to raise their children and keep their houses. Thoreau and Elizabeth Palmer Peabody were unmarried. Her mother's friend Lydia Maria Child, unhappily married and childless, had observed, "A woman of well-regulated feelings and an active mind, may be very happy in single life—far happier than she could be made by a marriage of expediency." Margaret Fuller remained single and childless until she was nearly forty. No one Louisa knew could accomplish both tasks. A man with a wife and children could write. A woman with a husband and children could not.

"A man's ambition with a woman's heart is an evil lot," Margaret Fuller had written of Louisa's predicament—and her own—in her best-selling manifesto, *Woman of the Nineteenth Century,* which was published when Louisa was twelve. "One should be either private or public. . . . Womanhood is at present too straitly-bounded to give me scope." Womanhood remained too restricted for Louisa, who agreed with Fuller's famous remark, "If you ask me what offices women may fill: I will reply—any. Let them be sea-captains, if you will." Like Fuller, she fantasized that marriage could be a union of equals, which was not possible so long as women were inferior to men in custom and law. Women's growing awareness of these inequities is one reason that the late nineteenth-century generation, according to Nancy Theriot, was "the least married group of women in United States history, with a record 13 percent remaining single."

A nineteenth-century woman who chose not to marry was expected to remain at home with her parents, caring for them as they aged. Louisa did this, but part of her longed to escape home, to be alone and creative. To satisfy this longing she sometimes took rooms in Boston without the pressure of seeking paid employment, simply to write. Later that fall, while quietly working in her Boston studio, the "old maid" received as a twenty-sixth birthday gift from her sister Anna and Anna's fiancé, John, a "peace-offering," a braided ring of their hair. Anna knew Louisa's character better than anyone except perhaps their mother. The sisters, only twenty months apart, had lived at close quarters their entire lives, sharing a room if not a bed and always, it seemed, supporting each other. It had pained Anna, who was devoted to Louisa, to see her so hurt by Anna's engagement.

The transition to adulthood was proving even more difficult for Louisa than it had been for Abigail thirty years earlier. Both women had goals in conflict with society's expectations. But Louisa, unlike her mother, had a most unusual upbringing. As a child she was asked to support her family. In her teens she vowed to pay the family's bills. As a young woman she yearned to accumulate cash. Moreover, Louisa's parents' marriage presented a powerful negative example. Louisa had "seen so much of . . . 'the tragedy of modern married life,'" she wrote a few years later that she was "afraid to try it." Accepting her fate as an unmarried woman, Louisa wrote, "Liberty is a better husband than love to many of us." Anna and John's future "nest" would be "very sweet and pretty, but I'd rather be a free spinster and paddle my own canoe." In sum, she felt, "The loss of liberty, happiness, and self-respect is poorly repaid by the barren honor of being called 'Mrs.' instead of 'Miss'." On account of her mother's experiences, Louisa knew that marriage can lead to misery. If she counted on no one but herself, then should she fail she could blame only herself. "Now that Mother is too tired to be wearied with my moods," she wrote in November 1858, "I have to manage them alone, and am learning that work of head and hand is my salvation when disappointment or weariness burden and darken my soul." Ironically, by choosing to go it alone in the world Louisa became even more dependent emotionally on her mother.

Louisa and Abigail's marriage-like bond was not unique. Because "an intensely close spousal relationship was not a part of many marriages," most of which were unhappy, according to Nancy Theriot, "women created intimacy . . . with their women friends and in their mothering." Many mothers and daughters of the period described "tremendous need" of each other and "a recognition of mutual confidence and friendship."

Louisa's story about Effie's near drowning brought in fifty dollars—more than she could earn from a month of sewing or teaching—from a new magazine called the *Atlantic,* which her father considered "far superior to any other literary journal." Emerson wrote for the *Atlantic,* which was read all over America. For each sensational or antislavery story she sold in this period, she usually earned between ten and a hundred dollars, often from the *Atlantic* or the *Saturday Evening Gazette.* So as not to offend "the proper grayness of old Concord," she published her stories

under pseudonyms, usually "A.M. Barnard," a masculine-sounding surname appended to the initials for *Alcott* or *Abigail May*. Louisa concealed
her gender for business reasons. Not only were books by men more
likely to sell, but also she desired privacy, particularly from older male
acquaintances and relatives. "Suppose [my favorite fictional characters]
went to cavorting at their own sweet will," she explained, "to the infinite
horror of dear Mr. Emerson" with his "chain armor of propriety. . . . And
what would my own good father think of me?" Discussing a manuscript
with an editor, she said, "My family laugh & cry over it, & think it fine—
they are no judges—neither am I. Mr. Emerson offered to read & give
his opinion long ago but I hadn't the courage to let him."

She was not afraid to discuss her stories with Abigail, however, who
encouraged her imagination no matter where it led. Perhaps because of a
long love affair with the written word, Abigail habitually gave Louisa her
own private journals and letters and suggested she study them for ideas
and let her fancy roam. On one of Louisa's visits to Concord, her mother
suggested it was better to invent fiction than to write history. "The writer
of fiction follows his characters into the recesses of their hearts," Abigail said, quoting a British writer she admired, Arthur Helps. "There are
no closed doors for" the fiction writer. "Could you have the life of any
man really portrayed to you, sun-drawn as it were, its hopes, its fears, its
revolutions of opinion in each day, its most anxious wishes attained, and
then, perhaps, crystallizing into its blackest regrets, such a work would
go far to contain all histories, and be the greatest lesson of love, humility and tolerance, that men had ever read. . . . It is not to be wondered at
that the majority of readers should look upon history as a task, but tales
of fiction as a delight." In Abigail's view, only fiction could fully portray
the life of any person, and Louisa likely agreed.

In Concord not long after Christmas, when none of her family but
Anna was home, Abigail became quite ill. Winter weather bothered her
in a poorly insulated house with only potbelly stoves and fireplaces for
warmth. She still mourned Lizzie and may have been depressed. Bronson had already gone west, stopping as usual in Syracuse, where Lucretia
had suffered a "relapse into the old malady" of frequent headaches and
possible depression, forcing Samuel Joseph to postpone a trip to Paris to
see their son Joseph. The Mays took Bronson to an elegant Christmas
party at which, Bronson reported to Abigail, "Sam told stories of your

father, and repeated some of your best ones of Fruitlands and the heroic periods of our history." Fruitlands was now a family joke, although the details of the stories are lost to history.

Anna, alone with her "invalid" mother, wrote to Louisa and May, who were spending the winter in a boardinghouse in Boston. Louisa rushed home to "cure" her, for she felt she was Marmee's best nurse. In Louisa's words, whenever "Mother fell ill . . . I corked up my inkstand and turned nurse." Bronson wrote to congratulate Louisa for her daughterly devotion, "I am glad you take things so bravely. It encourages your Mother under her trials, and . . . lightens the load with which she is so burdened." During the weeks she cared for her mother, Louisa wondered "if I ought to be a nurse, as I seem to have a gift for it." She cherished the arts, but "if I couldn't act or write I would try" nursing. "[I] May yet."

Once Abigail recovered, Louisa returned to her manuscripts and May in Boston. In April, not long after Bronson's return from his five-month trip, Abigail went to Boston to visit her two daughters, the Sewalls, and Hannah Robie, leaving Anna to keep house for Bronson in Concord. Anna's fiancé worked in insurance in Boston, as Grandfather May had done. A quiet, modest man, John Pratt had already taken "the family," Anna felt, "under his fatherly care."

At the Concord Town Hall on May 8, 1859, Louisa and her parents attended a lecture by the radical abolitionist John Brown. Bronson, whose view of slavery had evolved, was impressed by the tall, handsome vigilante in his late fifties, a Connecticut native like himself, with "hair shooting backward from low down on his forehead, . . . set lips, [and] countenance and frame charged with power throughout. I think him about the manliest man I have ever seen." Several scholars have theorized that Bronson "found John Brown physically attractive." And Bronson was now a convert to Brown's cause.

Five months after the lecture, John Brown's bloody raid on the U.S. armory in Harpers Ferry, Virginia, galvanized abolitionists across the country. Troops captured Brown and killed or captured his twenty cohorts. A jury in Virginia swiftly found him guilty of treason, rebellion, and first-degree murder. By early December 1859, when Brown was hanged, he had become a martyr for the antislavery movement. While some nonresistant abolitionists, including Frederick Douglass, were horrified by his violence, many, including Thoreau and Emerson, called Brown a "saint" and an "angel of light." Thoreau was a longtime abolitionist, and Emerson had begun to speak out against slavery in 1844. "Transcendentalists rushed to beatify Brown," John Matteson observed. Abigail's cousin Samuel E. Sewall, who had provided legal advice to Brown after the raid, "never felt . . . that the heroism of the attempt entirely obliterated its folly," yet "was deeply moved by [Brown's] self-sacrificing spirit." Even Garrison, long an "'ultra' peace man," called Brown a "hero." At home in Concord, Bronson composed a sonnet to Brown, "O Christian meek and brave!" Louisa wrote a poem praising Brown, "Saint John the Just," for making "death divine."

Samuel Joseph, however, reacted to Brown's raid with more trepidation. He did not learn of it until early November, when his ship from Europe arrived in Halifax. He had been at sea following a tour of England, France, Italy, Germany, Holland, and Wales with friends and his son John Edward. Hearing the news at anchor in Halifax Harbour, he felt shock and fear. The John Brown raid, "I apprehend, is but the beginning of sorrows," he wrote in his diary; "the pattering of the rain before a hurricane."

The mood was happier in Concord, as Abigail anticipated Anna and John's wedding, throwing herself into the role of mother of the bride. Her "usual vigor of thought and action" had returned, her husband observed happily at the end of 1859. She was "full of Anna's expected marriage" and "as energetic and busy as ever." Anna and John hoped to be married by Samuel Joseph the following June. Abigail spent several weeks in Boston planning the wedding, which for reasons unknown was moved forward to Wednesday, May 23, 1860, Abigail and Bronson's thirtieth wedding anniversary.

For her part, Louisa tried not to think about the wedding. She felt Anna was abandoning her. To distract herself, perhaps, she began a novel for adults. Her stories were finally bringing in enough money to support her family and even to send occasional gifts to her father's mother, who now lived in New York, and other relatives. Freed from sewing, teaching, and cleaning, Louisa had the luxury of writing longer, more challenging works.

At the desk by a window in the second-floor bedroom she shared with Anna at Orchard House, Louisa lost herself in her novel. "Genius burned so fiercely that for four weeks I wrote all day and planned [the novel *Moods*] nearly all night, being quite possessed by my work," she wrote in her journal in 1860. "I was perfectly happy, and seemed to have no wants." Whenever Louisa fell into this state, which she likened to a "vortex," her "Mother wandered in and out with cordial cups of tea, worried because I couldn't eat."

The novel *Moods* concerns the conflict at the heart of her mother's life, which Louisa would address again and again: how a woman can live in a world in which to marry is to enslave oneself. The heroine of *Moods,* Sylvia Yule, travels the world in search of love and finds two potential mates, one apparently modeled on Emerson and the other on Thoreau. She marries the wrong man, discovers her mistake, and considers suicide and divorce. As a slave to her husband-master, she has no choice but to join "that sad sisterhood called disappointed women, a larger class than many deemed it to be, though there are few of us who have not seen members of it. Unhappy wives, mistaken for forsaken lovers; meek souls, who make life a long penance for the sins of others; gifted creatures kindled into fitful brilliancy by some inward fire that consumes but cannot warm. These are the women who fly to convents, write bitter books, sing songs full of heartbreak, act splendidly the passion they have lost or never won. Who smile, and try to lead brave uncomplaining lives, but whose tragic eyes betray them, whose voices, however sweet or gay, contain an undertone of hopelessness." The novel's central issue, Elizabeth Lennox Keyser has written, is "whether Sylvia had the moral obligation to remain with her husband, whom she found impossible to love, or the moral obligation to leave him." She could have been describing Abigail.

Moods was not the only work that Louisa based on her mother's experiences, in Bronson's view. At the end of 1859, after "Love and Self-Love" appeared in the *Atlantic,* he observed that Abigail "partakes largely in [Louisa's] good fortune herself—[and is] a heroine in her ways, and with a deep experience, all tested and awaiting her daughter's pen." *Moods,* he added, was "attractive to us for the personal and family history, but slightly shaded, scattered along its pages."

Bronson spent this winter at home with his family, something he had not done for years. He had taken a job as superintendent of the town's public schools, which required his presence. His annual salary was one hundred dollars, which Louisa could now earn in a day or two. That winter he began to insulate the walls of their house.

As Anna's wedding approached, Louisa and May also stayed close to home. May, now nineteen, painted and gave drawing lessons to the sons of Horace Mann and his wife, the former Mary Tyler Peabody, and other Concord youth. Louisa worked on her novel and sewed a dress for May to wear to a ball. May, according to her father, was the "pink of a party" who with a female friend could "extemporize" entertainments at home for a throng of "very genteel young gentlemen." May had "many sweethearts," according to Anna. Sometimes Louisa struggled with jealousy toward her "fortunate" younger sister's serenity and ease, just as she envied Anna's ability to separate from the family by marrying. May "gets what she wants easily," Louisa lamented in her journal. "I have to grub for my help, or go without it. Good for me, doubtless, or it wouldn't be so; so cheer up, Louisa, and grind away!" Several years later, learning that an artist had given May free art lessons and a bouquet of flowers, Louisa wrote that May "always finds someone to help her as she wants to be helped. Wish I could do the same, but suppose as I never do that it is best for me to work & wait & do all for myself."

Less than two months before Anna's wedding, Louisa traveled to Syracuse to see her cousin Charlotte. On Friday, May 4, Samuel Joseph "took dinner at Charlotte's [house] with Cousin Louie." Two weeks later the minister, likely accompanied by his niece and daughter, traveled from Syracuse to Utica, Albany, Springfield, Worcester, West Newton, and Boston on his way to officiate at Anna's wedding. On Tuesday, May 22, after calling on relatives and the Garrisons in Boston, Samuel Joseph "went to Concord to my sister Alcott's." He "called on Mrs. [Horace] Mann and Miss [Elizabeth] Peabody. Emerson spent an hour with me." After sleeping at Orchard House, Samuel Joseph "rose at 6½, had a long and delightful conversation with Mr. Alcott." Decades of personal disappointment, especially on behalf of his adored Abigail, did not lessen Samuel Joseph's appreciation of Bronson's conversational gift. Another friend, James Russell Lowell, had described Bronson in a witty couplet, "While he talks he is great but goes out like a taper / If you shut him up closely with pen, ink, and paper." Samuel Joseph May's terse account continued, "At 11½, I married Anne B. Alcott to John B. Pratt."

Other observers provided more concrete details of the ceremony, which was attended by Henry David Thoreau, Elizabeth Peabody, the Emersons, the Alcotts, and the Mays. "All persons spoke of [the] fitness and beauty . . . [of] Mr. May's address and prayer," Bronson reported. Just before the ceremony, Anna and John crept up to the bedroom that Anna and Louisa had shared, to say their vows in private. The front parlor of Orchard House, where they all stood around the couple and their Uncle Sam, was "full of sunshine, flowers, friends, and happiness," Louisa said. But she herself was dressed in gray, "sackcloth, I called it, and ashes." In childhood she would have heard from Abigail that their ancestor the Salem witch judge had repented for his wrongful convictions by wearing sackcloth for the rest of his life. Louisa wore it symbolically, to "mourn the loss of my Nan. . . . Uncle S. J. May married them, with no fuss, but much love, and we all stood round her. She in her silver-gray silk, with lilies of the valley (John's flower) in her bosom and hair. . . . We had a little feast, sent by good Mrs. Judge Shaw; then the old folks danced round the bridal pair." Eight years later, in *Little Women,* Louisa created a similar scene:

> [T]he only ornaments she wore were the lilies of the valley which "her John" liked best of all the flowers that grew. . . . All three [sisters] wore suits of thin silver gray. . . . There was no bridal procession, but a sudden silence fell upon the room as Mr. March and the young pair took their places under the green arch. Mother and sisters gathered close, as if loath to give Meg up; the fatherly voice broke more than once, which only seemed to make the service more beautiful and solemn. . . . After lunch . . . Laurie . . . [said]: "All the married people take hands and dance around the new made husband and wife . . ." [prompting all to] dance around the bridal pair.

The flesh-and-blood bridal pair "left for their home in Chelsea at 1½," Samuel Joseph noted, to begin their married life in a house owned by John's maternal grandparents, the Bridges, near the beach just north of Boston. Then the mother of the bride took a nap.

The next day Samuel Joseph visited Frank Sanborn's school, which he was considering for his fifteen-year-old son, "Bonnie." To Sanborn, whose students included the offspring of Emerson, Hawthorne, John Brown, Henry James Sr., and Horace Mann, Samuel Joseph said, "I am desirous of removing my son George Emerson May from [a school in] West Newton to Concord. . . . My sister's maternal care, and her daughters' sisterly affection will cherish and quicken his domestic virtues. I wish him also to enjoy the benefits of your school. Can you receive him?" Bonnie began the term with Sanborn that fall and boarded with the Alcotts.

Later that day the Alcotts hosted a party for the family of John Brown. "A large party of antislavery ladies and gentlemen met at Mr. Alcott's," Samuel Joseph wrote. "Mrs. John Brown was there" with her baby, the youngest of John Brown's twenty children, who charmed Louisa and Charlotte. Louisa later reported, "C[harlotte] and I went and worshipped [him] in our own way . . . kissing him . . . and feeling highly honored when he sucked our fingers." She described Emerson and her Uncle Sam "cuddled into a corner" with their plates and teacups. The crowd of about forty people "had an earnest talk upon nonresistance," Samuel Joseph noted in his journal, but it is likely that he was the one who hewed most closely to that old faith. "Samuel J. May's plea for peace" before and during the Civil War "was most touching," according to Ednah Dow Cheney, "for he stood as truly an opponent of slavery as any man living, and firmly as ever he maintained his old faith in non-resistance." In early June, after he and Louisa attended a memorial service in Boston for the Reverend Theodore Parker, who had died of tuberculosis at forty-nine, Samuel Joseph brought his Harvard classmate George B. Emerson to Chelsea to visit the newlywed Pratts.

At her desk in Concord, Louisa spent the days after the wedding transforming her tangled thoughts into a short story based on her sister's courtship. Her emotions dictated the subjects of her work: whatever aroused her strong feelings worked its way into her fiction. The *Atlantic* paid her seventy-five dollars for the resulting story, "A Modern Cinderella." "Emerson praised it," she said with pride. Many "people wrote to me about it and patted me on the head. [I] paid bills and began to simmer another" story to sell. With both Anna and Elizabeth gone, Louisa felt even more strongly that she had to stay by and support her mother, so she and May remained in Concord for most of the summer, riding neighbors' horses in their free time. Louisa "had a funny lover," a handsome, forty-year-old southern man whom she eventually rebuffed. Privately she complained, "My adorers are all queer."

Louisa and May took over the housekeeping whenever Abigail was absent or sick. "My wife is very well, and does her own work" in the house, Bronson observed that summer. "My wife . . . lives in her family mostly as mothers and wives will." A year later he reported that "Louisa writes stories still and assists her mother about housekeeping."

Louisa and her parents spent the eventful winter of 1860–61 alone together at Orchard House, as Abraham Lincoln became president, the South seceded from the Union, and the nation anticipated war. May moved to Syracuse to live with her uncle and aunt and teach drawing at the insane asylum where Anna had worked. "More luck for May," Louisa wrote in her journal in December. "She wants to go to Syracuse and teach, and Dr. W[ilbur] sends for her, thanks to Uncle S. J. May. I sew like a steam-engine for a week, and get her ready. On the 17th [I] go to B[oston] and see our youngest start on her first little flight alone in to the world, full of hope and courage."

Aiming to be hopeful and courageous, Louisa worked long hours in the second-floor bedroom she now had to herself. She only "occasionally" appeared at the dinner table, her father noted, just "to vary a little the round of [her] work, by dashes of wit and amusement, for us chimney-corners ancients." Abigail seemed "very hopeful, only sick a day now and then, when she forgets how young she is at 60." Abigail— whose favorite sayings included "Cast your bread upon the waters, and after many days it will come back buttered" and "Hope and keep busy"— often muttered to her husband, "I hope good things of Louisa." No one encouraged Louisa's writing so much as her own "dearest critic."

One evening in February 1861, while Anna was staying with them in Concord, Louisa read aloud "several chapters of her book entitled *Moods,*" her father wrote. Anna, who seemed inexplicably to be going deaf, listened through an ear trumpet. The book "is entertaining and witty," Bronson felt, "her characters are drawn in lively colors, and there are several fine scenes," many drawn from family history. "The book has merits, and should be popular. . . . She writes with unusual ease, and in a style of idiomatic purity. Her culture has come from the writing of letters and the keeping of a diary, chiefly." Later that year Louisa gathered her parents and May in the parlor and read aloud the entire novel. "It was worth something," Louisa reported, "to have my three dearest sit up till midnight listening with wide open eyes to Lu's first novel." Her father proclaimed, "Emerson must see this. . . . Where did you get your metaphysics?" Her mother simply said, "Remarkable."

Abigail felt she was beginning to reap the fruits of her labors. "These girls," she wrote to her brother, are "full of life, aspiration, tact and talent." Louisa and May "both seem to have risen a peg or two" in the world's eyes "because one can write for the *Atlantic* and the other dipped so decidedly into the depths of the fine arts." Abigail had long known Louisa was special, but now observed that May, in her early twenties, "has a world of resource, and carries in her head a Mother wit and go-ahead-ativeness that beats all the Alcott family put together." Abigail's philosophy of raising children had always been to "stand as much out of the[ir] way" as possible "and try to keep myself from being a hindrance" to them. "I will never impose my experience upon them as the better guide or wisest way, tho' 30-40 years of a most varied life gives me an accumulated knowledge of the world and its requirements."

At the end of January 1861, she and Louisa heard, probably from May, that Samuel Joseph and a fellow abolitionist, a schoolteacher named Susan B. Anthony, had been hanged in effigy in downtown Syracuse. The two reformers, who had worked together for years, were preparing to address a meeting of the American Anti-Slavery Society in a building near his church when a mob stormed the building, shouting, "Put the niggers out." Following the secession of southern states, northern sentiment shifted against the abolitionists, who were believed to threaten the union. Among the well-to-do Syracuse residents opposing the anti-slavery meeting was Samuel Joseph's own son-in-law, Alfred Wilkinson, whose father, the president of the Syracuse Railroad, refused to allow any man accompanied by a manacled slave to ride his trains. To end the violence May and Anthony led the abolitionists from the hall and out to Hanover Square. Nevertheless, the riot raged for hours. A brass band arrived to serenade men parading through the city with effigies of the minister and Miss Anthony entwined in an obscene embrace. The mob built a bonfire and burned the effigies.

The brewing civil war finally erupted at Fort Sumter, in South Carolina, in April 1861. Young men from every corner of the nation headed to battle. Abigail wrote to Samuel Joseph, "Are we not beginning to reap in the storm what was there sown in the whirlwind? I dread a war, but is not a peace based on such false compromises and compacts much more disastrous to the real prospects of the country generally, and Freedom in particular? I think so. If the Border States secede . . . I think we can

call in aid from foreign powers, and may yet subjugate the whole brood
South and Border." Louisa, hearing the approaching drums of the Massachusetts Volunteer Militia, went out to stand alongside the road as the
men of the Concord Artillery of the state regiment marched by on their
way to the train depot. "I've often longed to see a war," she thought to
herself, "and now I have my wish." Yet she was frustrated, as her mother
at the same age had been, to be denied the worldly experiences of men.
"I long to be a man, but as I can't fight, I will content myself working
for those who can," she resolved. Alongside her mother, Louisa sewed
"night and day for the soldiers," according to Bronson. In October 1861
she wrote in her journal, "Sewing and knitting for 'our boys' all the time.
It seems as if a few energetic women could carry on the war better than
the men do it so far."

One fine spring day, Louisa went for a sail on Boston Harbor with
Anna and John. The boat stopped at an island with a fort. She climbed
the ramparts and "felt very martial and Joan-of-Arcy, as I stood on the
walls with the flag flying over me and cannon all about."

War seemed exciting. Not until a massive Union defeat at Bull Run
in July did most northerners begin to realize the actual cost of war.
President Lincoln determined not to interfere with slavery or to consider emancipation, even as numerous fugitive slaves offered to fight for
the Union and Samuel Joseph May and other abolitionists urged the
president to free and enlist them. A series of southern victories in 1862
changed Lincoln's mind. That September, immediately after General
Lee's surrender at Antietam, Lincoln signed the Emancipation Procla-
mation, freeing slaves in rebel states. As of January 1, 1863, all slaves in
all states were free, at least officially. Hundreds of thousands of male
former slaves became eligible to enlist for the Union.

Meanwhile, as she could not fight, Louisa gave in to her father's
encouragement and made another stab at teaching in early 1862. Sponsored by Elizabeth Peabody, who still taught in Boston, and the publisher James T. Fields, who was buying Louisa's stories, she opened a
kindergarten for poor children at the Warren Street Chapel. Her sister
Anna told a friend that "Miss Peabody . . . knowing Lu's peculiar faculty
with children proposed her." Louisa admitted to her journal, "[I] don't
like to teach, but take what comes; so when Mr. F[ields] offered $40 to
fit up with, twelve students, and his patronage, I began." The salary did

not cover room and board, so she commuted by train from Concord or stayed with Boston friends, among them Mr. Fields and his wife, Annie Adams Fields, a distant cousin of Abigail's. He was the junior partner in Boston's largest publishing house, Ticknor & Fields, which brought out works of Tennyson, Browning, Dickens, Wordsworth, Carlyle, Longfellow, Stowe, Emerson, Thoreau, Twain, Whittier, Lowell, Hawthorne, and Child, and the *Atlantic, Our Young Folks,* and the *North American Review.*

Delighted that she was pursuing his field, Bronson said to Louisa, "Your school promises good fruits."

"I do it against my own wishes," she responded. After only one term her labors "ended in a wasted winter and a debt of $40." But Mr. Fields agreed with her father that she should stay in the traditionally female profession. "Stick to your teaching, Miss Alcott," he told her. "You can't write."

Hurt, she scribbled in her journal, "I won't teach. I *can* write, and I'll prove it."

A month or so later, relieved to be done with teaching, she informed a friend jauntily, "I intend to [begin] with a blood & thunder tale as they are easy to 'compoze' & and are better paid than moral & elaborate works of Shakespeare. . . . So don't be shocked if I send you a paper containing a picture of Indians, pirates, wolves, bears & distressed damsels in a grand tableau over a title like 'The Maniac Bride' or 'The Bath of Blood. A thrilling tale of passion.'" She submitted more romantic thrillers to Frank Leslie, the editor of the *Illustrated Newspaper,* in New York City. Entranced, he paid her fifty to seventy-five dollars a story and soon wanted "more than I can send him. . . . I enjoy romancing to suit myself, and though my tales are silly, they are not bad, and my sinners always have a good spot somewhere."

That fall Louisa and May were back in Concord, where they planned to stay the winter. Abigail seemed "in the best of health" to Bronson, and Louisa was "as active as ever with her pen." It was her pen that provided solace from loneliness, Louisa suggested in a letter to a second cousin that contained a description of her "pathetic family." Her sister May "lives for her crayons and dancing." Anna, now pregnant with her first child, lived in a world "composed of John, and John is composed of all the virtues ever known, which amiable delusion I admire and wonder at from the darkness of my benighted spinsterhood." Bronson "lives for his garden." Abigail lives "for the world in general," assisting "every beggar that comes along," sewing for Union soldiers, and giving "lectures on Anti-slavery and peace wherever she goes."

Louisa felt she had to make a change. Like her mother at the same age, she wanted an escape from the life she knew. At nearly thirty, Louisa was now a confirmed old maid. She saw no path to combine a literary career, which she desired, with marriage and a domestic life. So she forswore domesticity except, of course, when Marmee needed her, and the rest of the time she dreamed of seeing the world.

There remained one profession open to women that Louisa had not yet tried. Margaret Fuller, one of her role models, had volunteered as a nurse at Rome's Fatebenefratelli Hospital during the Italian Revolution. Louisa never forgot Emerson's descriptions of Fuller's courage, especially his suggestion that a wartime nurse displays the gallantry of a soldier in battle. In nearly every respect, Louisa fulfilled the requirements for a Civil War nurse. By this time the reformer Dorothea Lynde Dix, superintendent of female nurses for the Sanitary Commission of the United States, had convinced the secretary of war that women could serve the Union as nurses so long as they were plain, modestly dressed, age thirty or older, and married without children. Except for the husband, Louisa was the perfect candidate, and she was sure that minor exceptions could be made.

On the verge of her thirtieth birthday, she made a fateful choice in pursuit of a certain kind of independence, as her mother had done a generation before. Abigail had married Bronson in the hope of forming an equal, loving partnership. Louisa went to war.

Chapter Thirteen

The Bitter Drop in This Cup

I never began the year in a stranger place than this," Louisa scribbled on the first page of her new journal on January 1, 1863. "Five hundred miles from home, alone among strangers, doing painful duties all day long, & leading a life of constant excitement in this greathouse surrounded by 3 or 4 hundred men in all stages of suffering, disease & death." She was in an army hospital in Washington, D.C., the capital of the nation and the Union war effort, where she was responsible for a forty-bed ward. Louisa had to "cork up" her feelings to avoid crying as she washed, fed, and consoled scores of injured and dying men. She had hardly a moment to stop and record her impressions. But this was something worth describing. "I . . . began my new life by seeing a poor man dying at dawn, and sitting all day between a boy with pneumonia and a man shot through the lungs. . . . [W]hen I put mother's little black shawl round the boy while he sat up panting for breath, he smiled and said, 'You are real motherly, ma'am.' I felt as if I was getting on. The man only lay and stared with his big black eyes, and made me very nervous. . . . I sat looking at the twenty strong faces as they looked back at me,—hoping that I looked 'motherly' to them, for my thirty years made me feel old, and the suffering round me made me long to comfort every one."

She had received her orders from Washington only a few weeks earlier. In haste she had filled a trunk with clothes marked "Louisa Alcott"

in indelible ink by Sophia Hawthorne and Abigail, who though she supported her daughter's decision confessed to her neighbor, "I shall feel
helpless without Louisa." She bid all a tearful good-bye and headed to
Boston, escorted by Julian Hawthorne, Sophia and Nathaniel's sixteen-
year-old son, and her sister May. After having a cavity filled and secur-
ing nursing credentials, Louisa purchased tickets for her trip: by train to
New London, Connecticut; by steamship to Jersey City, New Jersey; by
train to Washington, D.C.; and by cab to the filthy, disheveled former
hotel in which she now lived and worked on the main road in Georgetown, which she called "this big bee hive" or "Hurly-Burly House." Her
superior, Hannah Ropes of Boston, "cheered at the arrival of Miss Alcott
of Concord—the prospect of a really good nurse, a gentlewoman who
can do more than merely keep the patients from falling out of bed."

On December 16, 1862, Louisa's first full day as a nurse, cart after cart
of "legless, armless or desperately wounded" soldiers had arrived from
Fredericksburg, Virginia. They were victims of a Union defeat in which
nearly thirteen thousand men died. "In they came, some on stretchers,
some in men's arms, some feebly," Louisa reported. "I drowned my
scruples in my washbowl." Like many Americans, she could no longer
avoid the truth: war is grueling and awful, and in this war hundreds of
thousands of men would die. "When I peered into the dusky street lined
with what I at first had innocently called market carts, now unloading
their sad freight at our door . . . my ardor experienced a sudden chill, and
I indulged in a most unpatriotic wish that I was safe at home again, with
a quiet day before me."

Louisa had never been on such intimate terms with men. "Having
no brothers & a womanly man for a father I find myself rather stag-
gered by some of the performance about me . . . by dreary faced, dirty &
wounded men," she told a friend. At close quarters with scores of "dilapidated patriots, hopping, lying and lounging about," she found nearly all
of them "truly lovable & manly." Her "prince of patients" was a black-
smith from Virginia under whose "plain speech & unpolished manner
I seem to see a noble character, a heart as warm & tender as a woman's,
a nature fresh & frank as any child's. He is about thirty, I think, tall &
handsome, mortally wounded & dying royally, without . . . remorse.
Mrs. Ropes & myself love him & feel indignant that such a man should
be so early lost."

The opportunity to befriend men with whom she worked was another new experience. Dr. John Winslow, an army surgeon, invited Louisa on walks, to dinner, and to hear lectures and sermons in Washington, which she enjoyed. He also invited her to his rooms, "where I don't go." He seemed "odd, sentimental, but kind-hearted . . . amiable, amusing, & exceedingly *young.*"

At first her "chief afflictions" were bad odors and "bad air & no out of door exercise." But hardly a month into her nursing career she was laid up with a "sharp pain in the side, cough, fever & dizziness." Doctors feared typhoid fever, which Hannah Ropes now had. They ordered Louisa to stay in her room. A few days later Louisa was diagnosed with typhoid pneumonia and advised to go home. She felt it "ignominious to depart her post," so instead she chose to become a patient at the hospital. Doctors shaved her head and gave her the standard treatment for typhoid fever, daily doses of calomel, or mercury salts. Mercury, a heavy metal that affects the central nervous system and kidneys, causes tremors, inflammation of the gums, and psychiatric symptoms. She may have also received a "derivative of the opium poppy" that was freely available as a treatment for various ills.

In her delirium Louisa had nightmares, some of which she managed to record. Her most persistent dream, she recalled later, was of being married to a man who was a terrifying version of her mother. "I had married a stout, handsome Spaniard dressed in velvet with very soft hands & a voice that was continually saying, 'Lie still my dear.' This was mother, but with all the comfort I often found in her presence there was blended the awful fear of the Spanish spouse who was always coming after me, appearing out of closets, in at windows, or threatening me dreadfully all night long." In her unconscious, as in many of her sensational stories, marriage was alluring but ultimately enslaving. Above all, the dream suggests, Louisa depended on her mother, although she may have had mixed feelings about their intimacy.

In another dream Louisa "went to heaven & found it a twilight place with people darting thro[ugh] the air," seeming "busy & dismal & ordinary . . . dark and 'slow.' . . . I wished I hadn't come." Louisa dreamed she was a witch "worshipping the Devil" alongside other nurses. "A mob at Baltimore" was trying to capture, stone, hang, and burn them. Despite her soft spot for her ancestor the Salem witch judge, Louisa identified with the accused witches. Her uncle's experience of being hanged in effigy with Susan B. Anthony may have suggested the mob scene.

Hannah Ropes died in early January. Several days later Abigail and Bronson received a telegraph saying their daughter was near death. Abigail urged Bronson to depart for Washington without delay and bring her home. At the hospital on January 16, Louisa opened her eyes to find her father at her bedside. She went in and out of consciousness, and doctors informed him she was too weak to travel. However, a few days later, somewhat improved, she took a cab with her father into Washington, where Miss Dix met them and provided two nurses to accompany them on the train to Boston. "Enfeebled by her sickness and the long journey," Louisa spent a night with the Sewalls on Beacon Hill. Her father helped her onto the Saturday afternoon train to Concord on January 24, only six weeks after Louisa had left home.

Brief as it had been, this experience as an army nurse changed Louisa forever. It stole her health, which she had never before appreciated. At the same time, her wartime work fueled a remarkable literary productivity. To write stories, she no longer needed "to invent a clash of arms between a dark-robed scoundrel and a noble lord," Madeleine Stern observed. Louisa had "gazed on Truth, the never-failing source for storytellers." Years later Louisa would write, "I never have regretted that brief, yet costly experience . . . for all that is best and bravest in the hearts of man and woman comes out in times like those, and the courage, loyalty, fortitude and self-sacrifice I saw and learned to love and admire in both Northern and Southern soldiers can never be forgotten."

Louisa was one among hundreds of thousands of women whose professional lives were changed by the Civil War. With most American men engaged in the war, women were "taking over men's jobs in types of work that had not usually been associated with females," in hospitals, schools, newspapers, publishing houses, farms, government offices, and commercial firms, according to the historian Thomas O'Connor. Nevertheless, "It was clear that most men did not approve of 'the petticoats' moving into trades and occupations they traditionally considered the male worker's exclusive domain."

Publishing was particularly affected by the war. Centered in Boston, New York City, and Philadelphia, the field already attracted women because it was "a profession [that] could be made to look unprofessional," the historian Ann Douglas wrote. "It enabled its practitioners to do a man's job, for a man's pay, in a woman's clothes." Antebellum women writers had occupied a separate sphere from men, writing "pretty prattle" in which they were "discouraged from discussing politics or seeking literary fame." Nevertheless, women were "among the first to sense and develop [publishing's] business potential," according to Elaine Showalter. After the war "gentlemanly publishers were driven out by businessmen, who were indifferent to 'feminine' values and more interested in impersonal profits," and women writers came to see "themselves as artists rather than moralists."

On Louisa's return to Concord she could do nothing but sleep or rest. She was feverish, bald, frightened, and often delirious. Occasionally roused from her stupor, she complained of sore throat and exhaustion. She could not eat. She wanted to be left alone by everyone except Marmee, who often stayed at her bedside through the night. As she had done for Lizzie, Abigail now made nursing Louisa the center of her life.

Watching over her daughter, Abigail felt anxious but hopeful in a way she had not felt for Lizzie. Louisa had always been more vigorous than her sister. Josiah Bartlett, the family doctor, who came to see Louisa every day for weeks, reassured Abigail, "There is nothing against her getting well. All she needs is quiet and good nursing." With Louisa bedridden and Anna pregnant in Chelsea, Abigail needed household help, so May found her a part-time maid. In early February, according to Bronson, Louisa finally came "to her right mind." She was able to descend the stairs to breakfast on February 22, but soon returned to bed. She remained weak until late March, when she began to leave her room, join in the family's activities, and "clothe herself with flesh after the long waste of fever," her father said.

A few days later, on March 28, Anna gave birth to her first child, Frederic Alcott Pratt, whom they called Freddy. The new aunt composed a letter to Anna narrating Orchard House's reception of the news. Louisa, May, and their mother "were all sitting deep in a novel, not expecting Father home" from Anna's house in Chelsea "owing to the snowstorm, when the door burst open and in he came, all wet and white, waving his bag, and calling out, 'Good news! Good news! Anna has a fine boy!' With one accord we opened our mouths and screamed for about two minutes. Then mother began to cry; I began to laugh; and May to pour out questions; while Papa beamed upon us all,—red, damp, and shiny, the picture of a proud old Grandpa. . . . Father had told every one he met, from Mr. Emerson to the coach driver, and went about the house saying, 'Anna's boy! Yes, yes, Anna's boy!'" Six months later Bronson, who had pined for a son, boasted that his "little grandson . . . bids fair to grow and be somebody."

Abigail was overjoyed to be a grandmother. She delighted in the comings and goings of her grandson and the babies of her nieces and nephews, who were mostly married by the mid-1860s. Louisa both adored babies and also knew she was unlikely to have any of her own. Her books were her offspring, she felt, with regret and relief: relief because her literary creations gave her such satisfaction, and regret because she would have loved a family. As Margaret Fuller had described this paradox, "I have no child, and the woman in me has so craved this experience that it has seemed the want of it must paralyze me. But now as I look on these lovely children of a human birth what slow and neutralizing cares they bring with them to the mother. The children of the muse come quicker, with less pain and disgust, rest more lightly on the bosom," untainted with "earthly corruption." At the same time, as Louisa would realize after her sister became a mother, "I sell *my* children, and though they feed me, they don't love me as hers do."

Louisa experienced a burst of creativity as she recuperated from her long illness. In April, only a few weeks from her sickbed, she began a book based on the letters she had written to her mother from Washington, *Hospital Sketches: An Army Nurse's True Account of Her Experience During the Civil War*. Frank Sanborn offered to serialize it in *Commonwealth,* an antislavery journal published in Boston. Her jaunty description of herself in the preface to *Hospital Sketches* evokes a promise her mother had made to herself as a teenager, never to be found inferior to a man or incapable of anything. "I'm a woman's rights woman," Louisa wrote a half-century later in *Hospital Sketches,* "and if any man had offered [me] help in the morning, I should have condescendingly refused it, sure that I could do everything as well, if not better, myself."

When she was not resting or writing, Louisa received visitors. Samuel Joseph and his son Joseph, who was studying for the ministry in Cambridge, came to see her in May. Not long afterward Louisa spent "a pleasant day" with "Lottie May," her pet name for her cousin Charlotte, "& her boy," five-year-old Alfred Wilkinson Jr.

Hospital Sketches came out as a book in August 1863 and was received more positively by critics and buyers than anything she had published before. Her sketches had "uncommon merit," according to the *Boston Transcript*. "Fluent and sparkling in style, with touches of quiet humanity and lively wit, relieving what would otherwise be a topic too somber and sad, they are graphic in description." On walks around Concord, Louisa had "the satisfaction of seeing my towns folk buying, reading, laughing, & crying over it wherever I go." Her father remarked that "nothing could be more surprising to her or agreeable to us [than public] appreciation of Louisa's merits as a woman and a writer." But professional accomplishment was not always agreeable to Louisa. With a family to support, she told one publisher, she was impelled to devote her "time & earnings to the care of my father & mother, for one possesses no gift for money making & the other is now too old to work any longer for those who are happy & able to work for her. On this account I often have to deny myself."

Still, she loved to share with her mother her own amazed amusement at her success. "A year ago, I had no publisher and went begging with my wares," she said. Now three publishers "have asked me for something, [and] several papers are ready to print my contributions!" Sanborn told her that "any publisher this side of Baltimore would be glad to get a book from Louisa May Alcott." She detected "a sudden hoist for a meek & lowly scribbler who . . . never had a literary friend to lend a helping hand!" Louisa wrote in her journal, "Fifteen years of hard grubbing may be coming to something after all, & I may yet 'pay all the debts, fix the house, send May to Italy & keep the old folks cosy,' as I've said I would so long ago yet so hopelessly."

Louisa was herself again, Abigail observed with relief. Freed from housekeeping by illness and doted on by Marmee, she seemed hopeful, full of ideas, and eager to write. Abigail advised her to publish a collection of her popular stories, based on the printed copies she had saved. Boosted by her mother, she mined her war experiences in a short work of fiction, "My Contraband," that she set in an army hospital after the beginning of the siege of Charleston, in July 1863.

Like *Hospital Sketches*, "My Contraband" is narrated confidently by an army nurse. Louisa appears in *Hospital Sketches* as Miss Tribulation Periwinkle; in the story her alter ego is Miss Faith Dane. As the short story opens, a doctor asks Nurse Dane to watch over a new patient, a "drunken, rascally little" Confederate captain, "crazy with typhoid," who must be kept apart from Union soldiers at the hospital. "Out of perversity, if not common charity," she agrees. "Some of these people think that because I'm an abolitionist I am also a heathen, and I should rather like to show them that, though I cannot quite love my enemies, I am willing to take care of them."

In the teenage captain's room she encounters a slightly older servant, the "contraband" of the title, a former slave behind Union lines. The doctor describes the servant as "a fine mulatto fellow . . . too high and haughty" to be housed with "black fellows below."

Nurse Dane glances "furtively" at the "strong-limbed and manly" contraband, who has "all the attributes of comeliness belonging to his mixed race." Like the husband in Louisa's dream, he has a "Spanish complexion darkened by exposure." His eyes display "the passionate melancholy which in such men always seems to utter a mute protest against the broken law that doomed them at their birth." She wonders incessantly what he is thinking, and feels a love for him both maternal and romantic. She respectfully calls him "Robert" rather than "Bob." He has no surname, she learns, because he rejected his former master's. "I wanted to know and comfort him; and, following the impulse of the moment, I went in and touched him on the shoulder." Momentarily "the man vanished and the slave appeared."

A week later the doctor asks her to stay by the rebel captain until he dies. In his sleep that night, the captain cries out for "Lucy." To calm him "by following the fancy," Nurse Dane says, "I am Lucy." He murmurs that Lucy is dead; she "cut her throat."

The next morning Nurse Dane wakes to find Robert, who overheard their dialogue, preparing to kill the captain. Her "heart began to beat, and all my nerves tingled." The contraband reveals that Lucy was his wife and the captain his half brother because Robert is his former master's illegitimate son. The captain raped Lucy, who then killed herself, Robert now knows.

"Do not commit a crime and make me accessory to it," the nurse begs him. "There is a better way of righting wrong than by violence;—let me help you find it." Thinking of her New England ancestry, she wonders silently why Robert should "deny himself this sweet yet bitter morsel called revenge? How many white men, with all New England's freedom, culture, Christianity, would not have felt as he felt then? . . . Who had taught him that self-control, self-sacrifice, are attributes that make men masters of the earth, and lift them nearer heaven? . . . What did he know of justice, or the mercy that should temper that stern virtue, when every law, human and divine, had been broken on his hearthstone?"

Nurse Dane aims to use her clever tongue, "often a woman's best defense," to convince him not to kill the captain. "Do you believe," he asks her, "if I let Marster Ned live, the Lord will give me back my Lucy?" God will, she says, "in the beautiful hereafter, where there is no black or white, no master and no slave." Urging him to run away, she offers to "write you letters, give you money, and send you to good old Massachusetts to begin your new life a freeman." With her help Robert escapes to the North.

During the attack on Fort Wagner a few months later, Robert fights in one of the first all-black Union regiments, the 54th Massachusetts Volunteer Army under Colonel Robert Gould Shaw. At a Beaufort hospital Nurse Dane encounters "my contraband . . . deathly weak and wan." As he dies she notices his name written on a slip above his bed, "Robert Dane," and realizes that he has taken her name, as a woman usually takes her husband's. A similar reversal of tradition occurs in a story Louisa wrote three years later. In "Taming a Tartar," a confident young teacher subdues a tyrannical, chauvinistic man and then, after agreeing to marry him, vows to "love, honor and—*Not* obey" him.

Stories like "My Contraband" and "Taming a Tartar" were fun to write and easy to sell, and they paid the bills. Louisa published scores of thrillers with abolitionist and feminist themes in "penny dreadful" magazines throughout the 1860s. Melodramatic tales of murder, revenge, and interracial love affairs, like soap operas of a later era, allowed her to explore her recurring literary theme, sexual inequality. The central characters in these stories are angry, insane, or manipulative women who fight with men for power. "Alcott's feminism took the form of a power struggle between the sexes," Madeleine Stern observed. Androgynous pseudonyms concealed her identity, allowing her to live out her fantasies in secret. No one outside her family knew she wrote thrillers. Years later she told an interviewer, "I think my natural ambition is for the lurid style. I indulge in gorgeous fancies and wish that I dared inscribe them upon my pages and set them before the public."

Feeling somewhat improved after nearly a year in Concord with her family, Louisa began to plan a trip to the South. "I love nursing, and must let out my pent-up energy in some new way," she told a friend. "I am willing to enlist in any capacity. The blood of old Col. May asserts itself in his granddaughter in these martial times & she is very anxious to be busied in some more loyal labor than sitting quietly at home spinning fictions when such fine facts are waiting for all of us to profit and celebrate. . . . As I am no longer allowed to nurse the whites . . . [I will] help the blacks," cooking for troops or teaching freedmen on the Sea Islands. In the Carolinas she hoped to write a sequel to *Hospital Sketches* for the *Atlantic,* "Plantation Sketches."

The trip never occurred. Her application to teach was rejected "because I had no natural [male] protector to go with me." And her health remained unstable. Plagued by headaches, pain in her joints, and a weariness she could not escape, she was "a hollow-eyed, almost fleshless wreck," in Julian Hawthorne's words. Marmee's poor health may also have kept her home. Louisa observed in her mother an "irrepressible conflict between sickness and the May constitution." Perhaps this was an inherited condition that passed from Dorothy Sewall May to Abigail May Alcott to Louisa, a constitutional frailty they could not escape. Whatever the cause, the winter and spring found her at her desk revising *Moods* and working on another adult novel, this one about "the trials of young women who want employment & find it hard to get." In 1864 she sent the manuscript of *Moods* to the publisher A. K. Loring, made the cuts and revisions he suggested, and awaited its publication in December.

Moods was a disappointment to her, especially after the excitement aroused by *Hospital Sketches*. The novel neither sold well nor pleased many critics, although one review, in *Harper's Weekly,* compared Louisa to a neighbor whose writing she admired: "After Hawthorne we recall no love-story of equal power." Readers disapproved of the novel's love triangle and its unconventional portrayal of marriage. One reviewer alleged that she had based *Moods* on an actual love affair at Fruitlands between Charles Lane and Abigail, unaware that the affair, such as it was, was between the two men. "Some fear it isn't moral because it speaks freely of marriage," Louisa said of the novel, which in her view was "not a discussion of marriage, which I knew so little about, except to observe that very few were happy ones."

But Louisa's most important critic, Abigail, loved *Moods*. She read it more than twenty times, according to her journals. "I look upon this early effort of Louisa's as . . . quite remarkable. . . . Her descriptions of scenes [and] motives are admirable. I am charmed with it." Years later, after Louisa's remarkable success with *Little Women,* Abigail praised this "early effort," *Moods,* for its "indications of intellectual power hardly discoverable in any of her subsequent lesser writings" for girls.

Louisa, poignantly aware of her mother's thwarted ambition, dedicated *Moods* to Abigail. For Christmas that year, a full decade after making a gift of *Flower Fables,* she gave Abigail an early copy of her adult novel inscribed with a note: "I am happy, very happy tonight, for my five years work is done, and whether it succeeds or not I shall be the richer and better for it because the labor, love, disappointment, hope and purpose that have gone into it are a useful experience that I shall not forget. Now if it makes a little money and opens the way for more I shall be satisfied, and you in some measure repaid for all the sympathy, help, and love that have done so much for me in these hard years. I hope Success will sweeten me and make me what I long to become more than a great writer—a good daughter."

Abigail tried to stay awake all that night to read the new book. The next day Bronson read it and observed that Louisa "has succeeded better in her treatment of the social problem [of male-female relationships] than did Goethe or George Sand." Her style is "vigorous and clear," her theme dignified, and her characters "forcibly drawn. . . . She has written a better book than she knows, opening for herself . . . a career of wide usefulness, if not of permanent fame as a novelist and a woman."

Louisa's success was beneficial to him, too. It not only produced an income but also burnished his image. "Everywhere I am coming into importance . . . through that rising young lady," he wrote in 1864 in his diary. Recognized now as "The Father of Miss Alcott," he was "honored as never before." No one, he noticed, gave "the mother . . . her full share" of credit.

The author's mother was less sanguine about Louisa's future. Despite all that Louisa and the family had gained from her creative achievements since her recovery from typhoid fever, something essential had been lost. Louisa's vibrancy was gone. "I was never ill before this time, and never well afterwards," Louisa observed. To Abigail, writing in her journal, Louisa's mysterious affliction was "the bitter drop in this cup overflowing with success."

Chapter Fourteen

From May to March

A t Orchard House in January 1865, mother and daughter sat together beside the parlor fireplace. Abigail, wrapped in shawls and huddled in her comfortable chair, was writing in her journal, which her poor eyesight made challenging to read. Louisa sat nearby in her warm wrap, reading intently and occasionally stopping to write a quick note. Beside her was a stack of journals. There were ten, twenty, or more volumes of the diary that her mother had kept since 1811, one for each year. Abigail glanced at her thirty-two-year-old daughter the author with, one imagines, maternal pride and wrote, "Louisa is reading over my journals, from 1842, with many intermissions."

Louisa had often combed through her mother's journals for material. Indeed "Louisa learned to write from reading her mother's journals," according to Lisa Stepanski; "the biggest gift her mother gave Louisa was her voice." Louisa left no record as to why on that bitter January day she chose to start reading in 1842, the year she was nine. It was the year her father was gone for five months while she stayed in Concord with her sisters and mother. In the fall of 1842 Charles Lane and Henry Wright squeezed into Dove Cottage with the Alcotts, the beginning of the Fruit-lands debacle. That was the year in which her mother feared losing her mind and acted in a manner that later seemed "heroic." Eighteen forty-two was a time of drama, pain, loneliness, and triumph. Like Louisa's experience at the army hospital, this was something to write about.

Throughout the 1860s, while considering Abigail's powerlessness as a wife, Louisa populated short thrillers with powerful femmes fatales who "could manipulate whole families," scholars note. "Unbridled sensuality and principled struggles for equality vie in each [Alcott] heroine for pride of place. . . . Alcott's stories acknowledge that it is a man's world and woman must fight for a place in it. Losing her struggle, she must live alone or die uttering the battle cry of freedom."

In addition to these profitable tales, Louisa had begun another novel for adults, *Success,* which she later renamed *Work: A Story of Experience.* At the novel's center is a young single woman who ponders the questions, What is success? How do I create a meaningful life? She forgoes a traditional marriage, leaves home to work in the city, and asks only "for a chance to be a useful, happy woman." She tries every field a woman could—domestic service, nursing, teaching, and writing—and considers no marriage except that of equals. "Women who stand alone in the world, and have their own way to make, have a better chance to know men truly than those who sit safe at home and only see one side of mankind," she explains. "We who are compelled to be fellow-workers with men understand and value them more truly than many a belle who has a dozen lovers sighing at her feet."

Louisa's social criticism did not entice her publishers, so she always went back to churning out "rubbishy tales, for they pay best, and I can't afford to starve on praise, when sensation stories are written in half the time & keep the family cosy." Seventy-five dollars she received in February 1865 for a story called "A Marble Woman" made "things comfortable at home with wood, coal, flour, clothes &c." Poverty clearly motivated her "intense literary productivity," according to Madeleine Stern and Daniel Shealy. Louisa, like her heroine in *Work,* "tried every means then available of making money, from teaching to nursing, from domestic service to sewing, and especially, and always, writing." Louisa could only be satisfied when she had "paid up the debts . . . & made all things easy" for her parents. That spring she "paid debts of course, & went to work to earn more . . . sewed, cleaned house & and wrote a story." She was relieved that her mother, in her mid-sixties, could still enjoy reading, writing, and stationary housework. Bronson was also home that winter, having forgone his western tour because of his job superintending the Concord schools, which he would soon lose because parents complained that he did not attend church. Anna, who was pregnant again, often brought her toddler to visit his grandparents and Aunt Lu at Orchard House.

By April 1865 the Confederacy had fallen, William T. Sherman had marched across Georgia and South Carolina, and Robert E. Lee had surrendered to Ulysses S. Grant. After four years, more than six hundred thousand lives lost, innumerable wounded, and widespread despair, the Civil War was over. Less than a week after the surrender, President Lincoln was shot dead.

Three weeks later, on May 8, Lucretia May, who had become like a sister to Abigail, "nearer and dearer . . . than any female friend in the world," died at home in Syracuse, at roughly sixty years of age. It is unclear when Lucretia and Abigail had last seen each other, although Abigail noted frequent visits of Lucretia's children and grandchildren to Orchard House in the 1860s. Not long after Lucretia's funeral, Samuel Joseph visited with his wife's younger brother Charles Joy Coffin, according to a letter from Charlotte May Wilkinson to her brother. "Father . . . had a very touching time with Uncle [Charles, who] clung to him in a very affecting way & w[oul]d not let him go till the very last moment. Father said he seemed wonderfully like [our] mother. He came up in his room . . . in the morn and lay down on the bed and cried."

Samuel Joseph, in his late sixties, was unwell, too. He had difficulty walking and seemed "very delicate" to his old friend Garrison. Loath to rattle around his "Old House" on James Street Hill, Samuel Joseph invited Charlotte's family to join him. Like her unmarried cousin Louisa, Charlotte, the only May daughter, assumed the burden of caring for aging parents. Her banker husband, Alfred, had already "purchased the old but beautiful homestead now occupied by Mr. May—the house, grove, and eight acres of land, all for a little more than we gave for our birds' nest at Roxbury" near Boston, Garrison told his wife, adding that "Mr. Wilkinson must be doing a lucrative business." Charlotte, Alfred, their four small children, three maids, one cook, and two nurses moved in with Samuel Joseph, an arrangement that soon "exhausted" Charlotte, according to a daughter. The next year Charlotte and Alfred spent several months in Europe, courtesy of his rich father, who financed his son's increasingly lavish lifestyle. Their children stayed with Samuel Joseph, whom the grandchildren "adored," and Lucretia's sister Charlotte G. Coffin, who came from Boston to assist her brother-in-law.

Meanwhile, in Massachusetts, Abigail spent several months in the Chelsea home of her daughter Anna, who gave birth to her second child, John Sewall Pratt, in July 1865. This left Louisa to cook and scrub for her father at Orchard House. As she explained in her journal, "Mother passed most of the month with [Anna] so I had to be housekeeper & let my writing go." On one occasion, Louisa reported, her sister May agreed to "turn housekeeper" for a few months "when I offered to pay her $25," a third of her usual fee for a short story.

One sunny afternoon a band of Civil War veterans, replete with drums and fifes, marched along the road that passes Orchard House. Abigail, back from Chelsea, had set out fresh lemonade and plum cakes for them. The soldiers halted in front of the house and Louisa, who had been watching for them, became "the center and soul of the scene," her neighbor Julian Hawthorne observed. "Her greeting to the officer was cordial but brief; her chosen place was with the rank and file; she mingled and talked with them; those great black eyes of hers dimmed and brightened by turns." Talking with the soldiers, "she was far away on the battlefields and in the hospitals, amid the wounded and the dying. . . . A kind of grandeur and remoteness invested her simple, familiar figure. . . . During that ten minutes' halt she lived a lifetime." After the company marched away Louisa did not stir. "At last her old mother went up to her and put an arm gently round her waist. Then the tall girl faltered and drooped, and rested her forehead on her mother's shoulder; but she recovered herself quickly and passed hurriedly up the pathway to the porch of the old house and disappeared within."

That spring, according to Bronson, Louisa was "a good deal worn with literary labor" and eager for "some diversion to recruit her paling spirits and fancy." She dreamed of traveling to Europe, as many of her cousins were able to do. But a woman without means could not travel abroad without employment to pay her way. Margaret Fuller had first gone to Europe, at thirty-six, as a tutor. Louisa was now thirty-two. Learning that a wealthy young Bostonian named Anna Weld, an invalid, needed a paid companion for a yearlong tour of Germany, Switzerland, France, and England, Louisa, being "something of a nurse," accepted the post. She and Anna Weld and the latter's brother boarded a ship headed for Liverpool on July 19, 1865. The "dear home faces" of Louisa's cousins Lucy Sewall, Samuel E. Sewall's doctor daughter, and John Edward

May, who waved good-bye to her from the wharf, "made my heart very full as we steamed down the harbor & Boston vanished."

Louisa soon found Anna Weld "very hard . . . to manage," requiring "the patience and wisdom of an angel." For nine months they toured London, the Rhine region, and parts of Switzerland and France, ending up in Nice in the spring. On May 1, 1866, Louisa, having given her notice and found a replacement for herself, left the paid position, collected twenty-five dollars for the English publication of *Moods,* and wrote to relatives requesting money. Just before heading to Paris from Nice she received a hundred dollars from her uncle Sam, and other relatives likely contributed to her solo travels. In Paris she enjoyed a two-week romance with a young Polish man she had met in Switzerland. Then she returned to London for two months. "I suppose you will avoid [Charles] Lane" in England, her father surmised, correctly, in a letter.

At home in Concord, Louisa's absence left a crater. Bronson had returned from his annual trip exhausted. "The wicked West used you foully up," Abigail reproached him. He wrote to Louisa, "A little of that rare comfort which [Abigail] knows so well to administer will soon restore me. I find all [in the family] prosperous, [and our] debts never less. . . ." In fact, he was deeply in debt and eager for her return. He occasionally succumbed to guilt for not supporting his family. The previous year he had described "my wife over-burthened with household cares, and little [money] to do with. . . . Alas! I wish, for her sake and my children's, I could have had a pair of profitable hands and marketable wits." Still, his endeavors "in my Temple School and at Fruitlands" were divinely inspired; they "partook as largely of the spirit and ideas of the Nazarene Teacher, as any [endeavors] known to me in my time." But "I must pay the cost of such gifts as I have by . . . dependence on others."

Louisa, fully aware that a year was far too long for the Alcotts to be without their breadwinner, sailed home from England in July. "Dear" John Pratt, who was waiting on the wharf to meet her boat, accompanied her on the train to Concord, where she found her father, "Nan & babies [Freddy, age three, and twelve-month-old Johnny] at the gate" of Orchard House, "May flying wildly around the lawn & Marmee crying at the door." Louisa threw herself into her mother's arms. She had brought Marmee an olive-wood album of flowers and leaves she had collected and pressed across northern Europe. With it she gave Abigail a poem she had written:

> As children in the summer field
> Gather each flower they see,
> And hurry back with eager feet
> To lay it on their mother's knee,
> So I, by ruin, lake, and lawn,
> Found flowers in many lands,
> And gladly hasten home to lay
> My little nose-gay in your hands.

Abigail seemed "sick & tired," looking much older than Louisa remembered, and "Father as placid as ever. Nan [was doing] poorly," perhaps on account of her deafness, "but blest in her babies." Her sister May was "full of plans as usual." In her father's eyes, Louisa seemed "disabled" from her travels. She needed rest, he felt, to recover "strength and spirits for future works."

But there was no time for rest. Sensing her family's desperate need for money, Louisa set to work. Alone at her desk in her bedroom she imagined how it felt to be a woman locked in a passionate, brutal relationship, to consider murder or suicide, and to be compelled to torture her spouse. By the end of August she had sold a bodice ripper with a strong, vengeful heroine to *The Flag of Our Union,* which published it pseudonymously that fall. Jean Muir, in "Behind a Mask: or, A Woman's Power," is a governess of nineteen whose life was darkened by "some wrong, or loss, or disappointment." Driven to assume various roles in order to subdue powerful men, she exults, "There is a power in a woman's wit and will! What fools men are!" Like many heroines in Louisa's sensational stories, Jean Muir "uses the mask of femininity and the persona of a little woman to enact a devastatingly successful power struggle with a series of men who are clearly perceived as a single class and an enemy," Judith Fetterley observed. Louisa's ease in inventing such characters makes "clear the amount of rage and intelligence Louisa had." In the summer of 1867 Louisa allowed herself a short vacation with her sister May on the coast north of Boston, which she funded with half of a fifty-dollar gift from her uncle Sam. She "gave Mother the rest for bills." Several months later Abigail wrote Samuel Joseph a "painful letter," in his view, describing "all the [Alcott] family disabled." He promptly sent them a hundred dollars. Anxiety over money—where it went and how to earn more—plagued Louisa, too. "Bills accumulate and worry me," she wrote in her journal. "I dread debt more than the devil."

Thirty-five years old, Louisa had worked hard for twenty years. Still she did not have the luxury of following her grandfather May's familiar dictum, "Life is not given to be all used up in the pursuit of what we leave behind us when we die." Paradoxically, her own father's imperviousness to material objects had produced in her a lust for money. For years Louisa had been on a course antithetical to her grandfather's, using up life in the pursuit of wealth. Even as a teenager she had promised her friends, "I will write a good book, be famous, go abroad, and have plenty of money!" While she enjoyed writing and had earned more than anyone she knew, she feared that her success was coming too late to achieve her goal of providing her mother with comfort and security. She paid for an operation on her mother's bad eyes, yet Abigail remained "sick" and "feeble." Louisa wrote, "I never expect to see the strong, energetic 'marmee' of old times, but, thank the Lord, she is still here though, pale & weak, quiet & sad. All her fine hair gone & face full of wrinkles, bowed back & every sign of age. Life has been so hard for her & she so brave, so glad to spend herself for others."

Relief came in September with two offers of well-paid work. Horace B. Fuller, a Boston publisher for whom she had written, asked her to edit the children's magazine *Merry's Museum* for five hundred dollars a year. At the same time, an editor at the publishing firm Roberts Brothers, Thomas Niles, offered her the same sum "to write a girls book." He explained, "Lively simple books are very much needed for girls." Increased literacy among women in America, then estimated at 80 to 90 percent, had produced a new literary market. White women, according to the historian Barbara Sicherman, had "attained near literacy parity with their male counterparts, erasing a [significant] gender gap that had existed at the time of the nation's founding." In recent decades hundreds of female schools had opened. Women increasingly wrote textbooks, books of advice, poems, and novels. Nurses' influence grew after the

Civil War. Teaching, which had been largely a male profession in colonial America, was now 60 percent female. The "golden age of American children's fiction" had begun.

The idea of a girls' book did not thrill Louisa. Her first response, in private, was, "I could *not* write a girls' story, knowing little about any but my own sisters & always preferring boys." She told Niles, "I'll try," but accepted the job editing the children's magazine, which covered her expenses and paid her parents' recent debts. She "set up housekeeping for myself" in a Boston apartment on the top floor of 6 Hayward Place, which she called "Gamp's Garret," after a nurse in Dickens's *Martin Chuzzlewit,* near the office of *Merry's Museum.* May, who was painting and teaching drawing, joined her there for the winter. Louisa edited the magazine, wrote an essay on women's rights, and produced more pseudonymous thrillers for the editor Frank Leslie. She wrote a sentimental story for *Merry's Museum* about four sisters who donate their breakfast to the poor. She gave her fictional sisters her family's actual nicknames—Nan, Lu, Beth, and May. Louisa and May were "the two busiest young women in Massachusetts," their sister Anna wrote to a friend. "Louisa writes for a dozen different papers & magazines & is rapidly earning fame & fortune. Her European experience furnishes her with rich material, and everybody seems ready to buy everything she writes," while May "has settled down into a sober old lady, her whole soul absorbed in her art of which she is a most successful teacher."

The year began "cheerfully for us all," Louisa observed in January 1868. "Father and Mother [are] comfortable at home; Anna and family [are] settled in Chelsea; May [is] busy with her drawing classes of which she has five or six, and the prospect of earning $150 a quarter. . . . I am in my room, spending busy, happy days, because I have quiet, freedom, work enough, and strength to do it. . . . May and I are both earning." Louisa could even afford a housekeeper for Orchard House, refreshing Abigail's memory of luxuries she knew as a child. Learning at Christmas that Marmee "feels the cold in the Concord snowbanks," Louisa sewed her a flannel bathrobe. Louisa's health seemed restored. She accompanied her father to the annual meeting of the New England Anti-Slavery Society to hear a lecture by Wendell Phillips, her uncle's friend. "Glad I have lived in the time of this great movement, and known its heroes well," she said. "War times suit me, as I am a fighting May."

In February her father met with Thomas Niles in Boston to discuss *Tablets,* a volume of personal philosophy that Bronson had composed and hoped to publish. Niles mentioned his admiration of Louisa's "literary ability, rising fame and prospects," suggesting he might be more likely to publish *Tablets* if Bronson's daughter produced the book for girls. Bronson may have conveyed this to Louisa, who knew how deeply insecure her father was about his writing. "I wish I could write as I feel and think," he said in his thirties; a half-century later he added, "It [is] my settled conviction that I should not venture a sentence in print." Louisa may have concluded that she could help her father rehabilitate his image while earning five hundred dollars for less work than the magazine demanded. At the end of the month she "packed for home as I am needed there. I am sorry to leave my quiet room, for I've enjoyed it very much."

Meanwhile, Bronson commenced a flirtatious correspondence with another young woman. Ellen A. Chandler was a teacher of teachers at the Normal School in Framingham that Samuel Joseph once ran. At twenty-two, she was less than one-third Bronson's age and younger than his youngest daughter. He escorted Ellen to lectures and meetings and wrote to her, "I am delighted with my pupil's docility and could relish 'talking' long on such charming terms. . . . I am pleased too at finding an adept at dipping into books, and should like to get a glimpse at her. . . . Suppose she were to write me how that happens." He promised to attend a lecture by Emerson "on Monday evening when I hope to get a glimpse of your face again." He "value[d] her acquaintance above price." He praised her "charm. . . . I only wish—if I may write it—that you were nearer that I might partake the oftener. . . . My last Conversation I find gave much pleasure to a large and brilliant company. I only wished for a single young maiden." He sent Ellen a poem addressed to the "fair enchantress" who "reveals my youth's fond promise that my age conceals." Her visit to Orchard House was "the bright incident in my summer," he went on. "When young women cease to interest and charm me I shall know that it is time for me to withdraw from this world."

About two months after Louisa's return to Concord, she turned "the brains that earn the money" to plotting the book for girls. "Marmee, Anna, and May all approve my plan," she wrote in her journal in May. The plan was to create the happy family she had wished for at Fruitlands, when she was ten years old. The family would have four girls, like hers and her mother's. A single boy, more privileged and educated than the girls, would play a brotherly role. At the heart of the family would be a mother like Abigail.

The father would be a minister, away serving troops in the Civil War. The war seemed an effective backdrop because its effects lingered across America. Hardship was widespread in 1868. Families were decimated. Although the Thirteenth Amendment to the Constitution formally abolished slavery, living conditions for most of the four million people freed from bondage had not improved. The Fourteenth and Fifteenth Amendments gave black men full rights as citizens, but in truth they had few civil rights. Reformers who had worked together for decades were divided. Some abolitionists, including Garrison, felt "our work is done." Louisa's relatives and many others felt the battle was not over, that the war had not achieved their aims. Elizabeth Cady Stanton and Susan B. Anthony created the American Equal Rights Association in 1866 "to secure equal rights to all Americans, especially the right of suffrage, irrespective of race, color, or sex." Samuel Joseph, who organized an auxiliary Equal Rights Association in Syracuse, observed, "Had we such women as Lucretia Mott and Angelina Grimké in the Legislature, there would be more wisdom there than we have today. When I look through the nation and see the shameful mismanagement, I am convinced that it is the result, in part, of the absence of the feminine element in high stations." Samuel E. Sewall added, "The denial of this franchise is the most serious wrong done to women." At an 1867 Equal Rights Association meeting, the escaped slave and activist Sojourner Truth observed, "There is a great stir about colored men getting their rights, but not a word about the colored women; and if colored men get their rights, and not colored women theirs, you see the colored men will be masters over the women, and it will be just as bad as it was before."

In this time of chaos and upheaval throughout America, Louisa had an urge to create an idyllic portrait of family life, almost as if to salve the nation's wounds. Like her uncle Sam and her mother, Louisa was able to perceive injustice and to nurture and heal those who suffer as a result.

But before she began her girls' book, she had to give her fictional family a home. Louisa's childhood and youth had played out in a string of crowded boardinghouses and rented and borrowed homes, none secure. The girls in her story needed a stable home like the frame house on Federal Court in which her mother was raised, in a Boston that was a pretty country town. Louisa had fond memories of the minister's house in South Scituate in which she had spent several early summers, as well as the sprawling Victorian with the wraparound porch that she visited still in Syracuse.

Her fictional family also needed a name. May rolled off her tongue, but her own middle name, her mother's maiden name, would not do. She tried other months. June and July sounded strange. So did August. How about April or March?

As spring became summer the March family took shape. Her Christmas story for *Merry's Museum* suggested the opening scene in which one sister complains, "Christmas won't be Christmas without any presents." Louisa changed three of the girls' names: Nan became Meg, Lu became Jo, and May became Amy. Beth remained. They and their Marmee would manage triumphantly in a world devoted to "the gospel according to Abigail," in the words of Madeleine Stern. In addition to "temperance, woman's rights, and philanthropy," the Marches advocate "discarding medicine and the use of brown-bread pills instead, the substitution of new milk for strong coffee, and brown bread for hot biscuits. Dress reform that loosened tight belts and suggested the loose attire called freedom suits was championed, along with the three great remedies of sun, air, and water."

The book's heroine and Louisa's best-known alter ego is Marmee's tomboyish second daughter, Jo. A moody and imaginative young woman, Jo is a creative intellectual, a combination previously unknown in female characters in American literature. Jo manages her emotions by writing, as Louisa and Abigail did. She achieves a public voice by selling stories to magazines. Throughout the novel Jo voices dreams that Louisa and her mother shared: "I'd have a stable full of Arabian steeds, rooms piled with books, and I'd write out of a magic inkstand, so that my works should be as famous as Laurie's music. I want to do something splendid before I go into my castle—something heroic, or wonderful—that won't be forgotten after I'm dead. I don't know what, but I'm on the watch for it, and mean to astonish you all, some day. I think I shall write books, and get rich and famous."

The Reverend Mr. March is, as might be expected, largely absent from the book, appearing briefly at the end. The only significant male character is Laurie, the rich, charming, motherless boy next door who, according to Louisa, was inspired in part by several younger male friends. The quintet of Laurie and the March sisters evokes not only the May family of Abigail's childhood but also the five children at Fruitlands. There are hints of Colonel Joseph May in Laurie's imperious grandfather and in Mr. March, who has lost all his property before the novel starts. The sisters' judgmental Aunt March may be a partial portrait of Aunt Q. The story was "drawn from life," Louisa said later, "for I find it impossible to invent anything half so true or touching as the simple facts with which every day life supplies me."

During the nine weeks she spent composing the 402-page manuscript, Louisa felt "very tired." Her head was always "full of pain from overwork," and her heart was "heavy about Marmee, who is growing feeble." Abigail at sixty-seven was weakened by heart disease. No longer able to work outside the home, Abigail was severely restricted even within. As her world narrowed, her hopes focused even more on Louisa. When she felt well, she doted on her daughter, sewing caps to keep her warm and bringing her tea. When Abigail was unwell "she sits at rest in her sunny room," Louisa observed, "[which] is better than any amount of fame to me."

Louisa delivered the manuscript of *Little Women* to Niles on July 15. She admitted that it "reads better than I expected." In June Niles had found a partial manuscript "dull," and so had Louisa. Now, after showing the book to his appreciative young niece, Niles said, "[I have] read the whole of it & I am sure it will 'hit,' which means I think it will sell well."

A few weeks later, at his office on Washington Street in Boston, the publisher and Louisa discussed the terms of their contract. Niles offered her a choice: an advance of $1,000 and no royalties; or a smaller advance of $300 and royalties on each copy sold. She asked his advice. Years later she credited the "honest publisher" for suggesting she take royalties, which "made her fortune, and the 'dull book' was the first golden egg of the ugly duckling."

Niles made another clever suggestion. At the end of the book she could hint of a sequel. Louisa appended to the manuscript, "Whether [the curtain] ever rises again, depends upon the reception given to the first act of the domestic drama called 'LITTLE WOMEN.'"

It was soon clear that *Little Women* would have a sequel. Two weeks after its publication in October 1868, the first printing of two thousand books had sold out. Realizing its commercial appeal, Louisa immediately began Part Two. "I can do a chapter a day," she vowed on November 1. "A little success is so inspiring that I now find my 'Marches' sober, nice people, and as I can launch into the future, my fancy has more play."

Success did not allay her loneliness. "I never seem to have many presents, as some do, though I give a good many," she lamented that month on her thirty-sixth birthday. "That is best perhaps, and makes a gift very precious when it does come." Loneliness was a consequence of paddling your own canoe, she was aware. Marmee had been lonely, too, and perhaps that was worse, to be married and lonely. "I feel as if the decline had begun for her," Louisa wrote of her mother on the day Abigail turned sixty-eight, "and each year will add to the change which is going on, as time alters the energetic, enthusiastic home-mother into a gentle, feeble old woman, to be cherished and helped tenderly down the long hill she has climbed so bravely with her many burdens."

Bronson headed west again that fall, and Louisa had a "cold, hard, dirty time" helping her mother close Orchard House for the winter. Louisa was "so glad to be off out of C[oncord] that I worked like a beaver, and turned the key on Apple Slump with joy." She moved her mother to Anna and John's home in Maplewood, part of Malden, north of Boston, to spend the winter with them and their sons.

The working artists Louisa and May settled into an elegant "sky-parlor" on the top floor of the new Bellevue Hotel on Beacon Street in Boston, near their late great-uncle John Hancock's house. They had "a queer time whisking up and down in the elevator, eating in a marble café, and sleeping in a sofa bed, that we might be genteel." Louisa still felt poorly. "I was very tired with my hard summer, with no rest." But she still had work to do.

Innumerable readers sent her letters begging that the March girls marry, so she began Part Two with Meg's wedding to the teacher John Brooke. Louisa resisted her audience's drive toward marriage, "as if that was the only aim and end of a woman's life!" she told her mother. "I won't marry Jo to Laurie to please anyone!" Still, she satisfied her audience: by the end of Part Two all three surviving March sisters are happily married with children. "I haven't given up the hope that I may write a

good book yet," Jo March Bhaer says, "but I can wait, and I'm sure it
will be all the better for such experiences as" marriage and motherhood.
Like her creator, Jo must choose between marriage and a literary career.
In the world of *Little Women,* a woman cannot have both. Jo's mother
reminds her, "Hope and keep happy," and Jo thanks her for "the patient
sowing and reaping you have done." Marmee's seemingly satisfied reply
is "O my girls, however long you may live, I never can wish you a greater
happiness than this!" It is possible that for Louisa these words conveyed
some irony.

In many ways, *Little Women* accepts the very gender roles that
Louisa's mother had spent her life resisting. Jo and her husband start a
school that admits only boys. The twins born to Jo's sister Meg and her
husband could not be more stereotyped: "Daisy [the girl] demanded a
'needler,' and actually made a bag with four stitches in it; she likewise set
up housekeeping in the sideboard, and managed a microscopic cooking-
stove . . . while Demi [the boy] learned his letters with his grandfather. . . . The boy early developed a mechanical genius. . . . Of course,
Demi tyranized over Daisy, and gallantly defended her from every other
aggressor; while Daisy made a galley-slave of herself. . . ." Only the word
slave gives Louisa away.

In early January 1869, having sent off Part Two to Niles, she and
May "left our lofty room at Bellevue and went to Chauncey Street," also
downtown. "May & I are having a jolly winter boarding in Boston, she
teaching drawing & studying . . . I writing, editing and poking about in
my usual style," she told a friend. "My dream is beginning to come true,
and if my head holds out I'll do all I once hoped to do."

Louisa's head did not hold out. By March she felt poorly again. Her
joints hurt. She had pain in her head and her belly. Unable to sleep, she
displayed "that drawn tired look," May observed. Abigail urged Louisa
to come home. Bronson, just back from the West, "wanted his library"
at Orchard House, and Abigail "was restless at Nan's." So Louisa gave
up her rooms in April to join her parents in Concord, which seemed
"cold & dull." Still not feeling well enough to write, she "took care of
Marmee and tried to rest" as she awaited the publication of *Little Women,*
Part Two.

On an impromptu visit to her publisher, she found trucks, packing crates, and clerks swarming outside his building. Inside she found

Thomas Niles "curved like a capital G over his desk." Unnoticed, she stood quietly before him, thinking to herself, "Like the Duke of Marlborough, he is riding the whirlwind; something tremendous is evidently going on."

Seeing her there, he seemed to leap across the desk. "My dear Miss Alcott! You got my letter? No? No matter! Nothing to parallel it has occurred in my experience! All else put aside, street blocked . . . *Uncle Tom's Cabin* backed off the stage! . . . the triumph of the century!" The hubbub, it turned out, was for her book: three thousand copies of Part Two were already sold, days before its publication. "One leaves [*Little Women*] with the sincere wish that there were to be a third and a fourth part," a reviewer wrote in the *National Anti-Slavery Standard*. "Indeed he wishes he need never part company, with these earnest, delightful people." There "under the roof of a single New England home," another reviewer wrote, "could be discovered all the homes of America."

Niles pulled out his checkbook and asked Louisa what sum she desired. He anticipated selling twenty thousand copies by Christmas. Any amount, he said with a smile. That evening at home Louisa recounted her day to her mother, who was paring apples for a pie, and her sister May, on the piano stool. "Hard times for the Alcotts are over forever," she said. "I feel as if I could die in peace." Louisa paid all the debts, gave Samuel E. Sewall $1,200 to invest for her, and made sure Marmee had every comfort.

Her work seemed to be done. After "toiling so many years along the up-hill road, always a hard one to women writers, it is peculiarly grateful to me to find the way growing easier at last; with pleasant little surprises blossoming on either side, and the rough places made smooth," she wrote to Niles. Louisa's success vindicated her mother's hopes. Decades earlier Abigail had seen that her daughter was fond of writing and encouraged the habit. Her Lu had a nature too noble to curb, Abigail had said. There would soon be forty thousand copies of *Little Women* in print, more than any book by any male author of the day. For the first time ever, Odell Shepard wrote, the Alcotts enjoyed "comfort and . . . freedom from economic stress." Indeed they were rich.

As fiercely as Louisa had fought for success, though, she disliked fame. The pressure of an audience clamoring for more books for girls forced her to leave her true love, her sensational stories. In this way, according to Judith Fetterley, "the success of *Little Women* limited Louisa's artistic possibilities." Moreover, Louisa disliked celebrity. "People begin to come and stare at the Alcotts," she complained to Anna of the fans besieging her house. "Reporters haunt the place to look at the authoress, who dodges into the woods" to avoid them. "Success has its dark side," she realized, "& popularity is not half as delightful as it seems. Living in a lantern is very trying, to feel oneself suddenly dragged from obscurity to a pedestal, made public property." That summer she was determined to escape. She spent July in the village of Rivière-du-Loup on the Saint Lawrence River, more than a hundred miles north of Quebec City. This was the summer home of her second cousins the Frothinghams, of Maine and now Quebec, with whom her mother and uncle remained close. Frothinghams, like Mays, begat radical Unitarian divines. Louisa's slightly older "Cousin Fred," the abolitionist minister Frederick Frothingham, was a nephew of the ill-fated Samuel May Frothingham to whom Abigail had been engaged. Louisa and her sister May relaxed on Mount Desert Island in Maine during August. Niles reprinted *Hospital Sketches* and brought out *Fireside Stories,* a collection of Louisa's stories for adults, another best-seller.

Bronson was elated. His *Tablets,* published by Roberts the same month as *Little Women,* had sold well enough for a second printing and received respectful reviews. As for Louisa, critics across America now "place her in the first rank of writers of fiction," he said in September 1869. "It is an honor not anticipated, for a daughter of mine to have won so wide a celebrity, and a greater honor that she takes these so modestly, unwilling to believe there is not something unreal in it all. The public is not mistaken . . . and if she regains health and strength she will yet justify all her fame. I, indeed, have great reason to rejoice in my children, finding in them so many of their mother's excellencies, and have especially to thank the Friend of families and Giver of good wives that I was led to her acquaintance and fellowship when life and a future opened before me."

Even as he acknowledged his daughter's fame and his wife's "excellencies," Bronson still maintained a somewhat traditional view of women's role in society. "If women will only use their own tools simply and skillfully they may carry the world," he wrote a month later. "I don't like to see them taking to our [men's] ways as if all power lay in these. The platform and pulpit are efficient organs, but parlor and pen are still more, and graceful for women. An enthusiastic, intelligent, and earnest woman's eloquence in the parlor is irresistible. Let the women cultivate conversation and their day is sure to come." He had been bolder in *Tablets,* advocating that women "possess equal privileges with men."

In late October Louisa and her sisters closed Orchard House once again and moved their parents back to Anna and John's pleasant home in Maplewood. Louisa and May again took rooms, this time at 69 Pinckney Street in Boston, a few doors from the Louisburg Square home of their cousin, Elizabeth Willis Wells, who in the 1820s had been one of Abigail's orphaned charges. Louisa began writing *An Old-Fashioned Girl,* which, like *Little Women,* drew from May family history and began as a story for *Merry's Museum.* Its heroine, the humble Polly Milton, visits her wealthy cousins the Shaws, a noble Revolutionary War family, in Boston. The Shaws' teenage daughter rejects a suitor whom she does not love, as Abigail had done. Like the Mays, the Shaws lose their fortune, which frees the father from materialism.

Louisa, unlike Mr. Shaw, did seek greater profit. She asked Niles to raise her royalty percentage for the next book to 10 percent, three points higher than for *Little Women.* He refused. Around this time she made a strategic decision based on the market to stop writing thrillers and feminist tales and to produce more books for youth. Indeed, according to Sarah Elbert, Louisa "sought to distance herself from" her thrillers and feminist fiction so as to maintain her image as a children's author—a decision that doubtless undermined her posthumous reputation as a literary figure. The truth was, though, as Abigail observed a few years later, "The world craves entertainment, fun."

During the winter after the publication of Part Two of *Little Women,* Bronson spent five months touring fifteen cities across the United States. "Introduced as the father of Little Women," he wrote to his family, "[I] am riding in the Chariot of Glory wherever I go. . . . I have a pretty dramatic story to tell of [Louisa's] childhood and youth, gaining in interest as she comes up into womanhood and literary note." According to Frederick Dahlstrand, Bronson's audiences swelled because "lots of people were curious to hear about Louisa." Everywhere "promoted to the high places of honors on 'Jo's account,'" Bronson began singing the praises of poverty. "I can hardly conceive of anything more conducive to my spiritual advantage than the experience of those years at Fruitlands and return to Concord," he wrote in his journal during the tour. "I think I may say that my defeats have proved victories."

As the most popular author in America, Louisa now had the means to escape her family. She could afford to go anywhere and do just about anything. She dreamed of visiting Italy, which she had missed on her tour of Europe. She hoped to join her uncle Samuel Joseph on a trip to the South, a half century after his youthful voyage with his sister and her namesake, Louisa May. Niece and uncle planned to visit his friend Harrison Reed, Florida's new Republican governor, in Tallahassee that winter. The previous summer Samuel Joseph had presided at the governor's marriage to Chloe Merrick, an abolitionist and teacher from Syracuse.

But Louisa was "far from well," and traveled no farther than Boston that winter. She lost her voice and suffered from joint pain, headaches, boils, gastrointestinal pain, sore hands and legs, and swollen feet. A doctor cauterized her windpipe to restore her voice. She had consulted numerous medical experts over the years, and tried many treatments, including baths, massage, herbal remedies, homeopathy, iodine of potash, magnetic therapy, the mind cure of Christian Science, opium, and morphine. Her mysterious ailment, which twenty-first-century doctors conjecture was an autoimmune disorder, came and went and sometimes made her feel as old as her mother. Just as Louisa rushed home to nurse Abigail through every "sick-turn," Abigail nurtured and coddled her. Like an elderly couple, mother and daughter cared for each other as both experienced physical decline.

It had always been this way. In girlhood Louisa stood by Marmee when she abandoned Fruitlands. As a young woman she worked as domestic and teacher because her mother needed her help to survive. Now Louisa took pride in being her mother's best provider and helping her father realize his long-held dream of a public career. Like Edith Adelon in *The Inheritance,* Louisa would not break free from her family. She would continue as head of the household. Now and then, to be alone and work, she would rent rooms in Boston. She would have to find solace in writing, which allowed her mind if not her body to roam.

A $2,500 royalty check, the largest sum she had ever received, made Louisa's Christmas "unusually merry." The previous day, Abigail noted,

"S[amuel] J[oseph] and Louisa passed the day and night with us" in Concord. "Anna," who was visiting with her boys, was "full of hospitality, and 'kindness.' Uncle parted saying, 'Dear creature—lovely family—Goodbye darling.'"

Her heart full of pride in Louisa, Abigail continued, "The following notice appears in the Transcript of the 29th Dec. 1869: 'Her connexion with this firm of 'Roberts Brothers' has been most appreciable and profitable. Her book 'Little Women' has reached the 36 thousandth edition—a remarkable success for a book of so little pretension, and so free from sensational plot.'"

A few months later, a friend invited May on a European tour. Alice Bartlett, the only surviving member of a prominent Boston family, twenty-five years old and fluent in French and Italian, offered to pay for May's hotels, meals, and travel. May asked if Louisa could accompany them. Abigail's health was stable and she was happy to live with Anna and John while May and Louisa were abroad. So Louisa consented to join May and Alice as "duenna," an older chaperone, "hoping to get better."

She determined to make the voyage but feared the opportunity came too late. "I've lost the power of enjoying as I used to," she explained to Anna. "I get tired . . . very soon, and want to rest and be still. I feel so old and stupid and wimbly. . . . [I] only remember the weary years, the work, the waiting and disappointment" and feeling as if "the hounds were after me."

Chapter Fifteen

Welcome to My Fortune

S hall I stay, Mother?" Louisa cried, embracing Abigail, who had come to Beacon Hill to see her "girls" off to Europe. They were standing on the doorstep of the brick house on Pinckney Street where Louisa and May lived. The sisters, ages thirty-seven and twenty-nine, were about to "leave the nest," as Louisa put it. With Marmee's help they had spent a day packing their trunks. Now, on the morning of March 31, 1870, relatives gathered to say good-bye. Their parents and young cousin Louisa Wells, a granddaughter of Abigail's sister Eliza May Willis, were there, along with John Pratt, who would accompany his sisters-in-law as far as New York, where they would meet Alice Bartlett, their traveling companion, and begin their ocean voyage. Samuel Joseph, who was staying in Boston with his son John Edward's family, soon arrived with his niece Lizzie Wells, the mother of Louisa Wells. There were hugs all around.

Louisa couldn't shake the idea she might never see her mother again. Even if Marmee survived, Louisa—like Margaret Fuller—might not return. She "broke down," said, "We won't go," and held her mother tight.

"No," said Abigail. "Go!" She struggled to let her pale, gaunt daughter go. "And the Lord be with you."

Louisa released her mother and walked away, but "till I turned the corner she bravely smiled and waved her wet handkerchief." For Abigail, who had educated her girls, boosted their confidence, and encouraged them to explore the world, it was still agony to let them go.

Abigail and her brother parted that morning for the last time, it appears, although neither of them could have known it then. "At 11 I took leave of them," Samuel Joseph noted in his journal, "and walked across the Common to the AUA [American Unitarian Association] Rooms, 42 Chauncey St. There I lingered." Thinking his daughter and son-in-law were renovating his house on James Street Hill in Syracuse, he had spent several months in Boston, but he would soon return home to discover his lovely wood house razed and replaced by a new brick edifice. Several years earlier Charlotte's husband had mentioned to Garrison that he intended "pulling down the old house, and erecting a handsome edifice," but Alfred was not so explicit with his father-in-law. The new house was "fearfully modern," according to one of the Wilkinson daughters, "in that it had a bathroom, but only one, off my mother's dressing room behind double doors for fear of the emanations of silver gas from the pipes which in those days had no traps." Charlotte tried to make her father comfortable by giving him a study near the front door "so the miscellaneous lot who came to consult with him after his retirement—such as an ex-abolitionist, people interested in libraries (he founded the Syracuse Public Library), a couple who wanted to be married on the Friday the 13th of May by Dr. May—need not disturb the family life." Samuel Joseph donated thousands of documents concerning abolition to Cornell University so "the purposes and the spirit, the methods and the aims of the Abolitionists should be clearly known and understood by future generations." He told his friend Andrew White, Cornell's founder and president, that he hoped to leave the university his cherished oil portrait of his long-ago ally in school desegregation, Prudence Crandall. He had only one condition: Cornell must open its doors to women. As a result, Cornell began enrolling women that year, a shift that may have inspired Louisa's decision some years later to transform her fictional boys' school, Plumfield, into a coeducational university.

Two days after Louisa and May's departure from Boston, Abigail learned from John Pratt that her daughters had arrived safely in New York, met Alice Bartlett, and sailed for France. Their ship was *The Lafayette,* named for Aunt Q's old friend. "Let me gratefully acknowledge the propitious weather which prevails for my darlings—especially the poor invalid, Louisa," Abigail wrote in her journal. "Calm, bright, warm, Spring odors in the air; cheerfulness on every aspect."

"Poor invalid" or not, Louisa was America's best-selling author, as Niles informed Bronson that spring. No author anywhere had earned so much as Louisa earned that year. Her new juvenile novel, *An Old-Fashioned Girl*, came out on the day she sailed to Europe. Twelve thousand copies were already sold. In Syracuse her uncle Sam read the book cover to cover and remarked, "It is destined to a popularity almost as great as that of 'Little Women.'"

In a comfortable hotel in Dinan, a walled medieval town in Brittany, Louisa turned back to her task of describing just how she felt to her mother:

April 27, 1870 . . . I hope to stop aching soon. None of us are homesick yet but I often long for my marmee in the night when I fuss over my poor bones,
Adieu. Love to all. Your Lu.

April 29 . . . My Precious People . . . Stow away the $3000 [royalties for *An Old-Fashioned Girl*] when it comes and live on it as cosily as you can. Don't scrimp, Marmee; have clothes and good food and be as jolly as possible. Then I shant feel as if I was the only one who was spending money.

May 25 . . . We have . . . had fun about the queer food, as we don't like brains, liver, &c. &c. A[lice] does, and when we eat some mess, not knowing what it is, and find it is bowels or sheep's tails or eels, she exults over us.

July 31 . . . I am so tickled to wake every morning after a long sound sleep that I can't believe it is *me* . . . I can walk and ride and begin to feel as if a chain of heavy aches had fallen off and left me free. If this goes on without any [physical] break-down for a month or so I shall feel as if my trip was a brilliant success, and be satisfied if I never see Rome.

The trip was going well, far better than the trip with Anna Weld. In Vevey, Switzerland, in August, May wrote to Abigail from their large hotel room overlooking the lake, "As I lie in my bed till late these fine mornings, I imagine I heard mother saying at the foot of the stairs, 'Come girls, morning glories all out, and a beautiful day, breakfast nearly ready, come do get up for these are the most [lovely] hours of the day.' So I call to Lu, in remembrance of home, but we don't get up."

At four one morning in the Swiss Alps, as Louisa and her companions left a village in a horse-drawn carriage and cart, the traveling party seemed to her "something between a funeral and a caravan." It was "exciting, the general gathering of sleepy travelers in the dark square, the tramping of horses, the packing in, the grand stir of getting off; then the slow winding up, up, up out of the valley toward the sun, which came slowly over the great hills, rising as we never saw it rise before. The still, damp pine-forests kept us in shadow a long time after the white mountain-tops began to shine. Little by little we wound through a great gorge, and then the sun came dazzling between these grand hills, showing us a new world."

As was her habit, Louisa recorded many of her dreams and sent them home to her mother. Feeling healthier than she expected and perhaps guilty about being away from home so many months, Louisa enjoyed a particularly "droll dream" in Vevey. In the dream she was home in a Concord that felt strange. On the walk from the train station a familiar house was missing. Turning the corner, she "found the scene so changed that I didn't know where I was."

Orchard House was gone. "In its place," she wrote to her mother, "stood a great grey stone castle with towers and arches and lawns and bridges very fine and antique. Somehow I got into it without meeting any one of you, and wandered about trying to find my family." She came upon their neighbor Mr. Moore "papering a room" and inquired about the whereabouts of his house. Thinking her a stranger, he replied, "Oh! I sold it to Mr. Alcott for his school, and we live in Acton now."

"Where did Mr. Alcott get the means to build this great concern?"

"He took the great fortune his daughter left him, the one that died some ten years ago."

"So I am dead, am I?" she thought, feeling "so queerly."

"Government helped build this place," Mr. Moore continued, "and Mr. A. has a fine College here."

In wonderment, Louisa glanced into a mirror "to see how I looked dead." She saw "a fat old lady with grey hair and specs, very like E.P.P.," Elizabeth Palmer Peabody, a woman her mother's age.

Through a "Gothic window" she observed hundreds of boys "in a queer flowing dress roaming about the parks and lawns, and among them was Pa, looking as he looked thirty years ago, with brown hair and a big white neckcloth." He seemed "so plump and placid and young and happy." She nodded at him "but he didn't know me." Grieved to be "a Rip Van Winkle, I cried, and said I had better go away . . ." In the midst of this "woe" she woke up.

She analyzed the dream for her mother. She had just visited a lovely boys' academy in Vevey, which inspired the college. At a Swiss salon she had gotten a "top knot," talked about her gray hairs, and "thought how fat and old I was getting." She had shown friends a picture of her father, "which they thought saintly," she said.

"I believe in dreams," she went on, knowing her mother would understand. "I can't help thinking that it may be a foreshadowing of something real. I used to dream of being famous, and it has partly become true. So why not Pa's College blossom, and he yet young and happy with his disciples? I only hope he won't quite forget me when I come back, fat and grey and old. Perhaps his dream is to come in another [heavenly] world where every thing is fresh and calm," while "I was still in this work-a-day world, and so felt old and strange in his lovely castle in the air. Well, he is welcome to my fortune, but the daughter who did die ten years ago [Elizabeth], is more likely to be the one who helped him build his School of Concord up aloft."

Louisa fulfilled a waking dream in early November when she arrived for the first time in Rome. It was in Rome that Margaret Fuller had written war dispatches, worked as a nurse, fallen in love, and given birth to a child. Louisa did not expect so much of the city, no doubt, but part of her may have hoped. She would celebrate her thirty-eighth birthday in Rome, as Margaret Fuller had done not long before she met her Italian lover.

While Louisa and May settled into a six-room apartment with a servant girl on the Piazza Barberini, a crisis occurred at home. John Pratt, who had felt poorly for a few months, took to his bed with a bad cold. He developed pneumonia and on November 27 he died in Anna's arms. He was just shy of forty years old. They brought his body from Maplewood for burial in Concord on November 29, Bronson and Louisa's birthday. "It was a heart-breaking funeral," Ellen Emerson said, "all the more so for the calmness of poor Annie. . . . Freddy [age seven] sat at his mamma's feet. Mrs. Alcott didn't come, and kept Johnny [age five] at home with her." Bronson was in St. Louis on a winter tour that took him as far as Chicago and did not end until the following March. Anna moved into Orchard House, where her mother could help with the boys and solace her in her loss.

Louisa learned of John's death weeks later, at the end of December, when she read about it in a newspaper article in Rome. She immediately wrote to her cousin Lizzie Wells, asking her to "fill my place a little till I come [home]. . . . My heart is very anxious about mother & I ache to go to her, but winter, distance, health, & my duty to Alice [Bartlett] hold me till April. I think God will keep my Marmee for me because I couldn't bear to miss my Good bye & the keeping of my promise to close her dear eyes. Annie says she [Abigail] is not well & so I dread another loss before I have learned to bear the last."

The sad news from home impelled Louisa to finish another book for children, "that John's death may not leave A[nna] and the dear little boys in want. . . . John took care that they should have enough while the boys are young, and worked very hard to have a little sum to leave, without a debt anywhere," unlike her own father. She had "promised [herself] to try and fill John's place if they were left fatherless," and now she found that writing and thinking of them provided "comfort for my sorrow." The novel *Little Men* was for her nephews, Freddy and Johnny, "the little men to whom [the author] owes some of the best and happiest hours of her life."

This book, which she wrote in a room overlooking a Bernini fountain, was set at Plumfield, a school for boys run by her fictional alter ego Jo and her husband, Friedrich Bhaer. Plumfield is often seen as a nod to Fruitlands but may have had another inspiration. About a year before Louisa began writing *Little Men,* a school for orphaned and troubled youth had opened in Salem, Massachusetts. Called the Plummer Home for Boys, it was funded and named for Caroline Plummer, a wealthy,

intellectual spinster who at her death in 1854 had left large bequests to
Harvard for a professorship in Christian morals and to Salem for a Farm
School of Reform for Boys. Louisa may have read about the school's
opening or known of Miss Plummer though a relative or friend. Several years later her sister May would be close with a "Miss Plummer,"
perhaps a daughter or granddaughter of one of Caroline Plummer's
seven male Plummer first cousins. Louisa's nephew John Sewall Pratt
in 1909 would marry Eunice May Plummer. And reformers kept abreast
of each other's activities. Susan B. Anthony, who worked closely with
Louisa's uncle Sam, objected to the Plummer School's exclusion of girls.
"Whether in kitchen, nursery or parlor, all [girls] alike are shut away
from God's sunshine," Anthony wrote to a friend in Boston. "Why did
not your Caroline Plummer of Salem, why do not all of our wealthy
women leave money for industrial and agricultural schools for girls,
instead of ever and always providing for boys alone?"

   In June, having completed *Little Men,* witnessed the unfolding of the
Franco-Prussian War and a Tiber River flood, and enjoyed a few weeks
in England, Louisa prepared to sail home. Her mother, she had learned
from Anna, had been "ailing & despondent all winter," in need of her
Louie. On the theory that May "must be free and happy to cultivate her
talent," Louisa encouraged her younger sister to stay for another year of
studying and teaching art in London and Paris. So Louisa returned to
America alone. As her ship entered Boston Harbor, she could see her
father awaiting her on the dock. He escorted her to Concord, where she
found her mother "feeble and much aged by this year of trouble." Louisa
gave Abigail a wine-colored wool shawl she had bought in Europe and
vowed to herself, "I shall never go far away from her again."

   Anna painted a verbal portrait of her sister that day, in a letter to an
old friend. Louisa's "success has not spoiled her one bit. She is the same
old jolly generous simple Louie of your time, honest, outspoken and
quick, but the same warm heart, & straightforward goodness that made
her so loveable as a girl. The only change is the inevitable one which
age & sickness always bring & a certain elegance & stately grace which
we never thought to see in our topsy turvy boyish Louie. . . . She has
acquired an ease and polish which makes her (in my partial eyes) a most
beautiful woman." Anna felt tremendous relief to have Louisa home.

With John gone, Anna and Louisa would soon fall back into the supportive relationship they had enjoyed as girls and young women. Their bond was not unlike that between Abigail and her sisters and sister-in-law decades before.

Only a day after Louisa's return from Europe, the Alcotts received news that Samuel Joseph, age seventy-three, was "very sick at Syracuse." His daughter Charlotte was with him when he died, on July 1, 1871, leaving his sister the sole surviving May. The Alcotts learned of his death on the fourth. They were deeply saddened but Abigail could not tolerate a long train trip, Anna had her boys, and Louisa could not abandon Marmee, so only Bronson headed to Syracuse that afternoon. Abigail was unusually silent, Louisa observed, pressed "all the more into the embraces of her household, by this event." Alone with her journal, Louisa mourned "Dear uncle S. J. May . . . Our best friend for years."

On July 6, his "church could not contain the throngs who sought to attend the funeral exercises," a newspaper reported. Twenty Orthodox Protestant ministers, a Jewish rabbi, a Catholic priest, "an Indian chief and many colored people" filled the Church of the Messiah. Gerrit Smith called Samuel Joseph "the most Christ-like man I ever knew." Lydia Maria Child observed that he viewed women "not as charming creatures to be idolized for their personal attractions, or as helpless things to be condescended to on account of their weakness; but simply as living souls, into whom God had breathed the breath of spiritual life." William Lloyd Garrison, in poor health himself, paid tribute to the "Happy Warrior" who had been his closest friend. More than a century later, the scholar Catherine Rivard observed that "Samuel J. May had the unshakeable principles of Bronson Alcott without his crippling impracticality. He had Emerson's kindly temperament, without Emerson's distaste for humor. (Sam could be downright jolly.) He could stand up for an unpopular point of view without the noisy cage-rattling and often offensive tone of Garrison. Like Thoreau he was not afraid to take risks and appear different, but unlike Thoreau he was eminently likeable. Without any arrogance he could appeal to the gentle righteousness of people even while asking them to tear down injustice with firm purpose. In short, he had the best traits of the best of them." In 1897 Susan B. Anthony said, "Women suffragists to-day venerate Samuel J. May's

memory . . . [because he] took us by the hand and lifted us up," referring to herself and Elizabeth Cady Stanton. "It was he who helped the
women to grow into a knowledge of how to be and how to do."

Not long after his brother-in-law Samuel Joseph's funeral, Bronson
had a memorable dream. In the dream he was walking and talking with
the late Dr. Channing, to whom Samuel Joseph had introduced him in
1827. Channing was indicating to Bronson that Abigail was approaching
them "bearing a pail of water in each hand, tugging them up the lane,
leaving me to wonder where I was and why I was permitting her to do
what belonged to me." The dream suggests that Bronson felt he had not
carried his share of the family's load, unduly burdening his wife.

Louisa, settled back in Concord with her mother, sister, and nephews, could not avoid the effects of her celebrity, which she had largely
been spared in Europe. With more than 150,000 copies of her books of
juvenile fiction in print, she was besieged by "strangers swarming round"
Orchard House, Anna observed. In response, Louisa "panted for my garden hose and a good chance to blaz[e] away at 'em. Isn't it dreadful? . . .
O dear, what a bother fame is. . . . I hope the 'Jo Worshippers' were not
regaled with my [private] papers. Has the old box [of papers] ever been
nailed up? I squirm to think of my very old scribbles being trotted out."
From Europe she had warned Niles, "Don't give my address to any one.
I don't want the young ladies' notes. They can send them to Concord
and I shall get them next year."

She disliked adulation. "I can't entertain a dozen [fans] a day, and
write the tales they demand also," she complained. "Reporters sit on the
wall and take notes; artists sketch me as I pick pears in the garden; and
strange women interview Johnny as he plays in the orchard." She had
always felt "porcupiny," long before *Little Women*. In 1865 she described
herself privately as "busy writing, keeping house & sewing . . . & strangers begin to come demanding to see the authoress who does not like
it. . . . Admire the books but let the woman alone if you please, dear public." To her amazed father she seemed "almost indifferent to her fame."

Louisa's reticence impressed Lydia Maria Child. On a visit with the
Alcotts, Child admired Louisa's "straightforward and sincere" manner
and "hatred of lionizing" and "conventional fetters." Child never liked
Bronson but privately envied Abigail for having "such gifted daughters
to lean upon, after all the toil and struggles of her self-sacrificing life."

In contrast to his daughter, Bronson courted publicity, and in modern parlance he soon became her unofficial publicist. His yearly trip west became a sort of book tour. He spent four or five months in six or seven states delivering conversations on "Concord and Her Authors," foremost among them Louisa.

In her late thirties, Louisa had now accomplished the task she set herself at seventeen, "to make the family independent if I could." However, even though she often felt "frail," she could not rest. "As I still live, there is more for me to do." During the next fifteen years she rewrote *Work* for publication in 1873 (dedicated "to my mother, whose life has been a long labor of love"), revised and published a melodramatic novel called *A Modern Mephistopheles* (1877), published three short-story collections (*Aunt Jo's Scrap Bag, Proverb Stories,* and *Spinning Wheel Stories*), and composed five more novels for girls and boys—*Eight Cousins* (1875), *Rose in Bloom* (1876), *Under the Lilacs* (1878), *Jack and Jill* (1880), and *Jo's Boys* (1886). She also revised *Moods* for republication in 1882. While in her earlier version the heroine commits suicide at the end, in the revision Sylvia—like Louisa—lives on to develop a chronic illness and devote herself to the care of an aging parent. "At eighteen," Louisa explained, "death seemed [to me] the only solution for Sylvia's perplexities; but thirty years later, having learned the possibility of finding happiness after disappointment, and making love and duty go hand in hand, my heroine meets a wiser if less romantic fate than in the former edition."

On May's return from Europe in November 1871, Abigail rejoiced, "Thank God for these special mercies—My girls ALL home" under one roof. Orchard House would finally be warm in winter. Louisa was about to have a coal-burning, central furnace installed. "No more rheumatic fevers and colds," she vowed. "Mother is to be cosy if money can do it. She seems to be [cosy] now, and my long-cherished dream has come true, for she sits in a pleasant room, with no work, no care, no poverty . . . Thank the Lord! I like to stop and remember my mercies. Working and waiting for them makes them very welcome."

For years Bronson had pressed Louisa to write a book about his childhood and family life, as she had so often done for Abigail. To encourage this project, he gave her his letters and journals and shared "quaint" recollections. In 1872, to provide her "a picture for a background to her new story," he took her to see his boyhood home in Connecticut, where she had never been before and to which she never went again. She disliked it, remarking, "[I] Don't wonder the boy longed to climb those hills, and see what lay beyond." She told him she would try to write his book, which she would call *An Old-Fashioned Boy* or *The Cost of an Idea,* on one condition: "Pa, if you talk about Jo in public," she warned him, "I won't write 'The Cost of an Idea.' Say I forbid it, and don't cluck like an old hen over your ugly duckling." That year she showed him an account she had written of Fruitlands. "It surprises one by the boldness and truthfulness of the strokes," he felt. While she never completed *The Cost of an Idea,* she did publish her Fruitlands account several years later, under the title *Transcendental Wild Oats.*

Feeling somewhat better in the autumn of her fortieth birthday, Louisa moved to Boston to write. Bronson went west for the winter, while May, Anna, and the boys stayed in Concord with Abigail. "Another year is closing upon my life," Abigail wrote in her journal at the end of December. "The New Year finds us as a family somewhat separated. Mr. Alcott at the west. Louisa's in Boston. But having Anna and her children with us, makes us feel with May for our housekeeper, on the whole comfortable and happy; circumstances all easy and competent to the wants or even luxuries of life." Warmed by the furnace from Louisa in addition to the fireplace, Abigail mused on her character. "I fear little, [and] I hope much, for malice finds no place as an element in the composition of my character. I am impulsive but not *vindictive*. I love long, love much and hope to be forgiven." On the other hand, "My education was defective. My married life has been filled with trials. I was not prepared for it, and hardships I resisted rather than accepted or mitigated. I writhed under the injustice of society—and mourned my incompetency to *live above it*." Looking to the future, she continued, "If Louisa's health and capabilities for writing do not get exhausted, she has a fortune before her in her own gift. May has talent and industry to supply all her rational needs. Anna and her boys have got a good start in the world. Everything seems tending to independence."

May, who tended to even more independence, decided in the spring to return to England, to paint and draw. Louisa's goodbye gift to her May that spring was a thousand dollars. By late April, with her younger sister gone, Louisa felt obliged to go home to help Anna care for their parents. "Under Louisa's supervision our housekeeping for the last fortnight has sped quietly and tidily," Bronson wrote to Ellen Chandler in the summer of 1873. "And it is gratifying to find that she has lost nothing of her practical cunning while engaged in writing stories for the millions." It was not long before Louisa hired a temporary housekeeper so she could revise her unpublished novel *Work,* which sold twenty thousand copies when it came out later that year.

That summer Abigail became seriously ill, her mind clouded and her body weak. Fearing her mother was near death, Louisa spent weeks at her bedside. Some "dropsy of the brain [was] destroying her reason," Anna told a friend. "For several weeks she did not know us, or seem like mother. From this she at last recovered . . . [but] we feel that she will not be with us many years longer. Louisa, good soul, is devoted to her, and lives to provide, and lavish upon her every comfort & luxury. She pours out her money like water, and scarcely leaves her night or day . . . I sometimes fear [Louisa] will wear herself out. . . . She seems aged body & soul for a woman of 40 years." Although Abigail improved in August, Bronson was "not sure that Louisa can safely leave her mother even for a day."

Watching over her mother, as Abigail had watched over her, Louisa often sensed that she and Marmee were on parallel paths. Nevertheless, the world demanded Louisa's presence. Suffragists begged her to appear at their conventions. Not long after Abigail's recovery, her brother's old ally Lucy Stone, editor of the suffrage periodical *Woman's Journal* ("the only paper I take," Louisa said), wrote to solicit Louisa's support. After reading Stone's letter aloud to Abigail, Louisa asked her, "What shall I say to Mrs. Stone?"

"Tell her I am seventy-three," Abigail replied with what Louisa called "the ardor of many unquenchable Mays shining in her face." Abigail cried, "I mean to go to the polls before I die, even if my three daughters have to carry me!"

Louisa could not keep up with the public requests. "I am very lame & tied to my sofa for some weeks I fear," she wrote to the editor and writer Mary Mapes Dodge, who desired a children's story. "I am so busy with home affairs just now that I have no time even to think of stories. If I can get any leisure this winter I will try to send one or two [stories]. The state of my mother's health forbids my making any very binding engagements this year, so I can only say I will if I can."

In the fall of 1873 Louisa rented a large apartment for her three-generation family on Franklin Square in Boston's South End, at 26 East Brookline Street, facing the elegant St. James Hotel. Abigail enjoyed "the prospect of wintering in her native city," Louisa wrote to Bronson, who had already gone west.

Each spring the family returned to Concord. Anna and her boys spent summers now with John's relatives at the Pratt farm. Louisa and her parents lived in Orchard House. Bronson described his wife "reinstated in her chamber above my study. . . . She reads much, sews, as usual, and relinquishes household cares delightfully" to paid help or to Louisa. "I find myself inevitably alone much of the time," Abigail noted in her journal in early 1875, several months after May's return from Europe. "Louisa and May in Boston most of the time. Anna busy with her various duties. Not to be postponed for much gossip with the garrulous old Marmee. All right!!" she added, resignedly. "I am most comfortably situated, luxuries easily obtained, necessities anticipated. All in good health, fine weather . . . frequent letters, and propitious news from the dear old man at the West."

Abigail could finally relax and enjoy her old passions, reading and writing. "It makes me happy only to record all this. For a journal has its uses direct on the heart of the researcher." Considering her long habit of keeping a journal, she wrote, "I often feel happier after putting down some of my *own* experience than I do in *reading* much. Novels, even if they are good, pass out of my memory very rapidly. I enjoy it as I should a scene at the theatre; but am not essentially benefitted by the incidents or morals. What more desirable at this period of my life, than to find sources of daily peace and joy from within; that I think is true life. Let me not be selfish; but the best work done for others is that which proceeds from a contented mind."

For Louisa, it was fulfilling to see her old mother busily rereading old diaries and scribbling in a new one. As Abigail had difficulty walking, Louisa often invited her out for rides in a phaeton drawn by a horse named Rosa that May had purchased, partly for this purpose. May, too, enjoyed riding through the Concord woods "so deep and shady, . . . full of ferns, Solomon's seal, and field flowers . . . with the nice fresh smell so like the taste of wild strawberries," with "Marmee beside me," her "little crepe bonnet perhaps all on one side, but that handsome, pale face and soft hair so lovely to me."

One fair day in early 1875, as Louisa and her parents were driving toward the town of Lincoln, Abigail remarked to Bronson that Louisa's new book "surpasses its predecessors in power and brilliancy, and the author will not be easily recognized by its readers." Bronson, who had not read the manuscript or been told its title, was surprised that his wife had.

The new book, *A Modern Mephistopheles,* which only Louisa's mother had seen, was a Gothic thriller for adults, which is now believed to be the last sensational fiction she wrote. At the novel's center are a Faustian quartet—two men and two women, two young and two old—entangled by artistic longings, struggles for power, and sexual passion. The four are repeatedly compared to characters in *The Scarlet Letter,* a book that Louisa adored. There are indeed resemblances between Hawthorne's 1850 masterpiece and *A Modern Mephistopheles,* "Alcott's most elaborately disguised yet fullest disclosure of her artistic intents and purposes," according to Elizabeth Lennox Keyser. "By associating her artist hero, as well as his masculine and feminine alter egos, with Hawthorne's Dimmesdale, [Alcott] confesses that she, like that pillar of the patriarchal community, is an accomplished actor. . . . Dimmesdale time and again confesses publicly to his sin only to be canonized as a saint for his confession. . . . Alcott, too, repeatedly confessed her commitment to radical reforms for women only to be revered as a defender of [women's] traditional roles and values." Aware, perhaps, that she was and would be misunderstood, Louisa published *A Modern Mephistopheles* anonymously in Thomas Niles's 1877 No Name series. Reviewers "praised and criticized [it], and I enjoy the fun," she said, with a hint of irony, "especially when friends say, 'I know you didn't write it, for you can't hide your peculiar style.'" Ten years later, though, perhaps to reveal herself as a woman more layered than the "little woman" seen by the world, she reprinted *A Modern Mephistopheles* under her own name.

Another effect of Louisa's success was wealth, which enabled her to help relatives and friends. It was a pleasure, after so many years of accepting charity, to become a patron. She paid for several of her cousin Charlotte's children to attend college, sending Alfred Jr. to Harvard, and

Charlotte and Katherine to Smith. In 1875 she lent three sisters she knew three thousand dollars for the down payment on a house they wished to purchase in Roxbury, just west of Boston, where her seventeenth-century May ancestors had first settled. Of these sisters, the one Louisa knew best, Dr. Rhoda Ashley Lawrence, was a homeopathic therapist whom Louisa had encountered in her efforts to treat her long-standing ailment. Three years younger than Louisa, Dr. Lawrence was born in Lubec, Maine, the nation's easternmost town, trained in Boston as a schoolteacher, married and moved back to Maine, and had a son. A widow by her early thirties, Dr. Lawrence taught school before turning to the study of homeopathy and massage, which she provided Louisa. The doctor intended to start a convalescent home in the Roxbury house. "I very much want to help [her] . . . get a good start," Louisa explained to her mother.

"Life was always a puzzle to me," she observed in 1874, in considering her astonishing success. "When I had the youth I had no money; now I have the money I have no time; and when I get the time, if I ever do, I shall have no health to enjoy life. I suppose it's the discipline I need; but it's rather hard to love the things I do and see them [pass me] by because duty chains me to my galley. . . . If I can only keep brave and patient to the end."

Chapter Sixteen

Thou Excellest Them All

At nine in the morning on April 19, 1875, soldiers were marching, bands were playing, and it seemed the whole town of Concord had gathered to celebrate the centenary of the first battle of the American Revolution. President Ulysses S. Grant rode a barouche drawn by four bay horses at the head of the parade. The crowd was said to number fifty thousand, among them grandchildren and great-grandchildren of men who had fought in the war.

Louisa and Abigail arrived at the town center as men were taking their seats under a tent. The women were told to go to Town Hall, stand, and wait. After a while, Louisa asked a man if a few elderly ladies, including her mother, could occupy a corner of the tent until seats could be found for them. He replied, "They can sit or stand anywhere in the town except on this platform, for gentlemen are coming in to take these places." Another man "growled" at Louisa, "No place for women."

Women's participation in the celebration was limited to the festive ball that evening. Indeed at that point women had "six chairs apiece if we wanted them," Louisa remarked. Abigail had borrowed for the occasion the old Hancock punch bowl from a May cousin. She "enjoyed showing off the jolly old bowl immensely" at the ball, Louisa said afterward, "and I shall enjoy getting it off my hands still more" for fear of losing the cousin's "cherished treasure." Louisa had written to him requesting the loan, "Ma's dander is up and she is prancing like an old war horse, demanding that I should go to the ball as Madam Hancock."

The exclusion of women from most of the events angered both mother and daughter. "I was ashamed of Concord that day," Louisa said, echoing her uncle Samuel Joseph's remarks on racial discrimination: "I felt ashamed of Canterbury, ashamed of Connecticut, ashamed of my country, ashamed of my color." Two weeks later in an article in *Woman's Journal* Louisa predicted, "By and by, there will come a day of reckoning, and then the tax-paying women of Concord will not be forgotten. . . . Following in the footsteps of their forefathers, they will utter another protest that shall be 'heard round the world.'"

She was practically quoting Abigail, who, having failed to achieve female suffrage two decades before, was now composing another petition demanding the vote. "Women of this enlightened country," Abigail began, "Declare your right to freedom from Taxation without Representation and you will get it.

> You can do . . . as patiently and as wisely as the men of 1775. The parades and shot may be shared and the guns and glory less apparent yet if justice and righteousness *can* be reached a whole century after the men obtained *their* rights and the quarter of a century after the slaves obtained their freedom; 1900, shall witness women at the Polls, at Cabinet and Counsels of the Nation. By the side of the men, as aids to protect, legislate, to save the nation from Factions and Treachery. If ten men can do it, 20 wise, discreet, well cultured women can help them.

The women of Massachusetts were taxed without representation, Abigail pointed out. Citing recent state tax figures, she wrote, "In 1871 it appears that 33,961 women were taxed the previous year in the form of one million, nine hundred and fifty-three dollars." Concord's top female taxpayers included her daughter Louisa and Lidian Emerson. "This was nearly one eleventh of the entire tax upon property," Abigail observed. "This is an . . . extortion. Either the tax should be given up or the exclusiveness which surrounds the Ballot Box should be broken down." She urged "wives, mothers, daughters, sisters" to "protest, petition, clamor for the right of Suffrage. The vote is the power."

Abigail also proposed that women have educational and professional opportunities equal to men's. Young women should be "educated up to the knowledge of their rights." Having emancipated the slave, women "must work out their own emancipation. [Women] must help make the Laws, be educated as Jurists, Drs. Divine, Artists, Bankers. It will occupy and give dignity to their minds and lives. Rear for the nation beautiful girls and powerful boys. Learn to control their own homes, by love and discretion, never forgetting that the latter virtue is the better part of valor; and the proverb that he who controleth himself is greater than he that ruleth a nation." Abigail sent her petition to the state legislature, as she had done decades before. This time, with the call coming from the mother of Jo March, from Marmee herself, even more of Abigail's peers spoke out in support. "Our women are beginning to look after the justice of being taxed without representation, and are sending their protests," she said in early May, feeling hopeful. "They propose a convention to open the eyes of our women to the various degrees of Tyranny to which they are submitting." But her neighbors in Concord "seem wonderfully indifferent to the whole subject."

A few months later, the Massachusetts legislature "laid aside" Abigail's petition "with as little regard as the stump of a well worn cigar," she noted. Undeterred, she wrote seeking help from "our old friend Mr. Garrison." She hoped the petition might "be remembered for the next century as the test of our cause . . . for freedom to vote and liberty to choose our representative." Female suffrage would not come immediately, she predicted. "I cannot be here to see this, but I can leave my protest for my posterity."

Her posterity, meanwhile, continued to share the housekeeping and care of their parents. "Mother & Father are now 75," Anna wrote that year, "and their heads are snowy white, though their hearts keep young wonderfully. Mother is somewhat of an invalid owing to her extreme size, and inability to exercise, but she keeps very busy, still writes her diary as in old times, sews, and reads a great deal." Bronson, in contrast, was not even very hard of hearing. "With as few inherited ail[ment]s as most of my time," he wrote at seventy-six, "and these mostly held in check by habitual temperance during my later years (never indulged inordinately), I may possibly reach my hundredth birthday." He enjoyed gardening on "my little estate," taking tea with Emerson or dinner with Longfellow, corresponding with Walt Whitman, and visiting a fascinating young woman in Lynn, Mary Baker Glover, who is remembered as Mary Baker Eddy, the founder of Christian Science.

In October, renewed by her quiet summer, Louisa traveled to Syracuse to participate in a women's congress held by the Association for the Advancement of Women. She stayed with Charlotte and Alfred, who now had seven children, from seventeen-year-old Fred to ten-month-old Abby May, including a thirteen-year-old daughter called Jo, who had been named "Josephine May" after her grandfather, Colonel May. At the women's congress in the Syracuse opera house, "hordes of beaming girls all armed with Albums and cards" to sign begged Louisa to sit on the stage so everyone could see her. She signed autographs and answered questions but would not be "exhibited." With her cousin Charlotte she "finally had to run for my life."

Louisa spent part of that winter in New York City. More than ten thousand copies of her new novel, *Eight Cousins,* were already in print. Her health, according to her father, was "permanently restored." Rose Campbell, the heroine of *Eight Cousins* and its sequel, *Rose in Bloom,* which came out the next year, is a young woman blessed, it seems, with no parents and surrounded by male cousins who treat her as their equal. At the conclusion of *Rose in Bloom* Rose is happily married to her first cousin Mac, a more satisfying resolution to familial courtship than Abigail May and Samuel Frothingham experienced. Louisa herself attended a "co[u]sin dinner" one evening that winter at a relative's "fine" Upper East Side mansion. Louisa May Greele, "Mrs. John Sewall, E[dward B.] May, Alf[red], Lotty [Charlotte] & myself with the Goddards [her great-uncle Samuel May's relatives], made up the set," she wrote to her father. The meal entailed "seven or eight courses, canvas back ducks & green peas, venison & French messes, five kinds of wine & coffee & cigars." Most amusing to Louisa, relatives "who used to . . . [call her] an 'odd, grahamish, transcendental, half educated tom boy'" now greeted her as "Dear Louisa, old trump" and "My cousin the genius." She decided she felt closer to her Sewall relatives—the family of Abigail's mother—than to her May ancestors, as she explained in a letter to her "Blessed Marmee . . . Sewalls wear well & I like the breed better than the May."

Back in Boston in the spring of 1876, Louisa and her friend Maria Porter were seated in pews at the Old South Church as the abolitionist Wendell Phillips gave a stirring lecture on the need to save "this sacred landmark" from destruction. Old South, where many of Louisa's ancestors had worshipped and sung, was also the site of Judge Samuel Sewall's public repentance in 1697 for his actions during the Salem witch hunt. Louisa, "her face aglow with emotion," whispered to her friend, "I am proud of my foremothers and forefathers, and especially of my Sewall blood. Even if the good old judge did condemn the witches to be hanged, I am glad that he felt remorse, and had the manliness to confess it. He was made of the right stuff."

Two years earlier Louisa had taken her mother to visit another historic site in the city, King's Chapel. "A tablet to Grandfather May is put in Stone Chapel," Louisa noted in March 1874, "and one Sunday A.M. we take Mother to see it. A pathetic sight to see Father walk up the broad aisle with the feeble old wife on his arm as they went to be married nearly fifty years ago. Mother sat alone in the old pew a little while and sung softly the old hymns. . . . Several old ladies came in and knew Mother. She broke down thinking of the time when she and her mother and sisters and father and brothers all went to church together, and we took her home saying, 'This isn't my Boston; all my friends are gone; I never want to see it any more.'"

"And she never did," Louisa remarked later.

May Alcott, in her mid-thirties a serious painter working in oils and watercolors, hankered to return to Europe. In the summer of 1876 Louisa offered to pay May's way. Abigail encouraged her youngest daughter to go. During their goodbyes Louisa observed that May was "sober & sad, not gay as before. [She] Seemed to feel it might be a longer voyage than we knew. The last view I had of her was standing alone in the long blue cloak waving her hand to us, smiling with wet eyes till out of sight." On Saturday, September 9, Bronson accompanied May to the steamer in Boston and watched from the dock as she waved a handkerchief from the deck of the Cunard ship *China* until she disappeared.

With May abroad, Louisa's next task was finding a home for Anna and her sons, ages fourteen and twelve. The Thoreau house became available that winter after the death of the last member of that family, Henry David's sister Sophia. Henry David had died, in his forties, of tuberculosis, and Louisa and Anna had accompanied their father to his Concord funeral in 1862. The Thoreau house was a handsome, spacious colonial with a garden plot on Main Street, less than a mile from Orchard House. With Louisa's financial assistance, Anna purchased it on May 28, 1877, for $4,500. "She has *her* wish, and is happy," Louisa wrote in her journal.

"When shall I have mine? Ought to be contented with knowing I help both sisters by my brains. But I'm selfish, and want to go away and rest in Europe. Never shall."

Throughout the summer Louisa rarely left her mother's side. "I could not let any one else care for the dear invalid while I could lift a hand," she said, "for I had always been her nurse and knew her little ways." Sometimes Abigail still felt well enough to go out for early morning carriage rides with her. Louisa would coax Rosa to a spot where she knew Marmee liked to pick flowers. She would gather bouquets for her mother, who always replied with a smile. The little trips cheered Abigail, Louisa observed: "It keeps her young, and rests her weary nerves."

Jaunts with Marmee had a similar effect on Louisa, who thought she might finally have outlived her illness. Throughout June she kept house, attended to Marmee, and helped Anna to pack for the move to her new home.

In July, however, Louisa's symptoms returned. Too tired to write or do chores, she lay in her bedroom across the hall from her mother's, "happily at rest, wondering what was to come next." In August she forced herself to begin another juvenile novel, *Under the Lilacs*. Bronson felt she was well enough to serve as "our housekeeper during the summer mostly."

Abigail, her heart failing, slept most of the time. She was often so weak that she had to be carried in an armchair up the stairs. "This is the beginning of my ascension," she would say with a smile. Louisa, foreseeing "a busy or a sick winter," hurried *Under the Lilacs*. It was half done by early September, when Bronson—"the Concord sage . . . [and] Gifted Sire of Louisa May Alcott, the authoress of 'Little Women,'" who felt he had finally achieved "social standing" in "these later years"—commenced a solo conversational tour of New England.

Abigail had trouble breathing on September 7, while her husband was in Connecticut and Louisa was at her bedside. The doctor came and told Louisa that her mother's end was near. After the doctor departed, Abigail reached out to Louisa. "Stay by, Louie," she said, "and help me if I suffer too much."

How often Louisa had heard this . . . As a girl, when Marmee wept over having no money, Louisa determined to protect her. At ten, listening to her parents' discussions of a separation, she cried and vowed to stay by her mother. During her teens and twenties Louisa sewed, cleaned, taught, wrote, whatever would bring in cash. Her life and work reflected these very words: Stay by, Louie; help me if I suffer too much. Louisa and Anna called their father home, knowing that Marmee would want him there. In her mother's bedroom Louisa continued working on her novel. Even as she "forgot" herself to wait on Abigail, Louisa's brain felt "very lively" and her pen "flew," effects of stress she had seen before. "It always takes an exigency to spur me up and wring out a book," she observed. "[I] never have time to go slowly and do my best." She completed *Under the Lilacs* and wrote "My Girls," an essay about independent women that paid tribute to Abigail. It describes women successfully pursuing fields that had been closed to their sex. One, a doctor, "quietly and persistently carried out the plan of her life, undaunted by prejudice, hard work, or the solitary lot she chose." Another is a freed slave who teaches school. Yet another, a lawyer, "cleared the way for those who come after her, and proved that women have not only the right but the ability to sit upon the bench as well as stand at the bar of justice." And one is a "sister of charity," the very term that Abigail had used to describe herself.

On Abigail's seventy-seventh birthday, a sunny October 8, her two "girls," now forty-six and forty-four years old, built a pyramid of flowers on her bedside table. Her visitors that day included her niece Lizzie Wells and her adopted sister Louisa Greenwood Bond. Louisa read aloud a letter from May, with news that one of her paintings had been chosen for display in the Paris Salon. Once again she and Anna offered to send for May to come home. Abigail said no. Dr. Conrad Wesselhoeft, a homeopathic physician Louisa had consulted for years, was able to provide Abigail some "relief."

Louisa was so exhausted—"in danger of my life for a week" that month—she feared she might not be able to keep her promise to close her mother's eyes. She hired a nurse and forced herself to rest. By early November she was back at her mother's bedside around the clock. Abigail gave her the leather-bound King James Bible, published in England in 1803, that had belonged to her mother. Louisa undid the clasps to find inside its cover her grandmother's handwriting, "Dorothy May, 26th Sept. 1806," and her mother's "Abba May, Nov. 1825," a few days after Dorothy's death. Louisa added, "To LMAlcott Nov. 1877 . . . from her dearest Mother." Someone, either Abigail or her mother, had turned down a page in the thirtieth chapter of the Book of Isaiah that contained these comforting words: "For the people shall dwell in Zion at Jerusalem: thou shalt weep no more. He will be very gracious unto thee at the voice of thy cry; when he shall hear it, he will answer thee. And though the Lord give you the bread of adversity, and the water of affliction, yet shall not thy teachers be removed into a corner any more, but thine eyes shall see thy teachers."

On November 14, Louisa and Anna moved their dying mother to Anna's house, where it seemed easier to care for her. Louisa was to install a central furnace there, too. They carried Marmee upstairs to a sunny chamber with windows looking south, full of "flowers and the old fashioned furniture she loved," according to Louisa. Abigail said to her daughters, "The power that brought me here will take the kindest care of me wherever I may be hereafter." Closing the cover of a book by Samuel Johnson, "her favorite author," according to Louisa, Abigail added, "I shall read no more, but I thank my good father for the blessing this love of literature has been to me for 70 years." On Saturday, November 24, when her nieces Louisa May Greele and Lizzie Wells arrived, Abigail rejoiced to see the daughters of her late sisters Louisa and Eliza.

Louisa awoke at her mother's bedside on Sunday morning to a cold rain. She started a fire to warm the room and glanced outside. The leaves were mostly gone, the road muddy. Anna, Lizzie Wells, and Bronson joined her. All day, according to Bronson, Abigail "lay in a semi-conscious state, whispering to herself the unspeakable raptures she enjoyed as a foretaste of the bliss she was soon to partake in its fullness." Louisa thought Abigail seemed "very happy, thinking herself a girl again, with parents and sisters round her" at home on Federal Court, when she was the petted baby of the family. Early that evening Abigail looked up at her forty-four-year-old daughter and saw her own mother, Dorothy Sewall May, dead more than half a century. "Marmee," she said to Louisa.

Louisa reached down, embraced Abigail, and held her until seven thirty, when she "slipped peacefully away." As she had promised, Louisa stayed by and closed her mother's eyes. "She died in the arms of the child who owed her most, who loved her best, [and] who counted as her greatest success the power of making these last years a season of happy rest to the truest & tenderest of mothers," Louisa told a friend.

Thirty-five years before, at age ten, she had written the poem, "TO MOTHER, I hope that soon, dear mother, you and I may be in the quiet room my fancy has so often made for thee—the pleasant, sunny chamber, the cushioned easy-chair, the book laid for your reading, the vase of flowers fair, the desk beside the window where the sun shines warm and bright: and there in peace and quiet the promised book you write; while I sit close beside you, content at last to see that you can rest, dear mother, and I can cherish thee." Now she thought, "The dream came true, and for the last ten years of her life Marmee sat in peace, with every wish granted, even to the 'grouping together,' for she died in my arms." In her grief Louisa composed another poem for her mother, this one *in memoriam:*

TRANSFIGURATION

Mysterious death! who in a single hour
Life's gold can so refine,
And by thy art divine
Change mortal weakness to immortal power!

Bending beneath the weight of eighty years,
Spent with the noble strife
Of a victorious life,
We watched her fading heavenward, through our tears.

But ere the sense of loss our hearts had wrung,
A miracle was wrought;
And swift as happy thought
She lived again,—brave, beautiful, and young.

Age, pain, and sorrow dropped the veils they wore
And showed the tender eyes
Of angels in disguise,
Whose discipline so patiently she bore.

The past years brought their harvest rich and fair;
While memory and love,
Together, fondly wove
A golden garland for the silver hair.

Abigail was buried on November 27, 1877, at Concord's Sleepy Hollow Cemetery beside Lizzie's grave, where she had spent many hours. "Here I wish to be laid," Abigail had written in her journal several months earlier. "Although I often say it is of little consequence where we are finally laid in the flesh, for all is dust, and earth must receive our corruptible part; yet, I must own a preference . . . to rest among our kindred . . . even if we are insensible to the fact. After that the birds of the air, the dews from heaven, the Stars above us, even the snows of winter, are beautiful to contemplate as our companions in their seasons. The daisies will not forget to smile above me, and the sweet clouds of heaven moisten their throats with tender rain. Who can fear death and its consequences, if they have repented their sins, hope to be forgiven, and trust all to that power which created, sustained us here, and provides such beauty in the natural world to the end."

Lizzie was no longer alone, Louisa noted after the burial. She and Anna arranged a private memorial service at Anna's house the following day, at which Emerson sat beside Bronson and Lidian Emerson sat by Louisa and Anna. The Reverend Mr. Foote of King's Chapel read the Church Burial Service, and from Scripture the Unitarian minister Cyrus Bartol said her eulogy, and Garrison spoke fondly of "my first acquaintance with her and her saintly brother."

Not long after her mother's death, Louisa received a letter from Elizabeth Palmer Peabody. Noting that Louisa "must feel *identified* for ever more" with her "venerated Mother," Peabody recalled their friendship in the 1830s. "I lived with your mother in perhaps the most intense period of her suffering experience of life," Peabody wrote, "and feel as if I knew the heights & depths of her great heart as perhaps only you & Anna can do. For a few months we were separated by stress of feeling in most tragic circumstances—and she doubted my friendship. . . . But God gave me an opportunity to withdraw the veil & I have in her own hand her written expression of her conviction that I was *true to her* & her deepest worth *at that very time*."

Peabody attempted to sum up Abigail's character. "I have never known a great[er], more tender, more self-sacrificing human being; & it was all pure moral force & *character* for she owed nothing to the Imagination. . . . It was the tragic element in her that she could not *escape* on *that wing* [of imagination] the full painfulness of *experience*—There was no froth on the cup of life for her. It was all the reality down to its very dregs." Abigail displayed "uprightness & downrightness and plain speech—*but an infinitely tenderer heart*—such a heart as needs *the winged horse* which for fresh air takes daily excursions into the Ideal. . . . In all the time & especially the many years of the first part of the time I knew her she was too much without the 'Rose of Joy.'" Finally, Peabody addressed the relationship between mother and daughter:

> It was for you, dear Louisa, in these later years—indeed ever since you grew up, to gather these roses for her & crown her old age with them. You *understood* her—the first person perhaps who ever did sufficiently to do justice to her—Let me congratulate you—"Many daughters have done virtuously—but thou excellest them all." . . . I do not think I ever enjoyed anybody's fictions as I have enjoyed yours. I have enjoyed it in imaginative sympathy with both your father and your mother, but especially with the latter.

Louisa, staying with her father at Anna's house during those bleak early winter days, felt alone as she never had before. The person she loved best in the world was gone. "A great warmth seems gone out of life," she wrote in her journal in December, "and there is no motive to go on now." She felt adrift, almost as though she were a widow. Lacking the familiar, immediate goal of giving her mother material comfort, she said, "My duty is done. . . . No one understood all she had to bear but we, her children. I think I shall soon follow her, and am quite ready to go now she no longer needs me."

Chapter Seventeen

Stay By, Louie

Abigail's death reverberated in the London boardinghouse where May would receive the news a few weeks later, in a letter that Louisa wrote only hours after it occurred.

Sunday Eve Nov. 25th

Dearest May, Our Marmee is at rest after two months of pain and weariness as hard to bear as pain. A happy end, thank God! . . . Such sweet peace on her face now I wish you could see it. . . . I gave her a good-bye kiss for you. Yesterday she pointed up at your picture & said smiling "Little May," & nodded & waved her hand though only conscious at moments, then she looked up at us so sweetly & put up her lips to kiss us.

I wish I was with you my darling for I know how hard it will be to bear alone this sorrow, but dont think of it much till time makes it easier & never mourn that you didn't come. All is well & your work was a joy to Marmee. . . . God bless you dear, yr Lu.

May Alcott was now thirty-seven, long past the ordinary age of courtship for that period and "more than ever left behind in the race for matrimony," she had written to her family less than a year earlier. In the days after she learned of her mother's death, however, May grew close to a young Swiss man, Ernest Nieriker, who occupied the same boardinghouse. Ernest, who worked in a bank, was twenty-one years old. May told him she was only twenty-eight.

May had never seriously considered marriage, apparently, although she had been through what Anna referred to as her "75th love affair." Like Louisa, May feared that marriage would make her as unhappy as Abigail had been. But now Marmee was dead, and time and distance separated May from home and family. After a brief courtship Ernest asked May to marry him. In February 1878, less than three months after Abigail's death, May agreed.

She made a conscious decision to marry a man unlike Bronson. As May explained, "I think how [Abigail] married for love & struggled with poverty & all possible difficulties & came out gloriously at last, all the stronger and happier for so mastering circumstances, & this gives me courage, hoping her example will always be a safe guide for me. In my case it will be easier to be brave, because Ernest is a practical, thrifty business man; he is young, ambitious, with real faculty, instead of an impractical philosopher." A philosopher is "a man up in a balloon," Louisa once said, "with his family and friends holding the ropes, trying to haul him down."

The Alcotts learned of May's engagement only days before the wedding, which occurred on March 22, 1878, in London. No member of May's family was present. Somebody told Elizabeth Peabody that the Alcotts "do not seem to . . . like the marriage." Louisa sent the newlyweds a gift of one thousand dollars and observed in her journal, "May is old enough to choose for herself, and seems so happy in the new relation that we have nothing to say against it."

May and Ernest began their married life in a spacious Paris apartment with a studio in which she painted and taught, with a *femme de ménage* to manage the housekeeping. It was hard for Louisa to imagine May's married life, and when she did, it made her sad. "How different our lives are just now!" she thought. "I so lonely, sad, and sick; she so happy, well and blest. She always had the cream of things." Her jealousy toward Anna had evaporated with John's death. Now she felt resentment toward her sister who was happily married in France. Louisa hoped to visit May and Ernest, but did not yet feel strong enough to travel. Most of all, she missed her mother. "I need nothing but that cherishing which only mothers can give."

Her father asked her to join him in reviewing Abigail's journals and letters, many of which he had never read. With Louisa's help, he planned to "compile from [Abigail's] journals and letters a memorial worthy of her character." Aware that "biography is not in my line," Louisa spent months in 1878 rereading her mother's papers, her father at her side. Bronson found the experience unexpectedly painful. Abigail's accounts of him and their marriage filled him with shame. He had not known how unhappy she was. His "heart bled at the evidence of a long struggle for the first time clearly revealed," Odell Shepard wrote. Bronson observed that Abigail's papers "admit me, as daily intimacy hardly did, into the very soul of my companion, and . . . the memories of those days, and even longer years, of cheerless anxiety and hopeless dependence."

He decided to burn some of his wife's papers, particularly those that embarrassed him. There is no way to know the content of what he destroyed except to infer that it was less flattering to him than what survives. He also edited some of her papers and copied in his own hand portions of them to fill gaps in his own journals, which he intended to publish. "I copy with tearful admiration these pages," he wrote, "and almost repent now of my seeming incompetency, my utter inability to relieve the burdens laid upon her and my children during those years of helplessness. Nor can I, with every mitigating apology for this seeming shiftlessness, quite excuse myself for not venturing upon some impossible feat to extricate us from these straits of circumstance."

Unable to excuse himself, Bronson took consolation in the knowledge that his wife had found great happiness in her children. "Ah me! But it is past now. It is a sweet satisfaction that in her latter years she found in her daughters, if not in her husband, the compensations that fidelity to principles under the deepest tribulations always bring about and nobly reward. Under every privation, every wrong, and with the keen sense of injustice present, the dear family were sustained, the fair bond was maintained inviolate, and independence, a competency, honorable name, and even wide renown, was given at last. And but for herself this could not have been won."

Like her father, Louisa rewrote portions of her mother's personal writings and burned some of the originals, as she had burned some of her own papers and manuscripts, she revealed to a friend. "I . . . burned up a bushel of [my] diaries long ago fearing biographies when I was gone." Abigail's extant journal for 1842 displays some of Louisa's and Bronson's emendations. On November 29, 1842, Abigail had written of

Bronson, Lane, and Wright, "They all seem most stupidly obtuse on the causes of this occasional prostration of my judgment and faculties . . . [and are guilty of an] invasion of my rights as a woman and a mother." Bronson crossed out the word "all." Louisa, who wept when she read this passage, scribbled "Poor dear woman!!" on the margin of the page.

Louisa wrote inside the cover of another journal, "Leaves from Mother's diaries left me by her to use as I thought best. I looked them over and burned up all but these pages to be used for a life [biography] by and by. Burn these up if I die." More than thirty years earlier Abigail had observed, "I have serious objections to a Diary to be inspected after death, even if it could . . . help with exactness and truth." Pasted into another journal is a note she wrote on January 1, 1874, "To my Louisa! Beloved daughter—I place at the disposal of your judgment this, and all other of my Diaries; to keep for reference—or to destroy for safety— my hopes, fears, aspirations, have been uttered fearlessly—believing this utterance, or prayer or complaint should be known only to that power which can restore, protect, or relieve. May you Survive me, to consummate to perfection the work of Life you have so nobly begun, so successfully pursued, to generously share with those whose exertions have been thus far pursued with less success or reward. May you have good health as you have the good heart to live and love, *Long! Long!* [from] Marmee."

Another family member, probably Anna, later added the warning, "Do not loan this book or allow any use of it for publication. Keep in the family *always,* or *destroy*." A note on a bound volume of letters from Abigail to Samuel Joseph says, "Some [of Abigail's] letters have been destroyed by family as unnecessary and unsuitable for others' inspection—reflecting hardships and troubles often of a very personal nature." For the reader frustrated by this destruction and alteration of Alcott family documents, it may be some consolation to read in *Little Women* of Jo March's rage at her younger sister for burning a manuscript Jo has just completed. "You wicked, wicked girl!" Jo shouts at Amy. "I never can write it again and I'll never forgive you." Ironically, if not for *Little Women* and the renown it brought the Alcotts, they might have left all their personal papers intact.

In the fall of 1878, not quite a year after Abigail's death, Bronson informed Louisa that Robert Niles would publish their memoir of Abigail. In November Bronson gave the manuscript to Frank Sanborn "for criticism. . . . Mr. Niles is waiting to put it to press." Knowing that Louisa wished to travel to France as soon as possible to see May, he hoped "the Memoir will detain her with us till spring." The memoir was never published, and only a partial manuscript remains. Louisa reported in her journal that she "tried to write a memoir of Marmee, but it is too soon."

Louisa also penned a note requesting that all of her own journals be destroyed after her death, to protect her and her family from scrutiny. In 1882, four years later, she claimed in her journal to have "read over & destroyed Mother's Diaries as she wished me to do. A wonderfully interesting record of her life from her delicate, cherished girlhood through her long, hard, romantic married years, old age & death. Some time I will write a story or a Memoir of it." Having relied so heavily on Abigail's journals in her fiction, Louisa may have felt she already had. Several years later Louisa "sorted old letters & burned many. Not wise to keep for curious eyes to read, & gossip-lovers to print by & by."

In the fall of 1879 Louisa, who had hoped to be with her sister May when she gave birth, realized she was too weak to travel. "It is my luck," she wrote, mournfully, having to "[g]ive up my hope and long-cherished plan . . . I know I shall wish I had gone." Her father set off on an unusually short western tour to his Connecticut hometown and Columbus, Ohio, that enabled him to return in time for his eightieth birthday. Louisa, who turned forty-six on the same day, came from Boston to Concord to celebrate with him, Anna, Fred, and John. They were all together when the news arrived that May, attended by "the best accoucheur in Paris," had given birth to a healthy girl, Louisa May Nieriker, on November 8. "Two years since Marmee went," Louisa observed. "How she would have enjoyed the little grand-daughter & all May's romance."

Not long afterward they heard that May had a serious "brain disease." After the birth she had developed a high fever and fallen into a coma-like sleep, seldom opening her eyes. "The weight on my heart is not all imagination," Louisa said. "She was too happy to have it last, & I fear the end is coming. Hope it is my nerves, but this peculiar feeling has never misled me before." On December 31 a telegram from Paris arrived at the Emerson house in Concord. Emerson, infirm at seventy-six, read it, put on his overcoat, and hastened to Orchard House, where Louisa was reading in the parlor. No one else was home. Answering his knock, she knew from his face that something terrible had happened. "My child, I *wish* I could prepare you, but alas," Emerson said before handing her the telegram. "May is dead."

"I am prepared," she said, "and thank you."

May's death certificate cited no cause. American newspapers reported what Louisa believed and informed them—that May died of meningitis. It is more likely that May developed a generalized infection due to unsanitary conditions during childbirth, a condition called puerperal, or childbed, fever.

Early in the new year Louisa learned that May "wished me to have her baby & her pictures," meaning her paintings. "A very precious legacy. All she had to leave . . . I see now why I lived. To care for May's child & not leave Annie all alone." Like her mother six decades earlier, Louisa was expected to raise the child of her dead sister. On September 19, 1880, ten-month-old Lulu, as the Alcotts called her, finally arrived in Boston. This was another beginning for Louisa. She now had a child of flesh and blood, rather than of words. Lulu "always comes to me," she noted, "& seems to have decided that I am really 'Marmar.' My heart is full of pride & joy."

Unlike Abigail, who had cared for nieces and nephews in her twenties, Louisa was a sickly middle-aged woman. Her household consisted of two mothers, one baby, two teenage boys, an old man, and as many nurses and nannies as she and Anna desired. Each fall, Louisa and Anna closed the house in Concord and moved their dependents to Boston for the winter. Their burdens were shared. "Louisa's health still continues very uncertain, and the care of our large family falls upon me," Anna wrote in the spring of 1881, when they still occupied the former Thoreau house. "Although we have a faithful nurse" for Lulu, "either L[ouisa] or I must be always on the watch. I have a large house, endless company, a family of nine including three servants that are more care than all the rest put together. I am so busy."

In addition to everything else, Anna and Louisa shared a love of children. Not long after Anna's husband died, Louisa had written her a poem:

To Nan

I remember, I remember
A doll which once you had
A plaster head with numbered bumps
In long clothes sweetly clad.
And how you loved the funny thing
And bore it in your arms,
A tender mother even then
And proud of baby's charms.

Now living idols fill your heart
And be in your embrace;
Two yellow heads, bright-eyed & fair
Smile up in mother's face. . . .

Three weeks after Lulu's arrival from Europe, Bronson, hale at age eighty-one, departed again for the West. Anna described him as "perfectly well, busy & bright as a boy, enjoying a serene & beautiful old age," looking "far more youthful than his daughters who are thirty years younger." This winter tour lasted seven months, entailed conversations in thirty towns, and earned $1,200, more than ever before, according to Odell Shepard, "now that no one needed" it.

In the fall of 1882, six months after the death in April of his beloved friend Emerson, Bronson had a stroke, which incapacitated him. Lulu was now almost three. Each summer Louisa took her and her nurse to a house in Nonquitt, on the southern Massachusetts coast, to enjoy the ocean. Louisa was "entirely absorbed in her baby whom she loves passionately & on whom she lavishes all the strength & affection of her generous nature," Anna remarked. "It is beautiful to see them together."

Despite her love for her proxy child, Louisa never got over feeling that with Abigail's passing there was no longer any reason to live. She often wished Marmee were present. "I never go by [Orchard House] without looking up at Marmee's window where the dear face used to be," she said. As often as possible she visited her mother's grave, where an empty bird's nest she found one day seemed "a pretty symbol of the refuge that tender bosom always was for all feeble & sweet things." On

March 29, 1880, the first time women were ever permitted to attend the Concord town meeting, Louisa felt Abigail's presence as she became "the first woman to register my name as a voter" in Concord. She and nineteen other women voted for members of the local School Committee. "Next year," she said, hopefully, "our ranks will be fuller." She aimed "to stir up the women about suffrage," but they seemed "so timid & slow." That fall she was "ashamed . . . that out of a hundred women who pay taxes on property in Concord, only seven have as yet registered [to vote]. . . . A very poor record for a town which ought to lead if it really possesses all the intelligence claimed for it." Her father said he felt "much gratified in the fact that my daughters are loyal to their sex and to their sainted mother, who, had she survived, would have been the first to have taken them to the polls."

Around this time Louisa wrote a recollection of the gloomy November of 1848, when she and her mother and sisters "decided to move to Boston to try our fate again." With "the intense desire of an ambitious girl to work for those she loved," she had vowed to "do something by-and-by . . . anything to help the family; and I'll be rich and famous and happy before I die." She added, "So the omen proved a true one, and the wheel of fortune turned slowly, till the girl of fifteen found herself a woman of fifty, with her prophetic dream beautifully realized, her duty done, her reward far greater than she deserved." Louisa was rich and famous for sure, but happiness proved more difficult to achieve.

One of her late pleasures was mentoring admirers, mostly by mail. She encouraged one fledgling writer in a style reminiscent of her mother's: "There is enough in the facts to make a thrilling tale told briefly & dramatically. . . . Imagine you are telling it to children & the right words will come." To a Montana woman who wished to publish an account of Sioux Indians, Louisa wrote, "What is success given me after years of hard work if I cannot feel tenderly for others in need, & gladly help all I can. There is no more beautiful tribute to my books than the appeals that come to me from strangers who call me 'friend.' I wish you were nearer me. Write & tell me about the son. How old—does he like books, &c. I am 52, & an invalid but still able to do something thank God." Sounding like Abigail, Louisa added, "Hold fast, dear woman, to your faith, else all is lost. God does not forget us, & in time we see *why* the trials come. May He bless your loving effort & let me aid in its success."

To fans seeking tips, she quoted Michelangelo, "Genius is infinite patience." Many of her thoughts are near aphorisms, a gift her mother shared. "Everything in this busy world is so soon forgotten if let alone," she wrote to a colleague. "Never use a *long* word, when a short one will do as well," she advised aspiring writers; "express as briefly as you can your meaning. . . . The strongest, simplest words are best." To a curious colleague in 1887 she described her work habits: "My methods of work are very simple. My head is my study. . . . Any paper, any pen, any place that is quiet suit me, & I used to write from morning till night without fatigue when 'the steam was up.' Now, however, I am paying the penalty of twenty years of over work, & can write but two hours a day, doing about twenty pages. . . . While the story is under way I live in it, see the people, more plainly than real ones, round me, hear them talk, & am much interested, surprised or provoked at their actions." In her journal she was terser: "Very few stories written in Concord; no inspiration in that dull place. [I] go to Boston, hire a quiet room and shut myself up in it."

She carried on her mother's work for female suffrage. She appeared one day at the Boston office of *Woman's Journal* with a hundred-dollar donation. "I made this before breakfast by my writing," she told Lucy Stone, "and I know of no better place to invest it than in this cause." She wrote Thomas Niles, "I can remember when Anti slavery was in just the same state that Suffrage is now, and take more pride in the very small help we Alcotts could give than in all the books I ever wrote or ever shall write." She helped start a Temperance Society in Concord in 1882 and served as its secretary. Her letters often closed with the words, "Most heartily yours for woman suffrage and all other reforms," "Three cheers for the girls of 1876!" or "Yours for reform of all kinds." Her uncle Sam had frequently used the valediction, "Yours for Improvement in Everything."

In 1885, in response to widespread rumors that she and Julia Ward Howe had abandoned female suffrage, Louisa wrote to *Woman's Journal,* "It is impossible for me ever to 'go back' on woman suffrage." It is "a great cross to me that ill health and home duties prevent my devoting heart, pen, and time to this most vital question of the age. After a fifty years' acquaintance with the noble men and women of the anti-slavery cause, and the glorious end to their faithful work, I should be a traitor to all I most love, honor, and desire to imitate if I did not covet a place among those who are giving their lives to the emancipation of the white slaves of America."

Some day, she hoped, men and women could choose for themselves how to behave in public and in private. To her, women and men were fundamentally equal. She believed, with her mother and uncle, that gender is as arbitrary as race. She valued traits associated with both genders, and objected to the claim that women who support equal rights lose their femininity. "The assertion that suffragists do not care for children, and prefer notoriety to the joys of maternity is so fully contradicted by the lives of the women who are trying to make the world a safer and a better place for both sons and daughters, that no defense is needed. Having spent my own life, from fifteen to fifty, loving and laboring for children, as teacher, nurse, story-teller and guardian, I know whereof I speak, and value their respect and confidence so highly that for their sakes, if for no other reason, I desire them to know that their old friend never deserts her flag."

In her early fifties, Louisa sold her father's beloved Orchard House and returned with her family to Beacon Hill, the neighborhood her mother loved. The hill had begun its transformation to elegance in the year of Abigail's birth, when the real estate speculator Harrison Gray Otis began building "grand houses with beautiful gardens." By the 1830s, when the Alcotts lived in the slums above the wharves, "more than a third of Boston's richest families" resided on Beacon Hill. In 1884 Louisa leased a brick townhouse at 31 Chestnut Street, a street she had often visited in the hard years while boarding with her cousins Thomas and Mary Sewall at No. 98.

The following year Louisa moved into a lovely townhouse, No. 10 Louisburg Square, on a private garden square that replicated the tree-lined streets of the charming town in which Abigail was raised. In the early nineteenth century "proximity to a garden or other well-groomed green space made a building site highly desirable," according to Michael Rawson. Nine or ten servants helped her care for her "two babies," Lulu and Bronson, who never recovered from his 1882 stroke. With "both [of them] looking for me at once," she mused in 1883, "I feel like a nursing ma with twins."

Meanwhile, in Syracuse, her cousin Charlotte's husband, Alfred Wilkinson, who with his brother Forman ran a banking and investment firm called Wilkinson Brothers, was charged with grand larceny. The Wilkinsons had swindled more than half a million dollars, creating a "sensation in the city, as it had been supposed that their high social standing would protect them" from prosecution. Charlotte felt "utter surprise, shame, bewilderment, humiliation, and self-blame" to learn that her husband was "picked up in the street and brought home by kind strangers" because he had been "drinking too much and too long." She locked up her "table silver when not in use lest he sell it for whiskey." To support herself and her seven children, Charlotte opened a boarding school for girls in her home. Alfred was convicted of grand larceny but escaped imprisonment, presumably on account of family connections. Louisa's terse notation in her diary for July 28, 1886, was "A. Wilkinson dead. Relief to all."

In Boston, Dr. Lawrence, the homeopathic practitioner to whom Louisa had given a loan, still provided her with therapeutic massage. The doctor's touch reminded Louisa of her mother. "I have felt like an orphan ever since my mother went & with her the tender, protecting care which had been about me all my life," Louisa wrote. "Nothing takes its place." And yet, she added, "My mother is near me sometimes I am sure, for help comes of the sort she alone gave me."

Louisa paid tribute to Dr. Lawrence in the novel *Jo's Boys,* which she finished in 1886 on Beacon Hill. Nan, a "scientifically inclined" pupil of Jo's husband, cauterizes a dog bite suffered by Jo's son and treats him with homeopathic medicines. The adult Nan is a homeopathic practitioner and women's rights advocate. Dr. Lawrence, who studied at Boston University School of Medicine and graduated in 1885, worked closely with Conrad Wesselhoeft, the eminent homeopathic physician who treated Louisa for twenty years. Wesselhoeft, whose father had started the famous Brattleboro Water Cure in Vermont, was a graduate of Harvard Medical School and founder of the BU medical school.

It was Wesselhoeft to whom Louisa dedicated *Jo's Boys,* the last of the *Little Women* series. The figure of a dead Marmee hangs over the novel. Family portraits in a gallery at the mansion of Plumfield School hark back to Abigail's first family. "On the right, as became the founder of the house, hung the portrait of Mr. Laurence, with its expression of mingled pride and benevolence. . . . Opposite was Aunt March," in "her plum-coloured satin gown," and an "amiable simper on lips that had not uttered a sharp word for years." In "the place of honour, with the sunshine warm upon it, and a green garland always round it, was Marmee's beloved face, painted with grateful skill by a great artist whom she had befriended when poor and unknown. So beautifully lifelike was it that it seemed to smile down upon her daughters, saying cheerfully, 'Be happy: I am with you still.'" The three adult March "sisters stood a moment looking up at the beloved picture with eyes full of tender reverence and the longing that never left them; for this noble mother had been so much to them that no one could ever fill her place." A child was heard singing the aria "Ave Maria," as Marmee used to do. Louisa brought her March saga to a dramatic close at the end of *Jo's Boys,* when her narrator envisions "an earthquake which should engulf Plumfield and its environs so deeply in the bowels of the earth that" it can never be found.

Louisa, at only fifty-three, could no longer write. For more than two decades she had suffered from an unknown medical condition involving severe headaches, musculoskeletal pain, fatigue, vertigo, rheumatism, and rashes. Now she had severe dyspepsia with symptoms of gastrointestinal obstruction. She believed this mysterious condition resulted from mercury poisoning, a theory suggested to her in 1870 by an English doctor she had consulted in France. He had attributed her symptoms to the calomel administered to her in 1863 to treat typhoid fever. Medical experts now reject this theory because mercury is known to remain in the body no longer than about a year. "Mercury poisoning could not have caused her long-term complaints," two doctors who studied her records wrote in a medical journal in 2007. "We propose instead that Alcott suffered a multi-system disease, possibly originating from effects of mercury on the immune system," an autoimmune disorder such as systemic lupus erythematosus. Lupus is more common in women than in men, affects multiple organ systems, and is consistent with Louisa's symptoms.

That fall, unable even to care for herself, she left Anna in charge of Bronson and Lulu at Louisburg Square and moved into Dr. Lawrence's nursing home. At the Highlands, "a quiet retreat in Roxbury . . . entire rest, and care might give her the one chance of recovery that remains," Anna told a friend. The convalescent home was in a large house with a mansard roof and cupola on Dunreath Place, off Warren Street. Dr. Lawrence supervised Louisa's diet, read to her, and gave her daily massages and baths. Louisa occasionally rode to Beacon Hill to see her sister, nephews, father, and Lulu. Anna wrote to her twice a day, "morning & evening," and often brought the children to see her, bearing "flowers, books, and home news."

In the early summer of 1887, Louisa asked her cousin Samuel E. Sewall, who was retired from his law practice but continued to manage trusts, to draw up a new will. As the author of twenty-four books and hundreds of stories, she had a huge estate. Her royalties alone during the two decades after *Little Women* were equivalent to more than $2 million in 2000. Sewall arranged for her to adopt her younger nephew, John Sewall Pratt, so that he could renew her copyrights, which he would hold in trust. The income from the trust would be shared equally by him, Frederic, Lulu, and Anna. "John Sewall Pratt is now my 'legal son,'" Louisa said at the will signing. "A very easy process. I think I'll take a few more nice boys. Cant have too much of a good thing." She forgot to ask her elderly cousin what would happen "if John should die after me & unmarried what can he do about the copyrights? Adopt a child I suppose. . . . What a funny muddle a little money makes!" Dr. Lawrence witnessed the signing of the will, at which time Louisa canceled the long-ago loan to the doctor and her sisters.

Louisa's affairs settled, she took a vacation, accompanied by Dr. Lawrence, in Princeton, Massachusetts. She stayed at the Bullard Mountain House, overlooking Mount Wachusett, which Abigail had pointed out to her from Fruitlands forty-four years before. From the lodge she wrote a touching letter to her two nephews. "I have tried to spare you any probably future trouble which may arise from complications in regard to my money. If my wishes seem not unwise or impossible, I know you *will* respect and carry them out. Should conditions now unforeseen arise, I leave it to your judgment to arrange otherwise, believing the living can often judge better than any foresight of another 'gone before.' And my dearest boys, pray continue to be near each other, and live in harmony and good brotherhood, for the sake of MOTHER." Anna, for her part, despaired at the prospect of losing the last surviving member of her first family. "I have little hope," Anna told a friend, "that [Louisa]will ever be well. . . . She will not return home for a long time I fear. The household worries try her nerves, and she is better alone," but this "has been one of the saddest experiences of my life."

In October, when a new edition of *Flower Fables* minus some "plentiful adjectives" came out, Louisa longed to send her own mother a copy, as she had always done with each new book. Instead she sent the book to her mother's closest living female relative, Abigail's adoptive sister Louisa Greenwood Bond, who had been present at Abigail's final birthday a decade earlier. "I always gave Mother the first author's copy of a new book," Louisa explained to her aunt Bond. "As [you are] her representative on earth, may I send you, with my love, the little book to come out in November? The tales were told at sixteen to May and her playmates; then are related to May's daughter at five."

A doctor who was treating Louisa's ailments with plant-based remedies reassured her in November, "All is well."

"Now the oyster will go into her shell again," Louisa said to him.

"You mustn't call yourself that when you're doing so nicely. We will have some more fine books in a year or two."

"Do you honestly think so? I never expect to be well again, only patched up for a while. At fifty-five one doesn't hope for much."

Just before Christmas Louisa wrote to her friend and fellow author Mary Mapes Dodge, "I mend slowly but surely, & my good Dr. says my best work is yet to come. I will be content with health if I can get it." On New Year's Eve she wrote again to ask Dodge to consider publishing in her children's magazine a "well-written . . . pretty good" story by "my little cousin" Valentine, the thirteen-year-old daughter of John Edward May. This "grandchild of S. J. May" was a "bright lass who paints nicely & is a domestic little person in spite of her budding accomplishments . . . [who] longs to see it in print."

Louisa "improved all winter," Anna wrote hopefully to a friend, although her sister looked thin and frail. "We let ourselves hope." Louisa felt her only remaining hope was God, who had been revealed to her through poverty and pain, she wrote to a friend. She believed that the last veil separating her from God's love had been rent by sorrow when her mother died. Now, whenever she cried for Marmee, she felt God's presence. Faith "needs no logic, no preaching to make me SURE of it. The instinct is there & following it as fast as one can brings the fact home at last in a way that cannot be doubted."

On March 1, 1888, Louisa took a coach to Louisburg Square to see her eighty-eight-year-old father, who appeared to be dying. In his bedroom she knelt so her head was near his. "Father, here is your Louie. What are you thinking of?"

"Going *up,*" he said. "Come with me."

"Oh, I wish I could." Her oldest wish was to unite her father and mother in repose.

"Over all these years, serenely prosperous . . . still rises that dead image of my mother, still echoes that spectral whisper in the dark." These words, written in 1863 while she studied her mother's journals, conclude the story "A Whisper in the Dark"—which Frank Leslie paid forty dollars to publish pseudonymously in his *Illustrated Newspaper*— about a young woman victimized and enslaved by an older man. Sybil, the narrator, is a "willful," passionately independent, orphaned teenager who learns that her late father—like Abigail's—wanted her to marry her first cousin, Guy. Sybil says to Guy, who has offered to host parties for her, "I don't care for society, and strangers wouldn't make it gay to me, for I like freedom." The teenage Abigail had written, "I never cared much for society. Parties I disliked."

Intrigued by Guy, Sybil resolves to "try my power over" him. Like the adolescent Abigail, she is moody and rebellious. "What right had my father [to] mate me in my cradle? How did he know what I should become, or Guy? How could he tell that I should not love someone else better? No! I'll not be bargained away like a piece of merchandise, but love and marry when I please!"

Before the cousins' relationship is resolved, Sybil's middle-aged uncle, Guy's father, who covets her inheritance, attempts to marry her himself in spite of their thirty-year age difference. She rejects him. Furious, he locks her in her bedroom, drugs her into unconscious- ness, and imprisons her in a distant mansion. She awakes in a locked, barred room. Her hair is cut off, as Louisa's had been during her bout of typhoid fever. "For many weeks I lay burning in a fitful fever, con- scious . . . and rose at last a shadow of my former self, feeling pitifully broken."

Sybil hears a voice whispering at her door, and muffled sounds from the room above hers. She thinks her uncle has imprisoned someone else, too. Allowed to roam the mansion, she is drawn upstairs to the myste- rious room, which is locked and guarded by a hound dog. The room "haunted me continually, and soon became a sort of monomania, which I condemned, yet could not control, till at length I found myself pacing to and fro as those invisible feet paced overhead."

On Sybil's eighteenth birthday her uncle comes to claim her and her inheritance. Unable to flee, she resolves to kill herself because the "death of the body was far preferable to that of the mind." Briefly left unattended, she returns to the mysterious room, now unlocked. Entering, she finds on the bed the body of her mother, whom her uncle also imprisoned. Sybil feels she has discovered herself: "It was a room like mine, the carpet worn like mine, the windows barred like mine. . . .

> An empty cradle stood beside the bed, and on that bed . . . a lifeless body lay. . . . An irresistible desire led me close, nerved me to lift the cover and look below. . . . [T]he face I saw was a pale image of my own. Sharpened by suffering, pallid with death, the features were familiar as those I used to see; the hair, beautiful and blond as mine had been, streamed long over the pulseless breast, and on the hand, still clenched in that last struggle, shone the likeness of a ring I wore, a ring bequeathed me by my father. An awesome fancy that it was myself assailed me; I had plotted death, and with the waywardness of a shattered mind, I recalled legends of spirits returning to behold the bodies they had left.

Sybil finds a note her mother wrote to her but failed to deliver. "I implore you to leave this house before it is too late. Run away. Be free." Finally able to escape from her uncle, Sybil is "saved" by Guy, whom she marries. But this hasty resolution does not leave her happy. She is haunted by the memory of her mother, as Louisa was. "Over all these years, serenely prosperous, still hangs for me the shadow of the past, still rises that dead image of my mother."

Exhausted by her visit with her father, Louisa returned to her bed at the Highlands. She had lost more than thirty pounds since the fall. She was not at her father's side when he died, on Sunday, March 4, at the house on Louisburg Square, and may not have even known he died. It seemed to Anna, though, that "with his departure her last earthly care left her, & she felt free to follow, & be at rest."

Anna was called to the Highlands that day. Louisa "had taken ill the afternoon before," complaining of a pain like a huge weight on her head, which suggests she had a stroke, or cerebral hemorrhage. She grew "rapidly worse, and lay unconscious" by the time Anna arrived. "She never knew me, but drifted quietly away as she had always prayed she might. Painless, & unaware of her condition, and our grief, she lay till early Tuesday morning," March 6, 1888, "when just at dawn without a sigh she passed away." Fifty-five years old, Louisa had been in poor health nearly half her life.

"The loss of this talented writer will be felt far and wide among the many readers of her favorite books," the *New York Times* announced the next morning in a page-one obituary. The packaging of Louisa as a little woman—schoolteacher, nurse, and writer, devoted to the care of her parents—began immediately, along with the idea that her mother was irrelevant. "She was educated as a school teacher under the tutelage of her father and Henry D. Thoreau," the *Times* continued. "Mr. Alcott was stricken with paralysis in 1882, and since that time and up to that of her own fatal illness, she was his constant and loving nurse."

Anna, at fifty-seven "the only standby of this large family," in her words, was the last surviving Alcott. Like Abigail and Louisa, she found it "hard to be happy without mother or sisters." Fred and John Pratt were in their twenties; Fred was already married, and both young men were employed by their aunt's publisher Roberts Brothers. Eight-year-old Lulu soon returned to Zurich, at her father's request, to his custody. Anna and John spent nearly a year with Lulu in Switzerland, helping her adjust. Lulu later married, had a daughter, and died in Switzerland in 1975. Anna survived Louisa by only five years.

None of Louisa's survivors had to worry about money. At her death she was the country's most popular author, and had earned more from writing than any male author of her time. In the decade after *Little Women* was published, according to the *Boston Herald,* she sold more than half a million books in America alone. Ten years later, when Roberts Brothers was sold, it had printed nearly two million copies of her books. By the mid-twentieth century more than two million copies of *Little Women* alone were in print, and the most circulated books at the New York City Public Library were *Little Women* and Anne Frank's diary. Louisa's novel has been translated into scores of languages, including Flemish, Arabic, Portuguese, Urdu, Persian, and Japanese.

In Boston a few months after Louisa's death, the New England Woman Suffrage Association held a ceremony in honor of her eighty-eight-year-old cousin Samuel E. Sewall. The ancient lawyer and abolitionist, who had been born only a year before his first cousin Abigail May, rose from his chair to address the crowd. "Old Cato, whenever he was finishing a speech in the Senate, always added: 'This I say, and Carthage must be destroyed!' So I conclude, 'The emancipation of women must be carried!'"

Conclusion

I Believe in Dreams

F reedom was always my longing, but I have never had it," Louisa wrote near the end of her life. She accepted her place beside Abigail among that "Sad sisterhood of disappointed women," but never ceased hoping for the day when men and women could live equally and with mutual respect. Louisa dreamed of a world in which women would have the same public rights as men—to vote, travel, speak out, and run governments.

In the end, Louisa May Alcott was her mother's daughter. As willful, valiant, and loving as Abigail, she lived out her mother's hopes and fulfilled many of her mother's dreams. Neither woman achieved all she desired, but together they paved the way for modern women. Both wanted equal rights, but neither could find a way to live as men's equal. Each chose at age thirty to avoid a traditional female role. Abigail married a reformer who seemed to share her belief in gender equality; Louisa decided to have a career and go off to war. This decision to become a "self-made woman" had disastrous consequences for both women. Failing to create an egalitarian or satisfying marriage, Abigail leaned on her daughters for emotional and financial support. Louisa's decision to behave like a man in the world left her, ironically, lonely and dependent on her mother.

Unable to find a partner who was her equal, Louisa found comfort in Abigail who, more than anyone else, understood and sympathized with her. With her vivid imagination, however, Louisa would doubtless have preferred the kind of love that Margaret Fuller found in Italy. In a better world, Louisa believed, women would have the opportunity to work and be heard in the world, to "try all kinds" of lovers, to raise families, and to share the burdens and pleasures of domestic life. In short, they would be equal to men.

"There are plenty [of people] to love you," Marmee tells Jo in *Little Women,* "so try to be satisfied with father and mother, sisters and brother, friends and babies, till the best lover of all comes to give you your reward."

Louisa's alter ego replies, "Mothers are the *best* lovers in the world; but I don't mind whispering to Marmee, that I'd like to try all kinds. It's very curious, but the more I try to satisfy myself with all sorts of natural affections, the more I seem to want."

In Louisa's essay *Shawl-Straps,* written a few years before her mother died, she advised young women to explore the world, as Dr. Johnson in the eighteenth century had advised young men. Abigail had also told her daughters: learn your own country and culture, and educate yourself further through travel.

To Louisa, her lengthy tour of Europe with her sister May and Alice Bartlett had "proved," despite "prophecies to the contrary," that "three women, utterly unlike in every respect, [could travel] unprotected safely over land and sea . . . experience two revolutions, an earthquake, an eclipse, and a flood," and "yet [meet] with no loss, no mishap, no quarrel, and no disappointment . . .

> We would respectfully advise all timid sisters now lingering doubtfully on shore, to strap up their bundles in light marching order, and push boldly off. They will need no protector but their own courage, no guide but their own good sense and Yankee wit, and no interpreter if that woman's best gift, the tongue, has a little French polish on it. Wait for no man, but take your little store and invest it in something far better than Paris finery, Geneva jewelry, or Roman relics.
>
> Bring home empty trunks, if you will, but heads full of new and larger ideas, hearts richer in the sympathy that makes the whole world kin, hands readier to help on the great work God gives humanity, and souls elevated by the wonders of art and diviner miracles of nature. Leave . . . discontent, frivolity and feebleness among the ruins of the old world, and bring home to

the new the grace, the culture, and the health which will make American women what they just fail over being, the bravest, brightest, happiest, and handsomest women in the world!

Stand up among your fellow men, Joseph May had said to his son on the completion of his man's education. Improve your advantages. Go anywhere.

A woman can accomplish as much as a man, Abigail had told her daughters so often they came to believe her. Educate yourself up to your senses. Be something in yourself. Let the world know you are alive. Push boldly off. Wait for no man. Have heads full of new and larger ideas. And proceed to the great work God gives humanity.

Exploring the America of Abigail and Louisa May Alcott

Orchard House, a museum and educational center in Concord, Massachusetts, that receives tens of thousands of visitors each year, is a fine start to a tour of the landscapes of Abigail and Louisa May Alcott. My first visit to Orchard House was in the summer of 1968, exactly a hundred years after Louisa wrote *Little Women* there in her bedroom overlooking the front yard and the road. Nine years old, I arrived with my mother and our elderly aunt, Charlotte May Wilson, who announced on crossing the threshold, "Cousin Louisa's house!" Aunt Charlotte, a feisty Victorian spinster who ran an inn at the tip of Cape Cod, was a woman who wore a dress, nylon stockings, and leather shoes even to the beach. Proud keeper of the family tree, she was devoted to our ancestors but rarely amused by children.

"Well, well, here we are at Cousin Louisa's," Aunt Charlotte repeated. I wanted to hide, but the Orchard House guides rose to the bait and clamored for more. My aunt was the author's first cousin, two generations removed, she explained. Her grandmother and namesake, Charlotte May Wilkinson, was Louisa's first cousin and childhood playmate.

During our tour of the Orchard House parlor, where Anna Alcott had married John Pratt in 1860, Aunt Charlotte mentioned that her great-grandfather the Reverend Samuel Joseph May had performed the ceremony and signed the marriage license, which still hangs on the wall. Nearby, in the dining room, Aunt Charlotte quietly pointed out to my mother, "There's the sixth of your sister's dining-room chairs," which was somehow separated from its mates in the family shuffle.

It was clear even to a nine-year-old that Aunt Charlotte felt strongly about Cousin Louisa. Born in Syracuse, New York, and raised in 1890s Detroit, my aunt had listened rapt to her grandmother Charlotte's stories of growing up with her cousin Louisa, whom she outlived by more than three decades. Like Louisa, Aunt Charlotte was devoted to literature, to women's education, and to equal rights. After graduating from Smith College, in 1917, Aunt Charlotte made her own way in the world, as her cousin had. She emulated Louisa by serving as a Red Cross nurse in Europe during the First World War, and then followed her Aunt Abigail in becoming a city social worker. At least two other women in the family remained single and always worked: Katherine May Wilkinson, a history teacher at the Chapin School who was educated at Smith College (class of 1897) courtesy of the Alcotts ("in return," according to a family memoir, "for Grandpa [Samuel Joseph May]'s kindnesses" to Abigail), and Katherine's sister Marion, who ran an inn overlooking Provincetown Harbor. In the early 1930s Aunt Marion passed the inn to her niece Charlotte, my aunt, who hosted Mary Pickford, Eleanor Roosevelt, and many other guests at the Red Inn.

As a girl I often played on the parlor floor in Aunt Charlotte's little red house across the road from the inn. Occupied by the tiny wind-up toys adorning her window sills, I listened to my elderly, childless aunt cluck over our forebears like a hen over her brood. One memorable ancestor was scalped by Indians in seventeenth-century New York, along with all her little children, Aunt Charlotte added, ominously. Another ancestor was a Salem witch judge who realized his mistake and repented for hanging innocent people as witches. He wore penitential sackcloth for the rest of his life and became something of a feminist, according to Aunt Charlotte, who clearly loved the witch judge best. These ancestors seemed to be present and familiar to her, as if they were her friends, which in a way, I suppose, they were. While her fascination with dead people seemed ghoulish to a child, I see now that most families have an Aunt Charlotte, the relative who takes the time to learn and share stories about the family's past.

A few years ago, I found high on a bookshelf the family tree that Aunt Charlotte had handwritten and presented to me on my thirteenth birthday. This volume of names and dates as long ago as the sixteenth century arose from decades of genealogical research by my aunt in North America and even Europe, where she explored the Mays' Spanish-Jewish and Portuguese antecedents. It was only in recent years, as an adult beginning to research the lives of the ancestors she had first described, that I could appreciate Aunt Charlotte's gift.

Of late I have returned often to Orchard House to read documents, interview experts, and study its collections. The house, which the Alcotts occupied from 1858 until the late 1870s, is only one of many Alcott sites in Concord. Just up the road to the right of Orchard House is Hillside, the house Louisa lived in for three years as a teenager. Nathaniel Hawthorne later renamed it Wayside, the name it bears today. Open to the public and run by the National Park Service, Wayside is well worth a tour. Louisa's little room was in the left rear of the house, facing back toward the steep hill where Bronson built a rock garden. If you return from here to Orchard House and continue on for half a mile, just as Abigail and Louisa often did, you arrive at the Emerson house, which is now also a museum.

The house in which Abigail died is 255 Main Street, two and a half blocks west of Concord center on the left. Privately owned, it bears a historic marker indicating it was the Thoreau house; Henry David Thoreau and his siblings grew up and lived there. Louisa and Anna bought the house in the spring of 1877 for Anna and her boys. Abigail moved there that fall, a few weeks before her death, and Louisa and Bronson remained there with Anna's family that winter.

To see the Dove Cottage that the Alcotts occupied in the early 1840s, continue past the Thoreau house on Main Street, turn left at Route 62, and pass the Concord boatyard. Immediately after a railroad bridge you will see on your right the house that belonged to the Alcotts' landlords, the Hosmers, and beyond that the rental cottage. Their rear yards descend to the Concord River, where one can still row to view the cliffs the Alcott girls saw with their uncle Junius in the summer of 1842.

Louisa and Abigail are buried at Sleepy Hollow cemetery, on Author's Ridge, along with Elizabeth, Anna, Bronson, Emerson, and Thoreau. An American flag at Louisa's gravestone denotes her status as a veteran. There is a memorial stone for her sister May, who was buried in Paris, where she died.

Five miles east of Concord, just before Lexington's Town Green, is the pumpkin-colored eighteenth-century house in which Abigail's

Aunt Q experienced the first shots of the American Revolution, a house that Abigail may have visited later with her aunt. The Hancock-Clarke House, as it is known, is now a museum. It was built by John Hancock's grandfather the Reverend Thomas Hancock in 1737. John Hancock moved here as a boy in 1744, on the death of his father, and after 1750 he lived on Beacon Hill with his childless uncle and aunt, Thomas and Lydia Hancock. The house contains Hancock portraits and furnishings and relics of April 19, 1775: the first-floor bedroom where Dolly (later Aunt Q) slept that night alongside her fiancé's Aunt Lydia; the four-poster bed upstairs that John Hancock and Sam Adams shared; and the table at which the two men took tea.

The city of Boston contains many locations of Louisa and Abigail's lives. Indeed, their residences in the city seem too numerous to count. Their Beach Street boardinghouse was a stone's throw from the Chinese gate marking the entrance to Chinatown; their uncle Samuel May's "commodious" house at 88 Atkinson Street was a short block from the Rose Kennedy Greenway, above Rowes and India Wharves; and several of their boardinghouses were in the bustling commercial district along Washington Street. Abigail's birthplace is in modern-day Post Office Square, at the intersection of Congress and Milk streets in the city's financial district, where skyscrapers have replaced all the wooden houses and gardens of her day. A pillar topped with a golden eagle "in memory of George Thorndike Angell, 1823–1909," who founded the Society for the Prevention of Cruelty to Animals, adorns the square. The site of the house on Federal Court in which Abigail grew up, one inspiration for the setting of *Little Women,* is a few blocks away, near South Station. Federal Court, the cul de sac on which the May house stood, is now an alley in the shadow of the high-rise Winthrop Square parking garage, but Federal Street remains. Abigail's Aunt Q spent her final decade at 4 Federal Street, in the thick of the city's modern downtown.

King's Chapel, the eighteenth-century Georgian-style "Stone Church" in which Abigail and Bronson were married in 1830, is on Tremont Street a block west of Government Center. King's Chapel— which was both America's first Anglican church, in 1686, and also its first Unitarian church, in 1785—still offers Sunday services. Inside, past the double Corinthian columns and near the center of the main gallery, is the erstwhile May family pew, no. 20, with its mahogany rails and pink upholstery. There is a memorial plaque in the church to Colonel May, which Abigail and Louisa viewed at its installation in 1874. The pulpit of King's Chapel dates to 1717, the communion table to 1696. The busts in the chancel are of James Freeman, the friend of Colonel May who presided at the burial of six-year-old Edward May in 1802, and of the Reverend Francis Greenwood, who officiated at the Alcotts' wedding and whose daughter Colonel May adopted. The huge bell in the church tower is the last one made by Paul Revere. The church's burying ground, Boston's oldest cemetery, contains all that remains of John Winthrop, William Dawes, and Abigail's parents and most of her siblings. Just below the church at the other end of School Street is the Corner Bookstore building, 271 Washington Street, an early eighteenth-century structure where Louisa and her literary contemporaries visited the publishing house Ticknor & Fields.

The entrance to the Granary Burying Ground, where Abigail's mother pointed out to her children their ancestor Judge Samuel Sewall's grave, is across Tremont Street from King's Chapel. Toward the back of the cemetery, between the tomb of Paul Revere and that of Benjamin Franklin's parents and siblings, a large, rectangular nineteenth-century monument is marked "SEWALL . . . Judge Sewell [*sic*] tomb / Now the property of his heirs."

Returning to King's Chapel and turning left on Beacon Street, you approach the Massachusetts State House, built two years before Abigail was born. A large twentieth-century mural of Judge Sewall making his 1697 public repentance for hanging innocent people as witches adorns the Chamber of the House of Representatives. Beyond the State House on the same side is the site of the grand home of Abigail's Aunt Q and John Hancock, at what was then No. 30 Beacon Street. The house, built in 1739 on a two-acre plot owned by John Hancock's uncle Thomas, had magnificent gardens and views of Boston Common, which John Hancock was instrumental in improving. During Abigail's childhood cows still grazed on the Common, but they were banned in 1830, two years before Louisa's birth. As a small child Louisa played in the Common and fell into the Frog Pond. A few blocks away, on the north side of Beacon Hill, is the 1806 African Meeting House, at 46 Joy Street. The "oldest black church edifice still standing in the United States," this building was renovated to its former glory in the early twenty-first century. It was one of the 1832 meeting places of William Lloyd Garrison, Samuel Joseph May, Samuel E. Sewall, and other founders of America's first antislavery society. The meeting house is operated by the National Park Service and open to the public as part of the city's Museum of African-American History (www.maah.org). Boston's former Freedom Trail and Black Heritage Trail are now Boston's conjoined Trails to Freedom, with an office in Faneuil Hall. Just north of Beacon Hill, on Bunker Hill in Charlestown, you can climb to the top of the Monument to the Revolutionary dead whose first stone was laid by Aunt Q's old friend General Lafayette in 1825.

Beacon Hill boasts many addresses associated with Louisa and Abigail. Louisa purchased and lived during the last few years of her life at 10 Louisburg Square. Her first cousin Elizabeth Willis Wells, whom Abigail had cared for in the 1820s, also lived as an adult on Louisburg Square. Louisa's cousins Thomas and Mary Sewall lived for many years at 98 Chestnut Street. In the early 1850s Abigail rented 20 Pinckney Street, and nearly twenty years later Louisa and her sister May took rooms at 69 Pinckney.

The Mill Dam site where twenty-five-year-old Louisa considered suicide in 1858 is at the base of Beacon Hill at the intersection of Arlington and Beacon streets. This is now a corner of the city's Public Garden, which did not exist until 1860. The dam's path across the tidal waters of the original Back Bay was roughly that of Beacon Street heading west toward Kenmore Square.

On the eastern side of Boston Common, Bronson's Temple School was in a building at the corner of Tremont Street and Temple Place. The Alcotts lived on Temple Place in the summer of 1850. A block down Tremont Street is West Street, where Bronson took rooms in the 1830s. Elizabeth Peabody ran her bookstore and library and hosted Margaret Fuller's conversations to women at 13 West Street. That building, now number 15 West Street and a designated Boston landmark, is occupied by Max & Dylan's Kitchen Bar.

In Roxbury, where émigré Mays settled in the seventeenth century, no marker indicates the location of Louisa May Alcott's death, in March 1888. The house on Dunreath Street in which Dr. Rhoda Lawrence ran her rest home was torn down in the first half of the twentieth century.

A Baptist Church and its parking lot now occupy the site, at the corner of Dunreath and Warren streets, high on a hill overlooking the hills of Brookline to the west and the expanse of the Back Bay to the east. In the nearby South End neighborhood, the Alcotts' addresses include 81 West Cedar Street, 29 Dedham Street, and Franklin Square, at 26 East Brookline Street.

In Quincy, a city just south of Boston, the canary yellow house in which Aunt Q grew up is open to the public one Saturday afternoon a month each summer. The Dorothy Quincy House, also known as the Quincy Homestead, is "one of the few houses in Massachusetts in which the elements of a seventeenth-century building are still clearly visible," according to the National Society of the Colonial Dames of America. This National Historic Landmark is at the corner of Hancock Street and Butler Road about a quarter-mile north of the Quincy National Historic Site. It was built in 1685 by Edmund Quincy Jr. and occupied by five generations of Quincys. In the early twenty-first century one of John Hancock's decrepit chariots was still in its garage.

A half-hour south of Quincy, in the town of Norwell, Massachusetts, formerly South Scituate, Samuel Joseph's house and church are still standing. The house, a colonial at 841 Main Street known as the Elijah Curtis House or "May Elms" because of the trees planted by the minister, is privately owned. This is where Louisa and her sister spent several summers in the late 1830s. Less than a mile away, in the town center, is the First Church of Norwell, established in 1642 and looking much as it did in Samuel Joseph's day. The church building was erected in 1830, a few years before his arrival, and contains a Paul Revere bell, a pipe organ by Ebenezer Goodrich, and an Aaron Willard clock (www.firstparishnorwell.org).

The town of Melrose, home to Samuel E. Sewall and his family, whom the Alcotts often visited and with whom Louisa boarded, is north of Boston on the Mystic River. In the 1860s Anna and John Pratt moved from urban Chelsea to rural Melrose. To get a sense of nineteenth-century Melrose, visit the Middlesex Fells Reservation, which has several ponds and more than a hundred miles of trails. At the nearby border of Stoneham is Spot Pond, which the Mays and Alcotts knew well. Samuel Joseph May recalled in his memoir an 1817 trip to Spot Pond for a canal party hosted by Daniel Webster, who had just completed two terms in the United States House of Representatives. At the party the ladies asked the gentlemen to gather water lilies from the pond. "The more the probability of getting them seemed to recede," Samuel Joseph observed, "the more earnest became the desires of the young ladies to be possessed of the beautiful flowers." While the other young men left in search of a boat, the nineteen-year-old Harvard graduate, who was wearing his best suit, remained with Daniel Webster and the ladies, who began to glare at him. Urged on by Webster, Samuel Joseph waded into the pond to collect water lilies. "When I reached the shore, soaked from my waistcoat pockets downwards, and presented to each of the ladies one or more of the flowers they had so much desired, their thanks were to me quite as grateful as the fragrance of the lilies." Despite Samuel Joseph's "pleasant introduction to the great orator" in 1817, Webster's later defense of slavery, his "fearful recreancy to the cause of liberty, impelled me to lift my voice on the 4th of July, 1838, in earnest condemnation of one whom I had once so profoundly respected."

The hills and orchards of Walpole, New Hampshire, just over an hour's drive northwest of Boston, are much as they were in the 1850s, when Louisa and Abigail lived there. Heading east into Maine, you can still visit the 1797 Lake House in Waterford that housed the water-cure establishment where Abigail worked and lived in 1848. In the early twenty-first century the Lake House, at 686 Waterford Road, still operated as an inn in the historic district of this village in the foothills of the White and Mahoosuc mountains. Waterford, a vacation community for nearly two hundred years, is as lovely now as it must have been in the Alcotts' day. The remains of the tubs in which patrons of the spa soaked are said to be visible below the annex of the inn, across the lawn to the right. The farmhouse that belonged to Abigail's friend Ann Gage, whom Abigail often visited, is up the hill to the right of the inn, still occupied by Gage's descendants. Across the road from the inn are paths to nearby Keoka Lake.

In southern New England, Samuel Joseph's first church still stands in Brooklyn, Connecticut, near the Rhode Island border. A few miles south of Brooklyn on Route 169, at the Route 14 intersection, is Prudence Crandall's Canterbury house, the site of New England's first school for black girls. The house, now a museum and National Historic Landmark on Connecticut's Freedom Trail and Women's Heritage Trail, is open to the public Wednesdays through Sundays (860-546-9916). Each fall the

Prudence Crandall Museum hosts a "Tea with Prudence and Sarah" in which actors playing the teacher and her first black student, Sarah Harris, reenact the events of 1833 and 1834. A statue of Prudence Crandall, who at the end of the twentieth century was named Connecticut's state heroine, adorns the state Capitol, in Hartford.

Louisa enjoyed visits to New York City in the last decade of her life, when she was a media celebrity. In 1885, for example, she lived for a while at 41 West 26th Street. Her Goddard and Sewall cousins resided on 77th Street on the Upper East Side, and her cousin Charlotte May Wilkinson spent her final years with several of her grown children in an apartment at 129 East 76th Street.

Louisa's birthplace of Germantown is seven miles northwest of central Philadelphia. Germantown, a separate town from Philadelphia until 1854, was then a summer retreat for wealthy Philadelphians. The many extant historic houses along Germantown's cobbled streets include that of Reuben Haines, the Quaker who invited Bronson here in 1830. The Wyck house, as it is known, at the corner of Germantown Avenue and East Walnut Lane, is open to the public several days a week from April to December (www.Wyck.org). Louisa and her sister Anna as toddlers visited Wyck house with their mother and likely played in its rose garden. While some historians assert that Louisa returned to the house in 1876 while in Philadelphia for the installation of her cousin the Reverend Joseph May at the city's First Unitarian Church, at Chestnut Street, Louisa herself wrote to a friend in 1881 of "my birth-place, which I have never visited since I left it at the mature age of two."

Pine Place, the Germantown alley on which the Alcotts were living when Louisa was born, and their rented stone cottage surrounded by pine trees are long gone. Nevertheless, a historic sign marks the spot, at 5424 Germantown Avenue, which is now occupied by a piano factory. Around the corner, at 5501 Germantown Avenue in the old Market Square, the Germantown Historical Society has exhibits and information about the Alcotts and many local historic sites (www.germantownhistory.org). Germantown is a major stop on the African American Heritage Guide to Philadelphia's Historic Northwest (www.FreedomsBackyard.com).

The Union Hotel Hospital (later Georgetown General and Union Hospital), in which Louisa worked as a nurse, was torn down in the 1930s and replaced by a gas station. A SunTrust Bank office now sits on the site, at the northeast corner of M (then Bridge) Street and 30th Street NW (then Washington) in Georgetown. This part of M Street is now a thriving shopping district around Market House, Georgetown's market since 1751.

During the Civil War America's capital was filled with hospitals and wounded soldiers and surrounded by forts. Georgetown was a busy port, its population nearly a third African-American, some enslaved and some free. Louisa liked to walk up into the Georgetown hills and down to the nearby Chesapeake & Ohio canal to watch mules draw barges. The C&O canal was intended to connect to the Ohio River, but the rapid development of railroads made this method of transportation obsolete. A canal lock can still be seen on Jefferson Street, between M and K streets. On her walks Louisa would have passed the Old Stone House, built in 1765 on the same side of M Street as the hospital, and now considered the oldest standing building in Washington, D.C. Operated by the National Park Service and open to the public, the Old Stone House is part of the vast Rock Creek Park that runs north from Georgetown along the Rock Creek to the district's topmost corner (www.nps.gov/rocr).

Louisa knew canals well from her frequent visits to Syracuse, New York, the city in the Finger Lakes region where her uncle's family lived after 1844. Portions of the Erie Canal are still visible beneath Syracuse's Canal Street and Erie Boulevard. In the nineteenth century Syracuse was known as "that laboratory of abolitionism, libel, and treason" and "the great central depot" on the Freedom Trail. Residents of nearby towns included Frederick Douglass, Susan B. Anthony, Elizabeth Cady Stanton, Harriet Tubman, Matilda Joslyn Gage, and Gerrit Smith. The Fugitive Slave Law Convention in 1850 occurred in nearby Cazenovia. In Seneca Falls, where the first women's rights convention was held in 1848, the visitor center of the Women's Rights National Historical Park is open daily year round (www.cnyhistory.org).

Neither the May house nor Samuel Joseph's church here are standing, and it is difficult to see the bones of nineteenth-century Syracuse in the modern city. The Onondaga Historical Association Museum and Research Center offers exhibits and collections on Syracuse history, the Jerry Rescue, Samuel Joseph May, abolition, and women's rights. The society holds personal papers of Samuel Joseph May and Colonel Joseph May, although the bulk of Samuel Joseph May's extant papers are about

90 minutes to the north in the archives of the Division of Rare and Manuscript Collections of the Cornell University Library, where his painting of Prudence Crandall still hangs.

Louisa and Abigail often visited the Mays at their spacious home at 157 James Street, then a broad residential road less than a mile northeast of the center of Syracuse. James Street is now commercial, most of its mansions burned or razed. An apartment building occupies the site of the May house at what is now 472 James Street.

Samuel Joseph's Church of the Messiah was in the center of the city one block north of the Erie Canal at the corner of Burnet and Lock (now State) streets. The site is now a parking lot beside the elevated Interstate 690. In the mid twentieth century Samuel Joseph's former congregation moved to eastern Syracuse where it continues today as the May Memorial Unitarian Universalist Society, at 3800 East Genesee Street (315-446-8920 or www.mmuus.org). Its May Memorial Room contains several of Samuel Joseph's bibles, a two-volume Bible that his wife received from Colonel May's second wife in 1834, a bust and photographs of the minister, and some of his journals. Outside and to the right of the church is a large marble plaque in honor of Samuel Joseph that overlooks the May Memorial garden and a brook.

My final stop in Syracuse was the Oakwood Cemetery, adjacent to the campus of Syracuse University, at 940 Comstock Avenue. No one was present at the cemetery office when I visited, so it took me nearly an hour to find the Mays' graves. (I recommend calling 315-475-2194 for directions and then entering the cemetery from Colvin Avenue.) Down a winding, rutted road near the back of the cemetery, perched atop a lovely knoll, is a huge, ornate monument to the Wilkinson family. Arrayed beneath this sculpture and below many Wilkinsons are the graves of Samuel Joseph ("Born in Boston Sept. 12, 1797, Died in Syracuse July 1, 1871") and his wife ("Lucretia Coffin, Wife of Samuel Joseph May, Born in Portsmouth, NH, Died in Syracuse May 8 1865"), several of their children, their daughter Charlotte's sons and daughters (including Abigail's namesake Abby May Wilkinson, who died at age two), and, beneath a small granite slab surrounded by grass, my aunt "Charlotte May Wilson, 1895–1980."

Genealogy

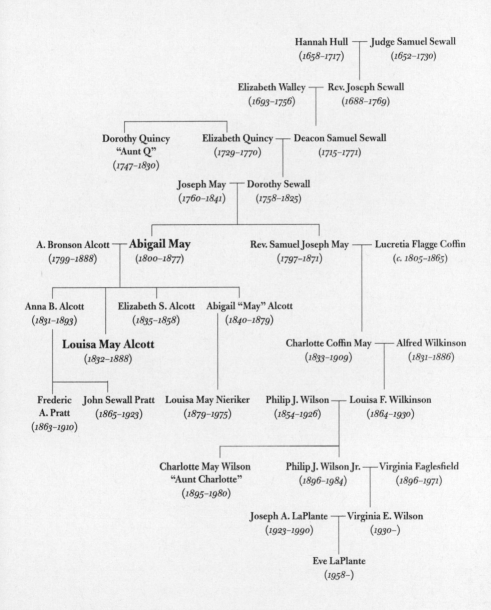

Hannah Hull (1658–1717) — Judge Samuel Sewall (1652–1730)

Elizabeth Walley (1693–1756) — Rev. Joseph Sewall (1688–1769)

Dorothy Quincy "Aunt Q" (1747–1830)

Elizabeth Quincy (1729–1770) — Deacon Samuel Sewall (1715–1771)

Joseph May (1760–1841) — Dorothy Sewall (1758–1825)

A. Bronson Alcott (1799–1888) — **Abigail May** (1800–1877)

Rev. Samuel Joseph May (1797–1871) — Lucretia Flagge Coffin (c. 1805–1865)

Anna B. Alcott (1831–1893)

Elizabeth S. Alcott (1835–1858)

Abigail "May" Alcott (1840–1879)

Louisa May Alcott (1832–1888)

Charlotte Coffin May (1833–1909) — Alfred Wilkinson (1831–1886)

Frederic A. Pratt (1863–1910)

John Sewall Pratt (1865–1923)

Louisa May Nieriker (1879–1975)

Philip J. Wilson (1854–1926) — Louisa F. Wilkinson (1864–1930)

Charlotte May Wilson "Aunt Charlotte" (1895–1980)

Philip J. Wilson Jr. (1896–1984) — Virginia Eaglesfield (1896–1971)

Joseph A. LaPlante (1923–1990) — Virginia E. Wilson (1930–)

Eve LaPlante (1958–)

Acknowledgments

I am most grateful to Lisa Stepanski, author of *The Home Schooling of Louisa May Alcott,* to Lis Adams, director of education at Orchard House, and to Rose LaPlante for their assistance in transcribing family papers and archival documents. Lisa Stepanski and Lis Adams also read the manuscript, made editorial suggestions, and guided me to important materials. Cynthia Barton, author of *Transcendental Wife,* shared her research notes and answered all my questions. Catherine Rivard provided several years of expert advice on the Alcott and May families. Megan Marshall, author of *The Peabody Sisters,* generously provided several of Elizabeth Peabody's letters that I might have overlooked. Virginia LaPlante, Liza Hirsch, and Alison McGandy read the manuscript and made invaluable suggestions. Jan Turnquist allowed me to roam the rooms and collections of Orchard House, of which she is executive director. The historian and curator Edward Furgol, D. Phil., continued to offer sage counsel. Alcott and May scholars whose work I relied on in addition to Cynthia Barton and Lisa Stepanski include Elizabeth Lennox Keyser, Joel Myerson, Daniel Shealy, Sarah Elbert, John Matteson, Madeleine Stern, Donald Yacovone, Madelon Bedell, and Ted Dahlstrand. I wish to thank Maria Powers of Orchard House for her help with images and permissions.

At the Houghton Library of Harvard University, the site of the May Alcott family papers, I am grateful for the assistance of Heather Cole, Emilie Hardman, Tom Lingner, Leslie Morris, Rachel Howarth, James Capobianco, Susan Halpert, Mary Haegert, Micah Hoggatt, Peter Accardo, Emily Walhout, and Joseph Zajak. At the Boston Public Library, I benefited from the expert assistance of Henry Scamell, Marta Pardee-King, and Patricia Feeley. At the Kroch Library of Cornell University, the site of the Samuel J. May Anti-Slavery Manuscript Collection, I wish to thank director and archivist Elaine Engst, Laura Linke, Katherine Reagan, Connie Finnerty, and Brenda Marston.

Local historians and others assisted me in the book's locations. Bruce Stoff guided me in Ithaca. In Syracuse, I am grateful to Roger Hiemstra, an expert on Samuel Joseph May and a member of the History Committee of the May Memorial Church. Harsey Leonard, Brian Betz, and George Adams showed me around that church. At the Onondaga Historical Association, in Syracuse, the curators Sarah Kozma, Dennis Connors, and Thomas Hunter were most helpful.

In Norwell (formerly South Scituate), Massachusetts: N. Dexter Robinson and Scott Babcock provided advice, Robert and Betsey Detwiler opened their home to me, and Sally and Owen McGowan showed me around Samuel Joseph May's house. I am grateful to the curator Kazimiera Kozlowski at the Prudence Crandall museum in Canterbury, Connecticut.

In northern New England, I am grateful to the late Robert Jasse, of Walpole, New Hampshire, and his wife, Susan, and especially to William "Whizzer" and Meg Wheeler, of Waterford, Maine, who opened to me their family archive. I am also grateful to the former proprietors of the inn at Waterford, and to Lilo Willoughby, of the Waterford Historical Society, for their assistance.

At the Germantown Historical Society, in Philadelphia, I received assistance from the librarian and archivist Alexander Bartlett, the volunteer Sam Whyte, and the historian Judith Callard. In Washington, D.C., my friends Mary and Ed Furgol and Howard Hyde and Nancy Paulu hosted me, and Jonathan Eaker at the Library of Congress assisted my research.

Other people from whom I have received support include the Rev. Jack Ahern, the Rev. Brian Clary, Emer ban i Chuiv and her family, Thomas and Eleanor Kinsella, Phoebe Hoss, Liza Hirsch, Diana Raffman, Carl Dreyfus and Virginia LaPlante, Deanie and Gerry Blank, Alex Reid, Jeanne McGowan, Lynne Jones, Cora and Sheldon Roth, Julianne Johnston, Michelle Rush, Leo Eguchi, and Bradford Wright.

I am particularly grateful to Lane Zachary, of Zachary Schuster Harmsworth, who expertly guided this book from start to finish. Rachel Sussman provided thoughtful editorial suggestions. At Free Press, I wish to thank Martha Levin, Dominick Anfuso, Hilary Redmon, Mara Lurie, Tom Pitoniak, Ellen Sasahara, Eric Fuentecilla, Jill Siegel, and especially Chloe Perkins and Millicent Bennett.

Finally, I could not have written this book without my family. Rose, Clara, Charlotte, and Philip provided advice on everything from covers to titles, and David, as always, considered every word.

Notes

Abbreviations

People: LMA (Louisa May Alcott), AMA (Abigail May Alcott), ABA (A. Bronson Alcott), AAP (Anna B. Alcott Pratt), AMAN (Abigail "May" Alcott Nieriker), SJM (Samuel Joseph May), LFM (Lucretia Flagge Coffin May), CMW (Charlotte Coffin May Wilkinson), EPP (Elizabeth Palmer Peabody), JM (Colonel Joseph May), and Samuel E. Sewall (SES).

Archival collections: HAP (Alcott Pratt Collection, Houghton Library, Harvard University), MHS (Massachusetts Historical Society), MFPCL (May Family Papers, SJM Anti-Slavery Collection, Cornell University Library), NEHGS (New England Historical and Genealogical Society).

Introduction

1   "Who is Louie?": LMA and her family spelled the nickname "Louie," "Louy," or "Louey." For the sake of consistency I use "Louie" throughout.
1   "little tales": LMA, *Journals*, 74.
1   a "lovely place": Ibid., 74.
2   "sister-in-love": CMW, unpublished memoir in the hand of her daughter Katherine May Wilkinson, family collection. CMW's "relations with Aunt Louisa were so close that Aunt Louisa always signed her letters to Mamma 'your sister-in-love.'"
2   "uncle father": LFM to SJM, May 19, 1843, quoting Louisa May Willis, MFPCL.
3   "nobility of character": Madelon Bedell, *The Alcotts*, 326.
3   "distinctly mother-centered": Monika Elbert, introduction, *Early Stories of Louisa May Alcott*, 11.
3   Abigail's birthplace: Previous biographies placed Abigail's birth in the house on Federal Court in which she was raised. But her family did not move to Federal Court until the year after she was born, according to the 1873 *Memoir of Colonel Joseph May, 1760–1841*. In 1800 the Mays lived on Milk Street at the corner of Atkinson, now Congress, Street.
3   biographer Susan Cheever: *Louisa May Alcott: A Personal Biography*, 5.
3   "his was the powerful personality": Bedell, *The Alcotts*, xii, x.
3   "Raised in Concord": Elizabeth Lennox Keyser, summary of *The Portable Louisa May Alcott*. Likewise, the editor of *Crosscurrents of Children's Literature: An Anthology of Texts and Criticism* described LMA as "the daughter of the American Transcendentalist philosopher Bronson Alcott and the neighbor in Concord, Massachusetts, of Ralph Waldo Emerson, Nathaniel Hawthorne, and Henry David Thoreau. . . ."

4   feminist study: Elaine Showalter, introduction, *Scribbling Women,* vii.
4   pregnant at least eight times: In *Transcendental Wife: The Life of Abigail May Alcott,*
    Cynthia Barton found evidence that Abigail had eight pregnancies, ending in 1831
    (Anna Bronson), 1832 (Louisa May), 1834, 1835 (Elizabeth Peabody/Sewall),
    1837, 1838, 1839 (stillbirth), and 1840 (Abigail May).
5   "instead of weaving": Matteson, *Eden's Outcasts,* 388.
5   Her claims of burning: Stern, introduction, *Selected Letters of LMA,* 3. Joel Myer-
    son, editor of LMA's letters and journals, agreed with Stern that LMA exaggerated
    the extent to which she burned her own papers. Bedell noted in *The Alcotts,* 336,
    that family members destroyed portions of LMA's journals after her death.
5   "My journals were all burnt": LMA to Louise C. Moulton, January 18, 1883, *Let-
    ters,* 267.
5   "In some ways, Abby": Bedell, *The Alcotts,* 335.
6   Her marriage was deeply distressed: Herrnstadt, introduction, *Letters of ABA,* xxi,
    describes Abigail and Bronson's 47-year marriage as "happy."

Chapter 1: A Good Child, but Willful

7   a large frame house: According to the *Memoir of Colonel JM,* the May house until
    1801 was on Milk Street on the western corner of Atkinson, now Congress, Street.
7   "She adored her husband": AMA journals, HAP.
7   Dorothy had been orphaned: Dorothy's mother, Elizabeth Quincy Sewall, died in
    February 1770. Dorothy's father, Samuel Sewall, died of an "apoplectic fit" while
    at a minister's house in January 1771, leaving their seven children orphans at ages
    eight to twenty.
7   The Harvard classes of Dorothy Sewall's male relatives: 1776 for her eldest brother,
    Samuel Sewall; 1733 for her father, Samuel Sewall; 1707 for her grandfather the
    Reverend Joseph Sewall; and 1671 for her great-grandfather Samuel Sewall. Dame
    schools, also called ma'am schools, were run at home by women instructing boys
    and girls in reading, writing, and arithmetic.
8   a library stocked with: Thomas J. Mumford, introduction, *Memoir of SJM,* 2.
8   "plain but comfortable": *Memoir of Colonel JM.*
8   prepared to descend from the barn: Details of the narrative of Edward May's death,
    including dialogue, derive from SJM's account in *Memoir of SJM,* 4–10. SJM de-
    scribed Edward as "my almost twin brother" whom he loved "more than anybody
    but my mother."
10 persuaded their parents: SJM, *Memoir of SJM,* 22–23.
10 "darling little sister": Ibid., 22. SJM's first dame school was run by Mrs. Cazeneau
    and her daughter on Milk Street, from which Abba was lost, as described here in
    chapter 4.
10 "rational, selfish, and intellectually superior": Eve Kornfeld, *Margaret Fuller: A Brief
    Biography with Documents,* 8.
11 "deficient": AMA, Diary for 1872, HAP.
11 Abigail's uncle: William Dawes was the husband of Colonel JM's older half-sister
    Mehetabel May.
11 "pretty country town": Edward Everett Hale, *A New England Boyhood,* 2.
11 "Town and Country seem married": Enock Wines, a late eighteenth-century visi-
    tor to Boston from Philadelphia, quoted in Rawson, *Eden on the Charles,* 32.
12 Lydia Maria Child: "Autobiography," SJM Anti-Slavery Collection, Cornell Li-
    brary, in Carolyn L. Karcher, *First Woman in the Republic: A Cultural Biography of
    Lydia Maria Child,* 199.
12 her "Aunt Q": Dorothy Quincy Hancock Scott (1747–1830), Abigail's great aunt,
    was an aunt of Abigail's mother, Dorothy Quincy Sewall (1758–1825), and the

youngest sister of Abigail's grandmother, Elizabeth Quincy (1729–1770). Aunt Q's parents were Judge Edmund Quincy and Elizabeth Wendell.

12 Grandma Shaw's late aunt: LMA, *An Old-Fashioned Girl*, 102–106.

12 "most petted": AMA, journals, HAP.

12 his "strong" mother: *Memoir of Colonel JM*. The May family genealogy notes that Abigail Williams May's mother "was of such strength that she could lift a barrel of cider from the ground (which few men can do)," and had "much experience in 'breaking in' colts."

13 Spanish, Portuguese, and Jewish forebears: My aunt Charlotte May Wilson described this to me in the 1970s. According to a genealogy of the May family, Mays in England were said to be "of the Portugal Race." In 2012 researchers at NEHGS were able to "confirm the existence of the tradition (dating back to at least 1684) that the May family in Sussex County, England, was from Portugal."

13 except at extreme high tide: Not only did the tides shrink the Boston to Roxbury Neck, but also storm tides completely covered the neck. The first stanza of a poem Emerson composed on the December 1873 centennial of the Boston Tea Party is: "The rocky nook, with hill-tops three, / Looked eastward from the farms, / And twice each day the flowing sea / Took Boston in its arms."

13 a "considerable" dealer in lumber: *Memoir of Colonel JM*. According to the May family genealogy, Samuel May, Abigail's grandfather, "had considerable skill" as an architect and built the Episcopal Church that still stands in Harvard Square. "His mansion on Orange, now Washington St., was still standing in 1854."

13 gift for singing psalms: Ibid.

13 left their church: Ibid.

14 Thomas Patten: He was born in Boston on April 4, 1734, and died on January 31, 1805. Patten's wife, Anna Woolson, was born on September 25, 1742, and died on January 5, 1800. The Pattens likely moved to Alexandria as adults. In 1793 their son Thomas Patten Jr., born in 1769 in Roxbury, married Mary Roberdeau of Alexandria, Virginia. Around 1810, after Mary's death, Thomas Jr., "having failed in business by his ships being lost at sea, and other misfortunes beyond his control," went to Louisiana with his eldest son, Joseph May Patten, to start a plantation, according to *Genealogy of the Roberdeau Family*. Thomas Jr. was not old enough to start a business with Colonel May in 1781, so his father must have collaborated with May in a business the son may have inherited.

14 "thrice related to the Quincys": AMA, Memoir of 1878, HAP.

14 Old South Church: *An Historical Catalogue of the Old South Church (Third Church) Boston, 1669–1882*.

14 According to a historian: Nina Moore Tiffany, *Memoir of SES*, 3.

14 equivalent to $310,000: All dollar equivalencies in the book were calculated at www.measuringworth.com using the Consumer Price Index.

15 "Mr. May gave up everything": *Memoir of Colonel JM*.

15 "sufferings which this disaster": Ibid.

16 "keenly alive to": Ibid.

16 "seriously ill": AMA, August 22, 1876, journals, HAP.

16 "this exquisite family-choir": George B. Emerson, "Memorial to Colonel JM," NEHGS Register, 27 (1873), 113–121.

16 "Dear Louisa [Abigail's sister] and SJ": AMA, August 22, 1876, journals, HAP.

17 "unusual attractions": David H. Fischer, *Paul Revere's Ride*. Donald Yacovone, *SJM*, 8, mentions that "according to family tradition [Dorothy Quincy] dallied with Aaron Burr before marrying John Hancock."

17 Boston in early April 1775: Historical details derive from Fischer, *Paul Revere's Ride*.

18 "modest decency, dignity": John Adams to Abigail Adams, November 4, 1775, in *Dames & Daughters of Colonial Days*, 192.

18 "houses by Bulfinch": Oliver Wendell Holmes, *Elsie Venner*, 1861.
18 "union of new wealth": George Frederickson, *Inner Civil War*, xi–xii.
18 active into his seventies: See the Gilbert Stuart portrait of Joseph May at Museum of Fine Arts, Boston.
19 portrait had always hung: A portrait of Judge Samuel Sewall still hangs in Abigail's bedroom at Orchard House, alongside pictures of her brother Samuel Joseph May and her father.
19 "the right of women": Samuel Sewall, *Talitha Cumi*, 1725. Judge Sewall wrote that "[so] many [women] are such good lawyers, and are of such quick understanding . . . they have no reason to be afraid" that they are inferior to men. The manuscript of *Talitha Cumi*, contained in Judge Sewall's diary for 1725, was donated in the early nineteenth century to MHS by AMA's cousin the Rev. Samuel Sewall of Burlington, Massachusetts.
19 "better faculty than I": Samuel Sewall, January 29, 1704, *The Diary of Samuel Sewall*, 496.
20 fundamentally equal: Samuel Sewall, *Talitha Cumi*, 1725, reprinted in LaPlante, *Salem Witch Judge*, 304–311.
20 Chauncy Hall: "IN MEMORIAM—Samuel Joseph May," Unitarian Congregational Society of Syracuse, 1871, 13–14.
20 Joseph May and other fathers: The founders of Chauncy School also included Otises, Parkers, and Eliots.
20 "puny": SJM, *Memoir of SJM*.
20 Samuel E. Sewall: a first cousin to AMA. Sewall's father was the younger brother of Abigail's mother. Many Alcott biographers have erroneously said that SES was related to AMA "by marriage," perhaps because the cousins did not share a surname. (For instance, see *Little Women Abroad*, Daniel Shealy, ed., 55.) Of course surnames, like land and property, passed through the male line, which is why during Abigail's youth the first Judge Samuel Sewall's famous diaries were owned by another first cousin, the Reverend Samuel Sewall, a Congregational minister in Burlington, Massachusetts.
20 sixty other young men gathered: SMJ's Harvard classmates included the diplomat Caleb Cushing, the Boston mayor and congressman Samuel Eliot, the historian George Bancroft, the educational reformer George B. Emerson, who was Ralph Waldo Emerson's cousin and SJM's closest college chum, and David Lee Child, the abolitionist husband of Lydia Maria Francis Child, Abigail's close friend. Details of SJM's education derive from his memoir and from Hale, *A New England Boyhood*.
20 brother read the classics: As a Harvard freshman SJM wrote a prize-winning essay on Hume and Montesquieu.
20 "Illness much interrupted": AMA, Diary for 1872, HAP.
20 2 Kings 4:32–37: This page is turned down in the family bible at Orchard House that was owned successively by Dorothy Sewall May, Abigail May Alcott, and Louisa May Alcott.
21 right hand had been badly burned: AMA, Memoir of 1878, Autobiographical Sketch, 1800–1882, HAP.
21 "Divines": ministers.
21 "Nothing is of unimportance": SJM to AMA, August 15, 1815, family letters, HAP.
21 device called a blackboard: "Rev. Samuel J. May," *American Jouranl of Education*, March 1866, vol. xvi, no. xlii, 142.
22 "Endeavor to accomplish": Louisa May to AMA, July 5, 1816, family letters, HAP.
22 of average height: SJM was 5 feet 8 inches tall, according to his biographer Donald Yacovone.
22 "kindness and cheer": Bedell, *The Alcotts*, 1.
22 "rather a favorite": SJM, *Memoir of SJM*, 4–12, 17–19.
22 "minister by nature": *Little Women*, Book 2, describing the Rev. Mr. March.

22 Anyone seen driving: Hale, *A New England Boyhood*, 106.
22 "a deep interest": *Memoir of Col. JM*.
23 "I cannot but pity": William Ellery Channing, 1828 essay on humanity's "Likeness to God."
23 Unitarians still experienced: Thomas O'Connor, *The Hub*, 88. O'Connor described enlightenment Unitarianism as "the best of two worlds" to the Mays and their community because it "accepted the lessons of scientific reason, while still acknowledging the traditions of Boston's Puritan religious heritage."
23 "perfectibility of human nature" : Hale, *A New England Boyhood*, 164.
23 "Liberal Christianity": "IN MEMORIAM—Samuel Joseph May," Unitarian Congregational Society of Syracuse, 1871.
24 "an emphatic pressure": SJM, in "Joseph May" chapter of *Lives of American Merchants*, vol. 1, Freeman Hunt, ed., footnote to 444 .
24 "To be good is to be happy": Colonel JM to AMA, September 6, 1811, family letters, HAP.
24 questioned the lawfulness: On May 7, 1696, Judge Samuel Sewall wrote in his diary, "the lawfulness of the intermarrying of Cousin-Germans [first cousins] is doubted," *Diary of Samuel Sewall*, vol. 1, 349.
25 Charles Windship: Abigail's sister Catherine's son, Charles May Windship, was born in 1809, attended Harvard Medical School, and become a doctor like his father, Charles Williams Windship.
25 "virtually betrothed": AMA, Memoir of 1878, HAP.
25 "radical new idea": Stephanie Coontz, *Marriage, A History: How Love Conquered Marriage*, 5.
25 "the bane of our family": LMA, "The Mysterious Key, and What It Opened," *Louisa May Alcott Unmasked*, 489–490.
26 "most valuable" supervision: AMA, Memoir of 1878, HAP.
26 Pythagoras: On November 29, 1861, ABA gave AMA a blank journal "with her favorite motto from the Golden Sayings of Pythagoras written on the title page." The motto is unidentified.
26 "until you can remember": SJM to AMA, May 19, 1819, family letters, HAP.
26 "a model worthy of imitation": AMA to her parents, March 25, 1819, family letters, HAP.
26 "I may yet earn": AMA to her sister Eliza May Willis, July 1819, family letters, HAP.
26 "flowing, full pen": ABA to AMA, August 3, 1857, *Letters*, 246.
26 "old passion": AMA to LFM, July 25, 1830, family letters, HAP.
26 what she wished to do: Cynthia Barton, in conversation with the author, fall 2010.
27 "not willing to be found incapable": AMA to her parents, October 10, 1819, family letters, HAP.

Chapter 2: Drawing Toward Some Ideal Friend

28 "be allowed to refuse visiting": AMA, ibid.
28 "those gay scenes": AMA, ibid.
29 friends had already started schools: AMA's friend Lydia Francis (later Child) in her early twenties taught at Madame Angeline Canda's academy for Young Ladies in Boston. The Peabody sisters had also started schools.
29 "Louisa's capability": AMA to Eliza May Willis, July 1819, family letters, HAP.
29 Samuel Greele: His surname was pronounced, and later in the century written as, "Greely." Lydia Maria Sewall Greele died in August 1822, without issue.
29 Eliza May Willis's death: SJM, *Memoir*, 78.
29 "Soon he will be rivaling": AMA to Eliza May Willis, July 1819, family letters, HAP.
29 "My time is expired": AMA TO SJM, February 4, 1829, ibid.
30 "I have felt a loneliness": AMA to SJM, August 1828, ibid.

30 SJM's 1820 sermon: SJM, Diary for 1870, MFPCL.
30 "Discover what moral evils": James Freeman, November 5, 1823, "Charge to the Pastor," *A Sermon Preached in Brooklyn, Connecticut, at the Installation of Rev. Samuel Joseph May*, 25.
30 he planned to travel: Some biographies say SJM and Louisa May traveled south in 1822, but his *Memoir* affirms that the trip was in 1821, before he moved to Brooklyn, Connecticut. The quotations about the slave gang are from SJM's *Memoir*.
31 Hancock's slaves: Woodbury, *Dorothy Quincy, Wife of John Hancock*, 114.
31 "half of colonial society": Gordon S. Wood, *Empire of Liberty*, 517.
31 "*not* brack": Nina Moore Tiffany, *Memoir of SES*, 10.
32 "her prompt decisions": Lydia Maria Child to LMA, June 19, 1878, *Collected Correspondence of Lydia Maria Child*, microfiche 90/2398.
32 "a cause worthy": AMA, January 2, 1836, journals, HAP.
32 "We shall shake hands": AMA to Mary Tyler Peabody, September 2, 1835. I am grateful to Megan Marshall, author of *The Peabody Sisters*, for sending me her transcription of this letter.
32 "democracy was premised": Fredrickson, *Inner Civil War*, xiv.
33 "wheels of the cotton-factories": Brooks, *Flowering of New England*, 173.
33 Lucretia Flagge Coffin: Her parents, Peter Coffin and Anne Martin, were born and married in Portsmouth, New Hampshire, and her paternal grandfather the Reverend Peter Coffin graduated from Harvard in 1733.
33 Lucretia Flagge Coffin May's age is estimated. According to her granddaughter Katherine May Wilkinson, Lucretia was "so vain" about her age that no family member ever knew the year she was born. "She had a complex about growing old, which seems to have been a Coffin [family] trait, for her sister suffered from it too." Lucretia's gravestone, in Syracuse, lacks a birth year. Lucretia's parents married in January 1797 and had five children, the last born in 1817. Lucretia, their third child, was likely born in Portsmouth, New Hampshire, in 1804 or 1805. Her family moved to Boston when she was about six, according to *Memoir of SJM*.
33 Samuel Joseph and Lucretia's wedding: In 2012 I found in my mother's attic a wedding gift to SJM and LFM, volume 11 of Maria Edgeworth's *Works*, published in Boston in 1825.
34 "conflict, hard work": SJM quoting his father, *Memoir of SJM*, 77.
34 heresy: SJM, ibid., 65, 99.
34 still had slaves: Slavery ended in Connecticut in 1857, when the state's last slave died.
34 his only prayer: "IN MEMORIAM—Samuel Joseph May," Unitarian Congregational Society of Syracuse, 1871.
34 "total abstinence": Ibid.
34 "customary hospitable kegs": Brooklyn, Connecticut, newspaper clipping, August 11, 1927, found in family copy of *Memoir of SJM*.
34 temperance: At the raising of the Mays' new house in Brooklyn, Connecticut, in 1829, laborers were served fresh water rather than the usual alcohol. If whiskey was required, SJM said, "Then it [the house will] lay upon the ground."
34 man drank on average: "Prohibition," a film by Ken Burns and Lynn Novick, PBS, 2011. The 1830 statistic is for American men sixteen and older. The historian is Michael Rawson, *Eden on the Charles*, 83.
34 "growing sea of workers": Rawson, *Eden on the Charles*, 93–94.
35 "time had wrought many changes": Crawford, *Romantic Days in Old Boston*, 10.
35 "by and by the general": LMA, *An Old-Fashioned Girl*, 104–106.
36 "She loved the doing": AMA, Memoir of 1878, HAP.
36 "tall and personable": ABA to AAP, September 23, 1861, *Letters*, 323.
36 Madam Cary was thirty-nine: Mary Ann Atkinson Cary May was born in November 1787 and died in early 1839. Joseph May's eldest children were Charles (1785–1786) and Catherine (1786–1815).

36 "very busy in conjugating": AMA to Thomas May, October 9, 1826, family letters, HAP.

36 their new house: The May house in Brooklyn, Connecticut, was a walk of a few hundred yards north along the Pomfret Road from his church at the center of town, on the left side of the road.

37 raising funds: SJM's salary in Brooklyn was often not paid in full, and his church almost dissolved in 1827–28 for lack of money, according to his *Memoir*.

37 a statewide convention: Herrnstadt, introduction to *ABA Letters*, xx.

37 "the grand diapason": AMA, July 8, 1842, in *ABA Journals*, 143. Jan Turnquist, Orchard House executive director, said on July 11, 2011, at School of Philosophy Summer Conversations that a contemporary journalist wrote, "To listen to Bronson Alcott speak is like going to heaven in a swing." Theodore Dahlstrand observed the same day that Bronson's listeners felt "they were soaring."

38 "treated like machines": AMA, April 27, 1829, journals, HAP.

38 "Women are not educated": AMA, September 27, 1827, journals, HAP.

38 chestnut hair: AMA referred to her hair as "my one beauty," in AMA to SJM, July 19, 1863, family letters, HAP.

38 "May character": ABA, September 21, 1828, *A. Bronson Alcott: His Life and Philosophy*, F.B. Sanborn, ed., 135.

38 This "young lady": ABA, August 2, 1828, *Journals*, 12.

38 self-made man: Odell Shepard, *ABA Journals*, xix.

38 "extreme" Calvinistic: ABA, September 12, 1880, *Journals*, 519.

39 "disgraced" and "disgusted": Odell Shepard, *ABA Letters*, xix.

39 "How knoweth this man": ABA, September 22, 1826, *Journals*, 2.

39 AMA reading Pestalozzi: AMA wrote in summer 1843, "Pestalozzi's letters . . . should be a study for every Mother," family letters, HAP.

39 "large fund": AMA, Memoir of 1878, HAP.

39 "sage and saint": SJM, *Memoir*, 122.

40 "my moral mentor": AMA, 1828, journals, HAP.

40 She hoped Bronson: Herrnstadt, *ABA Letters*, xx.

40 "abundant news": LFM to SFM, August 12, n.d., probably 1827, quoting AMA, MFPCL.

40 That fall, though: ABA, Autobiography 1799–1805, HAP.

41 "add much to my happiness": AMA to ABA, September 16, 1827, family letters, HAP.

41 letters of introduction: ABA, January 8, 1876, *Journals*, 464.

41 Boston mansions in 1820s: Hale, *A New England Boyhood*, 4–5.

41 "I was led providentially": ABA, July 25, 1871, *Journals*, 421.

41 "flattered by the prospects": ABA to his brother Chatfield Alcott, July 18, 1827, *Letters*, 15.

41 "strength & health": AMA to SJM, May 1828, MFPCL.

41 "it is quite pleasant": LFM to SJM, May 1, 1828, MFP.

42 "wifeless, childless, sisterless": AMA to SJM, May 1828, MFPCL.

42 "in relation to the Infant School": ABA, June 1, 1828, *Journals*, 9.

43 "I always do take a walk": *Little Women*, chapter 46, "Under the Umbrella."

43 "I shall hope": ABA to AMA, July 17, 1828, *Letters*, 16.

43 "too vacillating": ABA July 15, 1828, *Journals*, 11. ABA appears to quote AMA.

43 "peculiar temperament": ABA, June 14, 1828, *Journals*, 10.

43 he handed her his journal: Odell Shepard, Introduction, *ABA Journals*, xv, wrote, "Alcott showed a volume of his Journals to Miss Abigail May . . . thereby avoiding the embarrassment of an oral proposal of marriage."

43 "had the very effect": ABA, November 29, 1828, *Journals*, 15–16.

43 "he has been attached to me": AMA to SJM, August 1828, family letters, HAP.

43 "I am engaged": AMA to SJM, August 1828, family letters, HAP. While AMA

wrote years later, "I found I loved him. The pledge [to marry] was given and taken
in 1829," her letters and ABA's journal indicate the couple was engaged by August
1828. The delay in the wedding for nearly two years was due to ABA's inability to
secure a stable job.

44   "Give us much land & money": Emerson, in Barbara Packer, *Emerson's Fall,* 150.
44   enrollment had tripled: Odell Shepard, *ABA Journals,* Introduction, 8.
44   "we care little": ABA, June 14, 1828, *Journals,* 10.
44   "The connection I have found": AMA to SJM, January 3, 1829, AMA letters, HAP.
44   "with all the ardor": AMA, 1828, quoted by ABA, September 21, 1828, *A. Bronson
     Alcott: His Life and Philosophy,* F.B. Sanborn, ed., 135.
44   "With this temperament": AMA to SJM, January 3, 1829, family letters, HAP.
45   "woman's intelligence": AMA, 1828–1829, journals, HAP.
45   "Reason and religion are emancipating": AMA journal fragments, 1828–29, HAP.
45   "Servants!" Aunt Q exclaimed: ABA, October 26, 1828, *Journals,* 13–14.
46   "miserable" for months: LFM to SJM, May 1, 1828, MFPCL.
46   "nearer and dearer to me": AMA to LFM, January 1829, AMA letters, HAP.
46   "her love is more substantial": AMA to SJM, August 1843, family letters, HAP.
47   "fearless free-thinking": ABA, 1829, *Journals,* 18.
47   "$1200 per annum": ABA, December 22, 1829, *Journals,* 22. ABA quotes AMA's
     brother-in-law Dr. Windship.
47   Aunt Q died: Dorothy Quincy Hancock Scott died February 3, 1830. The young-
     est of ten children, she outlived her older sister Elizabeth, Abigail May's maternal
     grandmother, by sixty years.
47   five hundred dollars: about $10,000 in 2000.
47   "sundries": Joseph May, "Account of sundries given my Daughter Abigail at her
     marriage with Amos Bronson Alcott—May 1830," family letters, HAP. The wash-
     stand from AMA's father appears to be in the master bedroom at Orchard House
     today.
47   "We shall be mourning": LFM to AMA, April 1830, MFPCL.
48   "I never desire": LFM to her son Joseph May, undated, probably when Joseph was
     at Harvard in mid-1850s, MFPCL.
48   Boston as city: Crawford, *Romantic Days in Old Boston,* 3. In 1822 only one in six of
     Boston's adult inhabitants had the power to vote.
48   market economy: Donald Yacovone in *Samuel Joseph May* notes that Abigail's fa-
     ther was not too old-fashioned to have made sound investments in early manufac-
     turing concerns, railroads, and life insurance, 12.
48   factory system: Thomas O'Connor, *The Hub,* 86.
48   divide between public and private: O'Connor, *Civil War Boston,* 168: In the early
     nineteenth century Boston "revived its commercial economy, investing in the new
     textile industry, expanding its banking enterprises, experimenting with railroads,
     and transforming itself from a small colonial seaport town into a substantial urban
     metropolis."
48   plaid silk walking dress: Stern, *Louisa May Alcott,* 6.
49   a "noticeable" figure: "Memorial to Joseph May," NEHGS Register, vol. 27. ABA
     called Colonel JM "a gentleman of high standing, and of the old School," in ABA
     to AMA, November 23, 1856, *Letters,* 219.
49   Reverend Francis Greenwood: AMA, Memoir of 1878, HAP. While some biog-
     raphers of the Alcotts stated that SJM performed the wedding ceremony of AMA
     and ABA, Abigail's own papers contradict this. A bust of the Rev. Greenwood
     adorns King's Chapel today.
49   Food at wedding feast: Hale, *A New England Boyhood,* 198–99, 118. *Salisbury Letters,*
     244, describes typical celebratory feast in Boston at the time.

Chapter 3: Humiliating Dependence

50 "I am very well": AMA to LFM, July 15, 1830, family letters, HAP.
50 "all I expected": In regard to AMA's tendency to idealize her husband, she had written to him on June 10, 1929 (family letters, HAP), "My one fear is that I may cease to please you." Love, she believed, "is a mere episode in the life of man" but "a whole history in the life of woman." As a result, "I fear lest absence and [other] occurrences may convince you how unimportant the presence of a mere woman is to you."
50 "inadequate to our support": AMA, Memoir of 1878, HAP.
50 "diminished a good deal": AMA to LFM, June 15, 1830, family letters, HAP.
50 letters of recommendation: Judith Callard, "The Alcotts in Germantown," *Germantown Crier* (1996, vol. 47), no page numbers.
51 Garrison advertisement: *Boston Courier*, Tuesday, October 12, 1830.
51 Garrison's imprisonment: Nye, *Fettered Freedom*, 11.
51 "Too many Boston folk": Mary C. Crawford, *Romantic Days in Old Boston*, 87. Odell Shepard makes the same point in *ABA Journals*, 25, footnote.
52 met "strong resistance": Russel Nye, *Fettered Freedom*, 13.
52 "his eye for 'the good in everything'": Van Wyck Brooks, *Flowering of New England*, 390.
52 had no moral qualms: At the School of Philosophy at Orchard House in 2009, John Matteson, Joel Myerson, and other scholars discussed ABA's initial lack of support toward abolition, in contrast to the Mays. AMA and SJM promoted abolition from 1830 forward. By the 1840s ABA may have been influenced by Emerson's decision in 1844 to speak out against slavery.
52 "anything intolerable or outrageous": John Matteson, lecture on John Brown and abolitionism, School of Philosophy, Orchard House, July 2009, author's notes.
52 "serious, quiet manner": Dr. Marie E. Zakrzewska, in *Memoir of SES*, 132.
52 Julien Hall: at the northwest corner of Milk and Congress (formerly Atkinson) Streets.
52 "stronghold of the devil": Nye, *Fettered Freedom*, 11.
52 "a want of discrimination": ABA, October 16, 1830, *Journals*, 25.
53 "slept in slave quarters": Sarah Elbert, *A Hunger for Home*, 12.
53 "disciple and fellow-laborer": *Memoir of SJM*, 142.
53 "Never . . . was one man": Frederick Douglass, *Frederick Douglass' Papers*, October 9, 1857, Yale University microfiche, quoted in Yacovone, "Abolitions and the 'Language of Fraternal Love,'" in *Meanings for Manhood: Constructions of Masculinity in Victorian America*, by Mark C. Carnes and Clyde Griffen, 89.
53 "Garrison is a prophet": *Memoir of SJM*, 142.
53 "of one mind and heart with": Sarah Elbert, *A Hunger for Home*, 12.
54 excluded "from the benefits": Karcher, *The First Woman in the Republic*, 20.
54 "an Anti-Slavery party": Margaret Fuller, *Woman in the Nineteenth Century*, 1845.
54 men "made slaves of": Sarah Grimké, 1838 "Letters on the equality of the sexes, and the condition of woman," by Grimké and Mary S. Parker, 27.
54 "Little can be done": "Letter from Mrs. Child on the Present State of the Anti-Slavery Cause," *Liberator*, September 6, 1839, Collected Correspondence of Lydia Maria Child, 8/186.
54 "misguided": Crawford, *Romantic Days in Old Boston*, 99.
54 "pouring oil": Nye, *Fettered Freedom*, 13.
54 May approached Channing: Crawford, *Romantic Days in Old Boston*, 109. This dialogue between May and Channing occurred in Boston in 1834, according to *Memoir of SJM*.
55 "I have been prompted": Yacovone, *SJM*, 38.

55 "I hear your son went crazy": "IN MEMORIAM—Samuel Joseph May," Unitarian Congregational Society of Syracuse, 1871.
55 advocates of immediate abolition: Nye, *Fettered Freedom*, 14, 23.
56 "Our son, S. J. May": Mary Ann May, 1830 journal, MFPCL.
56 "few members": Yacovone, *SJM,* 3.
56 among Boston's free blacks: "Restoring cornerstone of Hub's black history," *Boston Globe,* September 20, 2011, B1. Also see Crawford, *Romantic Days in Old Boston,* 102–3, 105.
56 African Meeting House: Built in 1806, it later became a synagogue on Smith Court, off Joy Street, and at the turn of the twenty-first century it was restored and renovated alongside the city's museum of African-American history.
56 Women had been excluded from public meetings: This tradition in New England and America arose from the Puritans' literal interpretation of the injunction in the Gospel of Paul, "A woman must be silent in church." In 1831 the NEASS excluded women, an issue over which antislavery men split. In 1839 Garrison, SJM, and other men welcomed women to the movement, prompting some abolitionists to form a separate, all-male group.
56 Long-distance travel: Crawford, *Romantic Days in Old Boston,* 326. Before railroads the trip from Boston to New York took four or five days.
57 "The emotions produced": ABA, March 16, 1831, *Journals,* 27.
57 "good health, perfectly quiet:": AMA to LFM, March 27, 1831, family letters, HAP.
57 "narrated by the parent": ABA, June 1831, *Journals,* 28.
58 purchased for the Alcotts: Judith Callard, "The Alcotts in Germantown," *Germantown Crier* (1996, vol. 47), "The Alcotts Move into Pine Place," no page numbers.
58 "not the kindest": LFM to SJM, May 1, 1831, MFPCL.
58 anonymous donor: Most biographers presume this was Colonel JM. The gift may have been more than a thousand dollars.
58 settling ancient debts: Odell Shepard, *ABA Journals,* 23.
58 "infancy is when": ABA, July 31, 1831, *Journals,* 29.
58 "a goodly company": AMA to LFM, August 24, 1831, family letters, HAP.
58 "virtuous and sober": LFM, 1833, quoted in Yacovone, *SJM,* 47.
59 "leave the slaves alone": LFM to SJM, 1834, MFPCL.
59 "periods of mental depression": AMA 1842, journals, HAP.
59 "decaying": AMA to SJM, April 12, 1853, family letters, HAP.
59 "lot of the sex": AMA to Ann Gage, July 13, 1848, private collection, Waterford, Maine, viewed in August 2010.
59 "Lucretia I suppose": AMA to SJM, March 1831, family letters, HAP.
59 "fat" and "fine": ABA to his mother, November 29, 1832, *Letters,* 18.
59 "fair complexion": Miss Donaldson letter from Germantown, PA, December 16, 1832, quoted in Cheney, *LMA's Life, Letters and Journals,* 17.
60 "for domestic sentiment": ABA to Colonel JM, November 29, 1832, *Letters,* 20.
60 Bleeding was still: Theriot, *Mothers & Daughters in Nineteenth-century America,* 55.
60 Close female friends: Mary Ann McDonough and Mrs. Brown, AMA's second nurse, are quoted in Judith Callard, "The Alcotts in Germantown," 1996 *Germantown Crier,* no page numbers. The original letters are in the Wyck Papers at the Germantown Historical Society.
60 "eccentric": Charles Godfrey Leland, ABA's student in Philadelphia, in *ABA Journals,* 42, footnote. Judith Callard wrote in the 1996 Germantown Historical Society's *Germantown Crier* that Charles J. Wister, whose brother Owen was ABA's student there, "remembered Bronson Alcott as peculiar and eccentric. . . . Passing along the aisle [of the classroom] he would suddenly kick a seat from under a pupil. . . . He showed no cordiality [to visitors] and the visitors left in disgust."
60 "thankless employment": AMA to SJM and LFM, February 20, 1833, family letters, HAP.

60 "Dear Sam and Lu": Ibid.
61 separation would benefit them: Herrnstadt, *ABA Letters*, 19, footnote.
61 Coleridge, Wordsworth: Shepard, Note to 1833, *ABA Journals*, 34.
61 "My eyes are very uncertain": AMA to SJM, June 22, 1833, family letters, HAP.
61 "slowly gaining confidence": AMA to SJM, October 1833, family letters, HAP.
62 "minds are somewhat solitary": Ibid.
62 maternal aunt: Lucretia's sister Charlotte Coffin, who often stayed with the Mays and the Garrisons, and seems not to have married.
62 make him famous: Nye, *Fettered Freedom*, 106: the Crandall case projected SJM "into national prominence by his part in the proceedings."

Chapter 4: Sacrifices Must Be Made

64 "You and Miss Crandall": SJM, *Some Recollections of Our Antislavery Conflict*, 47f.
64 English grammar, history: Prudence Crandall Museum, Canterbury, Connecticut.
64 rejected biracial education: Ibid., 16.
64 "the Liberia of America": Canterbury Town meeting quoted in *The Liberator*, April 6, 1833.
64 reopened her school: CMW, unpublished memoir, family collection. Crandall's twenty or so black female students included Sarah and Mary Harris, Harriet Lanson, Eliza Glasgko, Ann and Sarah Hammond, Julia Williams, and Elizabeth Bustill, according to the Prudence Crandall Museum.
64 Black Law: Nye, *Fettered Freedom*, 106.
65 "I will dispute": SJM, *Some Recollections of Our Antislavery Conflict*, 49.
65 burned a cross: Ibid., 45–48.
65 Fearing for her students' lives: Nye, *Fettered Freedom*, 104–5, and *Memoir of SJM*, 148–51.
65 "the greatest disturbances": Ibid., 106, 103.
65 "propelled him": Yacovone, *SJM*, 43.
65 her reputation: Crawford, *Romantic Days in Old Boston*, 108.
66 "ashamed of Canterbury": SJM, *Some Recollections of Our Antislavery Conflict*, 1869.
66 "passed his life": CMW, unpublished memoir, family collection.
66 "minister has long preached": ABA, July 31, 1831, *Journals*, 29.
66 "reading for dear life": AMA to SJM, March 3, probably 1834, family letters, HAP.
66 "think and talk": AMA to SJM, January 19, 1834, family letters, HAP.
66 "elevate the people of color": *History of Women's Suffrage, 1848–1861*, 325.
67 "a growing realization": Nye, *Fettered Freedom*, 219.
67 "the mortifying fact": Ibid., 19.
67 "unkind, indifferent": AMA quoted by ABA, April 27, 1834, *Journals*, 41.
67 "too closely to the *ideal*": ABA, November 1837, *Journals*, 94.
67 "wife and children suffer": ABA, April 27, 1834, *Journals*, 41.
68 "unorthodox arrangement": Barton, *Transcendental Wife*, 37.
68 "blessed at last": ABA, April 27, 1834, *Journals*, 41.
68 suffered a miscarriage: Barton, *Transcendental Wife*, 36, 38.
69 Bronson learned of the miscarriage: Judith Callard, "The Alcotts in Germantown," *Germantown Crier*, no page numbers.
69 Boston "is the place": ABA, June 1832, *Journals*, 31. ABA to his mother, November 29, 1832, *Letters*, 19.
69 "I cannot bear to think": Mary Ann McDonough to Jane Haines, March 1833, quoted in Judith Callard, "The Alcotts in Germantown," 1996 *Germantown Crier*, no page numbers. The original letter is in the Wyck Papers at the Germantown Historical Society.
69 "wanted a separation": Judith Callard, ibid.

69 "much to myself": AMA to SJM, September 1, 1834, family letters, HAP.
69 "about 31 children engaged": Ibid.
69 "pleased and excited": AMA to SJM, September 9, 1834, family letters, HAP.
70 "great educational regeneration": AMA to SJM, September 1, 1834, family letters, HAP.
70 on Bedford Street: The Alcotts spent a few weeks at Mrs. Whitney's boarding-house on Morton Street, according to AMA's journal, before moving to the 19 Bedford Street boardinghouse.
70 Temple School description: Elizabeth Palmer Peabody, preface, *Record of a School,* 1835.
70 Temple School students: ABA, December 3, 1868, *Journals,* 389. The Quincy child was Mayor Josiah Quincy's grandson, who like his father and grandfather became Boston's mayor.
70 "not myself prepared to say": Peabody, *Record of a School,* Preface.
71 "more genius for education": displayed at Orchard House School of Philosophy, July 2011.
71 "methods of discipline": Shepard, *ABA Journals,* footnote, 476.
71 3 Somerset Court: Beacon Hill and Mount Vernon had already been leveled by 1834, when the Alcotts returned to Boston, but Pemberton Hill was not leveled until 1835. Somerset Court runs off Somerset Street, just below the State House. It is now Ashburton Street.
71 "particularly" Louisa: Shepard, *ABA Journals,* 47, footnote.
71 "has more sympathy": ABA, "Researches on Childhood," HAP.
71 "Some habits, I regret": ABA, September 19, 1835, *Journals,* 65.
72 "delicate and yet necessary": ABA, October 26, 1834, *Journals,* 47.
72 "domestic and parental relations": ABA, January 21, 1835, *Journals,* 55.
72 "If the Divinity wills": ABA, May 3, 1835, *Journals,* 56.
72 another "Record": ABA, June 24, 1835, *Journals,* 57.
73 "Abba is in trouble": SJM to LFM, August 14, 1835, MFPCL.
73 "most precarious contingencies": AMA to Mary Tyler Peabody, September 2, 1835, courtesy of Megan Marshall.
74 built "towers and bridges": LMA, "Recollections of My Childhood," *Lulu's Library,* vii.
74 "children are importunate": AMA to SJM, September 9, 1834, family letters, HAP.
74 "importance of *moral* education": AMA to SJM, September 1834, family letters, HAP.
74 "amount of mischief": Ibid.
75 "friend to the colored": LMA, "Recollections of My Childhood," in Shealy, *Alcott in Her Own Time,* 33.
75 "Newfoundland": Ibid.
75 "she had become so eager": SJM, *Memoir,* 23.
76 "accompany her to visit": ABA, Oct. 21, 1835, *Journals,* 69.
76 Garrison's pregnant wife: Helen Benson Garrison, at whose 1833 wedding SJM presided.
76 "the good man who helped": LMA, "Recollections of My Childhood," *Lulu's Library.*
76 "Some of your family": AMA to SJM, February 22, 1835, family letters, HAP.
77 Mobs in Rhode Island: Nye, *Fettered Freedom,* 125, 202.
77 "Private assassins": Ibid., 202.
77 Garrison stepped out: Ibid., 201.
77 mainstream Northern press: Ibid., 198, 103.
77 Samuel Joseph came to Boston: Ibid., 143–44.
77 American newspapers reported: Ibid., 177.
77 "the *higher classes*": William Goodell, ibid., 194.

77 America's "united South": James Freeman Clark, *Memorial History of Boston*.
78 "not made for . . . turmoil": SJM to LFM, May 13, 1835, MFPCL.
78 "one of the best men": *Portland Magazine* review in Matteson, *Eden's Outcasts*, 67.
78 "a wise man": Ralph Waldo Emerson to Frederic Henry Hedge, Concord, July 20, 1836, *Emerson's Letters*, II, 29.
78 "dispenser of moral truth": ABA, September 18, 1835, *Journals*, 63.
78 "an oracular style": Theodore Dahlstrand, talk on ABA, Orchard House School of Philosophy, July 2011.
78 "my little one": ABA, September 30, 1835, *Journals*, 67.
79 "As I was queen of the revel": LMA, Cheney, *LMA's Life, Letters and Journals*, 27.
79 "a happy breakfast": LMA, *Little Women*, chapter one.
79 "I could not!": AMA, quoted in EPP to Mary Peabody, April 1836, Bruce Ronda, ed., *Letters of EPP*, 163.
80 "made her very angry": EPP to Mary Peabody, April 1836, ibid., 161.
80 "heavy-handed": Ibid., 157.
80 this "breach of honour": EPP to Mary Peabody, May 15, 1836, ibid., 168.
80 arrogant "self-estimation": EPP to Mary Peabody, April 1836, ibid., 157–163.
81 Samuel Joseph baptized: ABA, Mary 2?, 1836, *ABA's Journal for 1836*, in *Studies in the American Renaissance, 1878*, Myerson, ed., 59.
81 generally "dissatisfied": ABA, October 5, 1828, *Journals*, 13.
81 abandoned formal religion: Odell Shepard, ed., *ABA Journals*, 3.
81 "Your Ascended Father": ABA to AAP, *Letters*, 97. See also ABA, September 22, 1826, *Journals*, 5.
81 "read about Jesus": AAP journal entry, October 1839, quoted in Caroline Ticknor, *May Alcott, A Memoir*, 8.
81 "Yes, often": ABA, in Matteson, *Eden's Outcasts*, 92
81 "I preach the Gospel": ABA, February 1837, *Journals*, 84.
81 "commune with God": ABA, June 24, 1835, *Journals*, 57.
81 "Sabbath exercises": AMA, January 8, 1843, in *ABA Journals*, 150.
81 "my own spirit": ABA, December 20, 1835, *Journals*, 71–72.
82 "feminine subculture": Kornfeld, *Margaret Fuller*, 10.
82 "We women": Margaret Fuller, ibid., 20.
82 to support her mother: Blanchard, *Margaret Fuller*, 107.
82 "distrust of Mr. Alcott's": Kornfeld, *Margaret Fuller*, 90.
82 class had shrunk: Herrnstadt, *ABA Letters*, xxii.
83 "age hath no": ABA, November 1837, *Journals*, 96.
83 "severely censured": ABA, April 1837, *Journals*, 88.
83 identified with martyrs: ABA, January 1838, *Journals*, 98.
83 "doomed": ABA, October 1837, *Journals*, 92.
83 "I see not my way": ABA, May 1837, *Journals*, 90.
83 visited with Emerson: Shepard, Note on 1837, *ABA Journals*, 80–81.
83 "Write!": ABA, May 1837, *Journals*, 90. Bronson quotes a letter from Emerson.
84 "in a large room": AMA, Memoir of 1878, HAP.
84 spent two weeks: LFM to SJM, June 13, 1838, MFPCL.
84 "native hills": ABA, March 13, 1839, *Journals*, 117.
84 "boarders and pupils": ABA, March 1838, *Journals*, 100. AMA to SJM, December 22, 1833, family letters, HAP, describes AMA's dislike of boarders.
84 "influences of Nature": ABA, March 13, 1839, *Journals*, 117.
84 "Mammon-king": ABA, February 26, 1839, *Journals*, 117.
84 finances: ABA, June 1838, *Journals*, 100.
84 Alcott House: Shepard, *ABA Journals*, footnote, 169.
85 "Friends in England": ABA to his mother, December 28, 1839, *Letters*, 44.
85 "cross the water": ABA quoting AMA, ibid.
85 ban of my scissors: ABA quoting AMA, February 2, 1839, *Journals*, 114.

85   closed school: ABA to his mother, March 17–18, 1839, transcribed in *Journals,* 118.
85   "short respite": ABA, March 23, 1839, *Journals,* 120.
85   "Every day we sewed": LMA to Louise C. Moulton, n.d., family letters, HAP.
86   Grandfather May's house: According to NEHGS register, Colonel JM and his second wife in early 1835 moved from the house on Federal Court to a house at the corner of Washington and Oak streets, where Elizabeth Alcott would have stayed in 1840. AMA to SJM, February 22, 1835, HAP, begins, "Dear Brother, The old house in Federal House is empty and desolate enough, and I never want to go there again."
86   "the creative jet!": ABA, March 31, 1839, *Journals,* 121.
86   "A young Hoper": ABA to his mother, March 17–18, 1839, *Letters,* 42.

Chapter 5: This Sharp Sorrow

87   "fine boy, full grown": AMA, 1839 journal, HAP.
87   message from God: see David Hall, *Worlds of Wonder, Days of Judgment,* and Eve LaPlante, *Salem Witch Judge.*
87   "death's bitterest beaker": AMA, journals, HAP.
87   "My thrill of Hope": ABA, August 1841, *Journals,* 119.
87   "poisons the fountain": ABA, April 1839, Ms. journals, HAP.
88   of the sixth generation: Harvard graduates in the four previous generations are Judge Samuel Sewall, Rev. Joseph Sewall, Samuel Sewall, and Rev. Samuel J. May. This legacy of access to higher education is an index of the Mays' affluence: less than 3 percent of Americans had such access in 1870, and only 4 percent did in 1900.
88   Colonel May in 1839: Bedell, *The Alcotts,* indicates Colonel JM was now senile.
88   "I go forth": ABA recounting dialogue with AMA, April 23, 1839, *Journals,* 125.
88   "Plato held": ABA, November 10, 1852, *Journals,* 258.
88   under whose "ministry": ABA, April 29, 1839, *Journals,* 126.
88   met fifteen years earlier: Lydia Maria Child to AMA, *Collected Correspondences of Lydia Maria Child, 1817–1880,* ed. Patricia G. Holland, Milton Miltzer, and Francine Krasno. Microform, 1980. 90/2398.
88   "Denied the education": Karcher, *First Woman in the Republic,* 3.
88   "entirely the prerogative": Ibid., 16.
88   "regarded as a *lady*": Ibid., 2.
88   "toiling for the freedom": Lydia Maria Child quoted in Deborah P. Clifford, *Crusader for Freedom: A Life of Lydia Maria Child,* 2.
89   "wrong, blind, and carnal": Luther Lee, *Autobiography of Luther Lee,* 221–22.
89   "preach from their texts": SJM to Garrison (BPL Ms. A.1.2.V8, 36), in Karcher, *First Woman in the Republic,* 259.
90   A Boston newspaper: *Boston Gazette,* March 9, 1838.
90   Grimké speech: SES, *Memoir of SES,* 130.
91   Lucretia's opposition to the cause of women's rights: In 1850, when her husband, her sister Charlotte G. Coffin, and her daughter, Charlotte, were conveners of the national women's rights convention in Worcester, Massachusetts, Lucretia declined to join them.
91   "threatens the female character": Crawford, *Romantic Days in Old Boston,* 133.
91   "country's first feminists": Yacovone, *SJM,* 4–5.
91   "are not appreciated": ABA, June 22, 1839, *Journals,* 131.
91   never taught schoolchildren again: ABA to his mother, June 21, 1840, *Letters,* 48.
91   "the Book of Nature": ABA, July 24, 1839, *Journals,* 133.
92   "I remember running": LMA, "Recollections of My Childhood," in *LMA's Life, Letters and Journals,* 29.

92   the character she created [Mr. March]: Catherine Rivard said in an email to the author in 2009, "When Louisa conjured up the minister 'Mr. March,' she had [her uncle] Sam in mind."

92   "black, white & grey,": LFM to Joseph May, June 10, 1854, MFPCL.

92   Cold Water Brigade: the chants and newspaper coverage are from the collection of documents concerning SJM at the First Parish Church of Norwell, Massachusetts, formerly South Scituate.

92   "Self-Culture": ABA, October 1838, *Journals*, 105.

92   return to peddling: ABA to his mother, December 28, 1839, *Letters*, 44.

93   "Dr. Charles Windship": either Abigail's nephew, Charles May Windship, who was thirty in 1839, or his father, Charles Williams Windship, who lived until 1852.

93   "Be a good Girl": ABA to LMA, December 1839, *Letters*, 45.

93   Wordsworth's influence on ABA: See ABA's published journals and Brooks, *Flowering of New England*, 232.

93   "Abba does all": ABA to his mother, June 21, 1840, *Letters*, 48.

94   "poetical wardrobe": Barton, *Transcendental Wife*, 71.

94   "I have planted myself": ABA to SJM, April 6, 1840, *Letters*, 47.

94   "time of Public Favor": ABA to SJM, August 10, 1840, *Letters*, 52–53.

94   "Two [children] make peace": ABA to AAP, May 14, 1841, *Letters*, 56.

94   "step lightly": ABA to LMA, June 21, 1840, *Letters*, 49.

94   Abby May: The baby was not actually named for several months, according to AAP's diary entry of November 8, 1840: "We are going to name the baby Abby, after Mother."

94   teenage nieces: Barton, *Transcendental Wife*, 73.

95   "anxious housewife": ABA to SJM, August 10, 1840, Letters, 53. ABA seems to quote AMA.

95   "a noble horse": AMA, journals, HAP.

95   "golden bees": Emerson to Margaret Fuller, August 12, 1842, *Letters of Emerson*, 81.

95   "gee and haw": AMA, journals, HAP.

95   "let the old man go": *Memoir of SJM*, 215.

95   Colonel May's estate: equivalency based on the Nominal GDP per capita, rather than the Consumer Price Index, for the year 2000.

95   Louisa Caroline Greenwood, born in 1810, married George W. Bond in 1843. She was a daughter of the Rev. Dr. Greenwood, who performed AMA and ABA's wedding in 1830. LMA and her sisters called her "Aunt Bond."

96   Marital law: Samuel E. Sewall, "Legal Condition of Women in Massachusetts in 1886," *Memoir of SES*, 133–34.

96   "beautiful little girl": Cheney, *LMA Life, Letters and Journals*, 18.

96   "Do write a little": AMA to LMA, c. 1846, quoted in Stern, *From Blood & Thunder*, 255.

97   "had no patience": Caroline W. Healey Dall, *Margaret and Her Friends: Or, Ten Conversations with Margaret Fuller upon the Mythology of the Greeks and Its Expression in Art*, xiii. Dall cites a letter c.1840 from Fuller to ABA rejecting a submission to the Transcendental journal she edited, *The Dial*: "The break of your spirit in the crag of the actual makes surf and foam but leaves no gem behind. Yet it is a great wave, Mr. Alcott."

97   "model children": LMA, "Recollections of My Childhood," *Lulu's Library*, xiii.

97   another depression: Joan von Mehren, *Minerva and the Muse*, 155.

97   "dreadful nervous excitation": AMA to SJM, January 1842, family letters, HAP.

97   "men icebergs": AMA, Memoir of 1878, HAP.

98   a "fine house": ABA to Junius Alcott, September 28, 1841, *Letters*, 57.

98   Bronson convinced: Herrnstadt, *ABA Letters*, footnote, 62.

98   "Here are my wife": ABA to Junius Alcott, February 19, 1842, *Letters*, 61.

98   "I will hope all things": AMA, May 7, 9, 1842, in *ABA Journals*, 142. The Biblical reference is 1 Cor. 13:7.

98   "my husband's wardrobe": AMA, April 1, 1842, in *ABA Journals*, 141.

99 ABA's trunk: ABA to AMA, May 7, 1842, *Letters,* 64.
99 "weight of responsibility": AMA to SJM, June 22, 1833, family letters 1828–1861, HAP.
99 "trembling hand": AMA, May 7, 1842, in *ABA Journals,* 142.

Chapter 6: Looking to My Daughter's Labors

100 "sick and sad": AMA, ibid. The Biblical reference is Isa. 10:13.
100 "second nuptial eve": ABA to AMA, May 7, 1842, *Letters,* 64. Bronson never fulfilled this promise of a second wedding ceremony on his return from England.
101 "Some flowers": AMA, May 22, 1842, in *ABA Journals,* 142–43.
101 no communication: Shepard, *ABA Journals,* 139.
101 "greeted by friends": AMA, June 20, 1842, in *ABA Journals,* 143.
101 "younger disciple": Matteson, *Eden's Outcasts,* 101.
101 "new plantation": ABA to Junius Alcott, June 30, 1842, *Letters,* 74.
102 "too crowded up": AMA, July 8, 1842, in *ABA Journals,* 143.
102 "swift duty": AMA, July 8, 1842, in *ABA Journals,* 143.
102 "Domestic life": AMA, November 20, 1844, journal fragments, HAP.
102 "the joy I feel": AMA, July 26, 1842, in *Journals ABA,* 145.
103 Depressive tendencies of LMA, AMA: AMA, Memoir of 1878, HAP.
103 "whether my capabilities": AMA, September 8, 1842, in *ABA Journals,* 147.
103 "must be benefited": AMA, June 18, 1842, Memoir of 1878, HAP.
103 "moved and embarrassed": Margaret Fuller journals (FJ 42–1, 328), in von Mehren, *Minerva and the Muse,* 157.
104 "ready at any moment": Emerson, March 1842, *Journals and Miscellaneous Notebooks,* VIII, 211–15.
104 "dear English-men": AMA, July 8, 1842, in *ABA Journals,* 143. AMA quotes ABA's letter on Lane's intellect.
104 Lane's library and family: Richard Francis, *Fruitlands,* 93.
104 "why am I so happy?": AMA, November 29, 1842, in *ABA Journals,* 148.
104 "I wished to breathe": AMA, October 23, 1842, in *ABA Journals,* 148.
105 "occasional hilarity": AMA, November 29, 1842, in *ABA Journals,* 148.
105 coverture: I am grateful for Cynthia Barton, author of *Transcendental Wife,* for introducing me to this legal concept, in conversation in 2009.
105 "profligate and idle": Margaret Fuller, *Woman in the Nineteenth Century.*
105 "traditional patriarchal view": Nancy Theriot, *Mothers & Daughters in Nineteenth-century America,* 34.
106 Bronson expected his wife: Herrnstadt, *ABA Letters,* xxxi.
106 "race of murderers": ABA, 1835, *Journals,* 115.
106 typical feast: AMA, January 22, 1843, in *ABA Journals,* 151.
106 "not favorably situated": AMA, August 22, 1842, in *ABA Journals,* 146.
106 "disrelish of cooking": AMA, November 29, 1842, in *Journals ABA,* 148.
106 contentious questions: ABA's biographer Theodore Dahlstrand said in 2010 Orchard House School of Philosophy lecture, "Bronson hated controversy and disliked being contradicted or having objections raised. He disliked when Garrison, Parker, or Pillsbury attended his lectures, because they were disputatious and confrontational. In one Buffalo, New York, conversation that former president Millard Fillmore and a congressman attended, Bronson felt useless because the politicians just wanted to debate. A good conversation, in his view, went 'two and a half hours and nobody [but him] said anything.'"
107 "I live, my dear": ABA to LMA, November 29, 1842, *Letters,* 93.
107 "the pencil-case I promised": AMA to LMA, November 29, 1842, Cheney, *LMA Life, Letters and Journals,* 23.
107 "safety valve": AMA, in Cynthia Barton, *Transcendental Wife,* 126.

107 "may this pen": AMA, ibid., 128.
107 "arduous and involved": AMA, December 24, 1842, in *ABA Journals*, 148.
107 "recreation": AMA, August 22, 1842, ibid., 146.
107 "for some weeks": ABA to Junius, December 26, 1842, quoting AMA, *ABA Letters*, 94. AMA's diary for that week indicates she took only William Lane and Louisa with her to Boston.
107 "Distance and absence": ABA to Junius Alcott, December 26, 1842, *Letters*, 95.
107 "quite electrified": Francis, *Fruitlands*, 113–114. The observer was Charles Lane and the speaker on education was Henry Wright.
108 "perfect trust": AMA, January 18, 1843, in *ABA Journals*, 150.
108 "practical philosophy": AMA, November 29, 1842, in *ABA Journals*, 148–150.
108 children's journals: Anna's extant journals began in 1839, when she was eight. There are no extant journals by Louisa before summer 1843, when she was ten.
108 "healing all differences": AMA, January 15, 1843, in *ABA Journals*, 150.
108 "notes of reconciliation": AMA, January 23, 1843, in *ABA Journals*, 151.
108 celibacy: Barton, *Transcendental Wife*, 86–87.
108 "overthrow": AMA, January 22, 1843, in *ABA Journals*, 151.
109 invited black parishioners: Karcher, *First Woman in the Republic*, 199.
109 employed by Horace Mann: Herrnstadt, *ABA Letters*, 51, footnote.
109 "little debts": AMA, March 6, 1843, in *ABA Journals*, 152.
109 "quite at a loss": AMA, March 6, 1843, Diary for 1841–1844, HAP.
110 disillusionment: Barton, *Transcendental Wife*, 85.
110 Emerson on ABA: Capper, *Margaret Fuller, An American Romantic Life: The Public Years*, 10. Emerson quotations are from his letter to Margaret Fuller, May 8, 1840, *Emerson's Letters*, II, 94.
110 "Alcott on the 17th October": Emerson, *Journals and Miscellaneous Notebooks*, VIII, 210–12.
110 "eventful years": AMA, June 1, 1843, in *ABA Journals*, 152.
110 "DEAR LOUIE": AMA, March 12, 1843, family letters, HAP.
111 "I hope that soon": LMA, 1843, Cheney, ed., *LMA's Life, Letters and Journals*, 23–24.

Chapter 7: To Drag Life's Lengthening Chain

112 "our little territory": AMA, June 1, 1843, in *ABA Journals*, 152. Details derive from this journal entry.
113 "This dell is the canvas": ABA to Junius Alcott, June 18, 1843, *Letters*, 103.
113 "prove a happy home": AMA, June 1, 1843, in *ABA Journals*, 152.
113 to visit Fruitlands: AMA to SJM, July 1843, family letters, HAP.
114 a hymn: The 64th hymn in J. W. Frothingham's *Universal Hymns*, Boston, 1894.
114 "Her pride is not yet": William Lane to William Oldham, 1843, quoted in Francis, *Fruitlands*, 110. See also Barton, *Transcendental Wife*, 95.
114 sleep apart: Barton, *Transcendental Wife*, 94–97. According to Barton, Lane "threatened [AMA's] very marriage . . . Lane was urging [ABA] to renounce the bondage of matrimony, leave his family, and join him in uniting with the Shakers."
114 he "forcibly illustrated": AMA, July 1843, in *ABA Journals*, 153.
114 threat to her marriage: Many scholars suggest that Bronson and Lane's relationship had a "homoerotic underpinning," as Richard Francis wrote in *Fruitlands*, 246. Other scholars who infer a homoerotic attachment between Bronson and Lane are Madelon Bedell, Frederick Dahlstrand, Harriet Reisen, and John Matteson. It is difficult to judge past intimacies by modern standards, however, and there is no actual evidence of a sexual relationship between the men.
114 "Lane was a subversive": Ronald Bosco, Summer Conversations, School of Philosophy, Orchard House, July 2009.

115 "strictly of the pure": LMA, "Transcendental Wild Oats," 38–39.
115 Fruitlands rules: ABA and William Lane, "Letter to Herald of Freedom," August–
     September 1843, in ABA, MS Autobiographical collections 1840–1844, 239–295,
     HAP.
115 "Only a brave woman's": LMA, "Transcendental Wild Oats," 39.
115 "spare the cattle": Samuel Sewall Greele, MS letter at Fruitlands, in Francis, *Fruit-
     lands,* 243.
115 The poet W. Ellery Channing: a nephew of the Rev. Dr. William Ellery Chan-
     ning, for whom he was named. Bronson and Lane's traveling companion, Henry
     Wright, had left the community, disillusioned, in the spring of 1843 and possibly
     returned to England; he died not long afterwards.
115 "amiable" and "active" Miss Page: AMA, journal for 1843, HAP. LMA later wrote
     in "Transcendental Wild Oats" that Ann Page, a "stout lady of mature years, senti-
     mental, amiable, and lazy, wrote verses copiously."
116 She alone was responsible: ABA to his brother Chatfield, August 4, 1843, *Letters,*
     107.
116 On Tuesday, July 18: AMA, July 24, 1843, in *ABA Journals,* 154.
116 train a black woman: SJM also offended the Normal School administration by tak-
     ing a class to a rally for a fugitive slave.
116 a "kind sympathy": AMA to SJM, August 1843, family letters, HAP.
116 "quite ill": AMA to Charles May, August 31, 1843, Memoir of 1878, HAP.
116 "by what human aids": AMA to SJM, August 1843, family letters, HAP.
117 "content to wait": ABA to Junius Alcott, April 6, 1845, *Letters,* 121.
117 "sepulchral tones": W. Ellery Channing, in AMA to SJM, August 1843, family let-
     ters, HAP.
117 never spent any time together: ABA to AMA, September 21, 1854, *Letters,* 184.
117 Elizabeth Willis Wells: this niece of Abigail's is probably the mother of Elizabeth
     May Wells, born August 20, 1839, who in 1866 married her first cousin once re-
     moved Samuel Sewall Greele, who was born October 11, 1824.
117 one visitor as he departed: James Kay.
118 "I told mother": LMA, November 29, 1843, *Journals,* 47.
119 "deport themselves": AMA, September 1, 1843, journals, HAP.
119 "must not tease my mother": LMA, September 1, 1843, *Journals,* 45.
119 "not very pretty": LMA to AMA, October 8, 1843, *Letters,* 3.
119 "I wish I were rich": LMA, October 8, 1843, *Journals,* 46.
119 "We saw but little": AMA, August 26, 1843, in *ABA Journals,* 154–55. Details of the
     following scene derive from that journal entry.
120 "A good remark and true!": Ibid.
120 "separation": Cynthia Barton, *Transcendental Wife,* 87.
120 "keep [at bay]": Bedell, *The Alcotts,* 241.
121 "The rule was to do": LMA, *Transcendental Wild Oats*, 52–53.
121 "I wish we could be together": LMA, January 1845, *Journals,* 46. LMA may be remi-
     niscing about Fruitlands.
121 "try to fortify myself": AMA to SJM, November 1843, family letters, HAP.
121 note to Anna: Barton, *Transcendental Wife,* 93.
122 Abigail singing: AMAN to AMA, August 10, 1870, *Little Women Abroad,* Daniel
     Shealy, ed., 184. May wrote to AMA from Vevey, Switzerland, "As I lie in my bed
     till late these fine mornings, I imagine I hear mother saying at the foot of the stairs,
     'Come girls, morning glories all out, and a beautiful day. Breakfast nearly ready,
     come do get up for these are the most [lovely?] hours of the day.' So I call to Lu, in
     remembrance of home, but we don't get up."
122 "not dead yet": AMA to her brother Charles, November 1843, family letters, HAP.
122 "Even our passions": Ibid.
122 "fortify" herself: AMA, Diary for 1841–1844, HAP.

122 "pitiable moodiness": Ibid.
122 "very unhappy": LMA, December 10, 1843, *Journals,* 47.
123 "Rosamond": poem by Christopher Pearse Cranch, poet born in Massachusetts in 1815.
123 "sifting everything": AMA to SJM, November 11, 1843, family letters, HAP.
123 "extreme mental depression": Herrnstadt, *ABA Letters,* 116, footnote.
123 he wished to die: Shepard, *ABA Journals,* Note on 1840–1841, 140.
123 "Then the tragedy began": LMA, "Transcendental Wild Oats," 55–58.
123 "Mrs. Alcott gives notice": Lane to Oldham, November 1843, in W. H. Harland, "Bronson Alcott's English Friends," *Resources for American Literary Study,* vol. 8 (1978), Joel Myerson, ed.
124 "quite uncomfortable": AMA to SJM, December 1843, family letters, HAP.
124 "In the morning mother": LMA, December 23, 1843, *Journals,* 48.
124 "a little merry-making": AMA, December 25, 1843, in *ABA Journals,* 155.
124 "appropriateness of this song": LMA, *Journals,* 50.
125 "Christmas is here": AMA, December 25, 1843, in *Journals of LMA,* 48.
125 "completely blocked up": AMA, December 25, 1843, in *ABA Journals,* 155.
125 "I have concluded": AMA, January 1–7, 1844, in *ABA Journals,* 156.
125 "I will not abide": ABA to Junius Alcott, January 2, 1845, and October 28, 1844, *Letters,* 117 and 115.
125 "There is nothing": AMA, February 3, 1844, in *ABA Journals,* 157.
126 "live [Bronson's] principle": AMA, January 1844, family letters, HAP.
126 "a great revolution": Samuel E. Sewall's *Legal Condition of Women,* 54, in *Memoir of SES,* 136.
126 Marital law improved: Ibid., 164. Sewall mentioned specific legal improvements: "1. To equalize the descent of real estate between husband and wife. 2. To equalize the descent of personal property between husband and wife. 3. To equalize the custody of minor children. 4. To legalize conveyances, gifts, and contracts between husband and wife. 5. To provide for testamentary guardians for wives as well as widows. 6. To repeal the act limiting the right of married women to dispose of real estate by will."
126 "very fault of marriage": Fuller, *Woman in the Nineteenth Century.*
126 "carve out our own": AMA, August 22, 1842, in *Journals ABA,* 146.
127 "hired a small house": AMA, Memoir of 1878, HAP.
127 her beloved books: a photograph of AMA's "Catalogue of my books—1844" appears in Barton, *Transcendental Wife,* 101.
127 the middle of January: in *Fruitlands,* 255, Francis concluded, based on a letter from Emerson to his brother and AMA letters to SJM, that Lane left the farm on January 6 and AMA and her girls left on January 16.
127 he moved with his family: Barton, *Transcendental Wife,* 97.
127 story that evokes this drama: "Pauline's Passion and Punishment," a thriller LMA wrote and published under a pseudonym in 1862, later that year won a hundred-dollar prize from *Frank Leslie's Illustrated Newspaper.*
128 "richly sexual *femme fatale*": Stern, *Critical Essays on LMA,* 55.
128 deemed "too sensational": LMA's novel *A Long Fatal Love Chase,* which James L. Elliot considered that year.
128 woman who had met the Alcotts: Mary Gove, of Lynn, Massachusetts, speaking in November 1842, in Francis, *Fruitlands,* 105–106.
128 "Abigail took control": Cynthia Barton, "The Ballast to Bronson's Balloon," unpublished essay shown to the author in 2010.
129 Louisa "suffered the most": Elbert, *Early Stories of LMA,* introduction, 10.
129 "Mr. Lane's efforts": AMA, January 16, 1844, in *ABA Journals,* 157.
129 "I love his faith": AMA, January 28, 1844, in *ABA Journals,* 157.
129 Hannah Robie: Born in Halifax in 1784, sixteen years before Abigail, Robie was

actually the aunt of Abigail's cousin SES. She was an unmarried sister of SES's mother, Mary Robie Sewall, who was the wife of Dorothy Sewall May's younger brother Joseph Sewall, who went into partnership with his nephew Samuel Salisbury, Jr., importing dry goods, as Sewall & Salisbury, a large and prosperous enterprise. As a sister-in-law of Abigail's mother, Hannah Robie functioned in the May-Alcott family as an aunt. She lived part-time in Halifax and part-time in Melrose with her sister, brother-in-law, and nieces and nephews, including SES. For more on the Robie family see *Memoir of SES,* 10.

129   "soul-sickness": AMA, March 22, 31, 1844, in *ABA Journals,* 158.
130   labor "unremittedly": AMA, April 24, 1844, in *ABA Journals,* 158.
130   "my Paradise at Fruitlands": ABA, April 6, 1850, *Journals,* 230–31.
130   "the sole person": ABA to Junius Alcott, June 15, 1844, *Letters,* 111.
130   "wish you success": AMA, July 15, 1844, in *ABA Journals,* 158–59.
130   "I am angry": LMA, *Little Women,* Chapter 8.
130   "two verses": LMA, *Journals,* 50–51.
130   "great thoroughfare": map of Syracuse in 1834, Onondaga Historical Association, Syracuse, NY.
131   sprawling Federal-style frame house: LFM and SJM to their son Joseph May, September 21, 1854, and SJM, Diary for 1860, MFPCL.
131   horse-drawn chaise: Yacovone, *SJM,* 21.
131   new baby: SJM and LFM's fourth child, George B. Emerson May, was named for his father's closest Harvard friend, Ralph Waldo Emerson's cousin George B. Emerson (1797–1881), a teacher, amateur naturalist, and president of the Boston Society of Natural History. After SJM's death George B. Emerson coauthored *Memoir of SJM* with Samuel May Jr. and Thomas J. Mumford.
131   rapidly growing city: Syracuse's population grew from 60 people in 1803 to 2,500 in 1830 and to 22,000 in 1852. The May family spent the entire summer of 1844 in Syracuse, returned to Lexington for a few months, and moved permanently to Syracuse in April 1845.
131   Underground Railroad: Nye, *Fettered Freedom,* 277.
131   "convenient shipping-point": Reverend Luther Lee, *Autobiography of Luther Lee,* 332.
131   "over a thousand fugitives": SJM collection, Onondaga Historical Association, Syracuse, New York.
131   accompanied some: Yacovone, *SJM,* 139–40.
132   "than Boston Gold": ABA to Junius Alcott, January 2, 1845, *Letters,* 117. Abigail's portion of the estate had now grown to about $3,100.
132   "as good to me": LMA, October 12 and December 23, 1843, *Journals,* 46, 47.

Chapter 8: The Best Woman in the World

133   "little room I have wanted": LMA, March 1846, *Journals,* 59.
133   Louisa's little room: Room location derives from a National Park Service tour of Wayside House, formerly the Alcotts' Hillside, July 2010.
133   arrived at Hillside: According to Herrnstadt, *ABA Letters,* 118, footnote, the Concord house purchased by the Alcotts for $1350 in 1845 and named Hillside was sold in 1852 for $1500 to Hawthorne, who renamed it Wayside, as it is known today.
133   male cousin: Frederick Llewellyn Willis, in *Alcott in Her Own Time,* Daniel Shealy, ed., 177.
134   "made a plan": LMA, March 1846, *Journals,* 59.
134   "half-educated tomboy": LMA to ABA, December 12, 1875, *Letters,* 206.
134   "to *work really*": LMA, March 1846, *Journals,* 59.
134   "making great effort": AMA, March 16, 1845, journals, HAP.

134 "DEAR MOTHER": LMA, January 1845, *Journals,* 55.
134 "God comfort thee": LMA to AMA, 1845, copied by AAP into her diary, in Barton, *Transcendental Wife,* 129.
135 "Bronson assigned great value": John Matteson, lecture on John Brown and the Alcotts, School of Philosophy, Orchard House, July 2009.
135 a "passion for the blond": Brooks, *Flowering of New England,* 277.
135 "Count thyself divinely tasked": ABA, March 16, 1846, *Journals,* 173. Editor Odell Shepard noted in a footnote, "In Mrs. Alcott and Louisa . . . he thought that he saw diabolic traits."
135 "I corrected their Journals": ABA, April 1846, *Journals,* 175.
135 "family exchequer": Caroline Ticknor, *May Alcott, A Memoir,* 26.
136 "I made [Louisa] write them": Ellen Emerson to a friend, December 21, 1854, quoted in Stern's *From Blood & Thunder,* 37. LMA later recalled writing her fairy tales at sixteen, but in 1848 she was fifteen.
136 Bronson desired a consociate family: ABA to Charles Lane, January 1846, *Letters,* 126.
136 "my own efforts to do and be": AMA, September 5, 1845, journals, HAP.
137 Sophia Ford lived: ABA to Charles Lane, January 1846, *Letters,* 126.
137 John Edward May: CMW and LFM to SJM, October 12, 1845. MFPCL. John Edward May while boarding with the Alcotts attended the Lexington Classical School, which his father had run.
137 "first clergyman to advocate": *History of Woman Suffrage,* eds. Susan B. Anthony, Elizabeth Cady Stanton, and Matilda Joslyn Gage, 518.
137 "Why do half": SJM, "The Rights and Condition of Women," *Commensurate with Her Capacities and Obligations Are Woman's Rights: A Series of Tracts,* 1–2,13.
137 masculine names: Cecile in "A Marble Woman" and Christy in *Work,* for instance. The quote is from the first chapter of *Little Women.*
138 abandon corsets: Jan Turnquist, executive director, Orchard House, in conversation, 2010.
138 "evils of Woman's life": AMA, "Sunday 19th" [probably 1848], journals, HAP.
138 "great big darling": LFM to SJM, August 25 [probably 1828], MFPCL.
138 "dull & lonesome": LFM to SJM, October 1845, MFPCL.
138 "No money comes": LFM to SJM, October 24, 1845, MFPCL.
139 "these prosaic ministers": LFM to SJM, December 11, 1846, MFPCL.
139 "quite out of place": ABA to Charles Lane, January 1846, *Letters,* 126.
139 "Though no son": Emerson, *Journals,* IV, 460.
139 "all victims": Blanchard, *Margaret Fuller,* 104.
139 "As was Eve": Miller, *Margaret Fuller, American Romantic,* 298.
139 "sentimental period": LMA, "Recollections."
140 *Jane Eyre*: LMA, 1852 "List of books I like," in Cheney, *LMA Her Life, Letters, and Journals,* 68.
140 "too noble to curb": AMA to SJM, February 29, 1848, family letters, HAP.
141 "constantly finding myself": AMA to SJM, December 31, 1846, journals, HAP.
141 "determined purpose": Cheney, *LMA Life, Letters and Journals,* 49.
141 "These arrearages," AMA, December 31, 1846, journal, HAP.
142 "bright active beings": AMA, January 22 [probably 1847], journals, HAP.
142 "meeting [with] God": AMA to SJM, December 31, 1846, family letters, HAP.
142 young fugitive: ABA, February 2, 1846, *Journals,* 188.
142 "the most intolerant": ABA, February 1846, *Journals,* 191.
142 "hermit": ABA to his mother, June 13, 1847, *Letters,* 130.
142 "Arrowheads": Brooks, *Flowering of New England,* 296.
142 summer of 1847: ABA to his mother, June 13, 1847, *Letters,* 130.
142 Edward May: In a June 13, 1848, letter to his mother, ABA mentioned "a boy now living with us, Edward May, from Boston," who studied in Anna's school. Born in

January 1838 to Abigail's first cousin the Rev. Samuel May Jr., of Leicester, Massachusetts, and his wife, this Edward May was later schooled in Boston for several years but apparently did not attend Harvard.

142 seraphine: Barton, *Transcendental Wife,* 124.

143 Elizabeth ("Lizzie") Willis Wells: Born in 1822, she gave birth in August 1839 to Elizabeth May Wells, who in 1866 married her first cousin once removed Samuel Sewall Greele, born October 10, 1824. In yet another union of first cousins, the Alcott girls'"Cousin Louisa" Windship, a daughter of Dr. Windship's second marriage, married her first cousin by marriage Hamilton Willis.

143 "dreadfully": LMA, July 1850, *Journals,* 63.

143 "with tearful eyes": AMA quoted in ABA to AAP, December 10, 1847, *ABA Letters,* 132.

143 "cold, heartless, Brainless": AMA to SJM, January 10, 1848, family letters, HAP.

143 "one of the dullest little towns": LMA to the *Springfield Republican,* May 5, 1869, in *Selected Letters,* 127.

144 water-cure establishment: The spa where Abigail worked was immortalized on an 1857 Seated Liberty Quarter counter-stamped "Dr. Shattuck's Water Cure, Waterford, Maine."

144 expanding railroad lines: Hale's *New England Boyhood* describes the first U.S. steam railway going nine miles from Boston to West Newton in 1833, and to Worcester the next year. By 1840 railroads linked all six New England states.

144 Mary Moody Emerson: Among the many charming accounts of Emerson's aunt is Carlos Baker's in the "Aunt Mary" chapter of *Emerson Among the Eccentrics.*

144 "head of a water cure": Ralph Waldo Emerson to Calvin Farrar, December 9, 1847, *Emerson's Letters,* VIII, 126, quoting AMA.

144 "cannot afford to feed": AMA, journals, HAP.

144 "Mrs. Alcott possesses": Emerson to Farrar, op. cit. Oddly, the editor of Emerson's letters, Elanor Tilton, writes that "nothing came of this scheme to provide a living for the Alcotts."

144 "family cares": ABA to Sylvester Graham, April 12, 1848, *Letters,* 134.

144 "*Action* is a duty": AMA, journals, HAP.

145 "By some chance as yet unforeseen": ABA to AAP, April 13, 1848, *Letters,* 135.

145 "work beyond myself": ABA to AAP, May 11, 1848, *Letters,* 138–39.

145 "fly" to her mother: ABA to AAP, June 23, 1848, *Letters,* 144.

Chapter 9: Mother, Is It You?

146 bedchamber that she shared: ABA to AAP, May 16, 1848, *Letters,* 140.

147 "scene in a theater": AMA to her family, May 27, 1848, Memoir of 1878, HAP. This letter is also the source of AMA's dream about LMA.

147 "*nation*alities": AMA to SES, June 14, 1848, family letters, HAP.

147 Daily spa schedule: AMA to ABA, May 20, 1848, Memoir of 1878, HAP. Although AMA mentions a Dr. Fisher, the doctor in charge of the spa that summer, according to *The Waterford Water Cure,* was Josiah Prescott, M.D., who had succeeded Dr. E. A. Kitteridge.

147 "the greatest thing": newspaper clipping pasted on letter from AMA to SJM, June 14, 1848, family letters, HAP.

147 "handsome, genial": Julian Hawthorne in Shealy, *Alcott In Her Own Time,* 205.

147 Ann Sargent Gage: Many of her papers have been donated to the American Antiquarian Society. I am indebted to her great-great-grandson William Wheeler for sharing with me the letters AMA sent her in 1848.

148 "dignity and character": AMA to Ann Sargent Gage, July 13, 1848, private collection, Waterford, Maine. In August 2010 the author viewed this and a second letter from AMA to Gage, dated a week later.

148 "selfish": AMA, May 18–21, 1848, journal for 1848, HAP.

148 "I had staid": AMAN to AMA, July 5, 1848, quoted in Ticknor, *May Alcott,* 28–30.
148 around July 10: Bedell and many other biographers of the Alcotts theorized that Abigail stayed at the water-cure spa for the three months to which she had agreed. But a newly discovered letter she wrote to Ann Gage from Concord, Massachusetts, on July 13, 1848, indicates she left the spa after about two months. The two-word quote about Eliza Stearns is from that letter.
148 "threshold of my Home": AMA to Ann Gage, July 13, 1848, private collection.
150 "Despair is the paralysis": AMA to SJM, September 17, 1848, Memoir of 1878, HAP.
150 "antique furniture": *Memoir of SES,* 149. His partner was George Dary.
150 influx of immigrants: Rawson, *Eden on the Charles,* 17. Irish immigration to Boston began in the 1820s and swelled in the 1840s with a massive influx of rural peasants to the urban environment. The city was one-third Irish by 1855, and by the end of the century Protestant Yankees were "outnumbered nearly three to one by people of other ethnic backgrounds," according to Rawson.
150 America's fourth-largest: Ibid., 86.
150 "dark lanes and alleys": Dr. Walter Channing, *Plea for Pure Water,* 14.
151 spread disease: According to *Eden on the Charles,* 82, an 1834 study by Boston's city council found that water from one-third of the city's 2,767 wells was undrinkable.
151 "Dr. Huntington's Society": The Rev. Dr. Frederic Dan Huntington (1819–1904), a Unitarian minister who preached in Boston, became Harvard's Plummer professor of Christian Morals, and in the 1860s joined the Episcopal Church.
151 "City Missionary": ABA to his mother, April 22, 1849, *Letters,* 149.
151 "a visitor of the poor": Mary Van Wyck Church, unpublished manuscript biography of Elizabeth Peabody, MHS, 339. I am grateful to Megan Marshall for pointing out this quotation.
152 thirty to eighty dollars: A few months after AMA started working in Boston, her monthly salary increased because the South Congregational Church Benevolent and Relief Fund directed by the Rev. Dr. Huntington employed AMA "to visit and distribute the alms of their society to the Destitute Poor of Ward 11."
152 impoverished South End: For eighteen months, from fall 1848 to spring 1850, AMA lived and worked in Boston's Ward 11, the rectangular portion of the South End including Harrison, Washington, and Tremont streets from Dover Street northwest to the Roxbury border.
152 Hillside tenant: Bedell, *Alcotts,* 271.
152 "we women folk": LMA, "Recollections of My Childhood," in *Lulu's Library,* xv–xvi.
152 "bustle and dirt": Ibid.
152 "fine free times": Ibid.
152 "all-absorbing poor": Ibid.
153 "drudgery": ABA to AMA, September 17, 1849, *Letters,* 152, quoting AMA.
153 "daily protest": AMA to SJM, 1850–1851, family letters, HAP.
153 88 Atkinson [now Congress] Street: ABA to his mother, April 28, 1850, *Letters,* 155. LMA said Uncle Sam's house had "many comforts about us which we shall enjoy." The editors of her *Journals* indicate that this Uncle Sam was SJM, the Alcotts' "longtime financial supporter," but in fact he was her great uncle Samuel May, Colonel JM's younger brother, who lived from 1776 to 1870. LFM to SJM, May 14, 1857, in MFPCL, mentions that this Uncle Sam "made millions of dollars by some lucky speculation." Bedell, *Alcotts,* 271, cites an anonymous 1846 pamphlet listing Samuel May's worth as $500,000, equal to more than a billion dollars in 2000.
153 ABA depression: ABA to AMA, September 17, 1849, *Letters,* 152.
153 "*A man once lived*": Ibid.
153 returned to slums: ABA to Chatfield Alcott, September 16, 1850, *Letters,* 159.
154 "poverty and Crime": AMA, 1851, journals, HAP.
154 "despondent": ABA, May 27, 1850, *Journals,* 231, quoting AMA.

154 "spared house rent": ABA, April 6, 1850, *Journals,* 230–31.
154 "implied indifference": ABA, May 27 and June 30, 1850, *Journals,* 231–32.
154 "family destitution": Ibid., 231.
154 "unmixed pleasure": ABA, February 14, 1850, *Journals,* 225.
154 "Webster's true place": ABA, March 23, 1850, *Journals,* 230. SJM preached about Webster on Sunday, November 29, 1852, after Webster's death, according to *The New York Times* the next day. "Rev. Samuel J. May, Unitarian, last night preached a sermon to the memory of DANIEL WEBSTER, in which he pronounced him licentious and intemperate. He was quite severe, saying, the least the Press says of him the better." The previous spring, not long after the Jerry Rescue, Webster, then U.S. Secretary of State, had given a speech in central Syracuse on the necessity of enforcing the Fugitive Slave Law.
155 "You have come together this evening": AMA, Fragments of Mrs. Alcott's Reports on her Missionary Work, March 1850, HAP.
155 smallpox: ABA, *Letters,* footnote, 156. See also ABA to Chatfield Alcott, September 16, 1850, Letters, 159.
155 "curious time": LMA, summer 1850, *Journals,* 62.
155 in New Hampshire: While scholars have thought Elizabeth Alcott contracted scarlet fever in the summer of 1856, an AMA letter at HAP dated July 29, 1855, mentions the family's experience with scarlet fever and how "very sick my Lizzy has been."
155 "children Mother nursed": LMA, June 1856, Journals, 79.
155 "maternal pelican": LMA, "Recollections of My Childhood," *Lulu's Library,* xiv.
156 "wonders of art": Margaret Fuller, "Farewell to New York," *The Tribune,* August 1, 1846, in Miller, *Margaret Fuller, American Romantic,* 251–52.
156 "beautiful finish": AMA, summer 1850, journals, HAP.
156 "*school-marm*": LMA, summer 1850, *Journals,* 63.
156 "imaginary children": LMA, February 3, 1865, *Letters,* 107.
157 "best American": Barton, *Transcendental Wife,* displays the broadside for AMA's Intelligence Office, 105.
157 "a shelter": LMA, Stern, *Critical Essays on LMA,* 101.
157 "flummery": Barton, "Ballast to Bronson's Balloon," unpublished essay.
158 her first novel: Scholars Myerson and Shealy write in the introduction to *The Inheritance,* xviii, "None of Alcott's extant letters or journals or the private writings of her family and friends provide any details of the novel's composition." Years after LMA wrote this novel she pasted a note on the manuscript, now at Houghton Library: "My first novel / written at seventeen / High St Boston." The Alcotts did not move to High Street until Louisa was eighteen, so it seems likely that she started it earlier and completed it at High Street.
159 "I don't *talk*": LMA, *Journals,* 61.
159 "safety valve": AMA to SJM, April 17, 1845, family letters, HAP.
159 "try not to covet": LMA, *Journals,* 61.
159 mental illness in LMA's stories: See, for example, Rachel R. S. Luckenbill's 2005 Villanova University dissertation, "Treating Insanity: Madness, Femininity, and Patriarchal Control in LMA's 'A Whisper in the Dark' and 'A Nurse's Story.'"
159 Charles May's insanity: Yacovone, *SJM,* 9.
159 "mother's notes": LMA, 1850, *Journals,* 63.
160 "Why don't you write?": LMA, *Little Women,* 481.
160 "romance": Bedell, *Journals of LMA,* Introduction, 35.
161 "Sexual qualities": ABA, January 18, 1850, *Journals,* 221.
161 "My dear Miss Littlehale": ABA to E. D. Littlehale, *Letters,* August 29, 1850.
161 "the unforgettable": Ibid.
161 "Louisa sat silent": Frank Sanborn, "Reminiscences of Louisa May Alcott," in Stern, *Critical Essays on LMA,* 215.
161 "inspiration of necessity": LMA to James Redpath, unknown date, in Stern, *From Blood & Thunder,* 178.

Chapter 10: A Dead, Decaying Thing

162 "confusing business": ABA to his mother, September 11, 1851, *Letters*, 162.
162 scrub floors: LMA, "How I Went Out to Service," in Stern, *From Blood & Thunder*, 95. LMA did not elaborate on this experience in her journals except in end-of-year notes for 1850.
162 "the connexion": AMA, January 11, 1850, journals, HAP.
163 angry: Stern, *From Blood & Thunder*, 94, states that LMA's "anger [in the 1850s] had traceable autobiographical causes," foremost among them "extreme" family poverty.
163 "male lords": LMA, 1851, *Feminist Alcott*, ed. Stern, vii.
163 "dead, decaying": AMA, April 1853, journals, HAP.
163 "fat and indolent": AMA to ABA, October 5, 1854, family letters, HAP.
163 Hawthorne paid: He repaired Hillside and renamed it Wayside. That house is a National Monument, open to the public, beside Orchard House.
163 her trustees: SES to AMA, November 3, 1852, family letters, HAP.
163 "more respectable": AMA to SJM, December 14, 1852, family letters, HAP.
163 "it is not clear": Shepard, *ABA Journals*, Note on 1852, 260.
163 "Father idle": LMA, summary for 1852, *Journals*, 68.
163 "opened a school": ABA to his mother, October 19, 1851, *Letters*, 162.
164 "Self-sacrificing": LMA, September 1855, *Journals*, 75.
164 "family contrive": LFM to Joseph May, December 21, 1856, MFPCL.
164 "hardscrabble years": Catherine Rivard, e-mail to the author, 2009.
164 "home bird": LMA, date, *Journals*, 69, 67.
164 "getting prizes": LMA, January 1854, *Journals*, 72.
164 "Raphael": LMA, April 1857, *Journals*, 84.
164 "more structured education": AMA, no date, journals, HAP.
164 "prospects somewhat fairer": ABA, October 6, 1851, *Journals*, 254. Although Bronson stated that AMAN's 1851 attendance at a Boston school was the first formal schooling for any of his children, he may have been exaggerating. Both he and Abigail referred to their older daughters attending schools in Concord in journals of the 1840s. AMAN still studied at the Bowdoin Grammar School in January 1853, when she was twelve.
165 "Sunlight": Stern, *From Blood & Thunder*, 256. Myerson and Shealy identify this as LMA's first published work.
165 "Great rubbish!": LMA, Cheney, *LMA's Life, Letters and Journals*, 68. The *Olive Branch* was the literary magazine that published this story. LMA later recalled that she wrote her first published short story at age sixteen at Hillside. As she was not yet sixteen when the family left Hillside, she likely wrote the story the next year, in Boston.
165 Only after her mother: LMA used nearly the same scene in *Little Women*, in a story also called "The Rival Painters."
165 hundreds of poems and stories: Stern, *From Blood & Thunder*, lists all known LMA periodical publications, 138–42. LMA sold about twenty serial pieces in the 1850s, more than forty such pieces in the 1860s, and even more during each of the following two decades.
166 "approaching crisis": AMA to ABA, December 25, 1853, family letters, HAP.
166 "laborious": LMA, "Alcott's Conversation on New England's Reformers," May 1863, in Stern, *LMA*, 67.
165 "not cold and formal": LMA, ibid.
165 "the best man": Theodore Parker to "Dear Poor Old Ladye," February 2, 1852, in O. B. Frothingham, *The Life of Theodore Parker* (1874), 299.
166 "the Collegian": ABA to AMA, September 21, 1854, *Letters* 184.
167 "Mother's undisguised favorite": CMW, unpublished memoir, private collection.
167 Charlotte's education: Ibid.

167 "those Peabody Sister schools": Ibid.
167 "being a school marm!" LMA to CMW, January 2, [1853?], *Letters,* 7.
167 "Dear Lottie don't": Ibid.
167 "Dear Jody": LFM to Joseph May, undated, probably September 29, 1853, MFPCL.
167 "go to your aunt Abba's": LFM to Joseph May, Saturday, September 30 [1853], MFPCL.
168 text of AMA's 1853 petition on suffrage: Stern, *From Blood & Thunder,* 152–154.
168 Similar efforts in Wisconsin: Sally G. McMillen, *Seneca Falls and the Origins of the Women's Rights Movement,* 71.
168 "*Be* something in yourself": AMA to SJM, April 12, 1853, family letters, HAP.
169 "good hours with Sam": ABA to AMA, January 15, 1854, *Letters,* 182–183.
169 Gerrit Smith: An antislavery candidate for president of the United States in 1848, 1856, and 1860.
169 public opposition: In 1855 the City of Syracuse was home to about 250 free blacks, according to "'That laboratory of abolitionism, libel, and treason': Syracuse and the Underground Railroad," an exhibition of the Special Collections Research Center, Syracuse University Library, July 2009.
169 "laboratory": Ibid.
169 Frederick Douglass: Jerry Rescue collection, Onondaga Historial Association, Syracuse, New York.
170 "Cozy home": AMA to ABA, November 18, 1853, family letters, HAP.
170 Anna in Syracuse: ABA to AMA, January 15, 1854, *Letters,* 182, mentions Bronson's plan to return homeward with Anna, who had been boarding in Syracuse.
171 quiet garret: LMA, April 1855, *Journals,* 73.
171 "glory cloak": LMA, February 1861, *Journals,* 103.
171 "retired from public life": LMA to CMW, January 2, [1853?], *Letters,* 7.
171 Anthony Burns case: Sanborn, *Bronson Alcott: His Life and Philosophy,* II, 441–44.
171 "propaganda weapon": Nye, *Fettered Freedom,* 281.
172 "contemptible president": SES, *Memoir of SES,* 102.
172 "triumphs of freedom": Ibid., 101.
172 railroad platform: The Syracuse depot was at the intersection of West Washington and Franklin Streets.
172 CMW's appearance: CMW, unpublished memoir, private collection.
172 LMA's appearance: although Edward Emerson said LMA had "black" eyes, Catherine Rivard stated that LMA's eyes were gray-blue like her father's and her sister May's. The April 1881 *Phrenological Journal* called her "tall and spare in frame," with a strong, "distinct" profile, nose, and chin, according to Stern, *From Blood & Thunder,* 243. LMA felt she had a "whopper jaw," according to LMA's note on her copy of *How to Read Character,* described in Ibid., 244, footnote.
172 still in Syracuse: ABA to AMA, September 21,1854, *Letters,* 185.
172 "exchanged your gloves": LFM and SJM to Joseph May, September 21–22, 1855, MFPCL.
173 "wifely washerwoman's": ABA to AMA, September 21,1854, *Letters,* 186.

Chapter 11: Left to Dig or Die

174 "all its faults": inscribed on the volume, HAP.
174 "her good fortune": ABA to AMA, April 26, 1856, *Letters,* 191.
174 invented for children: Some biographers placed her little school in the Emersons' barn, but LMA said in "Recollections" that she "had for a short time a little school in the barn" at Hillside.

174   pleasanter work: Stern, *From Blood & Thunder*, 4.
175   "topsy-turvy": LMA, April 1855, *Journals*, 73.
175   "very nervous": historical documents from Walpole, NH, viewed at Orchard House, October 2011.
175   "near poverty": Herrnstadt, *ABA Letters*, introduction, xxvi.
175   "cold and dull": LMA, December 1855, *Journals*, 76.
175   "Mother's blessing": LMA, November 1855, *Journals*, 75.
175   sent home most of her earnings: Stern, *From Blood & Thunder*, 4.
175   "dashing signature": LMA to Louise C. Moulton, n.d., family letters, HAP.
176   "business details": LMA, *The Critic*, March 17, 1888, in Cameron, *Concord Literary Renaissance*, 119.
176   fair skin: While many biographers said she had dark skin, there is no historical evidence of this, according to Catherine Rivard, in conversation, 2010.
176   "Louie Alcott Troupe": Stern, *LMA Unmasked*, xix.
176   convinced her Syracuse cousins: according to theatrical posters in Orchard House collection, viewed in 2011.
176   four small roles: on April 22, 1856, John Emerson May played the roles of Byron, Tremaine, Pelham, and Podge.
176   "such a hard life": LMA to AAP, November 6, 1856, *Letters*, 23.
176   Charles May's death: May-Windship-Barker-Archibald Papers, 1775–1922, at MHS, have Charles's April 1856 obituary. Charles likely returned to Massachusetts in 1842 to claim his inheritance. His four children with his wife, Caroline, were Eliza Dorothy Sewall May, Catharine Dodge May, Annie Bancroft May, and Joseph Sewall May. In *ABA Letters*, 829, to unknown recipient, June 8, 1881, ABA wrote that Charles's widow and son Joseph were in Dublin, NH, and that his daughter Kate married Robert Kirkpatrick and moved to Montana.
177   she worried: ABA to LMA, March 31, 1856, *Letters*, 191.
177   raced to New Hampshire: ABA, to his mother, August 5, 1856, *Letters*, 193.
177   water-cure establishment: ABA to AMA, November 13, 1856, *Letters*, 212.
177   Abigail . . . could not leave: Herrnstadt, *ABA Letters*, footnote, 244.
177   "Forlornites": LMA, winter 1856–1857, *Journals*, 85.
177   "poor child": LFM to Joseph May, December 21, 1856, MFPCL.
177   "Mr. Alcott's mark": LFM to SJM, "Wednesday evening," 1857, MFPCL.
178   "fidgets me": LFM to SJM, ibid.
178   "comfortable house": ABA to AMA, April 18–19, 1857, *Letters*, 242.
178   "supported myself": LMA, date, *Journals*, 85.
178   "The Lady and the Woman" quotation: LMA, *Early Stories of LMA, 1852–1860*, 165.
179   "a little something yet": LMA, July 1857, Cheney, *LMA Life, Letters and Journals*, 95.
179   thin, pale: ABA to his brother Ambrose, May 13, 1857, Letters, 244.
179   "Auntie and Uncle": LFM to SJM, July 21, 1857, MFPCL.
179   promised Anna and Louisa: ABA to AMA, April 29, 1857, *Letters*, 244.
179   "venerable of appearance": Odell Shepard, *ABA Journals*, introduction to 1857, 295.
179   sea air: ABA to AMA, August 3, 1857, *Letters*, 246. Mrs. Phillips, a relative of the Mays, is probably the wife of the abolitionist Wendell Phillips, Ann.
179   "brightening prospects": ABA to AMA, August 15, 1857, *Letters*, 248.
179   consulted medical experts: ABA to Abby May, January 2, 1859, *Letters*, 291.
179   "place to plant ourselves": ABA to his daughters, August 28, 1857, *Letters*, 251; ABA to AMA, August 15, 1857, *Letters*, 248.
179   repeated her reluctance: ABA to his daughters, September 16–20, 1857, *Letters*, 254–256. See also *ABA Letters*, introduction, xxvii.
179   "anxious and divided": ABA to AMA, November 16, 1857, *Letters*, 260.
180   "trust me for once": ABA to his daughters, September 17, 1857, *Letters*, 255.

180 "good home": ABA to AMA, August 23, 1857, *Letters*, 249.
180 "friendly competitors": ABA to AMA, August15, 1857, *Letters*, 248.
180 "investments": ABA to his daughters, September 9, 1857, *Letters*, 252.
180 "take the reins": ABA to AMA, April 29, 1857, *Letters*, 244.
181 "central figure" ABA to his daughters, September 9, 1857, *Letters*, 253.
181 "I . . . close my bargain": ABA, September 22, 1857, *Journals*, 301.
181 "Mother's money": LMA September 1857, *Journals*, 85.
181 Apple Slump: Lydia Maria Child said Orchard House was "fit for firewood," Jan Turnquist told the author in 2011.
181 Anna and Louisa helped: ABA to AAP, August 28, 1857, *Letters*, 251.
181 "I feel my quarter": LMA, November 1857, *Journals*, 86.
181 "Betty loves": LMA, ibid.
181 "Anxious and restless": ABA to AMA, December 1, 1857, *Letters*, 267.
181 "I don't relish 'the Governess'": ABA to AAP, November 21, 1857, *Letters*, 264.
182 old maids: Anna refers to being an "old maid" in letters to Alfred Whitman, August 1868 and July 21, 1872, family letters, HAP.
182 "lamentations": LMA, February 1858, *Journals*, 88.
182 "resurrection": ABA to his daughters, September 20, 1857, *Letters*, 256.
182 felt "right": ABA to AMA, November 16, 1857, *Letters*, 260.
182 "Sewall and May": ABA to AAAP, November 21, 1857, *Letters*, 263.
182 "Italian grammar": CMW, unpublished memoir, private collection.
183 "warm, comfortable, tidy": ABA to AAP, November 21, 1857, *Letters*, 262; ABA to AMA, January 1, 1858, *Letters*, 275.
183 "quite gay": LFM to SJM, "Wednesday evening, 1857," MFPCL.
183 housekeeping: Shepard, *ABA Letters*, footnote, 307.
183 "much hope": AAP to Bronson, January 9, 1858, family letters, HAP.
183 "no hope": LMA, January 1858, *Journals*, 88.
183 "best be spared": ABA, January 23, 1858, *Journals*, 303.
183 "too heavy": LMA, March 14, 1858, *Journals*, 88.
183 "kissed us": LMA, ibid.
184 "Elizabeth ascends": ABA, March 14, 1858, *Journals*, 307.
184 "freed soul fly": "Miss Louisa M. Alcott," *Boston Christian Register*, March 24, 1888.
184 picnic place: Jan Turnquist, June 2011, interview at Orchard House.
185 "a bereaved heart": AMA to SJM, March 19, 1857, family letters, HAP.
185 "stay longer": John E. May to his brother, April 1858, MFPCL. Samuel Greele, who is mentioned in the letter, died in 1861.
186 "little May": LMA, May 1858, *Journals*, 89.
186 taller, fairer: Catherine Rivard, in a 2010 interview with the author, described AMAN as 5' 8" with reddish-blond hair and a large bosom.
186 more than thirty: Shepard, *ABA Journals*, Note on 1858, 303.
186 Orchard House renovations: In June 2010 Jan Turnquist told the author that ABA had a carpenter remove one of the house's main corner posts, on the southeast side. This corner post has since been restored as part of extensive renovations to the house. ABA moved the entry of Orchard House to Wayside, where it remains. The well beneath the kitchen dates to the 1600s.
186 ABA gardens: Hope Ann Davis, *The Orchard House Landscape, Concord, MA, 1857–1868,* available at Orchard House.
186 "loved spot": ABA, August 26, 1869, *Journals*, 398.
187 Lizzy's Bible: The tiny Bible is in the Alcott collection at Orchard House.
187 "took faithful care": AMA, journals for 1872, "Fragment of an Autobiography," HAP.
188 "death and love": LMA, August 1858, *Journals*, 90.

Chapter 12: Paddle My Own Canoe

189 Junius's suicide: Occurred in upstate New York in 1852, when he was thirty-four.
189 "usual hunt": LMA, October 1858, *Journals,* 90.
189 "cared so little": LMA to her family, October 1858, *Letters,* 34. She wrote that "every one was so busy, & cared so little whether I got work or jumped into the river, that I thought seriously of doing the latter."
190 Mill Dam: An 1858 photograph of the Back Bay from the State House in Nancy Seasholes's *Mapping Boston* (126) shows what LMA would have seen from the Mill Dam on the day she considered suicide. In the 1850s developers began to dump gravel into the water south of the Boston Neck to create the South End. Late in the decade they were filling the muddy area north of the neck with soil from suburban Needham to create the Back Bay, nearly 600 acres of new land.
190 "thought seriously": LMA to her family, October 1858, *Letters,* 34.
190 "so cowardly": LMA to AAP, November 1858, *Letters,* 38.
190 inspired a scene: LMA's Mill Dam experience also inspired a scene in her novel *Work* in which the heroine, Christy, considers suicide on the Mill Dam.
191 "A woman of well-regulated": L. M. Child, *The Mother's Book,* 165.
191 "too straitly-bounded": Margaret Fuller, in Kornfeld, *Margaret Fuller,* 43.
191 "Let them be sea-captains": Ibid., 45.
191 "least married group": Theriot, *Mother & Daughters in Nineteenth-century America,* 117.
191 nineteenth-century woman: Megan Marshall, *Peabody Sisters,* 115.
191 "peace-offering": LMA, November 29, 1858, *Journals,* 91.
192 "free spinster": LMA, August 1860, *Journals,* 99.
192 "The loss of liberty": LMA, "Advice to Young Ladies: Being a Series of Twelve Articles by Twelve Distinguished Women. No. 3—Happy Women," *New York Ledger,* April 11, 1868.
192 "intensely close spousal relationship": Theriot, *Mothers & Daughters in Nineteenth-century America,* 37, 69.
192 "tremendous need": Ibid., 64.
192 "far superior": ABA, December 24, 1859, *Journals,* 311.
192 she usually earned: Dates and fees derive from Madeleine Stern, *LMA Unmasked,* xvii.
192 "proper grayness": LMA, in LaSalle Corbell Pickett's *Across My Path: Memories of People I Have Known,* 107–108. The possible sources for the initials in AM Barnard are consistent with Leona Rostenberg, *Critical Essays on LMA,* 44.
193 "infinite horror": LMA to James Redpath, n.d., in Stern, *From Blood & Thunder,* 214.
193 Arthur Helps quotation: AMA, Memoir of 1878, HAP, quoting Sir Arthur Helps in *Friends in Council: A Series of Readings and Discourse Thereon,* vol. 1, London: Pickering, 1848.
193 potbelly stoves: By the Victorian period, according to Jan Turnquist, there were black potbelly stoves inside the fireplaces.
193 "old malady": ABA to AMA, December 11, 1858, *Letters,* 283.
194 "invalid": ABA, January 1859, *Journals,* 293–96.
194 "corked up": LMA, January 1861, *Journals,* 103.
194 "so bravely": ABA to LMA, February 7, 1859, *Letters,* 298.
194 "fatherly care": ABA to AMAN, January 17, 1859, *Letters,* 294, quoting AAP.
194 attended a lecture: Brooks, *Flowering of New England,* 432. Later in 1859 John Brown left Frank Sanborn's house on his way to Harpers Ferry. Sanborn was arrested after the raid but released when townspeople protested.
194 "physically attractive": Ronald Bosco, School of Philosophy, Orchard House, 2009. At the same lecture series, John Matteson raised the possibility of a homosexual attraction between Bronson and John Brown. Ronald Bosco, editor of Em-

328 *Notes*

erson's papers, also suggested that ABA was attracted to Emerson, based on a late poem about skinny-dipping by ABA addressed to Emerson.

195 "angel of light": Tony Horwitz noted in his biography of John Brown that on October 30, 1859, Thoreau read aloud an oration, "A Plea for Captain John Brown," calling Brown an "angel of light." At the Music Hall, Emerson said Brown was like Christ, "the new saint awaiting his martyrdom" who will "make the gallows glorious like the cross."

195 begun to speak out: Ronald Bosco said at Orchard House School of Philosophy in summer 2009 that "Emerson moved toward the abolition movement kicking and screaming until the 1840s, and to the women's movement until the 1850s. Until the 1860s he thought 'better' women wouldn't want to vote."

195 "beatify": Matteson, lecture at Orchard House School of Philosophy, July 2009. Ironically, according to Matteson, Brown's raid effectively ended Transcendentalism.

195 "entirely obliterated": *Memoir of SES,* 103–4.

195 "hero": In Boston on the day of Brown's execution, SES presided over a Tremont Temple meeting at which Garrison read aloud Brown's "Address to the Court."

195 "Saint John": ABA wrote a sonnet and LMA wrote a poem to John Brown, according to LMA, 1859, *Journals,* 95.

195 "beginning of sorrows": SJM, Diary for 1859, MFPCL.

195 "usual vigor": ABA to William Russell, December 31, 1859, *Letters,* 307.

195 "Anna's expected marriage": ABA to his mother, April 12, 1860, *Letters,* 310.

195 bringing in enough money: ABA to his mother, August 1861, *Letters,* 322. Bronson wrote to his mother that Louisa "has been waiting almost since the year came in for her money, that she might send some to you. I wish it were more . . ."

195 "Genius burned": LMA, January 1861, *Journals,* 103.

196 "moral obligation to remain": Elizabeth Lennox Keyser, *Little Women: A Family Romance,* 9.

196 "partakes largely in": ABA to William Russell, December 31, 1859, *Letters,* 307.

196 "personal and family history": ABA, February 25, 1861, *Journals,* 337.

196 annual salary was $100: ABA to his sister Betsey, June 5, 1860, *Letters,* 313.

197 "pink of a party": ABA to AMA, October 29, 1860, *Letters,* 317.

197 "many sweethearts": Anna to Alfred Whitman, July 21, 1872, family letters, HAP.

197 "grub for my help": LMA, December 1860, *Journals,* 100.

197 "someone to help her": LMA, February 1864, *Journals,* 128.

197 "took dinner at Charlotte's": SJM, Diary for 1860, MFPCL.

197 "goes out like a taper": James Russell Lowell, *A Fable for Critics* (1848), 43.

197 "fitness and beauty": ABA, May 23, 1860, *Journals,* 326.

197 Anna and John crept up: Catherine Rivard, in conversation, 2010.

198 "Uncle S. J. May married them": Although "Mr. Bull the magistrate" made the marriage legal in the Commonwealth of Massachusetts, SJM performed the ceremony.

198 Bridge and Pratt house: The wooden structure near the Chelsea River known as the "Old Pratt house" was torn down in 1953.

198 took a nap: ABA to AAP, May 23, 1660, *Letters,* 311.

198 Sanborn's students: Brooks, *Flowering of New England,* 432.

198 "I am desirous": SJM, Diary for 1860, MFPCL. Later that year George E. May returned to the West Newton School.

199 "Mrs. John Brown": Anne and Sarah Brown, two of John Brown's older daughters, boarded with the Alcotts a few years later, according to Stern, *LMA,* 103.

199 "went and worshipped": LMA to AAP, May 27, 1860, *Letters,* 54.

199 "earnest talk": SJM, Diary for 1860, MFPCL.

199 "Samuel Jay May's plea for peace": Ednah Cheney, "Reminiscences of Ednah Dow Cheney," 83, 118.

199   the newlywed Pratts: SJM diary for 1860, MFPCL.
199   "A Modern Cinderella": published in the *Atlantic,* October 1860.
199   "people wrote to me": LMA, September and April 1860, *Journals,* 100 and 98.
199   "wife is very well": ABA to his sister Betsey, June 5, 1860, *Letters,* 314.
200   "lives in her family mostly": ABA to his mother, June 24, 1863, *Letters,* 342.
200   "Louisa writes stories still": ABA to his mother, November 1861, *Letters,* 324.
200   May moved to Syracuse: ABA to AMA, November 16, 1857, *Letters,* 260.
200   "More luck for May": LMA, December 1860, *Journals,* 100.
200   "to vary a little": ABA to AMAN, February 10, 1861, *Letters,* 320.
200   "very hopeful": Ibid.
200   "I hope good things": AMA, quoted in ABA to his mother, December 30, 1860, *Letters,* 318.
200   ear trumpet: Mentioned in several letters between the Alcotts. According to Catherine Rivard, in conversation in 2010, AAP was growing deaf by 1860.
200   "entertaining and witty": ABA, February 25, 1861, *Journals,* 337.
201   "life, aspiration, tact": AMA to SJM, March and September 8, 1858, family letters, HAP.
201   "wit and go-ahead-ativeness": AMA to SJM, December 8, 1860, family letters, HAP.
201   manacled slave: Yacovone, *SJM,* 139.
201   "beginning to reap in the storm": AMA to SJM, April 13, 1861, family letters, HAP.
202   "longed to see a war": LMA, April 1861, *Journals,* 105.
202   sewed: ABA, Note on 1861, *Journals,* 333.
202   "felt very martial": LMA, May 1861, *Journals,* 105.
202   Civil War: Three million men fought in the war, and more than 600,0000 died.
202   opened a kindergarten: ABA, January 6, 1862, *Journals,* 345.
202   "Lu's peculiar faculty": AAP to Alfred Whitman, December 1861, family letters, HAP.
203   a distant cousin: Hernnstadt, *Letters ABA,* footnote, 326.
203   "good fruits": ABA to William Russell, January 20, 1862, *Letters,* 326.
203   "against my own wishes": LMA, in *ABA Letters,* 326, footnote.
203   "I *can* write": LMA, May 1862, *Journals,* 109.
203   "blood & thunder tale": LMA to Alfred Whitman, June 1862, *Letters,* 79.
203   "I enjoy romancing": LMA, June, July, August, 1862, *Journals,* 109.
203   "best of health": ABA, September 1, 1862, *Letters,* 328.
203   "pathetic family": LMA to her second cousin Adeline May, July 1860, *Letters,* 57; and to her grandmother Anna Alcox, December 1862, ibid., 80.
204   Emerson's descriptions: Perry Miller, *Margaret Fuller, American Romantic,* xxv.

Chapter 13: The Bitter Drop in This Cup

205   "I never began the year": LMA, January 1, 1863, *Journals,* 113.
206   "feel helpless": Sophia Hawthorne to her daughter Una, December 1862, in Ticknor, *May Alcott,* 53–54, quoting AMA.
206   "big bee hive": LMA to Hannah Stevenson, December 26, 1862, MHS Online Collections, accessed at www.masshist.org, March 2012. Union Hotel Hospital was an imposing three-story building on Georgetown's main street.
206   "really good nurse": Myerson and Shealy, eds., *LMA Journals,* 112, footnote.
206   "When I peered": LMA, "Hospital Sketches," Ch. 3, in Elaine Showalter, ed., *Alternative Alcott,* 21.
206   "a womanly man": LMA to Hannah Stevenson, December 26, 1862. MHS Online Collections, accessed at www.masshist.org, March 2012.
206   "prince of patients": LMA, January 1, 1863, *Journals,* 113.
207   "odd, sentimental": LMA, January 4, 1863, *Journals,* 115.

207 "chief afflictions": LMA to Hannah Stevenson, December 26, 1862, MHS Online Collections, accessed at www.masshist.org, March 2012.
207 "sharp pain": LMA, January 1863, *Journals,* 115.
207 "ignominious to depart": ABA to AAP, January 25, 1863, *Letters,* 333.
207 shaved her head: Ibid.
207 "derivative": Stern, *Plots and Counterplots,* Introduction, 16.
207 "went to heaven": LMA, January 1863, *Journals,* 117.
208 opened her eyes: ABA, January 16, 1863, *Journals,* 353.
208 "Enfeebled": ABA to AAP, January 25, 1863, *Letters,* 332.
208 "clash of arms": Stern, *From Blood & Thunder,* 119.
208 "costly experience": LMA to Mr. Rand, October 24, [n.y.], *Letters,* 339.
208 "men's jobs": O'Connor, *Civil War Boston,* 168.
208 "look unprofessional": Ibid., quoting Ann Douglas, "The Literature of Impoverishment," *Women's Studies* I (1972), 6.
209 "pretty prattle": Caroline Kirkland, "Literary Women," in *Scribbling Women,* Elaine Showalter, ed., xxxvii.
209 "business potential": Showalter, ibid., xxxix.
209 except Marmee: ABA to AAP, January 25–February 4, 1863, *Letters,* 333–35.
209 anxious but hopeful: ABA, January 25, 1863, *Letters,* 354.
209 "nothing against": ABA to AAP, January 25, 1863, *Letters,* 333.
209 part-time maid: ABA to AAP, February 4, 1863, *Letters,* 335.
209 "right mind": ABA, February 6, 1863, *Journals,* 354.
209 "clothe herself with flesh": ABA, March 22, 1863, *Journals,* 354.
209 "sitting deep in a novel": LMA to AAP, March 28, 1863, quoted in *ABA Journals,* footnote, 355.
210 "little grandson": ABA, October 15, 1863, *Journals,* 359.
210 "I have no child": Margaret Fuller, *Memoirs of Margaret Fuller Ossoli,* vol. 1, 293, quoted in Blanchard, *Margaret Fuller,* 173.
210 "I sell *my* children": LMA, January 18, 1868, *Journals,* 163.
211 "her boy": LMA, June 1863, *Journals,* 119. CMW's five-year-old boy, Alfred Wilkinson Jr., as an adult would have a celebrated love affair with Winifred Davis, daughter of the president of the Confederacy during the Civil War. Alfred and Winnie were engaged in the 1880s, but because of her parents' objections to his family's politics the engagement was broken. She died soon afterwards. Alfred, my Uncle Fred, lived until 1918 but never married.
211 "satisfaction of seeing": LMA to James Redpath, August 28, 1863, *Letters,* 88.
211 "agreeable to us": ABA, August 26, 1863, *Journals,* 357.
211 "time & earnings": LMA to James Redpath, July 1863, *Letters,* 87.
211 a collection: Stern, *From Blood and Thunder,* 209.
211 "My Contraband": this story first appeared in the *Atlantic* in November 1863 under the title suggested by the editor, "The Brothers," but LMA always called it "My Contraband."
212 Faith Dane: This character, an upright spinster, also appears in LMA's *Moods.*
213 "power struggle": Stern, *LMA Unmasked,* xxvii.
214 "my natural ambition": LMA, quoted in LaSalle Corbell Pickett, *Across My Path: Memories of People I Have Known,* 107–8.
214 "I love nursing": LMA to Colonel Thomas Wentworth Higginson, November 12, 1863, in Stern, *From Blood & Thunder,* 188.
214 "Plantation Sketches": ABA, October 15, 1863, *Journals,* 360.
214 "irrepressible conflict": LMA, January 1861, *Journals,* 103.
214 another adult novel: The novel was called *Success* in 1863 and later, when published, *Work.*
214 *Harper's Weekly* review: Stern, *Critical Essays on LMA,* 66.

215 love affair at Fruitlands: Odell Shepard, *ABA Journals*, 368, footnote.
215 "Some fear it isn't moral": LMA, February 1865, *Journals*, 139. Also in Cheney, *LMA: Life, Letters and Journals*, February–May 1865, 165–66.
215 "very happy tonight": inscribed in *Flower Fables*, HAP.
215 stay awake: ABA, December 25, 1864, *Journals*, 367.
215 "forcibly drawn": ABA, December 30, 1864, *Journals*, 368.
216 "her full share": ABA, June 8, 1864, *Letters*, 356.

Chapter 14: From May to March

217 "many intermissions": AMA, January 14, 1865, Diary for 1865, HAP.
217 "gave Louisa was her voice": Author's interview with Lisa Stepanski, March 2012.
218 "manipulate whole families": *Plots and Counterplots*, ed. Stern, Introduction, 8.
218 "Unbridled sensuality": Sarah Elbert, Introduction to *Moods*, xxiii.
218 "useful, happy woman": LMA, *Work*, 268–69.
218 "rubbishy tales": LMA, February 1865, *Journals*, 139.
218 made "things comfortable": Ibid.
218 "tried every means": Stern and Shealy, *From Jo March's Attic*, xix.
218 "paid up the debts": LMA, Notes & Memoranda for 1865, *Journals*, 146.
218 "cleaned house & wrote": LMA, March–April 1865, *Journals*, 140.
219 "touching time": CMW to Joseph May, June 17, 1865, MFPCL.
219 "very delicate": WLG to SJM, December 10, 1865, *Letters of Garrison*, 1861–1867, 356.
219 "old but beautiful": WLG to Helen E. Garrison, September 10, 1864, ibid., 236–38.
219 "adored": CMW, unpublished memoir, private collection.
220 "turn housekeeper": LMA, May 1865, *Journals*, 140.
220 "the center and soul": Julian Hawthorne, in Shealy, *Alcott in Her Own Time*, 196–97, 207.
220 "something of a nurse": LMA, July 1865, *Journals*, 141.
221 "heart very full": LMA, 1865, *Journals*, 141. She indicates that her cousin John E. May's future wife, Kate Pomroy Horton, was also present on the wharf.
221 leaving Anna Weld: LMA, May 1866, *Journals*, 151.
221 "I suppose you will avoid": ABA to LMA, November 29, 1865, *Letters*, 378.
221 absence left a crater: LMA, 1865, *Journals*, 143. "My absence seems to have left so large a gap that I begin to realize how much I am to them in spite of all my faults."
221 "wicked West": AMA, quoted in ABA to LMA, March 18, 1866, *Letters*, 390.
221 "over-burthened": ABA, March 27–31, 1864, *Journals*, 363.
222 "children in the summer field": ABA, July 20, 1866, *Journals*, 383.
222 "sick & tired": LMA, July 1866, *Journals*, 152.
222 "disabled": ABA to Mrs. Francis Gage, April 14, 1867, *Letters*, 406.
222 "mask of femininity": Judith Fetterley, "Little Women: Alcott's Civil War," Stern, *Critical Essays on LMA*, 141.
223 "gave Mother the rest": LMA, July 1867, *Journals*, 157.
223 "painful": SJM to LFC, February 3, 1867, MFPCL.
223 "be famous, go abroad": AAP to Alfred Whitman, quoting LMA, July 21, 1872, family letters, HAP.
223 "feeble": LMA, July 1866, *Journals*, 152.
223 "strong, energetic 'marmee'": LMA, November 1866, *Journals*, 153.
223 "a girls book": LMA, September 1867, *Journals*, 158.
224 largely a male profession: Sicherman, *Well-Read Lives*, 39.

224 "golden age": Steven Mintz, *Huck's Raft,* 185.
224 "I could *not* write": LMA to Louise C. Moulton, "Note for Mrs. M," n.d., family letters, HAP.
224 Beth: Nicknames for Elizabeth Sewall Alcott included Lizzie, Betty, and Beth.
224 "busiest young women": AAP to Alfred Whitman, December 8, 1867, family letters, HAP.
224 Marmee "feels the cold": LMA, January 7, 1868, *Journals,* 162.
224 accompanied her father: ABA to William Russell, January 19, 1868, *Letters,* 426.
225 "literary ability": ABA to AMA, February 19, 1868, *Letters,* 427.
225 ABA insecure about writing: Shepard says ABA was a poor writer in his Introduction to *ABA Journals,* xix, and many other scholars concur.
225 "I wish I could write" and "my settled conviction": ABA, August 4, 1835, and June 13, 1880, 60 and 517.
225 Ellen A. Chandler: ABA's first correspondence with her is dated March 1868. The 1870 U.S. Census indicates Ellen Chandler was born in 1846, in Maine, and in 1870 lived in Framingham, Massachusetts, and worked as a Normal School teacher.
225 "on Monday evening": ABA to Ellen Chandler, November 11, 1868, *Letters,* 451.
225 "value[d] her acquaintance": ABA to William Harris, January 15, 1869, *Letters,* 458.
225 "that I might partake the oftener": ABA to Ellen Chandler, December 18, 1868, *Letters,* 456.
225 "fair enchantress": ABA to Chandler, July 25, 1869, *Letters,* 484.
225 "the bright incident": ABA to Frank Sanborn, September 2, 1869, *Letters,* 488.
225 "When young women cease": ABA, June 8, 1870, *Journals,* 411.
226 living conditions for former slaves: Fergus Bordewich, "How America's Civil War Changed the World," *Wall Street Journal,* April 9, 2011.
226 "our work is done": Frederickson, *The Inner Civil War,* 122.
226 "Had we such women": SJM, in *History of Woman Suffrage,* 578–79.
226 "denial of this franchise": SES, "Legal Condition of Women," *Memoir of SES,* 138.
226 Sojourner Truth quotation: *New York Tribune,* May 10, 1867, 8.
227 "gospel according to Abigail": Stern, *From Blood & Thunder,* 261.
227 creative intellectual: Barbara Sicherman used this term to describe LMA in *Well-read Lives.*
227 Mr. March: the minister enters the narrative at the very end of Part One of *Little Women,* which appeared in 1868. Part Two, published in 1869, and Part One are now published together as *Little Women.*
228 motherless boy next door: Laurie was apparently based on several people, including Alfred Whitman, Ladislaw Wisniewski, and Julian Hawthorne.
228 Aunt Q: A story that Aunt Q told Abigail, which Abigail surely told her daughters, may have inspired the scene in which Amy March falls through ice while skating. In Boston in 1787, "little Johnny Hancock," Aunt's Q's eight-year-old son, fell on ice while skating and died. Aunt Q's only other child, a daughter named Lydia, died in infancy.
228 "the first golden egg": LMA, 1885, footnote to August 1868, *Journals,* 166.
229 "gift very precious": LMA, November 29, 1868, *Journals,* 167.
229 "the decline had begun": LMA, October 8, 1868, *Journals,* 167.
229 "worked like a beaver": LMA, December 1868, *Journals,* 168.
229 "I won't marry Jo": LMA, November 1, 1868, *Journals,* 167.
230 some irony: See also Judith Fetterley's essay, "Little Women: Alcott's Civil War," *Feminist Studies* 5 (1979), 369–383.
230 Meg's twins: Caroline Heilbrun, "Jo March: Male Model—Female Person," in Stern, *Critical Essays on LMA,* 144.
230 "our lofty room": LMA to Ellen Conway, February 9, 1869, *Letters,* 123.
230 "if my head holds out": LMA, January 1869, *Journals,* 171.
231 "like a capital G": This story, its exact date unclear, derives from Julian Hawthorne's account in *Alcott in Her Own Time,* 200–201.

231 *National Anti-Slavery Standard*: Vol. 29, May 1, 1869, 3.
231 "single New England home": Stern, *From Blood & Thunder*, 259.
231 anticipated: ABA, April 30, 1869, *Journals*, 396.
231 Any amount: Julian Hawthorne, *Alcott in Her Own Time*, 200. Neither the exact date nor the amount LMA requested are known.
231 "Hard times": LMA, January 1869, Cheney, *LMA Life Letters and Journals*, 122. Details about May and AMA are from Julian Hawthorne.
231 "toiling so many years": LMA to Roberts Brothers, December 28, 1869, *Letters*, 129.
231 books in print: It is possible, according to Lis Adams of Orchard House, that Harriet Beecher Stowe had as many books in print as LMA.
231 "freedom from economic": Shepard, Note on 1869, *ABA Letters*, 393.
232 "limited Louisa's": Judith Fetterley, "Little Women: Alcott's Civil War," in Stern, *Critical Essays on LMA*, 141.
232 "Success has its dark side": LMA to Louisa M. Moulton, n.d., family letters, HAP.
232 Rivière-du-Loup: ABA to Ellen Chandler, June 27, 1869, *Letters*, 479.
232 "Cousin Fred": LFM to JM, undated, MFPCL.
232 *Tablets*: Matteson, *Eden's Outcasts*, 353.
232 "first rank of writers": ABA, September 4, 1869, *Journals*, 399.
232 "If women will only": ABA, October 11, 1869, *Journals*, 40.
233 "possess equal privileges": Matteson, *Eden's Outcasts*, 353.
233 LMA beginning *An Old-Fashioned Girl*: ABA to J. N. Pardee, September 3, 1869, *Letters*, 490.
233 Royalty rates: ABA to Mary Stearns, May 19, 1869, *Letters*, 475.
233 "distance herself": Elbert, Introduction to *Early Stories of LMA*, 16.
233 "entertainment": AMA, diary for January 1873, HAP.
233 "Chariot of Glory": ABA, December 1, 1869, *Journals*, 404. See also Shepard, Note on 1870, ibid., 405. Herrnstadt noted in *ABA Letters* (footnote, 430) that ABA brought home from that trip $700, more than ever before.
233 "people were curious": Theodore Dahlstrand, lecture at School of Philosophy, Orchard House, July 2011.
233 "high places of honors": ABA to Ellen Chandler, December 30, 1872, *Letters*, 580. See also ABA, April 25, 1869, *Journals*, 395.
234 most popular author: The early-twentieth-century author most similar to LMA in her lifetime is J. K. Rowling.
234 "far from well": ABA to Ednah Dow Cheney, October 12, 1869, *Letters*, 490.
234 numerous medical experts: LMA to her family, April–June 1870, *Little Women Abroad*, 10–86.
234 "unusually merry": LMA to Roberts Brothers, December 28, 1869, *Letters*, 129.
235 Abigail's health was stable: ABA to Frank Sanborn, November 4, 1869, *Letters*, 500.
235 as "duenna": LMA, Notes and Memoranda for 1870, *Journals*, 175.
235 "old and stupid": LMA to AAP, July 24, 1970, *Little Women Abroad*, 157, 159.

Chapter 15: Welcome to My Fortune

236 March 31, 1870: SJM, diary for 1870, MFPCL.
236 "till I turned": LMA, 1870, *Journals*, 110, 174.
237 "I took leave": SJM, Diary for 1870, MFPCL.
237 "erecting a handsome": Garrison to his wife, September 10, 1864, *Letters of Garrison*, 236–238.
237 "miscellaneous lot": CMW, unpublished memoir, private collection.
237 donated thousands of documents: That gift began the Samuel J. May Anti-Slavery Collection at the Anti-Slavery and Civil War Collections in the Division of Rare and Manuscript Collections at Cornell University Library. SJM's Crandall portrait, which he offered in exchange for the promise of opening Cornell to women,

now hangs in the library holding these collections. Many of SJM's personal papers were burned in a fire in his daughter Charlotte's house in Syracuse on August 21, 1890. Regarding the education of women then, "Although only one in fifty women attended college in the late-[nineteenth-]century period, the women who did were the first to receive educations comparable to their brothers'," Nancy M. Theriot, wrote in *Mothers & Daughters in Nineteenth-century America*, 79.

237   transform her fictional boys' school: In the novels *Little Men* and *Jo's Boys*.
238   "Calm, bright": AMA, Diary for 1870, HAP.
238   "Poor invalid": ABA, June 28, 1870, *Journals*, 414.
238   copies sold: ABA, April 1, 1870, *Journals*, 406. ABA to LMA, August 1870, *Letters*, 521. ABA to Ellen Chandler, October 3, 1870, *Letters*, 522.
238   "destined": SJM, Diary for 1870, MFPCL.
239   "As I lie in my bed": AMAN to AMA, August 10, 1870, *Little Women Abroad*, Shealy, ed., 184.
239   "between a funeral": LMA to AMA, October 8, 1870, ibid., 239.
239   "droll dream" in Vevey: August 21, 1870, ibid., 196–97.
241   into Orchard House: ABA to Frank Sanborn, December 3, 1870, *Letters*, 528. ABA later added a nursery for the boys adjacent to the master bedroom at Orchard House, where it remains.
241   "fill my place": AMA to Lizzie Wells, January 9, 1871, family letters, HAP.
241   "dear little boys": LMA, January 1871, *Journals*, 177.
242   Plummer School: I am indebted to Catherine Rivard, an expert on AMAN, for the information about the Plummer Farm School. Now known as the Plummer School for Boys, it is on Winter Island across a cove from the easterly point of Salem Neck, connected by a bridge to the mainland. It is still for boys only.
242   Plummer first cousins: The uncles of Caroline Plummer (1780–1854) who could have fathered (or grandfathered) the "Miss Plummer" who was close to AMAN in the 1870s were David, Joseph, William, Samuel, John, and Charles Plummer, all born in the 1750s and 1760s.
242   "wealthy women leave money": Susan B. Anthony, "The True Woman," in Ida H. Harper, *Life and Work of Susan B. Anthony*, I, 160.
242   "ailing": AAP to Alfred Whitman, January 29, 1871, family letters, HAP.
242   "free and happy": Caroline Ticknor, *May Alcott, A Memoir*, 99.
242   "feeble": LMA, July 1871, *Journals*, 178.
242   "not spoiled her": AAP to Alfred Whitman, June 18, 1871, family letters, HAP.
243   "very sick": AMA, June 21, 1871, Journal for 1871, HAP.
243   "embraces": ABA to SJM's son Joseph May, quoting LMA, July 16, 1871, *Letters*, 536.
243   "best friend": LMA, July 1871, *Journals*, 179.
243   SJM funeral: ABA to William Harris, July 4, 1871, *Letters*, 535.
243   "creatures to be idolized": Child, "Samuel J. May," August 30, 1873, *Woman's Journal*, 276, in *First Woman in the Republic*, 577.
243   "Happy Warrior": Eulogy of SJM by Charles de B. Mills at "Services in Honor of SJM in Syracuse, July 1871," published in Boston in 1886, 26–27.
243   "unshakeable principles": Catherine Rivard, email to author, 2009.
243   "suffragists to-day venerate": "Tribute to Mr. May," *The New York Times*, July 1897.
244   "bearing a pail": ABA, July 25, 1871, *Journals*, 421–22.
244   "panted for my garden hose": LMA, September 11, 1870, *Little Women Abroad*, 224.
244   "Reporters": LMA, July 1872, *Journals*, 183.
244   "strangers begin": LMA, June 1865, *Journals*, 147.
244   "indifferent": ABA, August 8, 1878, *Journals*, 491.
244   "straightforward": Child, *First Woman in the Republic*, 589.
244   "such gifted daughters": Child, *Selected Letters, 1817–1880*, 535.
245   "Concord and Her Authors": Shepard, Notes on 1870 and 1871, *ABA Journals*, 406 and 417.

245 "frail": ABA to Ellen Chandler, August 28, 1871, *Letters*, 537.
245 "Sylvia's perplexities": LMA, Preface to *Moods* (1882), in Stern, *From Blood & Thunder*, 195.
245 "Mother is to be cosy": LMA, December 1871, *Journals*, 179.
245 "quaint" recollections: Stern, *From Blood & Thunder*, 225.
245 "a picture for a background": ABA to William Harris, September 2, 1869, *Letters*, 490.
246 "Don't wonder the boy": LMA, September 1872, *Journals*, 183.
246 "boldness and truthfulness": ABA, August 30, 1872, *Journals*, 427.
246 Feeling somewhat better: ABA to Ellen Chandler, September 3, 1872, *Letters*, 562. Louisa stayed at "Mrs. May's boarding house" at 7 Allston Street, probably in Dorchester, possibly with May relatives.
246 Bronson went west: ABA to Mary Adams, October 4, 1872, *Letters*, 565.
246 "Another year is closing": AMA, December 1872, *Journals*, HAP.
246 "Under Louisa's supervision": ABA to Ellen Chandler, July 6, 1875, *Letters*, 599.
247 "writing stories for the millions": ABA, June 9, 1873, *Journals*, 435.
247 unpublished novel *Work*: ABA to William Harris, September 6, 1873, *Letters*, 605.
247 weeks at her bedside: ABA to Ellen Chandler, August 8, 1873, *Letters*, 601.
247 "dropsy of the brain": AAP to Alfred Whitman, February 2, 1874, family letters, HAP.
247 "can safely leave her mother": ABA to ADD, August 5, 1873, *Letters*, 600.
247 on parallel paths: Cynthia Barton, author of a biography of Abigail, said in 2009, "It seems likely" that Louisa sometimes resented her parents for having to care for them during these years.
247 "the only paper I take": LMA, in Stern, *From Blood & Thunder*, 147.
247 "Tell her I am seventy-three": Ibid., 154.
247 "I am very lame": LMA to Mary Mapes Dodge, October 8, [1874?], Stern, *From Blood & Thunder*, 220.
248 "the prospect of wintering": ABA to Mary Adams, October 27, 1873, *Letters*, 616.
248 "I find myself inevitably alone": AMA, *Journals*, January 25, 1875, HAP.
248 May had purchased: ABA, May 11, 1875, *Journals*, 458. AMAN now earned more than two thousand dollars a year from her art and teaching.
248 "so deep and shady": AMAN to AMA, November 1976, and AMAN to her family, spring 1878, Ticknor, *May Alcott, A Memoir*, 143, 172.
249 Abigail remarked to Bronson: ABA to AMAN, April 23, 1875, *Letters*, 686. ABA quotes AMA.
249 only Louisa's mother had seen: Ticknor, *May Alcott, A Memoir*, 190.
249 Nathaniel Hawthorne: He and LMA were not only neighbors but also shared Salem witch judge ancestry. The Mays descended from Samuel Sewall, and Hawthorne descended from Sewall's 1692 colleague, Judge John Hathorne. Nathaniel is said to have changed the spelling of his surname to distance himself from his ancestor, who never repented for Salem. Hawthorne died in 1864 while visiting in New Hampshire; his family still lived next door to the Alcotts.
249 "praised and criticized": LMA, April 1877, *Journals*, 204.
250 May ancestors: ABA to Rev. Samuel May (AMA's cousin), October 7, 1875, *Letters*, 657.
250 Rhoda Lawrence: It is not clear if Louisa already knew Rhoda Lawrence in 1868 when she gave the March family's neighbors the surname Laurence. Many scholars believe Rhoda Lawrence was a model for Dr. Nan in *Jo's Boys*. Louisa's cousin Lucy Sewall, a medical doctor and SES's daughter, may also have inspired Dr. Nan.
250 "I very much want to help": LMA to SES, September 28 [1875], *Letters*, 196.
250 "Life was always a puzzle": LMA, January 1874, *Journals*, 191.

Chapter 16: Thou Excellest Them All

251 Louisa and Abigail arrived at the town center: LMA, "Woman's Part in the Concord Celebration," in *Woman's Journal*, May 1, 1875.

251 "enjoyed showing off": LMA to her cousin Frederick W. G. May, April 20 [13], 1875, *Letters*, 191–92.

252 *Woman's Journal* article: LMA, "Woman's Part in the Concord Celebration," Stern, *LMA: Signature of Reform*, 198–202.

253 share the housekeeping: ABA, October 8, 1876, *Journals*, 40. ". . . cares of housekeeping falling to Anna and Louisa."

253 "Mother & Father are now 75": AAP to Alfred Whitman, 1875, family letters, HAP.

253 "few inherited ail[ment]s": ABA, January 25, 1876, *Journals*, 465.

254 Wilkinson family: Charlotte's daughter Jo, Josephine May Wilkinson, was born Oct. 22, 1862, "named after Gran'pa May," Colonel Joseph May, and died March 3, 1943. Little Abigail May Wilkinson, the baby named after AMA, died on December 21, 1876, at age two. CMW gave birth to nine children over twenty-one years, and was forty-three when her last child, Katherine May Wilkinson, was born on Oct. 24, 1876. Seven of her children survived to adulthood and six to old age, the last, my Aunt K, dying in New York City in 1959.

254 "hordes of beaming girls": LMA, in Stern, *From Blood & Thunder*, 148.

254 "finally had to run": LMA to *Women's Journal*, October 23, 1875.

254 More than ten thousand copies: ABA to AMA's cousin Samuel May, October 7, 1875, *Letters*, 658.

254 "permanently restored": ABA to C. L. Cole, December 2, 1875, *Letters*, 661.

254 "co[u]sin dinner": LMA to ABA, December 12, 1875, *Letters*, 206.

254 "Sewalls wear well": LMA to AMA, January 1, 1876, *Letters*, 214.

255 "her face aglow with emotion": Maria S. Porter, *The New England Magazine*, reprinted in Porter's *Recollections of Louisa May Alcott, John Greenleaf Whittier, and Robert Browning*. The Old South Meeting House was the 1730 stone structure built on the site of the seventeenth-century wooden South Church in which Judge Samuel Sewall repented in 1607. The stone building still stands today and is open to the public.

255 "A tablet to Grandfather May": LMA, March 1874, *Journals*, 192.

255 "sober & sad": LMA, July & August, 1880, *Journals*, 226.

255 she waved a handkerchief: ABA, January 31, 1880, *Journals*, 516.

255 AAP's purchase of house: ABA, May 28, 1877, *Journals*, 477.

255 "She has *her* wish": LMA, April 1877, *Journals*, 204–5.

256 In August she forced: ABA to Mary N. Adams, September 17, 1877, *Letters*, 697.

256 "our housekeeper": ABA to Mary N. Adams, September 17, 1877, *Letters*, 697.

256 "beginning of my ascension": Mary Hosmer Brown, in *Alcott in Her Own Time*, Daniel Shealy, ed., 219.

256 finally achieved "social standing": ABA, June 27, 1877, *Journals*, 477.

256 The doctor came: ABA to AMAN, November 25, 1877, *Letters*, 704. Three times a day Doctor Joseph Cook came to the house to see AMA.

256 "Stay by, Louie:" LMA, October 1877, *Journals*, 205.

257 "quietly and persistently": LMA, *Aunt Jo's Scrap-Bag*, 7–27.

257 display in the Paris Salon: ABA, October 8, 1877, *Journals*, 479–80, and LMA, "Notes & Memoranda for 1877," *Journals*, 206.

258 turned down a page: In Alcott family Bible at Orchard House, examined by author in 2011.

258 AMA moved to Anna's house: ABA to AMAN, November 18, 1877, and December 9, 1877, *Letters*, 703 and 706.

258 "The power that brought me": ABA to Mary Adams, January 27, 1878, *Letters*, 710, quoting AMA.

258 Abigail rejoiced: ABA to AMAN, November 25, 1877, *Letters,* 704.
258 closed her mother's eyes: ABA, November 25, 1877, *Journals,* 480.
258 "who owed her most": LMA to Louise Chandler Moulton, n.d., family letters, HAP.
259 "The dream came true": LMA, in Cheney, *LMA: Life, Letters and Journals,* 24.
260 AMA burial: ABA *Letters* give two different days for burial, November 26 and 27, 1877.
260 "wish to be laid": AMA, March 14, 1877, Diary for 1876–1877, HAP.
260 Louisa noted: LMA, November 1878, *Journals,* 206.
260 details of AMA funeral: ABA to AMAN, December 27, 1877, *Letters,* 707. ABA to Mary Adams, January 27, 1878, *Letters,* 710. ABA to Eliza Leggett, January 29, 1878, *Letters,* 712.
260 "must feel *identified* for ever": EPP to LMA, December 1877, *Letters of EPP,* Bruce Ronda, ed., 382–83.

Chapter 17: Stay By, Louie

262 "race for matrimony": AMAN to her family, December 12, 1876, in Ticknor, *May Alcott, A Memoir,* 153.
262 a young Swiss man: ABA to AMAN, November 18, 1877, *Letters,* 703.
262 only twenty-eight: Catherine Rivard told me that AMAN's death certificate gave her age at death as seven years younger than her actual age of 39. Her husband, who would have provided the year of her birth, apparently believed she was born in 1847.
263 "how [Abigail] married for love": AMAN to her family, spring 1878, displayed in the master bedroom of Orchard House in 2011. Quoted in Ticknor, *May Alcott, A Memoir,* 268.
263 definition of a philosopher: LMA, in Cheney, *LMA: Life, Letters and Journals,* 228.
263 "do not seem to . . . like the marriage": EPP to Ellen Conway, April 27, 1878, *Letters of EPP,* 385.
263 "May is old enough": LMA, March 1878, *Journals,* 209.
263 *femme de ménage:* Ticknor, *May Alcott, A Memoir,* 277.
263 "How different our lives": LMA, March 1878, *Journals,* 209.
263 "I need nothing but": LMA, January 1878, *Journals,* 209. See also ABA to AMAN, June 8, 1878, *ABA Letters,* 726, and ABA to Daniel Ricketson, April 24, 1878, *ABA Letters,* 719.
263 reviewing Abigail's journals: ABA to Mary Adams, January 27, 1878, *Letters,* 710. ABA to AMAN, June 8, 1878, *Letters,* 726. ABA to Daniel Ricketson, April 24, 1878, *Letters,* 719.
264 "biography is not in my line": LMA to W. T. Harris, January 7 [1881], *Letters,* 251.
264 unexpectedly painful: ABA to AMAN, November 29, 1878, *Letters,* 740.
264 His "heart bled": Odell Shepard, *ABA Journals,* introduction to 1877, 483.
264 copied in his own hand: Some entries from AMA's journals 1841–1844 appear in ABA's published diaries.
264 "Ah me!": ABA, June 10–14, 1878, *Journals,* 490–91.
264 "a bushel of diaries": LMA to Louise C. Moulton, n.d., family letters, HAP.
265 "Poor dear woman!!": LMA, footnote to November 29, 1843, AMA journals, in *ABA Journals,* 149.
265 Robert Niles would publish: ABA to William Harris, October 5, 1878, *Letters,* 737.
266 "Memoir will detain her": ABA to Mrs. M. D. Wolcott, November 10, 1878, *Letters,* 739.
266 partial manuscript remains: AMA's "Memoir of 1878," a partial manuscript of this memoir, mostly in Bronson's hand, is at HAP.

266 Louisa also penned a note: ABA, April 6, 1877, *Journals*, 474.
266 "Some time I will write": LMA, April 1882, *Journals*, 233 f.
266 "sorted old letters": LMA, August 1885, *Journals*, 262.
266 "long-cherished plan": LMA, October 1879, *Journals*, 217.
266 "best accoucheur": Rivard, in conversation, June 2011.
266 "Two years since Marmee": LMA, November 25, 1879, *Journals*, 217.
266 "brain disease": Medical details regarding May's death came from Catherine Rivard in conversation, June 2011.
266 "weight on my heart": LMA, December 1879, *Journals*, 218.
266 On December 31 a telegram: ABA to Ellen Chandler, December 31, 1879, *Letters*, 795.
267 puerperal fever: Catherine Rivard, in conversation, 2011.
267 "wished me to have her baby": LMA, Notes and Memoranda for 1879, *Journals*, 219.
267 "Louisa's health still continues": AAP to Alfred Whitman, May 15, 1881, family letters, HAP.
267 "Although we have a faithful nurse": AAP to Alfred Whitman, May 2, 1882, family letters, HAP.
268 "perfectly well, busy": AAP to Alfred Whitman, May 2, 1882, family letters, HAP.
268 "now that no one needed" it: Odell Shepard, Introduction to 1881, *ABA Journals*, 521.
268 "entirely absorbed": AAP to Alfred Whitman, May 15, 1881, family letters, HAP.
268 "Marmee's . . . dear face": LMA, May & June 1979, *Journals*, 215.
268 bird's nest: LMA, October 1879, *Journals*, 217.
269 "the first woman to register": LMA, August 1879, Cheney, *LMA's Life, Letters and Journals*, 321.
269 "our ranks will be fuller": Stern, *From Blood & Thunder*, 150.
269 "stir up the women": LMA, 1879, *Journals*, 28.
269 "my daughters are loyal": ABA, August 11, 1879, *Journals*, 508.
269 "decided to move to Boston": LMA, "Recollections of My Childhood," *Lulu's Library*, xv–xvi, xix.
269 "thrilling tale told briefly": LMA to Mrs. J. E. Sweet, September 11, 1885, *Letters*, 291–92.
270 Michelangelo: Stern, *From Blood & Thunder*, 206.
270 "Everything in this busy world": LMA to Caroline Healey Dall, November 10, 1875, *Letters*, 199.
270 "Never use a *long* word": Stern, *From Blood & Thunder*, 179.
270 "My methods of work": LMA to Frank Carpenter, April 1, 1887, *Letters*, 307.
270 "few stories written in Concord": LMA, undated, Cheney, *LMA's Life, Letters and Journals*, 286.
270 "I made this before breakfast": Stern, *From Blood & Thunder*, 151.
270 "I can remember": LMA to Thomas Niles, February 19, 1881, *Letters*, 253.
270 Her letters often closed: LMA to *Woman's Journal*, July 15, 1876, and October 11, 1879, in Stern, *From Blood & Thunder*, 151.
270 Her uncle Sam: M. J. and P. Buhle, *Concise History of Woman Suffrage*, 9.
270 "It is impossible for me": LMA to *Woman's Journal*, 1885, in Stern, *From Blood & Thunder*, 168.
271 "The assertion that suffragists": LMA to *Woman's Journal*, 1883, ibid., 166.
271 "Boston's richest families": Rawson, *Eden on the Charles*, 34.
271 "proximity to a garden": Ibid., 33.
272 charged with grand larceny: *The New York Times*, January 27, 1886.
272 "picked up in the street": CMW, unpublished memoir, private collection.
272 convicted of grand larceny: *The New York Times*, June 15, 1886.
272 *Jo's Boys* quotations: LMA, *Jo's Boys*, 33 f.

273 symptoms attributed to calomel: According to *Little Women Abroad,* 64, Dr. Kane, a doctor she met in 1870 in Dinan, France, told her the mercury she received in 1863 caused her chronic health problems. She wrote in 1870 to her parents, "The bunches on my legs are owing to that, for the mercury lies round in a body and don't do much harm till a weak spot appears when it goes there and makes trouble. . . . But I think Dr. K's Iodine of Potash will cure it in the end."

273 lupus diagnosis: Hirschhorn, Norbert, and Ian Greaves, "Louisa May Alcott: Her Mysterious Illness," *Perspectives in Biology and Medicine,* Vol. 50, no. 2, Spring 2007, 243–59.

273 Dunreath Place: "The house on Dunreath Place, in Boston, Where Miss Alcott died," is pictured in *The New England Magazine,* vol. 6, Sarah Orne Jewett, Cairns Collection of American Women Writers.

274 "morning & evening": AAP to Alfred Whitman, February 1889, family letters, HAP.

274 more than $2 million: The actual royalty figure at the time was $103,000.

274 "A very easy process": LMA to Thomas Niles, June 28, 1887, *Letters,* 316.

274 she took a vacation: Stern, *From Blood & Thunder,* 238.

274 "I have tried to spare you": LMA to Frederick Pratt and John Pratt Alcott, July 10, 1887, *Letters,* 317.

274 "I have little hope": AAP to Alfred Whitman, July 1887, family letters, HAP.

275 "I always gave Mother": LMA to Louisa Bond, October [25?], 1887, *Letters,* 322.

275 "All is well": LMA to AAP, November 27, 1887, *Letters,* 323.

275 "I mend slowly": LMA to Mary Mapes Dodge, December 22, 1887, *Letters,* 328.

275 "well-written . . . pretty good": LMA to Mary Mapes Dodge, December 31, 1886, Cheney, *LMA: Her Life, Letters, and Journals,* 375.

275 "improved all winter": AAP to Alfred Whitman, February 17, 1889, family letters, HAP.

275 "needs no logic": LMA to Florence Phillips, October 20, [1886?], *Letters,* 302.

276 "Father, here is your Louie": AAP to Alfred Whitman, February 17, 1889, family letters, HAP.

278 poor health: Catherine Rivard said LMA's last words were "Is it not meningitis?"—the disease she suspected had killed her sister May. Doctors now find that diagnosis unlikely in both women.

278 "hard to be happy": AAP to Alfred Whitman, May 29, 1891, family letters, HAP.

278 half a million books: *The New York Times,* "Miss LMA. Interesting Information Concerning the Popular Author. From the Boston Herald," April 28, 1880.

278 Sales figures and translations: Lavinia Russ, "Not to Be Read on Sunday," *Critical Essays on LMA,* ed. Madeleine B. Stern, 99–100.

279 "Old Cato": Henry Blackwell, *Woman's Journal,* December 29, 1888, quoted in *Memoir of SES,* 163.

Bibliography

Manuscript Sources, Archival Collections

Waterford (Maine) Historical Society, Abigail May Alcott letters, private collection.

Boston Public Library, Alcott and May papers.

Concord Free Public Library, Alcott papers, Franklin B. Sanborn papers.

Connecticut State Library, church records of Brooklyn, Connecticut.

Cornell University Library, Samuel J. May Anti-Slavery and Civil War Collection, May Family Papers.

First Parish Church of Norwell, Massachusetts, formerly South Scituate, Massachusetts, Samuel Joseph May collection.

Fruitlands Museum, Harvard, Massachusetts, Alcott papers.

Germantown (Pennsylvania) Historical Society, Alcott papers, Wyck papers.

Houghton Library, Harvard University, Alcott Pratt collections, including papers of Abigail May Alcott, Louisa May Alcott, A. Bronson Alcott, Anna Alcott Pratt, Elizabeth S. Alcott, A. May Alcott, Alfred Whitman, and the Pratt Alcott family.

Library of Congress, Civil War photographs and papers of Elizabeth Cady Stanton, Susan B. Anthony, Louise Chandler Moulton, and National American Women's Suffrage Association.

Louisa May Alcott Association, Orchard House, Concord, Massachusetts, Alcott papers, books, and artifacts.

Massachusetts Historical Society, collections of Sewall, May-Windship-Barker-Archibald, May, Alcott, Willis, Frothingham, and Hancock families.

May Memorial Church, Syracuse, New York, papers of Samuel Joseph May.

May, Samuel Joseph, unpublished letters, 1822–1865, private collection.

Norwell (formerly South Scituate), Massachusetts, Historical Society, Historic Homesteads collection.

Onondaga Historical Society, Syracuse, New York, collections of Samuel Joseph May, the Church of the Messiah, Abolitionism, and nineteenth-century Syracuse.

University of Rochester, Bragdon Family Papers, 1836–1968.

Schlesinger Library, May and Goddard family collection, 1766–1912.

Smith College Archives, Charlotte Coffyn [*sic*] Wilkinson Bragdon Papers, 1890–1962.

Wilkinson, Charlotte Coffin May, unpublished memoir and letters, private collection.

Published Primary Sources

Alcott, A. Bronson. *A. Bronson Alcott: His Life and Philosophy,* eds. F. B. Sanborn and W. T. Harris. 2 vols. Boston: Roberts Brothers, 1893.

———. *The Letters of A. Bronson Alcott*. Ed. Richard L. Herrnstadt. Ames: Iowa State Univ. Press, 1969.

———. *The Journals of Bronson Alcott*. Ed. Odell Shepard. Boston: 1938. Portions of Abigail's journals, transcribed by Bronson before burning, are included herein.

———. *Maternal Influence*. Boston: Allen & Ticknor, 1933.

Alcott, Abigail May. *Abigail May Alcott's receipts & simple remedies : best way of doing difficult things all tried and proved*. Concord, MA: Nancy L. Kohl and the Louisa May Alcott Memorial Association, 1980.

———. *Mrs. Alcott's Cookbook*. Concord, MA: Louisa May Alcott Memorial Association, 1976.

Alcott, Louisa May. *Alternative Alcott*. Ed. Elaine Showalter. New Brunswick: Rutgers Univ. Press, 1988.

———. *Aunt Jo's Scrap-Bag*. 3 vols. Published 1872, 1879, and 1882.

———. *Behind a Mask: The Unknown Thrillers of Louisa May Alcott*. Ed. Madeleine Stern. New York: William Morrow, 1984.

———. *Comic Tragedies*. Published 1893.

———. *Diana and Persis,* novella published posthumously.

———. *A Double Life: Newly Discovered Thrillers of Louisa May Alcott*. Eds. Madeleine Stern, Joel Myerson, and Daniel Shealy. Boston: Little, Brown, 1988.

———. *The Early Stories of Louisa May Alcott*. Intro., Monika Elbert. Forest Hills, NY: Ironweed Press, 2000.

———. *Eight Cousins*. Published 1875.

———. *Fairy Tales and Fantasy Stories*. Ed. Joel Myerson. Knoxville: Univ. of Tennessee Press, 1992. Composed 1854.

———. *The Feminist Alcott: Stories of a Woman's Power*. Ed. Madeleine Stern. Boston: Northeastern Univ. Press, 1996.

————. *From Jo March's Attic: Stories of Intrigue and Suspense.* Eds. Madeleine B. Stern and Daniel Shealy. Boston: Northeastern Univ. Press, 1993.

————. *A Garland for Girls.* Published 1887.

————. *Hospital Sketches.* Published 1863.

————. *The Inheritance.* Composed 1848, published posthumously.

————. *Jack and Jill.* Published 1880.

————. *Jo's Boys.* Published 1886.

————. *The Journals of Louisa May Alcott.* Eds. Joel Myerson and Daniel Shealy. Athens: Univ. of Georgia Press, 1997.

————. *Little Men.* Published 1871.

————. *Little Women.* Cleveland and New York: World Publishing Company, 1946. Composed and published 1868.

————. *A Long Fatal Love Chase.* Composed 1866, published posthumously.

————. *The Lost Stories of Louisa May Alcott: Stories of Intrigue and Suspense.* Eds. Madeleine B. Stern and Daniel Shealy. Seacaucus, NJ: Citadel, 1995.

————. *Louisa May Alcott Unmasked: Collected Thrillers.* Ed. Madeleine Stern. Boston: Northeastern Univ. Press, 1995.

————. *Lulu's Library.* 3 vols. Published 1885, 1887, and 1889.

————. *A Modern Mephistopheles.* Published 1877 anonymously.

————. *Moods.* Published 1864, 1882.

————. *Plots and Counterplots: More Unknown Thrillers of Louisa May Alcott.* Ed. Madeleine B. Stern. New York: Morrow, 1976.

————. *The Portable Louisa May Alcott.* Edited and introduced by Elizabeth L. Keyser. New York: Penguin, 2000.

————. *Rose in Bloom.* Published 1876.

————. *The Selected Letters of Louisa May Alcott.* Eds. Joel Myerson and Daniel Shealy. Athens: Univ. of Georgia Press, 1995.

————. *Silver Pitchers.* Published 1876.

————. *Spinning-Wheel Stories.* Published 1884.

————. *Transcendental Wild Oats.* Published 1873.

————. *Under the Lilacs.* Published 1878.

————. *Work. A Story of Experience.* New York: Schocken, 1997.

————, and May Alcott. *Little Women Abroad: The Alcott Sisters' Letters from Europe, 1870–71.* Daniel Shealy, ed. Athens, GA: Univ. of Georgia Press, 2008.

Allen, William G., Mary King, and Louisa May Alcott. *The American Prejudice Against Color.* Edited and introduced by Sarah Elbert. Boston: Northeastern Univ. Press, 2002.

Anthony, Susan B., Elizabeth Cady Stanton, and Matilda Joslyn Gage, eds. *History of Woman Suffrage.* 3 vols. New York: Fowler & Wells, 1881–1886.

Child, Lydia Maria. *Collected Correspondence of Lydia Maria Child, 1817–1880,* microfiche edition. Accessed online, April 27, 2012.

————. *Hobomok & Other Writings on Indians.* Ed. Carolyn L. Karcher. New Brunswick, NJ: Rutgers Univ. Press, 1986.

————. *Lydia Maria Child: Selected Letters, 1817–1880*. Eds. Milton Meltzer and Patricia G. Holland. Amherst, MA: Univ. of Massachusetts Press, 1982.

Dall, Caroline W. Healey. *Margaret and Her Friends: Or, Ten Conversations with Margaret Fuller upon the Mythology of the Greeks and Its Expression in Art*. New York: Arno, 1972.

Emerson, Ralph Waldo. *The Later Lectures of Ralph Waldo Emerson, 1843–1871*, 2 vols. Eds. Ronald A. Bosco and Joel Myerson. Athens, GA: Univ. of Georgia Press, 2001.

————. *Letters of Ralph Waldo Emerson*, 6 vols. Eds. Ralph L. Rusk and Eleanor M. Tilton. New York: Columbia Univ. Press, 1939.

————. *Selected Lectures of Ralph Waldo Emerson*. Eds. Ronald A. Bosco and Joel Myerson. Athens, GA: Univ. of Georgia Press, 2005.

Freeman, James. "Charge to the Pastor," *A Sermon Preached in Brooklyn, Connecticut, at the Installation of Rev. Samuel Joseph May,* November 5, 1823, by James Walker of Charlestown. Boston: John B. Russell, 1824.

Garrison, William Lloyd. *The Letters of William Lloyd Garrison*, 6 vols. Cambridge: Harvard Univ. Press, 1971–1979.

Garrison, William Lloyd. *William Lloyd Garrison, 1805–1879: The Story of His Life Told By His Children*. New York: Century, 1885.

Hunt, Freeman, ed. "Joseph May," *Lives of American Merchants*, vol. 1, 443–50. New York: Derby & Jackson, 1858.

A Liturgy for the Use of the Church at King's Chapel in Boston: Collected Principally from the Book of Common Prayer. Boston: Press of the Christian Examiner, 1828.

The Liberator, The Colonizationist, and other newspapers on nineteenth-century abolitionism and women's rights. Viewed at www.theliberatorfiles.com and on Internet archives.

Lee, Luther. *Autobiography of the Rev. Luther Lee*. New York: Phillips & Hunt, 1882.

May, Joseph. *Memoir of Colonel Joseph May, 1760–1841*. Boston: Clapp & Son, 1873. Compiled by Samuel May and published in *The New-England Historical and Genealogical Register and Antiquarian Journal*. Boston: April 1873, vol. 27, no. 2, 113–22.

May, Samuel Joseph. *Memoir of Samuel Joseph May*. Autobiographical essay, diaries, and memoirs compiled by George B. Emerson and Thomas J. Mumford, published posthumously. Boston: Roberts Brothers, 1873.

————. *Jesus the Best Teacher of his Religion, a Discourse*. 1847.

————. *Some recollections of our antislavery conflict*. 1869.

————. *Memorial of the quarter-centennial celebration of the establishment of normal schools in America*. 1866.

————. *What do Unitarians believe?* 1856, 1860, 1866, 1867.

————. *The true story of the barons of the South; or, The rationale of the American conflict*. 1862.

————. *On redemption by Jesus Christ*. Boston: Crosby and Nichols, 1847.

————. *Christian Monitor, and Common People's Advisor*. First volume of a serial publication, 1832.

———. *On prejudice*. 1831.

———. *The Revival of Education*. 1855.

———. *Memorial of the Quarter-Centennial Celebration of the Establishment of Normal Schools in America*. 1866.

———. *A Brief Account of his Ministry*. 1867.

———. *The right of colored people to education, vindicated: letters to Andrew T. Judson, Esq. and others in Canterbury, Conn., remonstrating with them on their unjust and unjustifiable procedure relative to Miss [Prudence] Crandall and her school for colored females*. Brooklyn, CT: Advertiser Press, 1833.

———. "Liberty or slavery the only question," oration delivered on the Fourth of July, 1856, at Jamestown, NY.

———. "The Rights and Condition of Women," sermon preached in Syracuse, November 1845, published as a chapter of *Commensurate with Her Capacities and Obligations Are Woman's Rights: A Series of Tracts*. Syracuse: Lathrop, 1853.

———. "Speech of Rev. Samuel J. May to the convention of citizens of Onondaga County, in Syracuse, on the 14th of October, 1851, called 'to consider the principles of the American government, and the extent to which they are trampled underfoot by the fugitive slave law,' occasioned by an attempt to enslave an inhabitant of Syracuse." Syracuse: Agan & Summers, 1851.

———. "Emancipation in the British W. Indies," August 1, 1834: an address delivered in the First Presbyterian Church in Syracuse, on August 1, 1845. Syracuse: J. Barber, 1845.

———. "A discourse on slavery in the United States," delivered in Brooklyn, Conn., July 3, 1831. 1832.

Mills, Charles de B. "Eulogy in Honor of Samuel J. May in Syracuse, July 1871." Boston: George E. Ellis, 1886.

Sewall, Samuel E. *Samuel E. Sewall; A Memoir*. Edited by Nina Moore Tiffany. Boston: Houghton, Mifflin, 1898.

Tributes to Theodore Park, Comprising the Exercises at the Music Hall, on Sunday, June 17, 1860, with the Proceedings of the New England Anti-Slavery Convention, at the Melodeon, May 31. Boston: The Fraternity & the 28th Congregational Society, 1860. Remarks by Samuel J. May, 36–38.

Secondary Sources

Abbott, John S.C. *The Mother at Home*. Boston: Crocker and Brewster, 1833.

Abel, Elizabeth, Marianne Hirsch, and Elizabeth Landland, eds. *The Voyage In: Fictions of Female Development*. Hanover, NH: Univ. Press of New England, 1983.

Abel, Elizabeth, ed. *Writing and Sexual Difference*. Chicago: Univ. of Chicago Press, 1982.

Abraham, Julie. *Are Girls Necessary? Lesbian Writing and Modern Histories*. New York: Routledge, 1996.

Adams, Charles Francis. *Three Episodes of Massachusetts History*. 2 vols. New York: Russell & Russell, 1965.

Adams, James T. *Dictionary of American History*. New York: Scribner, 1940.

Ahlstrom, Sydney E. *A Religious History of the American People*. New Haven: Yale University Press, 1972.

Aldrich, George. *Walpole as It Was and as It Is*. Claremont, NH: Claremont Manufacturing, 1880.

Atkinson, Clarissa W., Constance H. Buchanan, and Margaret R. Miles. *Shaping New Vision: Gender and Values in American Culture*. Ann Arbor: UMI Research Press, 1987.

Auerbach, Nina. *Communities of Women: An Idea in Fiction*. Cambridge: Harvard Univ. Press, 1978.

Bailyn, Bernard. *Faces of Revolution: Personalities and Themes in the Struggle for American Independence*. New York: Vintage Books, 1990.

Baker, Carlos. *Emerson Among the Eccentrics: A Group Portrait*. New York: Viking Penguin, 1996.

Bartlett, Irving H. *Daniel Webster*. New York: Norton, 1978.

Barton, Cynthia H. "Abigail May Alcott," talk delivered at Orchard House School of Philosophy, unknown year, courtesy of the author.

———. "The Ballast to Bronson's Balloon," 2005, unpublished essay, courtesy of the author.

———. *Transcendental Wife: The Life of Abigail May Alcott*. Lanham, MD: University Press of America, 1996.

Baym, Nina. *American Women Writers and the Work of History, 1790–1860*. New Brunswick, NJ: Rutgers Univ. Press, 1995.

———. *Novels, Readers, and Reviewers: Responses to Fiction in Antebellum America*. Ithaca: Cornell Univ. Press, 1984.

———. *The Scarlet Letter: A Reading*. Boston: Twayne, 1986.

———. *The Shape of Hawthorne's Career*. Ithaca: Cornell Univ. Press, 1976.

———. *Woman's Fiction: A Guide to Novels by and about Women in America, 1820–1870*. Ithaca: Cornell Univ. Press, 1978.

Bedell, Madelon. *The Alcotts: Biography of a Family*. New York: Crown, 1980.

Bercovitch, Sacvan. *The Puritan Origins of the American Self*. New Haven: Yale Univ. Press, 1975.

Blackmon, Douglas A. *Slavery by Another Name : The Re-enslavement of Black People in America from the Civil War to World War II*. New York: Doubleday, 2008.

Bordewich, Fergus. "How America's Civil War Changed the World." *The Wall Street Journal,* April 9, 2011.

Bowers, Q. David. *The Waterford Water Cure*. Wolfboro, NH: Bowers and Merena Galleries, 1992.

Brodhead, Richard H. *Cultures of Letters: Scenes of Reading and Writing in Nineteenth-century America*. Chicago: Univ. of Chicago Press, 1993.

Brooks, Geraldine. *Dames & Daughters of Colonial Days*. New York: Crowell & Co., 1900. New York: Arno Press, 1974.

Brooks, Geraldine. *March: A Novel.* New York: Viking, 2005.

Brooks, Van Wyck. *The Flowering of New England 1815–1865: Emerson, Thoreau, Hawthorne and the Beginnings of American Literature.* Boston: Houghton Mifflin, 1936.

Brown, Gillian. *Domestic Individualism: Imagining Self in Nineteenth-century America.* Berkeley: Univ. of California Press, 1990.

Buell, Lawrence. *Emerson.* New York: Belknap, 2003.

Callard, Judith. "The Alcotts in Germantown," *Germantown Crier,* vol. 47, 1996, Germantown Historical Society.

Cameron, Diane. "Connecticut Legislation Pertaining to 'Negroes,' Indians, Servants & Slaves." Wethersfield, CT: Webb-Dean-Stevens Museum, 2000.

Cameron, Kenneth W. *Concord Literary Renaissance: Ungathered Memorabilia of Emerson, Thoreau, Hawthorne, Sanborn, the Alcotts, Margaret Fuller and Their Connections.* Hartford: Transcendental Books, 1988.

Capper, Charles H. *Margaret Fuller: The Early Years.* Berkeley: Univ. of California, 1984.

———. *Margaret Fuller: An American Romantic Life.* New York: Oxford Univ. Press, 2007.

Carpenter, Delores Bird, ed. *The Selected Letters of Lidian Jackson Emerson.* Columbia: Univ. of Missouri Press, 1987.

Carroll, Michael P. *American Catholics in the Protestant Imagination: Rethinking the Academic Study of Religion.* Baltimore: Johns Hopkins Univ. Press, 2007.

Cheney, Ednah Dow. *Louisa May Alcott, Her Life, Letters and Journals.* Boston, 1889. Avenel, NJ: Gramercy Books, 1995.

Child, Lydia Maria. *The Mother's Book.* Boston: Carter and Hendee, 1831.

Chinkes, Margaret Barry. *James Freeman and Boston's Religious Revolution.* Glade Valley, NC.: Glade Valley Books, 1991.

Clifford, Deborah Pickman. *Crusader for Freedom: A Life of Lydia Maria Child.* Boston: Beacon Press, 1992.

Cohen, Charles L. *God's Caress: The Psychology of Puritan Religious Experience.* Oxford: Oxford Univ. Press, 1986.

Cohen-Solal, Annie. *Painting American: The Rise of American Artists—Paris 1867–New York 1948.* New York: Knopf, 2001.

Cole, Phyllis. *Mary Moody Emerson and the Origins of Transcendentalism: A Family History.* New York: Oxford, 1998.

Conforti, Joseph A. *Samuel Hopkins and the New Divinity Movement: Calvinism, the Congregational Ministry, and Reform in New England Between the Great Awakenings.* Grand Rapids, MI: Christian Univ. Press, 1981.

Conway, Moncure Daniel. *Autobiography: Memories and Experiences.* 2 vols. Boston and New York: Houghton, Mifflin, 1904.

Cook, Cita. "The Lost Cause Legend about Winnie Davis, 'the Daughter of the Confederacy.'" Chapter 1 of *The Human Tradition in the New South,* James C. Klotter, ed. New York: Rowman & Littlefield, 2005.

Cott, Nancy F. *The Bonds of Womanhood: "Woman's Sphere" in New England, 1780–1835.* New Haven: Yale Univ. Press, 1977.

Cox, Clinton. *Fiery Vision: The Life and Death of John Brown.* New York: Scholastic, 1997.

Crawford, Mary C. *Romantic Days in Old Boston.* Boston: Little, Brown, 1910.

Dahlstrand, Frederick C. *Amos Bronson Alcott, an Intellectual Biography.* Rutherford, NJ: Fairleigh Dickinson Univ. Press, 1982.

Dall, Caroline W. Healey. *Margaret and Her Friends: Or, Ten Conversations with Margaret Fuller upon the Mythology of the Greeks and Its Expression in Art.* New York: Arno, 1972.

Davidson, Cathy N., and E. M. Broner, eds. *The Lost Tradition: Mothers and Daughters in Literature.* New York: Frederick Ungar, 1980.

Deese Helen R., ed. "Louisa May Alcott's *Moods:* A New Archival Discovery. *New England Quarterly,*" vol. 76, no. 3 (Sept. 2003), 439–55.

Degler, Carl. *At Odds: Women and the Family in America from the Revolution to the Present.* New York: Oxford, 1980.

Douglas, Ann. "The Literature of Impoverishment." *Women's Studies I,* 1972.

Edes, Richard S. *A Genealogy of the Descendants of John May.* Boston: Franklin Press, 1878.

Elbert, Monika, ed. *Enterprising Youth: Social Values and Acculturation in Nineteenth-Century American Children's Literature.* New York: Routledge, 2008.

Elbert, Sarah. *A Hunger for Home: Louisa May Alcott and Little Women.* Philadelphia: Temple Univ. Press, 1984. Revised as *A Hunger for Home: Louisa May Alcott's Place in American Culture.* New Brunswick, NJ: Rutgers Univ. Press, 1987.

———. *Louisa May Alcott on Race, Sex, and Slavery.* Boston: Northeastern Univ. Press, 1997.

Eliot, Samuel A. *Heralds of a Liberal Faith,* Vol. 2. Boston: American Unitarian Association, 1910.

Emerson, Ellen Tucker. *The Life of Lidian Jackson Emerson.* East Lansing, MI: Michigan State Univ. Press, 1992.

Fahs, Alice. *The Imagined Civil War: Popular Literature of the North & South 1861–1865.* Chapel Hill: Univ. of North Carolina Press, 2001.

Faust, Drew Gilpin. *This Republic of Suffering: Death and the American Civil War.* New York: Knopf, 2008.

Fetterley, Judith. "Impersonating 'Little Women': The Radicalism of Alcott's *Behind a Mask.*" *Women's Studies,* 10, 1983, 1–14.

Fischer, David Hackett. *Paul Revere's Ride.* New York: Oxford Univ. Press, 1994.

Fitzpatrick, Tara. "Love's Labor's Reward: The Sentiment of Economy of Louisa May Alcott's *Work.*" *NWSA Journal,* vol. 5, no. 1 (spring 1993), 28–44.

Foote, Henry Wilder, John Carroll Perkins, and Winslow Warren. *Annals of King's Chapel from the Puritan Age of New England to the Present Day,* Vols. 1, 2. Boston: Little, Brown, 1900.

Franklin, John Hope, and Alfred A. Moss, Jr. *From Slavery to Freedom: A History of Negro Americans,* 6th ed. New York: Knopf, 1988.

Fredrickson, George M. *The Inner Civil War: Northern Intellectuals and the Crisis of the Union.* New York: Harper, 1965.

Friedman, Lawrence J. *Gregarious Saints: Self and Community in American Abolitionism, 1830–1870*. Cambridge and New York: Cambridge Univ. Press, 1982.

Frothingham, Octavius B. *Transcendentalism in New England: A History*. Boston: American Unitarian Association, 1903.

Furgol, Mary T., et al. "Creating the Celestial City: Social Work in Nineteenth-century Scotland." *Community College Humanities Review*, vol. 25, spring 2004.

Gage, Thomas Hovey. *Amos Gage of Bethel, Maine*. Worcester, MA, 1924.

————, ed. *Notes on The History of Waterford, Maine*, Worcester, MA: Collections of the Massachusetts Historical Society, 1913.

Galpin, W. Freeman. "Dr. Samuel May Active Abolitionist in Unitarian Pulpit Here." *Syracuse Journal*, March 20, 1989.

————. "God's Chore Boy: Samuel Joseph May." Unpublished ms., 1947. www.distance.syr.edu/galpin-may.html, 2007.

————. "Rev. S. J. May Outstanding Syracuse Citizen of Past, SU Historian Holds," *Syracuse Journal*, August 15, 1988.

Gaustad, Edwin S., ed. *A Documentary History of Religion in America to the Civil War*. Grand Rapids: Eerdmans, 1982.

————. *A Religious History of America*. New York: Harper & Row, 1966.

Geismar, Maxwell. "Duty's Faithful Child." Book review of Katharine Anthony's *Louisa May Alcott*. *The Nation*, 146, February 1938, 216.

Gilligan, Carol. *In a Different Voice*. Cambridge: Harvard Univ. Press, 1982.

Greene, Lorenzo J. *The Negro in Colonial New England, 1620–1776*. New York: Atheneum, 1968.

Greenwood, F.W.P. *A History of King's Chapel in Boston*. Boston: King's Chapel, 1833.

Grodzins, Dean. *American Heretic: Theodore Parker and Transcendentalism*. Chapel Hill: Univ. of North Carolina Press, 2002.

Habegger, Alfred. *Gender, Fantasy, and Realism in American Literature*. New York: Columbia Univ. Press, 1982.

Hale, Edward Everett. *A New England Boyhood*. Boston: Little, Brown, 1927.

Hall, David, editor. *Lived Religion in America: Toward a History of Practice*. Princeton, NJ: Princeton Univ. Press, 1997.

Hansen, Debra Gold. *Strained Sisterhood: Gender and Class in the Boston Female Anti-Slavery Society*. Amherst, MA: Univ. of Massachusetts Press, 1993.

Harding, Walter. *The Days of Henry Thoreau: A Biography*. Princeton, NJ: Princeton Univ. Press, 1992.

Harper, Ida Husted. *The Life and Work of Susan B. Anthony*. 3 vols. Indianapolis: Bowen-Merrill, 1899.

Hartman, Saidiya V. *Scenes of Subjection: Terror, Slavery, and Self-making in Nineteenth-century America*. Oxford: Oxford Univ. Press, 1997.

Hawthorne, Nathaniel. *The Scarlet Letter*. 1850. Boston: Houghton Mifflin, 1960.

Heilbrun, Carolyn. *Reinventing Womanhood*. New York: Norton, 1979.

Helly, Dorothy O., and Susan M. Reverby. *Gendered Domains: Rethinking Public and Private in Women's History*. Ithaca: Cornell Univ. Press, 1992.

Hersh, Blanche Glassman. *Slavery of Sex: Feminist-abolitionists in America*. Urbana: Univ. of Illinois Press, 1978.

Hirschhorn, Norbert, and Ian Greaves. "Louisa May Alcott: Her Mysterious Illness." *Perspectives in Biology and Medicine,* vol. 50, no. 2 (spring 2007), 243–259.

Horwitz, Tony. *Midnight Rising: John Brown and the Raid that Sparked the Civil War*. New York: Holt, 2011.

Hosmer, Horace. *Remembrances of Concord and the Thoreaus: Letters of Horace Hosmer to Dr. S. A. Jones*. George Hendrick, ed. Urbana: Univ. of Illinois Press, 1977.

Howe, Daniel Walker. *What Hath God Wrought: The Transformation of America, 1815–1848*. New York: Oxford, 2008.

Isenberg, Nancy. *Sex and Citizenship in Antebellum America*. Chapel Hill: Univ. of North Carolina Press, 1998.

Jarvis, Edward. *Traditions & Reminiscences of Concord, Massachusetts, 1779–1878*. Sarah Chapin, ed. Amherst: Univ. of Massachusetts Press, 1993.

Jeffrey, Julie Roy. *The Great Silent Army of Abolitionism: Ordinary Women in the Antislavery Movement*. Chapel Hill: Univ. of North Carolina Press, 1998.

Jeynes, William H. *American Educational History: School, Society, and the Common Good*. Thousand Oaks, CA: Sage Publications, 2007.

Johnson, Allen. *Dictionary of American Biography*. New York: Scribner, 1933.

Jurmain, Suzanne. *The Forbidden Schoolhouse: The True and Dramatic Story of Prudence Crandall and Her Students*. New York: Houghton Mifflin, 2005.

Karcher, Carolyn L. *The First Woman in the Republic: A Cultural Biography of Lydia Maria Child*. Durham: Duke Univ. Press, 1994.

Kelley, Mary. *Learning to Stand and Speak: Women, Education, and Public Life in America's Republic*. Chapel Hill: Univ. of North Carolina Press, 2006.

Kent, Kathryn R. *Making Girls Into Women: American Women's Writing and the Rise of Lesbian Identity*. Durham: Duke Univ. Press, 2003.

Kerber, Linda K. *Women of the Republic: Intellect and Ideology in Revolutionary America*. Chapel Hill: Univ. of North Carolina Press, 1980.

———. *Toward an Intellectual History of Women: Essays*. Chapel Hill: Univ. of North Carolina Press, 1997.

Kerber, Linda, Alice Kessler-Harris, Kathryn Kish Sklar, eds. *U.S. History as Women's History: New Feminist Essays*. Chapel Hill: Univ. of North Carolina Press, 1995.

Keyser, Elizabeth Lennox. *Little Women: A Family Romance*. New York: Twayne, 1999.

———. *Whispers in the Dark: The Fiction of Louisa May Alcott*. Knoxville: Univ. of Tennessee Press, 1993.

Kirschmann, Anne Taylor. *A Vital Force: Women in American Homeopathy*. Trenton, NJ: Rutgers Univ. Press, 2004.

Kornfeld, Eve. *Margaret Fuller: A Brief Biography with Documents*. Boston: Bedford Books, 1997.

Krieger, Alex, and David Cobb, eds. *Mapping Boston*. Cambridge, MA: MIT Press, 2001.

Lader, Lawrence. *The Bold Brahmins: New England's War Against Slavery: 1831–1863*. Westport, CT: Greenwood Press, 1961.

Lang, Amy Schrager. *The Syntax of Class: Writing Inequality in Nineteenth-Century America*. Princeton, NJ: Princeton Univ. Press, 2003.

LaPlante, Eve. *American Jezebel: The Uncommon Life of Anne Hutchinson, the Woman Who Defied the Puritans*. San Francisco: HarperOne, 2004.

———. *Salem Witch Judge: The Life and Repentance of Samuel Sewall*. San Francisco: HarperOne, 2007.

Lemire, Elise. *Black Walden: Slavery and Its Aftermath in Concord, Massachusetts*. Philadelphia: Univ. of Penn. Press, 2009.

———. *Miscegenation: Making Race in America*. Philadelphia: Univ. of Pennsylvania Press, 2002.

Levander, Caroline F., and Carol J. Singley. *The American Child: A Cultural Stsudies Reader*. New Brunswick, NJ: Rutgers Univ. Press, 2003.

Loring, James S. *The hundred Boston orators appointed by the municipal authorities and other public bodies, from 1770 to 1852; comprising historical gleanings illustrating the principles and progress of our republican institutions*. Boston: Jewett, 1853.

Lutz, Alma. *Crusade for Freedom: Women of the Antislavery Movement*. Boston: Beacon Press, 1968.

Macleod, Anne Scott. *American Childhood: Essays on Children's Literature of the Nineteenth and Twentieth Centuries*. Athens, GA: Univ. of Georgia Press, 1994.

Marcus, Steven. *The Other Victorians: A Study of Sexuality and Pornography in Mid Nineteenth Century England*. New York: Basic Books, 1964.

Marshall, Megan. *The Peabody Sisters: Three Women Who Ignited Romanticism*. Boston: Houghton Mifflin, 2005.

Matteson, John. *Eden's Outcasts: The Story of Louisa May Alcott and Her Father*. New York: Norton, 2007.

May Memorial Unitarian Universalist Society website, www.mmuus.org/who-we-are/history/smjay.html.

May, Samuel. *A Genealogy of the Descendants of John May, Who Came From England to Roxbury, in America, 1640*. Boston: Franklin Press, 1878.

May, Samuel J., and James M. Smith. "An Abolitionist Discusses Racial Segregation and Educational Policy During the Civil War." *The Journal of Negro History*, vol. 41 (Apr. 1956), 138–147.

Mayer, André. *King's Chapel, The First Century, 1686–1787*. Boston: King's Chapel, 1976.

Mayer, Henry. *All on Fire: William Lloyd Garrison and the Abolition of Slavery*. New York: St. Martin's, 1998.

McDougall, Walter A. *Freedom Just Around the Corner: A New American History, 1585–1828*. New York: HarperCollins, 2004.

———. *Throes of Democracy: The American Civil War Era, 1829–1877*. New York: HarperCollins, 2008.

McManus, Edgar. *Black Bondage in the North*. Syracuse, NY: Syracuse Univ. Press, 1973.

McMillen, Sally G. *Seneca Falls and the Origins of the Women's Rights Movement*. New York: Oxford Univ. Press, 2009.

McPherson, James M. *The Struggle for Equality: Abolitionists and the Negro in the Civil War and Reconstruction*. Princeton, NJ: Princeton Univ. Press, 1964.

Melish, Joanne Pope. *Disowning Slavery: Gradual Emancipation and "Race" in New England, 1780–1860*. Ithaca, NY: Cornell Univ. Press, 1998.

Mendelsohn, Jack. *Channing: The Reluctant Radical*. Boston: Little, Brown, 1971.

Michaels, W. B., and Donald E. Pease, eds. *The American Renaissance Reconsidered*. Baltimore and London: Johns Hopkins Univ. Press, 1985.

Miller, John. *The Colonial Image: Origins of American Culture*. New York: George Braziller, 1962.

Miller, Perry, ed. *Margaret Fuller, American Romantic: A Selection from her Writings and Correspondence*. Gloucester, MA: Peter Smith, 1969.

Mintz, Steven. *Huck's Raft: A History of American Childhood*. Cambridge: Harvard Univ. Press, 2004.

Morey, Ann-Janine. *Religion and Sexuality in American Literature*. New York: Cambridge Univ. Press, 1992.

Morison, Samuel Eliot. *The Founding of Harvard College*. Cambridge: Harvard Univ. Press, 1935, 1995.

Mott, Frank Luther. *Golden Multitudes: The Story of Best Sellers in the United States*. New York: Macmillan, 1947.

Mott, Wesley. *Biographical Dictionary of Transcendentalism*. Westport, CT: Greenwood Press, 1996.

Myerson, Joel, ed. *Studies in the American Renaissance*. Charlottesville: Univ. Press of Virginia, 1984.

———. *Transcendentalism: A Reader*. New York: Oxford, 2000

Myerson, Joel, Sandra Harbert Petrulionis, and Laura Dassow Walls, eds. *The Oxford Handbook of Transcendentalism*. New York: Oxford Univ. Press, 2010.

New York history website: www.nyhistory.com/central/sjmay.htm.

Norton, Mary Beth. *Liberty's Daughters: The Revolutionary Experience of American Women, 1750–1800*. Boston: Little, Brown, 1980.

Nye, Russel B. *Fettered Freedom: Civil Liberties and the Slavery Controversy, 1830–1860*. East Lansing: Michigan State Univ. Press, 1963.

O'Brien, David J. *Isaac Hecker: An American Catholic*. New York: Paulist Press, 1992.

O'Connor, Thomas H. *Civil War Boston*. Boston: Northeastern Univ. Press, 1997.

———. *The Hub: Boston Past and Present*. Boston: Northeastern Univ. Press, 2001.

The Old South Church. *An Historical Catalogue of the Old South Church (Third Church) Boston, 1669–1882*. Boston: David Clapp & Son, 1883.

Packer, Barbara. *Emerson's Fall*. New York: Continuum, 1982.

Pease, Jane H., and William H. Pease. *Bound with Them in Chains: A Biographical History of the Antislavery Movement*. Westport, CT: Greenwood Press, 1972.

The penultimate chapter concerns "The Gentle Humanitarian: Samuel Joseph May."

Perry, Lewis. *Antislavery Reconsidered: New Perspectives*. Baton Rouge: Louisiana State Univ. Press, 1979.

————. *Radical Abolitionism: Anarchy and the Government of God in Antislavery Thought*. Ithaca: Cornell Univ. Press, 1973.

Petrulionis, Sandra Harbert. *"Swelling That Great Tide of Humanity"*: The Concord, Massachusetts, Female Anti-Slavery Society. Boston: New England Quarterly, 2001.

Pickett, LaSalle Corbell. *Across My Path: Memories of People I Have Known*. New York: Brentano, 1916.

Pierpont, Claudia Roth. *Passionate Minds: Women Rewriting the World*. New York: Knopf, 2000.

Piersen, William Dillon. *Black Yankees: The Development of an Afro-American Subculture in Eighteenth-Century New England*. Amherst, MA: Univ. of Massachusetts Press, 1988.

Pinar, William. *The Gender of Racial Politics and Violence in America*. New York: Lang, 2001.

Porter, Maria S. *Recollections of Louisa May Alcott, John Greenleaf Whittier, and Robert Browning*. Boston: New England Magazine Corporation, 1893.

Puleo, Stephen. *A City So Grand: The Rise of an American Metropolis, Boston 1850–1900*. Boston: Beacon, 2010.

Rawson, Michael. *Eden on the Charles: The Making of Boston*. Cambridge: Harvard Univ. Press, 2010.

Remini, Robert V. *Daniel Webster: The Man and His Time*. New York: Norton, 1997.

Reynolds, David S. *Waking Giant: America in the Age of Jackson*. New York: Harper, 2008.

Richardson, Robert D. *Emerson: The Mind on Fire*. Berkeley: Univ. of California Press, 1995.

————. *Henry Thoreau: A Life of the Mind*. Berkeley: Univ. of California Press, 1986.

Robbins, Paula Ivaska. *The Royal Family of Concord: Samuel, Elizabeth, and Rockwood Hoar and Their Friendship with Emerson*. Philadelphia: Xlibris, 2003.

Robbins, Sarah. *Managing Literacy, Mothering America: Women's Narratives on Reading and Writing in the Nineteenth Century*. Pittsburgh: Univ. of Pittsburgh Press, 2004.

Rusk, Ralph L. *The Life of Ralph Waldo Emerson*. New York: Scribner's, 1949.

Russ, Lavinia. "Not to Be Read on Sunday," in *Critical Essays on Louisa May Alcott,* ed. Madeleine B. Stern. Boston: G. K. Hall, 1984.

Salyer, Sandford. *Marmee: The Mother of Little Women*. Norman, OK: Univ. of Oklahoma Press, 1949.

Sanborn, Franklin B. *Recollections of Seventy Years*. Boston: R. G. Badger, 1909.

————. *Bronson Alcott at Alcott House, England, and Fruitlands, New England*. Boston: Roberts Brothers, 1893. New York: Biblio & Tannen, 1965.

Sanborn, Franklin B., and William T. Harris. *A. Bronson Alcott: His Life and Philosophy*. 2 vols. Boston: Roberts Brothers, 1893.

Savage, James. *A Genealogical Dictionary of the First Settlers of New England, Showing Three Generations of Those Who Came Before May, 1692*. 4 vols. Boston: Little, Brown, 1862.

Saxton, Martha. *Louisa May: A Modern Biography of Louisa May Alcott*. New York: Farrar, Straus, & Giroux, 1977.

Schlereth, Thomas J. *Victorian America: Transformations in Everyday Life, 1876–1915*. New York: HarperCollins, 1991.

Schreiner, Samuel A., Jr. *The Concord Quartet: Alcott, Emerson, Hawthorne, Thoreau, and the Friendship that Freed the American Mind*. New York: Wiley, 2006.

Scovel, Carl, and Charles Conrad Forman. *Journey Toward Independence: King's Chapel's Transition to Unitarianism*. Boston: Skinner House, 1993.

Seasholes, Nancy. *Gaining Ground: A History of Mapmaking in Boston*. Cambridge, MA: MIT Press, 2003.

Sedgwick, Eve Kosofsky. *Epistemology of the Closet*. Berkeley: Univ. of California Press, 2008.

Shannon, Martha A. S. *Boston Days of William Morris Hunt*. Boston: Marshall Jones, 1923.

Shattuck, Lemuel. *History of the Town of Concord*. 1835. Boston: Goodspeed's, 1985.

Shealy, Daniel. *Alcott in Her Own Time*. Iowa City: Univ. of Iowa Press, 2005.

Shepard, Odell. *Pedlar's Progress: The Life of Bronson Alcott*. Boston: Little, Brown, 1937.

Showalter, Elaine. *A Jury of Her Peers: American Women Writers from Anne Bradstreet to Annie Proulx*. New York: Knopf, 2009.

———. *Scribbling Women: Short Stories by 19th-century American Women*. New Brunswick, NJ: Rutgers Univ. Press, 1997.

Sicherman, Barbara. *Well-Read Lives: How Books Inspired a Generation of American Women*. Chapel Hill: Univ. of North Carolina Press, 2010.

Speicher, Anna M. *The Religious World of Antislavery Women: Spirituality in the Lives of Five Abolitionist Lecturers*. New York: Syracuse Univ. Press, 2000.

Stampp, Kenneth M. *America in 1857: A Nation on the Brink*. New York: Oxford Univ. Press, 1990.

Stange, Douglas C. *Patterns of Antislavery among American Unitarians, 1831–1860*. Rutherford, NJ: Fairleigh Dickinson Univ. Press, 1977.

Stauffer, John. *Giants: The Parallel Lives of Frederick Douglass and Abraham Lincoln*. New York: Twelve, 2008.

Stepanski, Lisa M. *The Home Schooling of Louisa May Alcott: How Her Father and Her Mother Educated an American Writer*. Lewiston, NY: Edwin Mellen Press, 2011.

Sterling, Dorothy. *Ahead of Her Time: Abby Kelly and the Politics of Antislavery*. New York: Norton, 1991.

Stern, Madeleine B. *Louisa May Alcott*. Norman, OK: Univ. of Oklahoma Press, 1950.

———. *Louisa May Alcott: From Blood & Thunder to Hearth & Home*. Boston: Northeastern Univ. Press, 1998.

———, ed. *Critical Essays on Louisa May Alcott*. Boston: G. K. Hall, 1984.

Story, Ronald. "Harvard Students, the Boston Elite, and the New England Preparatory System, 1800–1876." *History of Education Quarterly*, vol. 15, no. 3 (autumn 1975), 281–98.

Stout, Harry S. *The New England Soul: Preaching and Religious Culture in Colonial New England*. New York: Oxford, 1986.

Stowe, William W. *Going Abroad: European Travel in Nineteenth-Century American Culture*. Princeton: Princeton Univ. Press, 1994.

Strane, Susan. *A Whole-Souled Woman: Prudence Crandall and the Education of Black Women*. New York: Norton, 1990.

Sullivan, Constance. *Landscapes of the Civil War: Newly Discovered Photographs from the Medford Historical Society*. New York: Knopf, 1995.

Sutherland, Daniel E. *The Expansion of Everyday Life, 1860–1876*. New York: Harper, 1989.

Thayer, George B. *Pedal and Path: Across the Continent Awheel and Afoot*. Hartford, CT: Case, Lockwood & Brainard, n.d.

Theriot, Nancy M. *Mothers & Daughters in Nineteenth-century America: The Biosocial Construction of Femininity*. Lexington, KY: Univ. Press of Kentucky, 1996.

Thwing, A. H. *The Crooked and Narrow Streets of Boston*. Boston: Brown, 1949.

Ticknor, Caroline. *May Alcott, A Memoir*. Boston: Little, Brown, 1928.

Traister, Rebecca. *Big Girls Don't Cry: The Election That Changed Everything for American Women*. New York: Free Press, 2010.

Unger, Harlow Giles. *John Hancock: Merchant King and American Patriot*. New York: Wiley, 2000.

Unitarian Congregational Society of Syracuse. "IN MEMORIAM—Samuel Joseph May," July 1871, docsouth.unc.edu/neh/maysamuel/maysamuel.html, accessed online in April 2012.

Ward, Geoffrey C. *Not for Ourselves Alone: The Story of Elizabeth Cady Stanton and Susan B. Anthony*. Based on documentary film by Ken Burns and Paul Barnes, with preface by Burns, introduction by Barnes, and contributions by Martha Saxton, Ann D. Gordon, and Ellen Carol DuBois. New York: Knopf, 1999.

Warren, Rev. William. *The History of Waterford, Oxford County, Maine*. Portland, ME: Hoyt, Fogg & Donham, 1879.

Waterford Historical Society. *Waterford, Maine, 1875–1976*. Somersworth, NH: New Hampshire Printers, 1977.

Waterford, Town of. *History of Waterford, Maine, 1775–1875*. Portland, ME: Hoyt Fogg & Donham, 1879.

Wayne, Tiffany K. *Woman Thinking: Feminism and Transcendentalism in Nineteenth-century America*. Lanham, MD: Lexington Books, 2005.

———. *Women's Roles in Nineteenth-century America*. Westport, CT: Greenwood, 2007.

Welch, Marvis Olive. *Prudence Crandall: A Biography*. Manchester, CT: Jason Publishers, 1984.

Welter, Barbara. *Dimity Convictions: The American Woman in the Nineteenth Century*. Athens: Ohio Univ. Press, 1976.

Wheeler, William W. "A Country Doctor's Ledger: Leander Gage, 1791–1842," and "Ann Sargent Gage," presented to the Waterford (Maine) Historical Society, August 1996.

Wills, Garry. *Lincoln at Gettysburg: The Words that Remade America*. New York: Simon & Schuster, 1992.

Winik, Jay. *April 1865: The Month that Saved America*. New York: HarperCollins, 2001.

Wood, Gordon S. *Empire of Liberty: A History of the Early Republic, 1789–1815*. New York: Oxford, 2009.

Woodbury, E.C.D. *Dorothy Quincy, Wife of John Hancock*. Washington: Neale, 1901.

Wright, Conrad. *The Beginnings of Unitarianism in America*. Boston: Beacon, 1955.

———. *The Liberal Christians: Essays on American Unitarian History*. Boston: Beacon, 1970.

———. *Three Prophets of Religious Liberalism: Channing, Emerson, Parker*. Boston: Beacon, 1961.

Yacovone, Donald. *American National Biography*. New York: Oxford, 1999.

———. *Samuel Joseph May and the Dilemmas of the Liberal Persuasian 1797–1871*. Philadelphia: Temple University Press, 1991.

———. "Samuel Joseph May, Antebellum Reform, and the Problem of Patricide" in *Perspectives in American History*, n.s. 2 [1985], 99–124.

Yee, Shirley. *Black Women Abolitionists: A Study in Activism, 1828–1860*. Knoxville: Univ. of Tennessee Press, 1992.

Yellin, Jean Fagan. *Women and Sisters: The Antislavery Feminists in American Culture*. New Haven: Yale Univ. Press, 1992.

Zagarri, Rosemarie. *Revolutionary Backlash: Women and Politics in the Early American Republic*. Philadelphia: Univ. of Pennsylvania Press, 2008.

Ziegler, Valarie H. *The Advocates of Peace in Antebellum America*. Bloomington: Indiana Univ. Press, 1992.

Zorn, Roman J. "The New England Anti-Slavery Society: Pioneer Abolition Organization." *The Journal of Negro History*, vol. 42, no. 3 (July 1957), 157–76.

Permissions and Credits

Quotations in text are reprinted with permission from:

Houghton Library, Harvard University: Amos Bronson Alcott papers (MS Am 1130.9-1130.12); Louisa May Alcott additional papers (MS Am 1817, MS Am 2114, MS Am 1130.13); Louisa May Alcott papers (MS Am 800.23); Alcott family additional papers (MS Am 1130.14-1130.16); Alcott family additional papers (MS Am 2745); Alcott family additional papers (MS Am 1817.2); Alcott family letters (MS Am 1130 and MS Am 1130.1-1130.2); Alcott family papers (MS Am 1130.4).

The May Anti-Slavery manuscript collection, #4601. Division of Rare and Manuscript Collections, Cornell University Library.

Quotations from papers at Orchard House used by permission of Louisa May Alcott's Orchard House.

Illustration credits:

Insert page 1: Map of Boston, 1840 Map reproduction courtesy of the Norman B. Leventhal Map Center at the Boston Public Library.

Insert page 2: Etching of Abigail May Alcott and photograph of Bronson Alcott used by permission of Louisa May Alcott's Orchard House.

Insert page 3: Photograph of young adult Louisa May Alcott used by permission of Louisa May Alcott's Orchard House.

Insert page 4: Photograph of Anna Alcott, painting of May Alcott, drawing of Lizzie Alcott, photograph of Fred and Johnny Pratt, and photograph of Lulu Nieriker used by permission of Louisa May Alcott's Orchard House.

Insert page 5: Photograph of Orchard House used by permission of Louisa May Alcott's Orchard House; painting of King's Chapel, Boston: Photograph © 2012 Museum of Fine Arts, Boston.

Insert page 6: Photograph of Charlotte May Wilkinson and portrait of Samuel Joseph May courtesy of Eve LaPlante; engraving of Syracuse, 1852 courtesy of the Onondaga Historical Association Museum & Research Center.

Insert page 7: "Heralds of Freedom" courtesy of Boston Athenæum; photograph of Mill Dam, 1860 courtesy of the Boston Public Library, Print Department.

Insert page 8: Photograph of older Louisa May Alcott used by permission of Louisa May Alcott's Orchard House.

Index

About the Author

EVE LAPLANTE is a great-niece and a cousin of Abigail and Louisa May Alcott. The author of *Seized, American Jezebel,* and *Salem Witch Judge,* she is also the editor of *My Heart Is Boundless,* a collection of Abigail's writings. She lives with her family in New England and can be contacted at www.EveLaPlante.com.